NAME	DATE RECEIVED	DATE RETURNED
Patricia Alexander	12/20/17	

Please remember to return this book at the end of the year to the Program Coordinator. If you fail to do so, you may be subject to reimbursing the program for the cost of the book.

BOOK NUMBER FB1 13

J. Edgar Hoover's
FBI Wired
The Nation

By
Dempsey J. Travis

 URBAN RESEARCH PRESS, CHICAGO 2000

URBAN RESEARCH PRESS, INC.

www.urbanresearchpress.com

Copyright© 2000 Urban Research Press, Inc.
840 East 87th Street, Chicago, Illinois   60619 USA
Printed in the United States of America
First Edition
ISBN 0-941484-31-9

Library of Congress Cataloging-in-Publication Data.

Dedicated To

The brave souls who opted not to sacrifice their Civil Liberties for a false promise of National Security.

Special Thanks

American Civil Liberties Union Of Illinois

Photo Credits

Lois M. Walker Chicago Daily Defender Librarian
The Illinois Blue Book 1965-66
Urban Research Press, Inc.
Johnson Publishing Company
Schomburg Collection, NYPL

Acknowledgements

A good coach never changes the front line of a winning team. Therefore, with great pride, I salute the following players: My wife, Moselynne Travis, my motivator; Dr. Deloris Lipscomb, English Professor and Editor; Ruby Davis, senior researcher; Ken Kittivanich, cover and book designer; Jewell Diemer, and Jasmine Dunning, a student trainee from Chicago Vocational High School.

Introduction

In the early morning of December 4, 1969 Chicago police Sergeant Daniel Groth led a raiding party of officers armed with shotguns, a Thompson submachine gun, an automatic carbine rifle and other weapons to the Illinois Black Panther Party apartment at 2337 West Monroe where Fred Hampton and other Panthers lay sleeping. Groth carried a .38 caliber revolver in his right hand and a duly issued search warrant in his left hand authorizing the police officers to search the apartment for weapons. The warrant had been issued at the request of States Attorney Edward V. Hanrahan. The raiding party had been briefed before the raid. Among the documents referred to in the briefing was a diagram of the apartment which specifically identified the bedroom and bed on which Fred Hampton slept.

Sergeant Groth, noting that all of the lights were out in the building, climbed quietly up the front stoop accompanied by Officers Jones, Hughes, Garmon and Davis. Offices Carmody, Ciszewiski, Broderick, Kelly, Joseph and Corbett tiptoed around to the back door of the two apartment building. Officers Marusich, Harris and Howard remained on the street with riot guns and rifles. There were other officers stationed on the roof of 2337 West Monroe and others stationed themselves nearby on rooftops. Officers from the Woods Street Police Station cordoned off both ends of the 2300 block on Monroe.

At 4:46 A.M., four of the Cook County State's Attorney's police officers were standing in the foyer of the 2337 West Monroe dwelling with deadly weapons that were loaded and unlocked: Sergeant Groth had a .38 caliber revolver and his own 12 gauge, double-barreled shotgun. Garmon had a .357 caliber revolver in his holster and cradled a .45 Thompson submachine gun in his arms. Davis had both a .38 caliber revolver and his own .30 caliber carbine rifle.

At this point, Groth knocked on the door to the first floor apartment. A woman who lived in the second floor apartment above Hampton at 2337 West Monroe confirmed that she heard somebody knock on the first floor door. According to this woman, the sound of the knock was instantly followed by a bellowing male voice that shouted, "Open up! Police!" There was a moment of deadly silence, and then World War II broke out in the Hampton apartment. A loud cannon blast at the front door literally shook the building and that nerve-shattering impact was followed by rapid machine gun fire followed by the intermittent loud barking sound of small firearms. Simultaneously, shots were heard coming from the rear of the apartment.

The raiders fired at least 42 shots through the south living room wall into the north bedroom where three Panthers slept. About seven of those shots continued through the south wall of the north bedroom and into the south bedroom where Fred Hampton and his fiancee Deborah Johnson were sleeping. Numerous shots were fired through the doors and doorways into the north and south bedrooms. At the conclusion of the raid Fred Hampton and Mark Clark were killed and four other Panthers were wounded.

It was the sound of the gunfire that awakened Verlina Brewer, a sixteen-year-old kid from Ann Arbor, Michigan, who had run away from home to join the Black Panther Party in Chicago. Verlina was sleeping in the front bedroom which was located adjacent to the living room with two other Panthers. She told her lawyer, R. Eugene Pincham, that when she heard the shooting she and the two others in the bed simply rolled out of the bed onto the floor and then rolled under the bed. When Verlina attempted to stand, it was then that she realized for the first time she had been shot. She fell to the floor. The State's Attorney's police picked her up and carried her out into the hallway. Her two roommates stood in the hall with their hands held high above their heads, while she sat on the floor. While sitting there, Verlina heard one officer say, "There's a Black son-of-a-bitch back here, and he's in pretty bad shape." She then heard two shots and a voice say, "If he wasn't dead, he's dead now." The voice had come from the second bedroom which was the room where Chairman Fred Hampton had been sleeping.

It was not learned until 1973 that this entire raid had been instigated and orchestrated by the Chicago office of the F.B.I. under the direction of case agent Roy Martin Mitchel. Mitchel was operating pursuant to the F.B.I.'s counter intelligence program known as COINTELPRO. COINTELPRO was initiated by J. Edgar Hoover on March 4, 1968. Dempsey Travis describes the historical origins and purposes of Hoover's COINTELPRO initiative and Hoover's penchant for targeting some of America's great political leaders, musicians, composers, writers and producers for surveillance. The December 4th raid was orchestrated to destroy the Black Panther Party and to murder the young charismatic and fearless Fred Hampton. Fred Hampton had become a national figure in the Black Panther Party. He had the ability to bring together and motivate young Blacks from every economic spectrum of Black society. His well honed oratorical skills even captivated the admiration of older and middle class Blacks who saw in Hampton a potential for leadership in the struggle for Black liberation and empowerment. It was Hoover's keen insight into this potential that led to the targeting of Fred Hampton and other Black Panther Party leaders.

The Black Panther Party was an organization which espoused arming its members for self-defense against the brutality visited upon the Black community by the police. The Party openly threatened to "off the Pig" in their defense and that of the Black community. The Panthers provided free breakfast for children and free health clinics in the Black community. They published and sold a Party newspaper which provided a vehicle to mobilize the community and a source of revenue for the Party's activities. The legal framework under which Hoover rationalized his assault upon the Party was to "discredit, disrupt and destroy" groups bent on the violent overthrow of the United States. This same rationale was used to justify the targeting of the Honorable Elijah Muhammad, Stokely Carmichael, Dr. Martin Luther King, Malcolm X, and other leaders who did not espouse violence as a means of liberation for Black people.

Dempsey Travis provides us in his work a group of persons, Black and white, who incurred the wrath and attention of J. Edgar Hoover who in no sense espoused the use of violence to effect social change. In fact, most of them were little concerned with the politics of social change. Adam Clayton Powell and Governor Adlai Stevenson were advocates of a free and democratic society. John Lennon, Charlie Chaplin, Leonard Bernstein, Louis Armstrong, Josephine Baker, Nat King Cole, Duke Ellington and Billie Holiday were actors and entertainers. They were in no way activists in the pursuit of devising ways and means to destroy a democracy. The sole rationale for targeting them was the fact they may have been considered "uppity Niggers" or "Nigger Lovers" by a dyed-in-the-wool racist such as J. Edgar Hoover. Hoover's targeting of white musicians, producers and writers seems to flow from their liberal and/or offbeat lifestyles. James Baldwin, Lorraine Hansberry, Ernest Hemingway, Tennessee Williams and Richard Wright represent persons who personify the kind of communication and dialogue in a free society that was espoused by our founding fathers. Dempsey's biographical sketches of these fine men and women who incurred Hoover's interest go a long way to demonstrate the abuses of governmental power that occurred during his time.

There is great value added to Dempsey's book. His easy style and journalistic accuracy profile the lives and times of a panorama of personalities whom we are given the opportunity to know. J. Edgar Hoover's F.B.I. Wired the Nation is a tremendous addition to Dempsey Travis' prodigious contribution to the landscape of American literature.

James D. Montgomery, Principal of James D. Montgomery and Associates, LTD, and a partner in the National Law Firm of Cochran, Cherry, Givens, Smith and Montgomery.

He served as Corporation Counsel of the City of Chicago under Mayor Harold Washington from May 1, 1983 to February 1986.

August 2000

Table of Contents

Chapter 1

Hoover: The Keeper of The Nation's *Secret* Files

J Edgar Hoover, the future Director of the Federal Bureau of Investigation, first saw the light of day on Sunday morning January 1, 1895 in a whitewashed frame house located in a lower middle class neighborhood at 413 Seward Square in S. E. Washington, D. C. He was the last of four children born to Dickerson and Annie Hoover. His father worked as a printmaker for the federal government's map-making department. His mother was a housewife. The family homestead was approximately eight city blocks from the White House where President Grover Cleveland hung his hat for two four-year terms.

Weekly lynchings below the Mason-Dixon Line were common in 1895 and Jim Crow in the nation's capital was and remained tighter than Dick's hatband for the first fifty-five years of Hoover's life. Everything in the District of Columbia was off limits to Colored people including the theaters, many downtown stores, and the "Whites Only" water fountains in the Union Train Station and throughout the city.

Wounded and disabled Colored World War I & II veterans, returning from the European and Pacific theaters of war found that all the toilet doors above the basement level of Walter Reed Veterans Hospital had "For Whites Only" signs posted on them. The racial climate of Washington, D. C. umbrellaed all of the 48 states and its territories. Colored taxicab drivers were prohibited from entering the horseshoe circle in front of the Union Train Station to drop off or pick up Colored travelers because of the District of Columbia's Jim Crow laws. Thus, Colored women, men, and children were forced to lug or drag their luggage almost a half city block before they could get a Negro driven cab, hitch a ride in a jitney, or catch a streetcar on Massachusetts Avenue, a location in front of the Union Station which afforded the newcomers a postcard view of the gleaming white dome of the nation's capital building. All of the seats in the United States Senate and the House of Representatives were occupied by white men, although ten percent of the nation's population was Black and over 50 percent were white women.

There was a brief aberration from the Color bar, when twenty-two Colored gentlemen were elected by the carpetbaggers from the former Confederate states and seated in the hallowed halls of Congress from 1869 to 1901. President Ulysses S. Grant, served four two year consecutive terms during the Reconstruction period. He also served as General of President Abraham Lincoln's Union Army during the Civil War. Among the Negroes who served in the Congress during the post Civil War era were U. S. Senators H. R. Revels and Blanche K. Bruce, both representing the state of Mississippi, J. T. Walls of Florida, Benjamin S. Turner of Alabama, Jefferson H. Long, of Georgia, Joseph H. Rainey, and Robert C. DeLarge, of South Carolina.

George H. White, the last Black Congressman of that period, stood in the well of the House of Representatives and said the following in his farewell speech on January 29, 1901:

> "This, Mr. Chairman is perhaps the Negro's temporary
> farewell to the Congress, but let me say, he like Phoenix will
> rise up again someday . . . "

Hoover like most Southern gentlemen, held Negroes in low esteem and that was just one rung above the American Indians, two hundred of whom were massacred at Wounded Knee, South Dakota in 1890. As was the custom Hoover tolerated Negroes as houseboys, cooks, gardeners, and chauffeurs. For the Director to refer to a Negro male by any title other than "boy" was as painful as swallowing a fish bone. His skin would turn as crimson as a ripe strawberry on the occasions when ordinary civility obligated him to address a Negro male as "Mister". To Hoover nothing was more dangerous than intellectual Negroes and liberal thinking white folk such as James Baldwin, the author of Tell Me How Long The Train Has Been Gone, John Lennon of the Beatles, Ernest Hemingway, who penned For Whom The Bell Tolls, Sinclair Lewis, the great novelist who created in his novels characters like "Babbit" and "Elmer Gantry", and because of his creativity became the first American to receive a Nobel Prize for Literature. Also among the nation's brightest and best were Arthur Miller, the writer of Death Of A Salesman, Tennessee Williams, the playwright whose works include The Glass Menagerie, Carl Sandburg, the poet who in his poem "Chicago" tagged Lincoln's city by the lake, the "Hog Butcher of the World", Charlie Chaplin, the British actor who gained international fame in American movies for his role as a comic, a cane carrying tramp who wore oversized shoes, in which he walked slew foot, in draped baggy trousers. A black derby hat was his sky piece. Some additional talented, and unlimited, individuals were Truman Capote, society's darling, whose works include Breakfast at Tiffany's and In Cold Blood, Aldous Huxley, whose best work was Brave New World, Thomas Mann, the German Nobel prize winner who wrote The Magic Mountain, John O'Hara who wrote short stories for the New Yorker and novels such as, Ten North Frederick, Richard Wright, who wrote Native Son, Canada Lee, the actor who appeared in the movies Body & Soul and Life Boat, Ralph Waldo Ellison, the writer of the epic novel, Invisible Man, Sam Greenlee, author of The Spook Who Sat By The Door, Countee Cullen, leading poet of the Harlem Renaissance and the author of Copper Sun and last but not least the talented Arna Bontemps, the poet and novelist who wrote Black Thunder. Hoover held Baldwin, Capote, and Williams in complete contempt because their known sexual preferences, mirrored his own.

J. Edgar Hoover was appointed Director of the Bureau of Investigation on December 22, 1924 eight days before his thirtieth birthday. James Amos, the only Black agent in the Bureau at the time Hoover was elevated to the top office, was described by White members of the Bureau as an Uncle Tom type darkie. He had been appointed an agent by William Burns, Hoover's predecessor. His primary job was to baby-sit and protect President Theodore "Captain of the Rough Riders" Roosevelt's six children. If Hoover had had his druthers, Amos would have been the Alpha and Omega of Negro agents. Amos was also used from time to time as an undercover agent to spy on Black activists, such as Dr. W. E. B. DuBois, the Harvard trained Secretary of the NAACP, A. Philip Randolph, the organizer of the Pullman Porters Union, and Paul Robeson, the famous singer, actor, lawyer, and Phi Beta Kappa scholar who blew a fortune because he chose to be in the forefront of the civil rights struggle to free his Black brothers and sisters.

A second gentleman of color, James Crawford was hired by Hoover, in late 1934 shortly before the word Federal was added to the name of the Bureau of

Investigation. Mr. Crawford was the holder of a Howard University degree and had formerly been employed as a truck driver in President Franklin D. Roosevelt's Work Progress Administration program. His duties for the Director were that of a head chauffeur and handyman. As chauffeur, he was on standby duty from 7:00 A. M. to sometimes as late as midnight if the Director attended a cocktail or dinner function.

Crawford remained Hoover's main man until he was forced to retire from the Bureau after thirty-eight years of service because of failing health. However, because of his loyalty, Hoover kept him on his personal payroll as a domestic and gardener until he died. The Dr. Jekyll side of Hoover's personality was paternal in a Great White Father versus Colored boy relationship. The Hyde side of his personality reflected a 180 degree turn on matters dealing with racial equality and integration.

On New Year's Eve 1936, Hoover was a guest at Sherman Billingsley's Stork Club in Midtown Manhattan, along with Walter Winchell and other V. I. P. guests. Winchell a New York newspaper journalist, wrote the national syndicated column, "On Broadway" from 1924 to 1963. Following dinner, Winchell suggested that members of their party go uptown to the Cotton Club in Harlem and catch the Duke Ellington Orchestra and see a Jungle style floor show.

Initially, Hoover rejected the suggestion to go uptown with the party but changed his mind after Clyde Tolson, his male constant companion, nudged him several times. He had objected to being in an interracial social environment. Juan Tizol a white valve trombonist from Puerto Rico and featured star in the otherwise all Negro Ellington orchestra, was co-composer of the popular 1930's hit "Caravan" with Duke Ellington. The Cotton Club scene was difficult for Hoover to digest. It was a symbol of his worst nightmare.

Under Hoover's stewardship, the Bureau treated Black agents as if they were something that the dog had left. When the civil rights struggle was igniting across the South and the North during the middle 1950's, some FBI instructors were still openly referring to Black trainees as "Niggers" during their class sessions.

Shortly, after John F. Kennedy was elected President in 1960 and Robert Kennedy was appointed Attorney General, the FBI Director came under pressure to hire more Black agents. Hoover felt that the full court press to hire Blacks was a plot to satisfy the National Association for the Advancement of Colored People, an organization that he considered a Communist front. The writer was the President of the Chicago branch of the NAACP in 1959 and 1960, at a time when the chapter's active NAACP membership exceeded fifty thousand card carrying members. The Chicago branch during that period was the largest in the country.

On June 1, 1960, a month prior to the Los Angeles march on the Democratic National Convention, America's two foremost civil rights leaders A. Phillip Randolph and Martin Luther King sent the following telegram to Chicago:

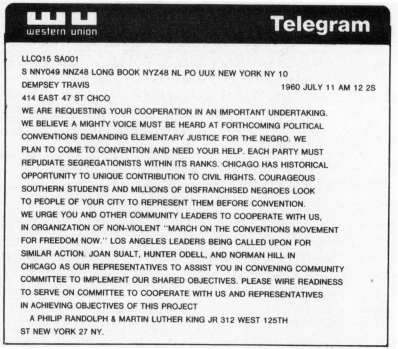

The initial meeting of the Chicago March on the Convention Committee assembled in the Blue Room of the Parkway Ballroom at 45th and South Parkway (Martin Luther King, Jr. Drive) and was called to order on June 21, 1960, at 3:55 p. m. by Bayard Rustin, executive assistant to A. Phillip Randolph. Mr. Randolph said: "Johnson was a hypocrite, and Clarence Mitchell attempted to justify his position when he stated that if Lyndon Johnson believes in the Democratic pledge to eliminate poll taxes as a requisite for voting, why doesn't he start in his native Texas. "

The week of July 11, 1960 when Senator Lyndon Baines Johnson was selected as Kennedy's vice presidential candidate, seven thousand blacks and whites marched and rallied outside of the Democratic convention in Los Angeles for a strong civil rights plank and an elimination of the southern poll tax. Dr. Martin Luther King flew in from South America to join the marchers. The NAACP's Clarence Mitchell observed that while they were waiting for Congressman Powell to join the march, the U. S. representative drove up in a white Cadillac. "If he had to join us that way, " Mitchell declared, "he could have used a car with an integrated paint job. "

Students held a round-the-clock "Freedom Vigil" to dramatize the sit-in movement. Dr. Martin Luther King Jr. , Congressman Adam Clayton Powell, Roy Wilkins and A. Phillip Randolph who had been active participants and leaders of the Los Angeles march, demanded that the Democratic party write ironclad civil rights guarantees into its platform and expel segregationists from the party ranks. From A. Phillip Randolph, to Dr. Martin Luther King, Jr. , to Roy Wilkins and Adam Clayton Powell, the civil rights issues were being painted in iridescent colors, sketched in bold strokes which left not a particle of doubt as to their intent and purpose. Their demands were aired before the 108 member Democratic platform committee. The delegates to the convention approved the suggested civil rights plank almost intact despite a last minute effort by some southern delegates to scuttle it. A minority report against the civil rights plank had been presented on behalf of the states of Georgia, North Carolina, Arkansas, South Carolina, Florida, Mississippi, Virginia, Tennessee and Alabama. An Alabama delegate who was asked by a reporter for his reaction to the electrifying civil rights plank that had just been passed replied with thunder in his voice: "No comment, suh! Go to hell! No comment! "

The Southerner's minority report struck its hardest blow at voting rights for Negroes and the implied endorsement of "sit down" demonstrations. Some forty Chicago leaders attended. Rustin expressed his appreciation for their presence on the part of those community leaders in the hall and introduced A. Phillip Randolph. In his remarks, Randolph, often called the "Father of the Modern Civil Rights March, " discussed both the purpose and the program of the "March on the Convention Movement for Freedom Now. " He stressed the importance of the march in Chicago and in Los Angeles as a demonstration on the part of Black people and their supporters in the labor conventions. Randolph said "This demonstration shall be a protest against the conspiracy of silence on civil rights characterized by both the Republican and Democratic parties. "

Randolph, who had been called the most dangerous man in America by President Woodrow Wilson, continued:

> The 'March on Convention Movement' would emphasize the need for a presidential executive order to implement court decisions ending segregation in housing and guaranteeing the right to vote. He wanted the march in Chicago to be a huge mass demonstration that would leave no doubt that Black people stood firmly behind their leaders in the demands for an end to equivocation on the civil rights question.

Federal Bureau of Investigation

COINTELPRO

Counter-Intelligence Program

When infiltration of Black organizations did not get the kind of results that Hoover wanted, he was prompted to write the following memo to various FBI offices across the country.

> *Prevent the coalition of Black nationalist groups. In unity there is strength, a truism that is no less valid for all of its triteness. As effective coalition . . . might be the first step towards a real "Mau Mau" in America, and the beginning of a true Black revolution.*
>
> *Prevent the rise of a "messiah" who could unify and electrify the militant Black nationalist movement. Malcolm X might have been such a "messiah"; he is a martyr of the movement today . . . Elijah Muhammad is less of a threat because of his age. King could be a very real contender for this position should he abandon his supposed "obedience" to "white" liberal doctrines (nonviolence) and embrace Black nationalism. Stokely Carmichael has the necessary charisma to be a real threat in this way.*
>
> J. Edgar Hoover, Director
Federal Bureau of Investigation
March 4, 1968

Dr. Martin Luther King, Jr. was assassinated on April 4, 1968, exactly thirty days after J. Edgar Hoover issued the aforementioned directive.

In the absence of high profile leaders, Hoover used his FBI Countelpro (Counter Intelligence Program) to provoke warfare between organizations such as the Black Panthers and the Blackstone Rangers. The objective of this tactic was to promote the risk of serious bodily harm or death to the target as evidenced in this letter to Jeff Fort, leader of the Black Stone Rangers.

> *Dear Jeff:*
>
> *I spent some time with some Panther friends on the west side lately. And I know what's been going on. The brothers that run the Panthers blame you for blocking their thing, and there's supposed to be a hit out for you. I am not a Panther, or a Ranger, just Black. From what I see these Panthers are out for themselves, not Black people. I think you ought to know what they're up to. I know what I'd do if I was you. You might hear from me again.*
>
> *(Signed) A Black brother you don't know*

The FBI's Chicago office believed that the letter to Jeff Fort would intensify the degree of animosity between the two groups and cause Fort to take retaliatory action which would disrupt the Black Panther Party or lead to reprisals against its leadership.

To further its efforts of disruption and dissension between the Stones and the Panthers, the Chicago FBI field office, in March 1969, approved the following anonymous letter:

> *Dear Hampton:*
> *Just a word of warning. A Stone friend tells me (name deleted) wants the Panthers and is looking for somebody to get you out of the way. Brother Jeff is supposed to be inter-ested. I am just a Black man looking for Blacks working together and not more of this gang-banging.*

A page that had not found its way into the Federal Bureau of Investigation's Counter-Intelligence scenario was that of a possible affiliation with the Mau Mau, a self-defense organization, with the Black Panther Party. The Mau Mau joined the Panther Party in mass and was subsequently having trouble following the Illinois Black Panther Party's orders. Therefore, the FBI saw this as another opportunity to cause dissension. Hence, it sent the following letter:

> *Brother Kenyatta,*
> *I am from the South Side and have some Panther friends that know you and tell me what's going on. I've known these two that run the Panthers for a long time and those mothers been with every outfit going where it looked like there was something in it for themselves. I heard, too, they are sweet-hearts and that has worked for the man, that's why he's not in Vietnam. Maybe that's why they're not playing like real Panthers. I hear a lot of the brothers are with you and want those mothers out but don't know how. The Panthers need real Black men for leaders, not freaks. Don't give up broth-ers.*
>
> > *A Black Friend*

Federal Bureau of Investigation documents also indicated that during this letter- writing period, a FBI informant within the Black Panther Party was involved in keeping a kettle on the front burner that would further divide the Panthers and the Blackstone Rangers.

According to a report reviewed by the Senate Intelligence Committee, the FBI through the use of anonymous letters and dirty tricks succeeded in provoking unrest in the Black Panther Movement thus causing the Cook County States Attorney's police to raid Fred Hampton's Chicago apartment at 2337 West Monroe Street on Thursday, December 4, 1969 at 4:46 A. M. by breaking through the front door. FBI agent, Roy Mitchell, had furnished States Attorney Edward Hanrahan with a detailed map which showed the layout of the apartment.

Fourteen members of a raiding party under the supervision of the States Attorney Hanrahan fired eighty- nine bullets inside the apartment as compared to a single shot fired by a Black Panther. Fred Hampton was killed in cold blood as he slept in a back bedroom with his girlfriend Debra Johnson 18, who was 8 1/2 months pregnant. She was not injured. Mark Clark was killed, Brenda Harris 18, and Velma Brewer 17, were both shot in the leg.

In 1982, after persistent litigation by Attorneys James Montgomery and R. Eugene Pincham, the survivors were awarded $1. 85 million in damages from the Chicago Police Department. The killings were a direct result of the FBI providing detailed information on Hampton's whereabouts.

In March 1971, a group that fashioned itself as an adhoc Citizens Commission to Investigate the FBI broke into the east coast field office of the Bureau in Media, Pennsylvania and removed more than a thousand documents that revealed the Bureau's tactics of surveillance of some of the individuals and organizations on the FBI's hit list. One document pulled the cover off Cointelpro, the code word for the covert section of the Bureau's bag of dirty tricks. Included in the large haul were skeletons of the kind of anonymous letters that were cranked out and used in their efforts to cause the Stones and Panthers to self destruct. Copies of the documents were sent to newsmen and politicians. As a result of these disclosures, Hoover had to close down Cointelpro. (Counter Intelligence Program)

Senator George McGovern said in the well of the senate:

> *"We don't want our great nation to become a land where our personal privacy and our personal freedom are jeopardized by the abuse of power by a police official who seems to believe he is a law unto himself. "*

Under the cloak of darkness, Hoover pulled out his bag of dirty tricks and fine tooth combed McGovern's record only to find that the Senator was as clean as a pot of greens. Edgar privately called McGovern a psychopathic liar.

Back on the congressional ranch, Senator Edmund Muskie discovered that the FBI had recently surveilled a series of countrywide rallies by environmentalists including himself. Congressman Henry Reuss learned from the documents that were stolen in Pennsylvania by the Citizens Commission to investigate the FBI that agents had investigated his daughter, a student at Swarthmore College. The protests of Muskie and Reuss were a cat's meow compared to the lion's roar of House Majority Leader Hale Boggs. In April 1971 he made speeches accusing the FBI of wiretapping members of Congress and infiltrating the universities. He said, *"When the FBI adopts the tactics of Stalin's Soviet Union and Hitler's German Gestapo, then it is time, as a matter of fact- way past time, Mr. Speaker for the present Director J. Edgar Hoover to let the doorknob hit him where the sun don't shine. Yes! It is time for the Attorney General of the United States to ask for the resignation of Mr. Hoover."*

Following Boggs' speech the next edition of Life magazine adorned its red and white cover with a cartoon of Hoover, as a disgruntled old man looking like a statue from the days of imperial Rome. The headline read: The 47 Year Reign of J. Edgar, the Emperor of the FBI Should End. The headline in the Newsweek cover story read, "Hoover's FBI: Time For A Change?"

President Richard M. Nixon had to make a move on Hoover in spite of all the material that Hoover had gathered on him and some members of his cabinet. Hoover had tapes on Nixon loaded with enough material to blow up the east wing of the White House. Fortunately for the President the material was never used because J. Edgar Hoover died in the early morning May 2, 1972 following a midnight telephone call from the President advising him that he had to retire.

Left to right: Asst. Secretary H. R. Crawford, Congressman Walter Fauntroy, Dempsey J. Travis, Chairman of Housing for Operation PUSH, Secretary of HUD James L. Lynn, and Rev. Jessie L. Jackson, President of Operation PUSH. This picture was taken in September 1972 in Washington, D. C.

Chicago Police Department

"Red Squad" Files

Subject: Dempsey J. Travis

NAME				DATE		
TRAVIS, Dempsey J.				1956		
ALIAS		SEX	RACE	DATE OF BIRTH		
aka -Denney		X F	N	DAY	MONTH	YEAR
HOME ADDRESS				PHONE NO.		
BUSINESS ADDRESS Travis Realty Co. 414 E. 47th St. (1961)				PHONE NO. KE 6-0155		
SOCIAL SECURITY NO.	I.R. NO.		HEIGHT	WEIGHT	COLOR EYES	COLOR HAIR
PECULIARITIES, MARKS, SCARS, ETC.						

PHOTO:A.7,p. 90 & 91   **090584**

REMARKS: Chairman of Freedom of Residence "REPORTER"
Committee,'61-One of honorary co-chairman of the
American Friendship Club's Annual Friendship Day-1964
PRESIDENT: Sivart Mortgage Corporation.-OWNER-OF THE
TRAVIS REALTY & MORTGAGE CO. -BOARD MEMBER OF OPERATION
PUSH.

TRAVIS, Dempsey J.   **Colored**   1956
5428 Indiana Ave.
Chicago, Ill.
414 E. 47th St. (1961)

On file with ASF, Dec. 1955, file X-6, p32.
  PHOTO: in "Chicago" magazine, Jan.1958, page 7,
  National & Foreign Publ.
Subject is a candidate for the presidency of the
Chicago Branch of the NAACP: he is being backed by
Theodore A. JONES, present president, who is not seek-
ing re-election: see the Tribune, 12/4/59.
Member of the Board of Directors of the Home
Opportunities Made Equal (a racial integration in
housing organization); File 843 item 1, pages 1 & 4, ?
report, Feb. 11, 1960.
                    (OVER)   msg **090585**

Spoke at the Installation luncheon of the Chicago
Branch of the NAACP, 1-28-60; Daily News, 1-28-60.
Spoke at the Parkway Ballroom, 420 E. 45th St.;
File 462-A, item 10.
Chicago Coordinator of "March on the Convention Movement
for Freedom Now" - demonstrated against the Republican
National Convention beginning July 25, 1960; see report,
and letterhead, file 462-A, items 16 and 17, and
   item #22.
Slated to speak at mass mtg, Sun. July 24, 1960, Liberty
Baptist Church , 4849 S. Parkway, Chgo; see report,
file 462-A, item 18.   090586

Chairman of Freedom of Residence "Reporter" Committee;
File #904, item 3-8, p 1, leaflet, Oct. 1961.
Past president of the Chicago Branch, NAACP and
president of the newly formed Sivart Corporation
established to furnish FHA and VA mortgage loans to
Negroes. Given award by the American Friendship Club,
Dec. 9, 1961, for his fight to abolish segregation
in housing, etc; Hyde Park Herald, Dec. 6, 1961, p 17.
              SEE CARD #2

TRAVIS, Dempsey J.   CARD #2   1964
414 E. 47th Street '61'   AFG
Chicago 53, Ill   KE 6-0155
President of SIVART Corp. 1965   090587

    One of the honorary co-chairmen of the American Friend-
ship Club's Annual Friendship Day, which will be Aug. 2,
1964. File #792, item 18, See Clpg. dtd 7/27/64.
    Background investigation and attached material rela-
tive to Travis Realty Company. See file 964-B, item
23 to 23-3, rpt 9 Oct 1964.
    Name appears on mailing list of CORE. See File CO-402,
item 4, Oct. 64.
    Participated at the Natl.Assembly on Progress in
Equality of Opportunity in Housing held March 18 thru 20,
1965 at Holiday Inn East in Springfield, Ill. SEE FILE:
904, it. 9, dtd 18 MAR 65.   nat'l.boycott
"CHI NAACP TO PICKET METROPOLITAN LIFE". Organized
by subj.Pres. of the United Mortgage Bankers of Amer, Inc.
set to begin 21 May 65. - protesting "Jim Crow lending
policies" of the Ins.firms, participation will be mainly
picketing and demos at branch Metropolitan Offcs on the
South & West Sides of Chgo. See File 462-B, it.26, Del.

Chicago Police Department "Red Squad" file

Participated in American Friendship Club Eighth Annual
Awards Dinner, Ascot House, Chicago (Defender, 1 Jan 66):
photo, Album 7, p 90, 91.

Chicago American newspaper clipping Dated 18-Feb. 1966, Subject
Charged the Chicago Real Estate Board With Containment of the
Negro people. See File 462-B Item 39 — ms8.

Pledged $1,000 support for the first Chicago Freedom — no
Festival, Dr. King's fight to end slums & segregation in
Chicago. DEF 28 Feb. 66. File 940 it 83.

Sub mentioned in rpt of Coordinating Council of
Community Organ as person financing a housing rehabilita-
tion program. File 951 Item 47. Rpt. dtd. 3Jan67. ms8

Series of news clippings re: Pilot Project for
$4-Million Slum Rehabilitation in Chicago. Subject is
Preisident of Sivart Mortgage Corporation, a negro-owned
firm who will handle the financing. File: 940-G items
103 thru 103-4 clippings dated Dec. 1966.

PICTURE of Subject re: above item in item 103-4.
Name appears on mailing list of CORE. See File CO 402, ms8
it.4, Oct.64.
SEE CARED #3090588

TRAVIS, Dempsey J.   CARD #3
414 E. 47th Street (67)   1967
Chicago 53, Ill.

REAL ESTATE BROKER COUNTERS MARKHAM BIAS CHARGE - Times Clpg dtd
21 Feb 1967. Dempsey J. Travis, Negro broker licensed to sell homes
in Markham charged that city officials are trying to block him instead
of instituting positive programs for integration. File 1065, it 30.

CLPG:FILE:853-D, it.15, dtd.31 July 1967.DAILY DEFENDER.

CLPG & PICTURE: Subject one of persons on a program
called "FOR BLACKS ONLY", presented on Channel 7, 27
January 1970, re: problems families have in finding
decent black housing. FILE: 1134. It. 41-1 thru 41/2,
Daily Defender, dtd 27 January 1970.
OVER   090589

CLFG: SUBJECT, President of UMBA announced that SALK, WARD & SALK, INC., had become the Nation's first white mortgate bankers to join the UNITED MORTGAGE BANKERS OF AMERICA. FILE: 964-J, It. 2-1, Daily Defender, dtd 11 December 1969.

LEADERS BLAST CONTRACT BUYERS LEAGUE EVICTIONS. JACKSON, TRAVIS JOIN FIGHT. Brennetta Howell and Rev. Charles Koen to participate. FILE: 1134, item 78 thru 78/3, Daily Defender Clpg., 4-10 April 1970. *items 76*

CONTRACT BUYERS LEAGUE PACT. ACCORD STILL IN DISPUTE. PUSHES MORTGAGE PLAN. SUBJECT and Allen Oakley HUNTER, presidents fo Federal National Mortgage Assn., in Washington, D. C., hope CBL., will approve plan. File: 1134, item 91 and 91/1, Daily Defender dated 13 April 1970.

090590

TRAVIS TO WASHINGTON, D.C., CONTRACT BUYERS LEAGUE OKAYS MORTGAGE PLAN. Subject willing to join Sidney Clark in returning to the Mayor's office. Rev. Charles Keon has established a survival fund; and it may be reached by calling Checkpoint Charlie at 651-4950. File: 1134 item 92, Daily Defender clpg., dated 14 April 1970.
SEE CARD No. 4

TRAVIS, Dempsey J.   M/N   CARD #4   1968
Sivart Mortgage Corp.
Chgo.Ill.

090591

BOOK: dtd Dec.67-File 1052, Vol.#1, Exhibit File TOWARD RESPONSIBLE FREEDOM-A PROPOSAL OF THE COMMUNITY RENEWAL SOCIETY, Pages 1 thru 70 written by Donald L. Benedict, Executive Director, See Item 9/120, page 5 of Appendix VII, Suject on the Board.

INTV.RPT: 18 Apr.70-Mtg. of Operation Breadbasket-79th Halsted St. Re: Senator Percy who will also meet with Subject regarding the Contract Buyers League. File:940-P, It.4-1.

PERCY ASKS U.S. AID FOR CONTRACT BUYERS. Plan revealed at Operation Breadbasket's meeting held at Capitol Theater, 7941 S. Halsted St., 25 April 1970. Subject present. FILE: 1134-A, item 4, Chicago Today, 26 April 1970.

OVER

Chicago Police Department "Red Squad" file

INTV.RPT: 20 Apr.70-INFO.Re. SILVERCUP INC.-5324 S. Federal St. Chgo.Ill. is being refinanced by SIVART MORTAGAGE COMPANY-840-E. 87th St. of which Subject is President. File:940-P,It.6-1.

INTV.RPT: 25 Apr.70-SUBJECT was identified at meeting of Operation Breadbasket-Capitol Theater-79th Halsted St. File:940-P, It.7-1 thru 7-2. Also see It.11-1 thru 11-10.

CLPG: THE LEADERSHIP COUNCIL FOR METROPOLITAN OPEN COMMUNITIES HAS STARTED PROGRAM TO OPEN WHITE NEIGHBOR-HOODS TO BACK HOME BUYERS. THE SUBJECT MENTIONED. FILE: 1065-A, It. 69-1, News, dtd 9 April 1970.

SUBJECT shown in group photo receiving an award as new President of Dearborn Real Estate Board, Inc., at banquet held at Palmer House. Mrs. Josephine Walker Jackson and Edward Holmgren mentioned. FILE: 479-U, item 79, Daily Defender clpg., dated 18-24 April 1970.

msa.

CARD NO. 5   090592

CARD NO.5   1970

TRAVIS, Dempsey J.   090593

CLPG:"LEAGUE BUYERS GET $200,000 AID FUND". They are the Seaway National Bank and Supreme Life Ins.Co., 3501 King Dr., Each committed $100,000 for the purchase of the contracts from Midstates Homes, Inc., 234 E. 95th St. which will be mortgated thru the Sivart Mortgage Corpora-tion, E. 87th St., according to the SUBJECT, who is President of Sivart and a Director of Supreme Life. FILE: 1134-A, It.25-1, Tribune, dtd 26 June 1970.

INTV.RPT:SUBJECT WAS IDENTIFIED AT MEETING OF OPERATION BREADBASKET-Capitol Theater-7941 S. Halsted St. on 22 August 1970. File:940-R, It.25-1 thru 25-3. (Also see File:940-R, It.46-1/19 Sept.1970.

SURV.RPT:SUBJECT WAS IDENTIFIED AT OPERATION BREADBASKET BLACK BUSINESSMAN'S CONFERENCE HELD AT THE CENTER FOR CONTINUING EDUCATION-1307 E. 60th St. File:940-S, It. 20-1 thru 20-2, dtd 10 Nov.1970.

OVER

Chicago Police Department "Red Squad" file

REPORT RE: NEWLY FORMED CHICAGO WEST BUSINESS ASSOCIATION
3014 W. Madison St., headed by George Durham and assisted
by Rev. James L. Bevel, Dempsey Travis and Mr.
Sullivan of Philadelphia on 15 Mar.1971.BLACK SOULS AKA:
MAD BLACK SOULS NATION, a west side gang. FILE: 964-0,
item 53-1; report dated 16 May.1971.

INTV.RPT:SUBJECT SPOKE AT MEETING SPON BY OPERATION
BREADBASKET HELD AT KING'S WORKSHOP-7941 S. Halsted St.
on 29 May 71,concerning the unfair practic in the black
neighborhood by large auto insurance agencies . File:
940-U, It.38-1.(Also see File:940-U, It.39&40 dtd 29 May
1971.)

INTV.RPT:FILE:1185-item 35-1/5, dtd 15 Jan.72-SUBJECT
WAS IDENTIFIED AT A MEETING SPON BY OPERATION PUSH HELD
AT TABERNACLE CHURCH-4130 S. Indiana Ave.(BOARD MEMBER
OF OPERATION PUSH)

SEE CARD #090594

TRAVIS, DEMPSEY J.   CARD #6   1972

INTV.RPT.FILE:1190,it.4-1/4-26, dtd. 17,18,19 March 1972]
SUBJECT was one of the panel members at the NATIONAL REAL
ESTATE CONFERENCE, sponsored by WEST SIDE COALITION at
Schwinn Auditorium, 3027 W. Palmer Street, Chicago, Ill.
RELATED MATERIAL ATTACHED.

FILE: 1185-I ITEM 21-1 thru 21-12 SURV & INTV RPTS DTD 25 thru 28
JULY 73 OPERATION PUSH held 2nd annual convention at Dr. King's
Workshop, 930 E. 50th St. SUBJECT identified. RELATED MATERIAL
ATTACHED.

090595

NOTE: ALSO TO BE USED FOR OVERHEARD INFORMATION

INTELLIGENCE DIVISION

CHICAGO POLICE DEPARTMENT

INTERVIEW REPORT

CASE _____

DATE OF REPORT 20 Apr. '70

SUBJECT MATTER OF INVESTIGATION	PERSON INTERVIEWED
OPERATION BREADBASKET % Capitol Theatre 79th Halsted St. Chicago, Illinois	C.I. ▆▆▆

DATE & TIME INTERVIEWED	OTHER PERSONS PRESENT
18 April 1970 4:00 PM	None

PLACE OF INTERVIEW	INVESTIGATORS:
On the street	▆▆▆

PURPOSE OF INTERVIEW OR INFORMATION

To attend SUBJECT'S meeting and obtain any information that would be of interest to the Intelligence Division. This meeting was held on 18 April 1970, from 8:30 AM to 12:30 PM, at the indicated location.

STATEMENT OF INTERVIEW OR INFORMATION

Approximately four thousand (4,000) persons were in attendance at this meeting. Almost one thousand of this figure were white. There was one unidentified male/white, and one unidentified female/white from the United Farm Workers Organizing Committee of Chicago on the speakers platform. Also on the speakers platform was Rev. Ralph Abernathy M/N and Rev. Jesse Jackson M/N . Rev. Jackson was very angry about a "young white boy" around twenty three (23) years old, by the name of Richard Devine M/W who has just been appointed Deputy Mayor of Chicago. Rev. Jackson further stated that this young man has only been in Chicago one (1) year, and he was appointed to this position when there are several qualified blacks in Chicago who should have that position.

Rev. Jackson said that at this time he is trying to find the home address of Deputy Mayor Devine for the purpose of leading a protest march at his home. He also appealed to all black Policemen to get themselves together and support Officer Renault Robinson M/N in all his endeavors. He mentioned that Stokely Carmichael M/N will be at the First Congregation Church 40 N. Ashland Avenue, on Sunday 19 April 1970, at 6:00 PM, and he encouraged all blacks to attend.

Rev. Jackson announced that he had been appointed a Vice President of the Southern Christian Leadership Conference, AND TOOK issue with the Chicago Daily Defender article that said that he had been kicked upstairs in the organization in order to get him out of the way.

It was announced that on 20 April 1970, at 9:30 AM, Senator Charles Percy, and Senator George Mc Govern will conduct hunger hearings at the People's Church 941 W. Lawrence Avenue . It was also announced that Senato Percy will also meet with Dempsey Travis M/N regarding the Contract Buyers League. Rev. Jackson concluded by saying that this summer there will be many demonstrations at all food stores in the Chicago area, and he is determined to see to it that they hire blacks on a large scale or ship out of the city. There was many members of the Black Panthers in attendanc and both Rev. Abernathy and Rev. Jackson thanked them for their help.

CPD 35.361 (REV. 7/68)

128706

1-1

Chicago Police Department "Red Squad" file

940

NOTE: ALSO TO BE USED FOR OVERHEARD INFORMATION

INTELLIGENCE DIVISION   CHICAGO POLICE DEPARTMENT

INTERVIEW REPORT   CASE

DATE OF REPORT 23 April '70

SUBJECT MATTER OF INVESTIGATION	PERSON INTERVIEWED
SILVERCUP BAKERIES INC. 5324 S. Federal St. Chicago, Illinois	C.I. ████

DATE & TIME INTERVIEWED	OTHER PERSONS PRESENT
20 April 1970 4:00 PM	None

PLACE OF INTERVIEW	INVESTIGATORS:
On the street	████

PURPOSE OF INTERVIEW OR INFORMATION

Information received that SUBJECT organization was reportedly purchased by Operation Breadbasket or an agent of that organization in 1969.

STATEMENT OF INTERVIEW OR INFORMATION

Operation Breadbasket or one of it's agents reportedly purchased SUBJECT in 1969. A check of credit sources reveal that SUBJECT was purchased by a Alton A. Davis M/N, for $911,000, in August 1969. Davis was born in 1907, is married, and employed by National Bible Guild Inc. 2600 W. Lexington Ave. Chicago, Illinois, for twenty years as general manager and director. He is also chairman for the board of Gran-Mother Bakeries 2608 W. Lexington Ave. Chicago, Illinois.

Mr. Davis is reported to be in poor health, and a William Atkins M/N is reported to be in complete control. He is also reported to be closely associated with the leaders of Operation Breadbasket. Mr. Atkins is using pressure tactics on chain food stores to take Silvercup and Gran Mothers bread.

It was also determined that SUBJECT is being refinanced by Dempsey Travis M/N through the Sivart Mortgage Company 840 E. 87th Street, Chicago.

Chicago Police Department "Red Squad" file

NOTE: ALSO TO BE USED FOR OVERHEARD INFORMATION

INTELLIGENCE DIVISION

CHICAGO POLICE DEPARTMENT

INTERVIEW REPORT

CASE _____

DATE OF REPORT 27 April 1970

SUBJECT MATTER OF INVESTIGATION	PERSON INTERVIEWED
OPERATION BREADBASKET Capitol Theater - 79th & Halsted St Chicago, Illinois	# ▓

DATE & TIME INTERVIEWED	OTHER PERSONS PRESENT
On Street - 27 April 1970	None
PLACE OF INTERVIEW	INVESTIGATORS:
On Street	# ▓

PURPOSE OF INTERVIEW OR INFORMATION   To obtain information regarding the activity of the SUBJECT at a meeting held on Saturday 25 April 1970 at 8:30 AM at the indicated location.

STATEMENT OF INTERVIEW OR INFORMATION

At 8:30 AM the SUBJECT's regular weekend meeting began. There were approximately three-thousand (3000) persons in attendance including about five-hundred (500) whites.

Individuals identified were as follows: SAMUEL JACKSON M/N, REV. JESSE JACKSON M/N, REV. CALVIN MORRIS M/N, REV. WILLIE BARROWS F/N, REV. GEO. E. RIDDICK M/N, LEONARD SENGALI M/N, DEMPSEY TRAVIS M/N, SIDNEY TRAVIS M/N and the REV. TOM SKINNER M/N.

The first speaker to address the crowd was Dempsey Travis who told those present not to be afraid of contracts when they are buying houses. He said that only when these contracts are put into the hands of evil people do you begin to have problems.

Sidney Clark, chairman of the south side CBL then spoke breifly and he spoke of the recent evictions and how some of the people are paying up their contracts but that they still have a solid front and as long as they remain together, they will be able to win their suit in court.

The next speaker of the day was Leonard Sengali who touched on the structure of the gangs. Sengali said that people should not think bad of

Con't.

CPD 35.361 (REV. 7/68)

7-1   ▓   128694

PACE **2** OF _____

SUBJECT MATTER OF INVESTIGATION: **OPERATION BREADBASKET**
(TITLE ONLY)

INVESTIGATORS # ████   DATE OF REPORT **27 April 1970**

all members of the gangs. He added that when you think bad of a gang member, then you had better look into your own closet and check your own child
out.

Rev. Willie Barrows then spoke and she talked about her hunger campaign. Rev. Barrows told those present that she was asking for volunteers
to help in the feeding of children. She said too that Mayor Daley had released five-hundred-thousand (500,000) dollars to help in the feeding of the
poor, adding that Dayley's program is set up for from 10:00AM to 2:00 PM
but these hours do not help out the children in school however.

The next speaker was Rev. Jesse Jackson who at this time stated
that relative to Mayor's program, if the feeding hours were not changed,
then the people would have to take the children out of school. Jackson
then talked about the contract buyers league and how there is a conspiracy
against poor blacks. Then Jackson talked about how precinct captains handle their new jobs in locating hungry people in their wards but he said
however, all you have to do is open up your telephone book to the west
side and you will find all the hungry people you want.

Samuel Jackson followed Rev. Jesse Jackson to the stage and he told
those present that the Federal Government may help Chicagos contract buyers
obtain mortgages. He told them also, that Sen. Chas. Percy had contacted
H.U.D. secretary George Romney and asked him to look into the contract
buyers dispute.

Following Samuel Jackson was an out of town visitor Rev. Tom Skinner
an evangelist minister who offered his apoligies for the way that ministers
lead their people in the wrong path. After some prayer the meeting ended.

C P C ?? ?65 (REV. 7/68)   128695

Chicago Police Department "Red Squad" file

q40

NOTE: ALSO TO BE USED FOR OVERHEARD INFORMATION

INTELLIGENCE DIVISION   CHICAGO POLICE DEPARTMENT

INTERVIEW REPORT   CASE

                                                        DATE OF REPORT 28 Apr. 70

SUBJECT MATTER OF INVESTIGATION	PERSON INTERVIEWED
OPERATION BREADBASKET (OB) Capitol Theater 7941 So. Halsted Street	C.I. #

DATE & TIME INTERVIEWED	OTHER PERSONS PRESENT
28 April 1970	None

PLACE OF INTERVIEW	INVESTIGATORS:
On the Street	

PURPOSE OF INTERVIEW OR INFORMATION

To obtain information regarding the regular Saturday meeting of SUBJECT, held on 25 April 1970, at the above indicated location.

STATEMENT OF INTERVIEW OR INFORMATION

The meeting was opened at 8:30 A.M. with approximately 3,000 persons in attendance. Of this total, about 75% were Negroes, and 25% whites, with all ages represented. This assemblage was evenly divided between males and females. About two or three Negroes were observed wearing African style hairdos. All of the ushers wore African style darshikies.

About a dozen literature tables were set up in the lobby containing OB and related material. Other activity in and about the lobby consisted of leaflet distribution, circulation of petitions, and the selling of publications, buttons, and trinkets. Also observed inside the hall were members of the "straight" and Negro press, photographers, and TV camera crews.

The meeting was called to attention at 9:00 A.M. by Rev. Edgar Riddick M/N, who acted in the capacity of "Master of Ceremonies." Riddick conducted the meeting until Rev. Jesse Jackson M/N arrived. On stage at this time were about 40 persons, including speakers and guests.

Persons identified in attendance were: Kim Weston F/N, Thomas Biety M/W, Sam Jackson M/N, Rev. Thomas Skinner M/N, Leonard Sengali M/N, Jesse "MA" Houston F/N, Dempsey Travis M/N, Irina Hampton F/N and Jesse Jackson M/N.

Rev. Thomas Skinner was the first speaker. He spoke on radicalizing Christianity. Compared America's present day leaders to the Roman rulers who occupied the Holy Land when Jesus lived, and compared the present day militants to the Apostles, and other associates of Jesus.

Next to take the speakers stand was Dempsey Travis. The most significant of his remarks was the accusation that the federal, state, and city governments are conspiring to defraud Negroes by holding

Chicago Police Department "Red Squad" file

PAGE ___ OF ___

SUBJECT MATTER OF INVESTIGATION: OPERATION BREADBASKET (OB)

(TITLE ONLY)

INVESTIGATORS   **DATE OF REPORT** 28 April 1970

them responsible for contracts they sign, particularly for the purchase of a home.

Jesse "Ma" Houston reported on the breakfast program in schools. She said the city is paying the cost for the food. However, she strongly objected to the hours set aside for feeding the children. The feeding begins at 10:00 A.M. which is too late to do any good, said Houston. She will seek an earlier hour.

Next to speak was Leonard Sengali. He said that his trial is coming up in Criminal Court, and is currently out on bond. He informed the group that the Black P Stone Nation will support "Breadbasket" in future demonstrations.

Mrs. Irina Hampton, mother of the late Fred Hampton M/N, was introduced by Rev. Riddick. She did not speak, but chose to remain seated on stage. Along with Mrs. Hampton, a Negro author and doctor were also introduced, but neither spoke. Next to be introduced were about a dozen visiting Soviet journalists. This Russian contingent departed the meeting after several hours had passed since the opening.

The final speaker of the evening was Rev. Jesse Jackson. He began by accusing Mayor Richard Daley of "tricking" Negroes, and criticized the Mayor at every opportunity. Along this line, he referred to Negro politicians as "Uncle Toms."

The following are highlights of points made by Jackson while addressing the audience: He praised Sengali for his work in the freedom movement and stated that he (Jackson) would "stick" by him in event of need. - Negro children may boycott schools if the feeding hours at school are not held earlier in the day. - There must be police to deal with persons "committed to not working." - Urged the audience to support the Contract Buyer's League (CBL) in every possible way. - Negro merchants are not cooperating with Breadbasket in number as desired, and those that have refused will be picketed and boycotted until they beg forgiveness. - When in church, revolutionary ideas should be left at the door. -"God is Black."

In his closing remarks, Jackson appealed for funds from those in attendance. Plastic buckets were then passed among the audience for small money donations. Large sums were hand delivered in person to Jackson. "Breadbasket is seeking a new office, and expects heavy legal expenses - also numerous picket signs must be paid for," said Jackson. The audience remained fairly quiet in response to this request, although some individuals expressed their approval by yelling and hand-clapping. Jackson then announced that next Saturday plans will be made public naming banks and other financial institutions in downtown Chicago that hold mortgages on Negroes' homes.

CPD 35.365 (REV. 7/68)   128659

Chicago Police Department "Red Squad" file

PAGE __3__ OF __3__

SUBJECT MATTER OF INVESTIGATION: __OPERATION BREADBASKET (OB)__
(TITLE ONLY)

INVESTIGATORS ▬▬▬▬ DATE OF REPORT __28 April 1970__

    Sam Jackson M/N, the government official from Washington, D.C. was one of the guest seated on stage. He made the announcement that the Government is studying ways to improve housing for Negroes in Chicago.

    The meeting ended at 12:00 P.M. (noon). It ran for about three hours without incidents, disturbances, or arrests. The next meeting of this type will be held on 2 May 1970, same time and location.

Chicago Police Department "Red Squad" file

l l

NOTE: ALSO TO BE USED FOR OVERHEARD INFORMATION

INTELLIGENCE DIVISION   CHICAGO POLICE DEPARTMI

INTERVIEW REPORT   CASE _____

DATE OF REPORT 3 June 71

SUBJECT MATTER OF INVESTIGATION	PERSON INTERVIEWED
OPERATION BREADBASKET (Meeting) King's Workshop 7941 S. Halsted Chicago, Illinois	C.I.# ███

DATE & TIME INTERVIEWED	OTHER PERSONS PRESENT
Saturday 29 May 71 1930 hours	None

PLACE OF INTERVIEW	INVESTIGATORS:
On the street	███████████

PURPOSE OF INTERVIEW OR INFORMATION

    To obtain information concerning the regular meeting of the SUBJECT, that was held on 29 May 71, at 0830 hours, at the above location, that will be of importance to the Intelligence Division.

STATEMENT OF INTERVIEW OR INFORMATION

    On 29 May 71, at 0830 hours, the SUBJECT conducted ITS regular Saturday meeting at King's Workshop, 7941 South Halsted. This meeting was attended by approximately eighteen hundred(1800) persons. Of the persons present, fifteen hundred(1500) were black, and three hundred(300) were white. The following persons were identified: The Rev. Calvin Morris M/ the Rev. Jesse Jackson M/N, the Rev. Earl Simmons M/N, Bobby Rush M/N, Deloris Elliott F/N, Dempsey Travis M/N, the Rev. Ed Riddick M/N, Ron Burke M/N, Mrs. Iberia Hampton F/N, Bill Robinson M/N, and Ramsey Lewis M/N.

    Deloris Elliott opened the meeting by giving a talk on the Consumers Education Program of the SUBJECT. She stated that the average person on welfare receives only five dollars and eighty-two cents($5.82) a week for a family with four(4) children. She then encouraged the people to join the Consumers Club to find out just how wisely they can spend their money and to join, they should contact the SUBJECT.

    Dempsey Travis was the next speaker and his topic concerned auto insurance. Travis said the blacks should stand behind the Insurance Brokers Association of Chicago, because this company has done more to help the blacks with their auto insurance. He then added that blacks pay more for their insurance than do the whites not living in the black area, and that his facts had come from the Wall Street Journal.

    The Rev. Calvin Morris spoke of the "Housing Bill", now before the State Legislature. He said the bill would take the power away from the Chicago, and place the power in the hands of Congress. He then mentioned the Newhouse Bill, and stated that this bill would let Congress do what Chicago could not do for housing. He added that many of the Congressmen had the power to pass the bill but they didn't, and he was wondering why. He also mentioned the bill that Hanrahan was trying to get passed, which contained some twenty(20) items. This bill according to Morris has conotations of a police state, and that the words law and order mean nothing to Hanrahan.

contd.

CPD-41.104 (3/71)   129358

40-1

SUBJECT MATTER OF INVESTIGATION: OPERATION BREADBASKET (Meeting)
(TITLE ONLY)

INVESTIGATORS ▮▮▮▮▮▮▮▮▮▮▮▮▮▮▮▮ DATE OF REPORT 3 June 71
contd.,

The Rev. Jesse Jackson was introduced and began his talk concerning the young black girl who had been shot and killed in Mississippi, and about having a black president. He also addressed the audience on the Fred Hubbard situation, and stated that Hubbard is innocent until proven guilty, but the newspapers have convicted him already, as well as many of Hubbard's office workers and officials. Jackson then said there is a conspiracy on the black leadership.

Bill Robinson then addressed the audience and told the people that they now have a leader in the Rev. Jesse Jackson, and the people can stand behind Jesse in this white racist society. Robinson said that a black man in public office is in trouble in the white man's society, because in the white racist society a black man is not supposed to be a man, and that we all live in a society that says the blacks are slaves. Robinson ended by saying that Jesse is the answer for todays blacks.

Ron Burke spoke to the audience about the film of Fred Hampton, and that the film is to be shown at King's Workshop in the near future. He then introduced Mrs. Iberia Hampton to the audience and asked them to contribute to help buy a headstone for the grave of Fred Hampton, and all money should be sent to Mrs. Hampton.

It was also announced that the SUBJECT is going to picket the National Food Stores as well as the Jewel Food Stores, and Sears. The people were asked to volunteer to be sent to the picket locations.

The meeting ended at 1230 hours without incidents.

Chicago Police Department "Red Squad" file

Dr. Martin Luther King, Jr. returned to Chicago on the occasion of the Chicago Freedom Movement's unveiling of a $4, 500, 000 Housing and Urban Development mortgage commitment for the rehabilitation of apartment buildings on the loan starved west side. Seated left to right at the December 20, 1966 unveiling in the lower auditorium of the Liberty Baptist Church are: Dempsey J. Travis, mortgage banker, and author; Al Raby, convener of the Coordinating Council of Community Organizations; Dr. Martin Luther King, president of the Southern Christian Leadership Conference; Ernest Stevens, director of the local insurance office, of the Federal Housing Administration; Frank B. Palmer, board chairman of the Community Renewal Foundation and Jess Gill, project director.

Chapter II

Louis Armstrong: The Down Home Boy Who Hollered Foul

Although Louis Armstrong had been busted by the Los Angeles police for smoking pot in the parking lot of The Sebastion Cotton Club on March 9, 1931, his name did not surface on the Federal Bureau of Investigation files until November 30, 1950 when he hollered foul because of the Jim Crow policy being practiced against him and the men of the orchestra at the Flamingo Hotel in Las Vegas, Nevada.   Joe Glaser, his agent and manager told the Flamingo Hotel owners that he would pacify Armstrong by giving him a case of scotch whiskey and a couple of cigar boxes full of giant size reefers. Louis's next entry in the FBI files was dated September 10, 1951.   This was the day that a FBI informant furnished the Bureau with a copy of a letter received by Louis from The Negro Actors Guild of America, Inc. , headquartered at 1674 Broadway, in New York City.   Among the names appearing on the letterhead of the organization was Louis Armstrong, he was listed as vice president.   J. Edgar Hoover considered the Negro Guild a Communist front. He placed the Guild in the same Communist category as that of the National Association for The Advancement of Colored People.   In the mind's eye of Hoover any organization that was slightly left of center was smeared with the red paint of Russia.

Armstrong never considered himself a Twentieth Century version of Uncle Tom although some of his contemporaries believed that to be true. He proved them all wrong on September 19, 1957 at a press conference in Grand Forks, North Dakota when he criticized President Dwight Eisenhower for not supporting the Little Rock Nine students when they attempted to enroll at the lily-white Central High School in Little Rock, Arkansas. Armstrong's blood pressure figuretively spiraled up to 250/110 when Arkansas Governor Orval Faubus defied the United States Supreme Court's order to desegregate Little Rock Central High School. Governor Faubus had exercised his power as the chief executive of the state and mobilized the Arkansas National Guard to block the entry of the Black children.

President Eisenhower had not taken a stand on the Little Rock school desegregation dilemma. However, when violence erupted, the President reluctantly federalized the National Guard and dispatched one thousand members of the 101st Airborne Division and ten thousand federalized Arkansas guardsmen to ensure that the nine Black children were permitted to register at the Little Rock Central High School. Armstrong was not satisfied with Ike's action. He said, "President Eisenhower was "two faced" and had "no guts"; otherwise he would go down to Little Rock and take those little Colored children by the hand and lead them into the school.

When the reporters told Joe Glaser, Armstrong's manager, what Louis had said, Glaser called Louis from New York City and said, "You didn't say that, did you?" Louis softly retorted "Oh! Yes I did."

Glaser prevailed upon Armstrong to apologize to the President. Louis in turn sent a telegram to the White House which read, "Mr. President, if you decide to walk into the school with those little Colored children, take me along Daddy, God will bless you."

As a result of Armstrong's expressing his gut feeling about racism in America, he was thought to be Communist inspired. His actions and movements were put under FBI surveillance, like that of a Nazi agent. This action was not sanctioned by Eisenhower although he was a diehard racist. His racism was evident by the way he treated Black soldiers in the European theater during World War II. In spite of this, he was concerned that loyal American citizens should not be persecuted for alleged communist affiliation.

As a result of Louis playing the role of the "mouse that roared", many of his concerts and theater engagements were cancelled throughout the South and the North, but the Europeans welcomed him with open arms.

While in Rome, Ernie Anderson one of his booking agents and a practicing Catholic, made a routine request for a papal audience for Baptist Louis Armstrong and his Catholic wife Lucille. When Anderson told Louis he would have to get down on his knees before the Pope, Louis rescinded an invitation he had not yet received. Louis declared, "I won't get down on my knees for any man." Lucille tearfully persuaded Louis to accept the honor of a meeting with the Pope, if the opportunity presented itself.

The American Embassy reported to Anderson that there had been no response to his request. The Vatican has its own private mail system; Mail is hand delivered by Swiss guards, wearing costumes designed by Michelangelo.

Some 24 hours later the guards delivered a formal invitation to the Armstrongs that indicated that the Pope would give them a private audience the next morning at 10 A. M. at the papal summer residence, Castel Gondolfo, an hour's drive south of Rome.

When the Pope came through the door of the salon, Louis was the first one to hit the floor on his knees. During the half-hour audience, the Pope wanted to know where they were from. Lucille responded, "Long Island." The Pope indicated that he had been there. He then asked Louis, "Do you have any children?" Louis replied, "No, but we sure are having fun trying." Ernie Anderson, who was in the salon with Louis and Lucille, said, "You could see the Pope trying to translate Louis's remarks. As he did so he began to chuckle, and the chuckle grew into a hearty laugh."

This tour, like Armstrong's previous two tours of Europe, was not sponsored by the U. S. State Department. During the period that Cordell Hull, a Roosevelt appointee, headed the U. S. State Department, he recruited a large number of young Southern gentlemen for his staff. Their upbringing would not permit them to see a person of Armstrong's color as anything other than a black jelly bean stuck at the bottom of a jar. Therefore, a number of years and several presidents passed before the State Department officially recognized Louis Armstrong as a Cultural Ambassador.

The Truman White House did not have a monopoly on slighting Colored people. In 1956, Glaser's public relations people arranged to get Armstrong an invitation to the White House for lunch. Louis assumed he was going to have a meal with President Eisenhower. The President never showed. Sherman Adams, the White House chief of staff, came into the room where the lunch was to be served and shook hands with Louis and Lucille and then faded away down a long corridor.

America's Ambassador of Jazz some years later played at a party for President John F. Kennedy in 1963 at the Waldorf Astoria Hotel in New York City.

However, he never did perform at the White House during his lifetime.

Federal Bureau of Investigation

Freedom of Information/Privacy Acts Section

Subject: <u>Louis Armstrong</u>

CORRELATION SUMMARY

SECRET   Date: **August 8, 1962**

Main File No:

Subject: Louis Armstrong

Date Searched ALL INFORMATION CONTAINED
HEREIN IS UNCLASSIFIED EXC
WHERE SHOWN OTHERWISE.

Searched And Identical References Found As:

Louis Armstrong
Louie Armstrong
Satch Armstrong

. Satchmo Armstrong
. Satcho Armstrong

Also Searched And No Identical References Found As:

One Armstrong*   Classified by _____ /lmw Louis D. Armstrong
L. Armstrong   Declassify on: OADR 7/09/8 One Satchmo
Lewis Armstrong

This is a summary of information obtained from a review
of all "see" references to the subject in Bureau files under the
names and aliases listed above. All references under the above
names containing data identical with the subject have been included
except those listed at the end of this summary as not having been
reviewed, or those determined to contain the same information as
the main file.

This summary is designed to furnish a synopsis of the
information set out in each reference. In many cases the original
serial will contain the information in much more detail.

THIS SUMMARY HAS BEEN PREPARED FOR USE AT THE SEAT OF
GOVERNMENT AND IS NOT SUITABLE FOR DISSEMINATION.

Analyst   Coordinator   Approved

* Not completely searched; see search slip page 7

CLASSIFIED AND
EXTENDED

100 - 438995 -

ENCLOSURE

7 AUG 8 1962

SECRET

F. B. I. Secret Files

This reference is the "Current Biography" for September, 1944, published by the H.W. Wilson Company, NYC, which contained a lengthy biographical sketch of Louis Armstrong, musician.

SECRET 94-3-4-1115-36 encl. p.3
(2)

ONI report, dated 7/13/48, on the subject of ███████████ **b2**
███████, revealed that ██████ address book contained the name of ███ **b7c**
Louis Armstrong, 9200 Wilshire, Beverly Hills, Calif.

████████████████████████ **b2**
(3)

On 11/30/50, ████████████████████████ |
████████████████ which indicated that Louis Armstrong and his **b2**
orchestra were playing at the Flamingo Hotel and Armstrong was dis- **b7D**
satisfied with the situation. ████████████████ he would take care
of Armstrong by calling him on the telephone and by sending him "a
bottle of Scotch or a couple of reefers."

62-75147-26-370 p.8
(1)

████████████████████████████ furnished a copy of a letter received by him from
the Negro Actors Guild of America, Inc. (62-95433), 1674 Broadway, **b7D**
NY 19, NY, dated 9/10/51. ████████████████

████████████ Appearing on the letterhead of this organization as a
vice-president, was the name of Louis Armstrong.

62-95433-2 p.2
(1)

SECRET

-2-

6

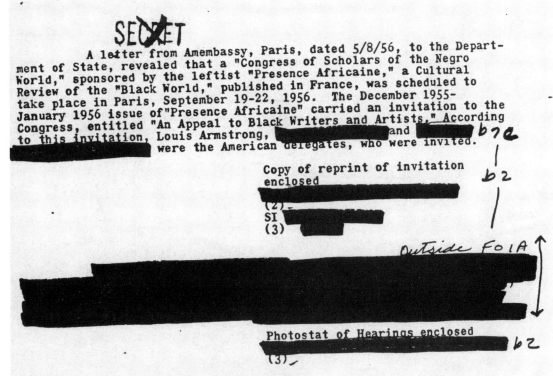

SECRET

A letter from Amembassy, Paris, dated 5/8/56, to the Department of State, revealed that a "Congress of Scholars of the Negro World," sponsored by the leftist "Presence Africaine," a Cultural Review of the "Black World," published in France, was scheduled to take place in Paris, September 19-22, 1956. The December 1955-January 1956 issue of "Presence Africaine" carried an invitation to the Congress, entitled "An Appeal to Black Writers and Artists." According to this invitation, Louis Armstrong, ███████████ and ███████ b7a were the American delegates, who were invited.

Copy of reprint of invitation enclosed

b2

(2)
SI
(3)

Outside FOIA

Photostat of Hearings enclosed

b2

(3)

* Negro History Week held February, 1956.

The "Washington News," dated 1/10/57, in an article entitled, "No Bid for Elvis- Murphy Stands Pat," revealed that George Murphy, director of entertainment for the inaugural committee, advised that he was trying to get Louie Armstrong to entertain at the Inaugural Ball in Washington, D.C.

62-66098-A "Washington News"
(5)   1/10/57

SECRET

-3-

Knoxville teletype, dated 2/20/57, captioned "Dynamite Explosion, Chilhowee Park, Knoxville, Tenn., 2/19/57," advised that an unknown person exploded dynamite approximately 100 yards from Chilhowee Park Auditorium, where Louis Armstrong and band were playing.

> 100-135-24-103
> (2) ✓
> SI 100-135-24-A "Washington Star"
> (2,6) ✓   2/20/57

furnished on 9/19/57, a newspaper clipping from the 9/19/57 issue of the "Southeast Missourian," printed in Cape Girardeau, Mo., entitled, "Satchmo" Gives Integration Views" and datelined Grand Forks, N.D. The article reported that Louis Armstrong, while in Grand Forks for a concert, declared that he was dropping plans for a government-backed trip to Russia, "because of the way they are treating my people in the South, the government can go to hell." Armstrong called Eisenhower "two-faced" and had "no guts" and was letting Governor Orville Faubus "run the country."

> 100-135-374
> (2;6) -
> SI 105-47652-162 encl. p.3
> (4;7) "The Evening Star", Washington, D.C.
>   9/19/57

An anonymous letter, dated 9/21/57, with envelope postmarked Boston, Mass., revealed that the writer was concerned about the NAACP (61-3176) and various well known Negroes, who according to the writer, were associated with CP members. The writer stated "Louis 'Satcho' Armstrong is a communist, why does State Dept. give him a passport?"

> 61-3176-2085
> (1;6) -

-4-

The 9/26/57 issue of the "NY Herald Tribune" datelined
Davenport, Iowa, 9/25/57, in an article captioned "Satchmo Lauds
President for Action at Little Rock," revealed that Louis (Satchmo)
Armstrong, greeted the news of President Eisenhower's action in the
Little Rock situation by proclaiming "this is the greatest country."
He indicated he might change his mind about abandoning a government
sponsored tour of Russia.

62-101087-A "NY Herald Tribune"
(1,6)   9/26/57
SI 100-351585-A "Washington Post
(2)   and Times Herald"
            9/26/57

The 10/16/57, issue of the "Washington News," datelined
"Fayetteville, Ark. 10/16/57, entitled "Satchmo Is Scratched," reported
that the student senate of Arkansas University withdrew a prom date
invitation to jazz artist Louis Armstrong because of his "unfortunate"
remarks about the engagement. Armstrong, a vehement critic of Gov.
Orval Faubus, had said he would be glad to play at Arkansas, but would
be sorry if Gov. Faubus were to hear any of the "beautiful notes
coming out of my horn."

100-135-25-A "Washington News"
(2)   10/16/57

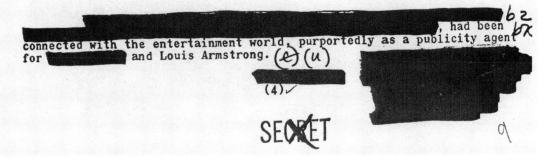

, had been
connected with the entertainment world, purportedly as a publicity agent
for _____ and Louis Armstrong. (e) (u)
(4)

SECRET

A letter from USIA, dated 2/24/59, enclosed a copy of allegatic
made by ████████████████████ against the Persian Service of USIA
Broadcasting Service, and a copy of the reply memorandum from the
Broadcasting Service. ██████████ alleged that material depicting the
achievements of the Negro " is seldom if ever, used in the Persian
Service." The Broadcasting Service advised that the Persian Service
had carried special feature items on William Warfield, Ralph Bunche,
Marion Anderson, Louis Armstrong, Harlem Globe Trotters, San Francisco
Golden Gate Quartette and George Washington Carver.

b2

(4)

The "NY Post," dated 3/19/59, in an article captioned "It
Happened Last Night," by Earl Wilson, reported that Louis Armstrong was
taking his group into Poland and Yugoslavia the following week.

100-351585-A "NY Post
(2) 3/19/59

(S)

(S)

(S)

b1

b2

(4;7)

SECRET

F. B. I. Secret Files

A letter from Amembassy, Accra, Ghana, to the State Department, dated 6/17/60, advised that Ghana had extended invitations to the Republic Inauguration Ceremonies to a number of Americans. Among those extended on invitations was Louis Armstrong, musician.

109-12-366-32
(4)

The 10/6/60 issue of the "Daily Defender," datelined Hollywood, contained an article entitled "Satchmo Asks Russia Tour." The article stated that Trumpeter Louis Armstrong would leave for a 6 month tour of Europe and Africa and he had asked the State Department for a visa to include Russia in the trip.

100-351585-A "Daily Defender"
(2)   10/6/60

A letter from Amembassy, Lome, Togoland, Africa, to the State Department, dated 12/9/60, on the subject "Distribution in Togo of Communist Propaganda Booklet Attacking US Racial Policy," advised that a booklet identified as a publication of the "Association of Friends of Africa," which presented a vicious attack on US racial policy, was distributed to members of the Togo Chamber of Deputies. It was noted that the document made its appearance at approximately the dates on which Louis Armstrong performed in Lome.

64-175-372-3
(1)

The following references in the file captioned "Visit of US Concert Artists to the USSR, file #105-39762, contain newspaper articles concerning a proposed government-sponsored trip to Russia by Louis (Satchmo) Armstrong. Plans for this trip were made and then cancelled by Armstrong because "the way they are treating my people in the South, the government can go to hell." After President Eisenhower sent troops into Little Rock, Armstrong changed his mind and stated that he was ready to make the proposed Ambassadorial trip.

TITLE OF ARTICLE	REFERENCE NUMBER	SEARCH SLIP PAGE NUMBER
"Satchmo Wants to Set Fire Under Soviet 'Cats'"	-A "Washington Post and Times Herald" 11/7/55	(3)

(continued on next page)

SECRET

12

Memorandum

TO   :DIRECTOR, FBI   DATE: 1/28/71

                                    ATTN: National Stolen
FROM :SAC, LOS ANGELES (87-33177) (P)   Property File

SUBJECT:UNSUB;
        THEFT OF $30,000 WORTH OF JEWELRY,
        11/4 - 5/70
        Century Plaza Hotel,
        Los Angeles, California;
        Mr. and Mrs. LOUIS ARMSTRONG -
        VICTIMS
        ITSP
        00: Los Angeles

          Captioned loss was reported ███████████
███████████ by Mrs. ARMSTRONG, on 11/5/70. Victim,
LOUIS "SATCHMO" ARMSTRONG's name was not reported initially,
to prevent unwanted publicity, in view of his status as a
nationally-known entertainer. The ARMSTRONG's were staying
at the Century Plaza Hotel during an engagement in Los
Angeles. Captioned loss occurred during their absence from
their hotel room.

          Investigation ████████ has developed no information
which would identify the unknown subject, indicate the whereabouts or disposition of the missing property, or indicate an
Interstate Transportation of Stolen Property (ITSP) violation.
Informants and sources of the Los Angeles Division have
furnished no information of value on such points, in this case.

          Mrs. ARMSTRONG has been interviewed by Bureau Agent
concerning captioned loss. She is unable to furnish any more
specific information than that which she originally reported

3 - Bureau
2 - Los Angeles
█████████
(5)

114728

20 FEB 4-1971

LA 87-33177

    It is requested that the following items, among those reported stolen in this case, be indexed in the National Stolen Property File:

    Ring, woman's diamond, five-carat, dome-shape stone, canary-yellow color, one tier of diamonds below main stone, another tier of baguettes below diamonds, platinum mounting; Value $8,000

    Bracelet, diamond, approximately $\frac{1}{2}$" wide, platinum, chain link with diamonds, clasp in shape of link; Value $10,000

- 2 -

Louis and Lucille Armstrong shortly after they were married in St. Louis in the fall of 1942.

Chapter III

Josephine Baker:
The Lady Who Never Escaped
The FBI's "*St. Louis Blues*"

At age 11 shabbily clothed Josephine Baker lived in the "Black Belt" section of the Carondele area on the South side of St. Louis. In her neighborhood, she felt the heat of hell and smelled burning human flesh resulting from the fire and ashes of the 1917 bloody race riot in East St. Louis, Illinois which is located on the east bank of the Mississippi River just across the Free Bridge from where she was born in St. Louis, Missouri on June 3, 1906. She first saw the light of day at the St. Louis Social Evil Hospital, a treatment center for poverty stricken, pregnant, Colored prostitutes suffering from venereal disease.

The white mobs literally burned down hundreds of houses owned or occupied by Negroes in East St. Louis on July 2, 1917. It was midmorning on that blistering hot summer's day when the first firebomb was thrown into an occupied home. There were no survivors. The only escape routes for the Coloreds who chose to abandon the city were via the Eads Bridge and the Free Bridge, the two bridges that spanned the Mississippi River and geographically tied St. Louis, Missouri and East St. Louis, Illinois together. The New York Times estimated that 9 whites and between 40 and 75 Negro men, women and children were killed, and hundreds were seriously injured in the riot.

The smoldering origin of the riot was caused by the escalating number of southern Negroes moving into the area in search of World War I jobs in the stockyards and packing plants of Swift, Armour, and the Morris meat slaughtering companies. The Negro presence in East St. Louis represented cheap labor. White folks' faces turned strawberry red with just the thought of losing their jobs to the Black migrants.

The other sparks underlying the riot were strictly political in that the Republican Party's local organization was working overtime actively recruiting and colonizing Negroes from Mississippi, Alabama, Georgia and Tennessee for the sole purpose of swinging the potential Abraham "He Set You Free" Lincoln Loyalists to their side of the ticket. (Northern Negro registered voters, voted decisively for the Lincoln Party from the late 1860's up until 1936 when they switched to President Franklin Delano Roosevelt and his "Happy Days Are Here Again" Democrats.)

Several years after the East St. Louis blood bath, Miss Baker hit the road with Bob Harris' Vaudeville Troupers. Although she had never sang or danced professionally, her spunk and personality made up for her lack of experience. Thus, Mr. Harris hired her. She was assigned by Mr. Harris to appear and study under the wings of Clara Smith and hence become her protegee. Smith was billed on the theater marquees as the south's favorite "Coon Shouter". Clara was a known lesbian, or ladylover as they were known in those days. She treated Josephine like a daughter for a short period and at the same time taught her how to sell a song and excite an audience and become her young lover.

The spontaneity of Baker's act was aided by her large repertoire of Saturday and Sunday afternoon movies that she had seen. In addition, she poured an enormous amount of energy into each dance step she had learned on the sidewalks of St. Louis. Her favorite dances were the Mess Around, the Itch, Tack Annie, Charleston, Snake Hips, Jelly Roll and the Shimmy. She literally had rhythm in her feet, hips, thighs and eyes. While traveling on the road with Clara Smith, she was recruited to join Shuffle Along produced by the talented vocalist and composer Noble Sissle and Eubie Blake the pianist and composer of "Memories of You" and "I'm Just Wild About Harry. Shuffle Along was a hit on the road and was bound for Broadway in New York City where it played to SRO houses for a year. When Shuffle Along closed, she was invited by Sissle and Blake to become the end girl in the chorus line of the "Hot Chocolate" Revue. As the end girl, she was the last person to leave the stage. This position enabled her to strut her stuff using all of her dance skills and bring the house down with her comedic showmanship and roving, flirting eyes. Thus, Josephine Baker did not simply emerge, she exploded to stardom on the Broadway stage before she was old enough to vote at the age of 16 in 1924.

In 1924, a young Louis Armstrong who was six years Baker's senior left Chicago, Illinois' musically thriving "Black Belt" for a gig in New York City with the very popular piano player, composer and arranger Fletcher Henderson's Black Swan Troubadors at the "for whites only" Roseland Ballroom, located Off Broadway in Midtown Manhattan. Duke Ellington seven years her senior and the leader of the Five Washingtonians was working at the Kentucky Club (Hollywood Cafe) in a basement speakeasy at 49th Street between Broadway and Seventh Avenue, in the heart of the "Big Apple" two blocks from the Roseland. The Kentucky Club had an all Colored floor show produced by Leonard Reed an Octoroon (12. 5% Black), but the club did not accept Colored patronage.

Both J. Edgar Hoover and Josephine Baker became bright lights on the American Landscape in 1924. Hoover became Director of the Bureau of Investigation in Washington D. C. , and Josephine Baker became the toast of New York's "Great White Way". Only the Shadow knew that they would be on the opposite side of the political fence for the balance of their lives.

Josephine Baker sailed from New York City on Wednesday, September 16, 1925 as a passenger on the Berengaria. In 1937 she gave up her United States citizenship and married for the third time to a French broker by the name of Jean Lion. Her first two husbands were American Negroes. Her fourth was Jean Bouillon a homosexual. This marriage was dissolved by divorce in 1940. During World War 11 she worked with the French Resistance Army and helped General Charles de Gaulle propagandize North Africa.

It was not until the early 1950's that Baker got a whiff of democracy sans the Cotton Curtain in the country of her birth. The alleged birthright was quickly yanked from her when she refused to accept racist snubs in public places. Baker absolutely refused to accept anything other than first class treatment in New York's Stork Club, the watering hole and the chow trough for the rich and the famous. Walter Winchell and J. Edgar Hoover dined there frequently. Both men were famous but neither was rich by Wall Street standards. The other thing that Hoover and Winchell had in common was the overwhelming desire to dethrone the first African American woman who achieved international stardom. Both men died in 1972, thus, preceding Baker in death by three years.

Although Josephine Baker became a living legend, her life ended, like it began in poverty. She never forgot or forgave America for the hurt it had inflicted upon her and her people.

A photo of Josephine Baker taken in Paris, France in 1927.

Federal Bureau of Investigation

Freedom of Information/Privacy Acts Section

File Number 62-95834

Subject: <u>Josephine Baker</u>

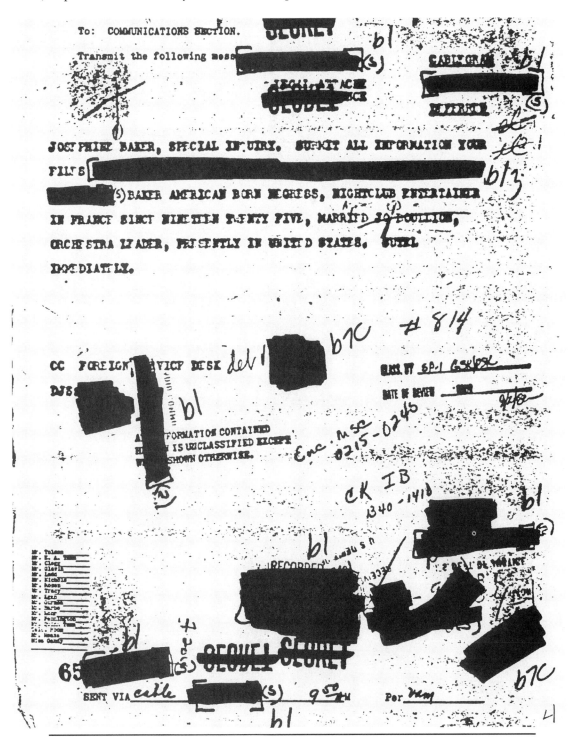

DO-8

OFFICE OF DIRECTOR
FEDERAL BUREAU OF INVESTIGATION
UNITED STATES DEPARTMENT OF JUSTICE

November 5, 1951

Jo Baker

The attached letters were sent in
by Walter Winchell. They concern
Josephine Baker, the colored
singer who was recently involved
in the incident at the Stork Club.

Concerning the top letter, which
is from one ████████████ and
alleges that he saw Josephine Baker in Leningrad,
as a guest of the Soviet Union, in 1936, Mr.
Winchell states: "Hoover, can we check this please?"

Attachments
eff

Mr. Tolson
Mr. Ladd
Mr. Nichols
Mr. Belmont
Mr. Clegg
Mr. Glavin
Mr. Harbo
Mr. Rosen
Mr. Tracy
Mr. Laughlin
Mr. Jones
Mr. Mohr
Tele. Room
Mr. Nease
Miss Holmes
Miss Gandy

SE 43

RECORDED - 5

NOV 14 1951

ALL INFORMATION CONTAINED
HEREIN IS UNCLASSIFIED
DATE 9/4/82 BY SP-1 GSK/kr

50 DEC 6 1951

b7c

Monday
October 29th, 1951

Dear W. W. (Walter Winchell)

Just read your column on J.B. (Josephine Baker) in today's Daily Mirror, in your last paragraph Mr. Rayburn gives a summation of J.B.'s attitude in the year 1935, In 1936 I visited Leningrad from Helsinki, Finland on a 3 day visit. The month was June "I think"? Anyhow the correct dates on, still on, the U.S.S.R. visa issued in Helsinki on my old passport, a British passport, I'm a Scotchman. Well I wandered into the Russian bar at the hotel one night of the 3 I was there & who was the "Big Shot" of the evening, surrounded by Red Commisars & French Reds, & actually singing & drinking with them to her heart's content, but J.B. The only colored person there. She came to the U.S.S.R. with a large group of French Reds, who in 1936 were being rewarded by the Politbureau for their work in the French Elections that year by a free trip to the U.S.S.R. "as guests of the Soviet Union." If you with your connections "check up" you will probably find J.B. is just a highly colored copy & a poor one at that, of Mati Hari. But still doing her stuff for Uncle Joe The Reds wined & dined her no end & were laughing up their sleeves at her, as they have no Negroes in the U.S.S.R. she was just a novelty, & a good stooge. Looks to m she is still following the line everywhere she goes.

Sorry she implicated you Walter, but that might have been one of her assignments? You know how the Reds "love you."

Sincerely,

b7c

COPY-eff

Office Memorandum • UNITED STATES GOVERNMENT

TO : *The Director*   DATE: *November 2, 1951*

FROM : *D. M. Ladd*

SUBJECT: *JOSEPHINE BAKER*   CLASS. BY SP·IC·SK/DL

DATE OF REVIEW ...

PURPOSE:

> To advise you, pursuant to your request, of information appearing in our files relative to Josephine Baker, Negro singer and entertainer.

SCOPE OF SEARCH:

> In the preparation of this memorandum Baker's name was searched through the single initial and with a combination of the first name with various middle names and initials. Baker's known married names were also searched. The search was not limited to locality and included a search of both criminal and subversive references.

PERSONAL HISTORY:

> According to the April 2, 1951, issue of "Life" magazine, Josephine Baker is the daughter of a St. Louis, Missouri, Negro washer woman. This article stated that Baker, who as of the time of the article, was alleged to be 45 years of age, began her Paris night club career in 1925, and has spent most of her life since that time in France.

> This "Life" article further stated that Baker was reported to have at one time been married to a Negro tap dancer and supposedly married one Pepito Albertino in the 1920's. In 1937, Baker gave up her United States citizenship and married a French broker by the name of Jean Lion. This marriage was dissolved by a divorce in 1940. Baker married her present husband, a Frenchman, band leader Jo Boullion, in 1947.

> According to the March 12, 1951, issue of "Time" magazine, Baker has been a French citizen since 1937, and during the occupation of France by the Germans, during World War II, spent her time in North Africa. This article further stated that while in North Africa, Baker became a Lieutenant in the Free French Air Force, did intelligence work, drove an ambulance, and entertained troops.

DJS:djb:dm

RECORDED - 122

INDEXED - 122   62-9583   1951

COPIES DESTROYED

11 DEC 1 1964

DEC 12 1951

16

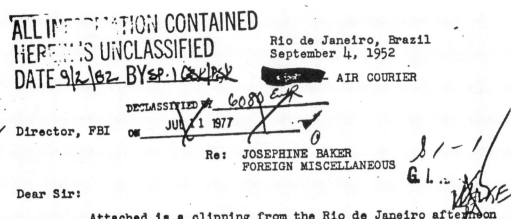

ALL INFORMATION CONTAINED
HEREIN IS UNCLASSIFIED
DATE 9/2/82 BY SP·1CSK/PSK

Rio de Janeiro, Brazil
September 4, 1952

AIR COURIER

DECLASSIFIED BY 6080 EWR
on JUL 11 1977

Director, FBI

Re: JOSEPHINE BAKER
     FOREIGN MISCELLANEOUS

Dear Sir:

Attached is a clipping from the Rio de Janeiro afternoon newspaper, "O Globo," dated August 29, 1952.

The article, with two photos of JOSEPHINE BAKER, is headed "Josephine Baker A Serviço De Uma Grande Causa" (Josephine Baker at the Service of a Great Cause). JOSEPHINE BAKER is the United States night club and musical comedy star who went to France in the '20s and became a big attraction there. It is believed that she became a French citizen. It will be recalled that some months ago, when she was in the United States, she became involved in an incident at the New York night club, The Stork Club, in which she accused the management of racial discrimination. In some way, Walter Winchell, the newspaper columnist, came into the picture in opposition to her. The writer knows of the incident only through sparse newspaper attention given it here in Brazil.

The attached article tells of her intention to form a Rio de Janeiro branch of the World Association Against Racial and Religious Discrimination. (Newspapers September 4, 1952, announce that the event took place.) The president of the organization in Rio is to be AFONSO ARINOS DE MELLO FRANCO, sponsor of an anti-racial law, and presently a member of the Federal House of Deputies, and just named House leader of the UDN (União Democrática Nacional - National Democratic Union - conservative party in opposition to the present government).

The article reports the results of an interview with JOSEPHINE BAKER, who is presently in Rio, where she has had a

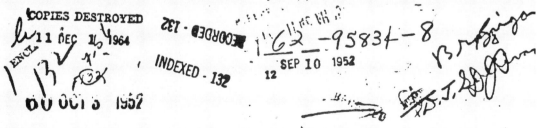

COPIES DESTROYED
11 DEC 14 1964

RECORDED - 132
INDEXED - 132

62-95834-8

SEP 10 1952

OO OCT 3 1952

successful run in/at least two night clubs and one theater in
a small revue. Other names in the World Association are ELEANOR
ROOSEVELT, RALPH BUNCHE, ARTHUR GARFIELD HAYS, BARRY GRAY and
TED POSTON. She refers to the Stork Club incident, and to
Winchell. As to that incident, she said that she and her friends
won out, "Today there is a law against racial discrimination in
the State of New York."

The closing paragraph states that she will attend the
official installation ceremonies of the association in Haiti
and in Cuba. It does not state when this will be. At another
point in the article, it states that from Rio she will go to
Uruguay.

The above is for the completion of the Bureau's files.

Very truly yours,

MARTIN CARLSEN
LA

Attachment
MC:jar

-2-

ALL INFORMATION CONTAINED
HEREIN IS UNCLASSIFIED EXCEPT
WHERE SHOWN OTHERWISE.

~~SECRET~~

November 12, 1952

JOSEPHINE BAKER
Born June 3, 1906 at
St. Louis, Missouri

CLASS. BY SP-1 GSL/BK

DATE OF REVIEW

CC TO: _____
REQ. REC'D _____
NOV 13 1962
ANS.
BY: _____

SECURITY INFORMATION - CONFIDENTIAL

According to the April 2, 1951, issue of "Life" magazine,
Josephine Baker is the daughter of a St. Louis, Missouri, washer woman.
This article stated that Baker, who as of the time of the article, was alleged
to be forty-five years of age, began her Paris night club career in 1925, and
has spent most of her life since that time in France.

The article further stated that Baker was reported to have at
one time been married to a tap dancer and supposedly married one Pepito
Albertino in the 1920's. In 1937, Baker gave up her United States citizenship and married a French broker by the name of Jean Lion. This marriage
was dissolved by a divorce in 1940. Baker married her present husband,
a Frenchman, band leader Jo Bouillon, in 1947.

According to the March 12, 1951, issue of "Time" magazine,
Baker has been a French citizen since 1937, and during the occupation of
France by the Germans, during World War II, spent her time in North
Africa. This article further stated that while in North Africa, Baker
became a Lieutenant in the Free French Air Force, did intelligence work,
drove an ambulance, and entertained troops.

Josephine Baker took a great interest in and engaged in
extensive activity in the defense of Willie McGee, a Negro who was convicted
in the State of Mississippi on the charge of rape of a white woman and,
subsequently during May, 1951, was executed by the State of Mississippi
for that offense.

RECORDED - 57
INDEXED - 57

162 -75834 -15

"Counterattack," a publication of "Facts to Combat Communism,"
55 West 42nd Street, New York City, in letter No. 200 dated March 23, 1951,
carried an item entitled, "Josephine Baker Won't Support Communist Fronts."
According to "Counterattack" Baker cancelled a speaking engagement at a
"Save Willie McGee Rally" scheduled for March 19, 1951, when she learned
that the rally was sponsored by the American Labor Party and that Paul
Robeson, well-known entertainer and Communist Party apologist, and former
United States Representative Vito Marcantonio of New York City would also
speak at the rally. (100-350-512-393)

Attachment
Original to INS-Washington, D. C.

SECURITY INFORMATION - CONFIDENTIAL

SECRET

SECURITY INFORMATION - CONFIDENTIAL

b1

Criminal Div (100-3-3866 p. 11) Diss:
5-7-52) In a report dated March 29, 1944, the Special Committee on
Un-American Activities, House of Representatives, stated that "For years
the Communists have put forth the greatest efforts to capture the entire
American Labor Party throughout New York State. They succeeded in
capturing the Manhattan and Brooklyn sections of the American Labor
Party, but outside of New York City they have been unable to win control."

b1

(S)

b1

(S)

100-270288-6 Diss: D/R, 7-13-51)
Relative to Baker's interest in the Willie McGee case while
in Detroit, Michigan, the May 16, 1951, issue of the "Daily Worker,"
east coast Communist newspaper, carried the story under the by-line of
William Allan, State Board member, District No. 7, Communist Party,
and Michigan correspondent for the "Daily Worker," entitled "'Pulitzer
Prize' Paper Gagged Josephine Baker." According to this story Baker,
who at that time was appearing at the Fox Theater in Detroit, Michigan,
contacted the editor of the "Detroit Free Press" and advised him that she
would like to make a statement on the "legal murder" of one of her people,
Willie McGee, who she stated was an innocent man framed on a charge of
raping a white woman. This article went on to state that after receiving
assurance that her statement would be printed in the "Detroit Free Press,"
the statement never appeared. (100-3-90-216)

- 2 -

SECRET

SECURITY INFORMATION CONFIDENTIAL

01026637

62-95834

Date: April 21, 1954

To: Legal Attache
Paris, France

From: Director, FBI

Subject: JOSEPHINE BAKER
INTERNAL SECURITY - FR

SECRET AIR COURIER

ALL INFORMATION CONTAINED
HEREIN IS UNCLASSIFIED EXCEPT
WHERE SHOWN OTHERWISE.

CLASS. BY

DATE OF REVIEW

The following appeared in Walter Winchell's
column of April 9, 1954, in the "New York Daily Mirror":

"How does the U. S. Consul at Paris, France,
explain issuing an American visa to anti-American speech
maker, Josephine Baker? Isn't he acquainted with her rantings
against the U. S. in Argentina and elsewhere? Isn't he familiar
with the regulations at U. S. Immigration? They stopped
admitting persons to these shores for being a Nazi, Commy or
Fascist sympathizer...We aided in getting this Ingrate into
the U. S. a few years ago. After her manager said: 'She
asked me to find out what you would do or say about her giving
up her U. S. citizenship,' to which we said: 'Oh, how's her
act?'...we plugged her act into $26,000 a week until she
staged a 'show' at the Stork Club...When her trick boomeranged,
she staged some 'shows' against the U. S. and has been since."

You should determine from the U. S. Embassy, Paris,
if the captioned individual has recently been issued a U. S.
visa or if the foregoing information pertains to a U. S. visa
which she was issued when coming to the United States in 1953.
You should also be alert to furnish the Bureau any information
reflecting her return to the United States.

cc - 1 - Foreign Service Desk

elc

NOTE: Legal Attache has background information in this case.

RECORDED - 78 62-95834

EX - 122 APR 23 1954
132

LEGAT
2 7 APR 23

APR 28 1954 MM-FBI

TO : Director, FBI (62-95834)　SECRET　DATE: 8/30/54

FROM : SAC, New York (105-8241)

SUBJECT: JOSEPHINE BAKER　　　　　　CLASS. BY
IS - FR

Rebuair tel, 6/11/54 and NY air tel to Bureau,

Record of the Clerk of Court, SDNY, under Civil
Docket No. 72-74, reflects that on 12/21/51, JOSEPHINE BAKER,
represented by Attorneys HAYS, ST. JOHN, ABRAMSON and
SCHULMAN, filed a libel action against WALTER WINCHELL,
Hearst Corporation and King Features, Inc. individually and
jointly charging that defendant WINCHELL indicated in his
syndicated column that the plaintiff, JOSEPHINE BAKER, was
a Fascist, Communist or one who consorts with Communists,
an Anti-Semite, an Anti-Negro, an enemy of the people of her
own race, intellectually dishonest, a fraud and a person of
low or doubtful character.

A claim for $400,000 damages was filed as follows:

1. Damage for unemployment　　　　$100,000
2. Publication caused damage　　　　200,000
3. Punitive damage　　　　　　　　100,000

The complaint filed by ARTHUR GARFIELD HAYS, 120
Broadway, Attorney-at-Law, alleged that on or about 10/16/51
JOSEPHINE BAKER, in company with friends, visited the Stork
Club, was treated discourteously. It continued that friends
of BAKER formed a picket line for a few evenings thereafter.
It alleged that WALTER WINCHELL was present on 10/16/51
at the Stork Club and resented publicity and thereafter
embarked upon a public campaign to vilify, libel and damage
BAKER in her reputation and professional standing in the
community. Further, the complaint alleged that on or about
10/22/51 and day to day up to 12/21/51, WALTER WINCHELL
maliciously, wantonly and recklessly printed and published
information of and concerning BAKER in the "NY Daily Mirror"
and in various papers throughout the US.

Further that on 10/28/51 an article was written
by WINCHELL intended to mean that BAKER was an Italian Fascist
or a sympathizer of Italian Fascists, that she invited and

COPIES DESTROYED

11 DEC 1964

RECORDED 94

INDEXED 94

62-95834 - 50

SECRET-125

55 SEP 13 1954

SEP 3 1954

ALL INFORMATION CONTAINED
HEREIN IS UNCLASSIFIED

SECRET

Letter to Director
NY 105-8241

planted incidents for purposes of publicity and self-display;
that on 10/29/51 an article by WINCHELL intended to mean that
BAKER has "horn swoggled", deceived and cheated colored
people into accepting her as a heroine and champion; that
she has in some improper way been connected with Communism,
pro-Communists and fellow travellers; and that she approved
of their views and philosophy; that she did not protest
against discrimination in Cuba; that the Stork Club incident
was a "job"; that she engaged in lascivious dancing; that
the places where she performed did not want colored patronage;
that she did not mix with colored people and did not want
to be associated with them and that she was anti-Negro
and wanted to be only with the white people.

The complaint further alleged that an article
written by WINCHELL on 11/4/51 intended to mean that
JOSEPHINE BAKER planned to act in a disorderly fashion in
a Washington, D.C. Department Store in order to incite
publicity against discrimination, but the newspapers having
failed to help her in a false endeavor she did not go ahead.

It alleged that an article written by WINCHELL
on 11/5/51 intended to mean that there was something illegal
or suspicious in connection with the status of BAKER in
the US and that she was under surveillance by the Government
and might be prevented from ever entering the US again; that
she was intellectually dishonest and a complete opportunist.

According to the complaint, an article written by
WINCHELL on 12/9/51 intended to mean that JOSEPHINE BAKER
hates Jewish people.

The record reflected that the Attorney for
defendants WALTER WINCHELL, Hearst Corporation and King
Features, Inc. was MC CAULEY and HENRY, 959 8th Ave., NY, NY.

The following notations appeared on the docket:

12/21/51 filed complaint and summons issued.

12/27/51 issued additional summons as of 12/21/51.

SECRET

-2-

Office Memorandum • UNITED STATES GOVERNMENT

~~SECRET~~

TO : MR. R. R. ROACH

DATE: December 10, 1954

FROM : L. V. PHILCOX

61356

ALL INFORMATION CONTAINED
HEREIN IS UNCLASSIFIED EXCEPT
WHERE SHOWN OTHERWISE.

SUBJECT: JOSEPHINE BAKER
INTERNAL SECURITY – FR
(Bureau File 62-95834)

On December 8, 1954, Mr. Mario Noto, Immigration and
Naturalization Service (INS), advised that Commissioner Swing
of INS has taken a personal interest in the case of Josephine
Baker and has directed that INS obtain sufficient information
with which to order her exclusion from the U. S. Mr. Noto
explained that recently the Department ruled that there was
insufficient derogatory subversive information to use as a
basis for her exclusion, and, therefore, INS is conducting
additional inquiry in order to attempt to obtain additional
information.

Mr. Noto has requested that Bureau files be reviewed
to insure that all pertinent derogatory information in possession
of the Bureau has been furnished to INS. Mr. Noto also directed
attention to Bureau memorandum dated November 14, 1952, page 4,
paragraph 5 (Serial 15).

Mr. Noto stated that he would forward this request
to the Bureau in a formal communication.*

ACTION:

It is requested that this memorandum be furnished
to the Espionage Section for handling.

ADDENDUM:

WP:hke
(3 copies) VTKS:mg

1-Mr. Philcox
1-Section Tickler

RECORDED - 17 62-95834-53

13 DEC 29 1954

* LETTER ATTACHED EX-109
  i NO 12/15/54

~~SECRET~~

UNITED STATES DEPARTMENT OF JUSTICE

FEDERAL BUREAU OF INVESTIGATION

In Reply, Please Refer to
File No.

ALL INFORMATION CONTAINED WASHINGTON 25, D. C.
HEREIN IS UNCLASSIFIED   June 9, 1960
DATE 9/10/80 BY SP-1GS/DK

JOSEPHINE BAKER

Released er State Dept.

On June 8, 1960, Mr. CHARLES SELAK, Visa Section,
U. S. Embassy, Paris, advised that his office in mid-1959
received information which indicated Miss BAKER would soon
request a visa to enter the United States. In order to
forestall any difficulty involved in the issuance of a visa
to Miss BAKER, it was deemed advisable by the Visa Section,
U. S. Embassy, Paris, to furnish Miss BAKER's complete background history to the Department of State so that the Department would have sufficient time to examine her case prior to
an actual request in order to ascertain whether Miss BAKER
qualified for a nonimmigration visa.

Mr. SELAK stated his Department by Department of
State Cable No. 1250, dated September 18, 1959, advised that
Miss BAKER was not considered ineligible under Section
212(a)(27)(28) or (29) of the Immigration and Nationality Act
of 1952 which authorized the issuance of a visa to Miss BAKER
in the event she so requested one.

Miss BAKER, according to Mr. SELAK, applied for a
visa to visit the United States in early February, 1960. On
February 8, 1960, an H-1 visa (issued to temporary visitors
of distinguished merit) was given to Miss BAKER. She departed
from Orly, France, at 1 p.m. on February 10, 1960, via Air
France, and arrived at New York City on February 10, 1960,
at 3 p.m.

Mr. JOHN DIGGINS, U. S. Consul, Visa Section, U. S.
Embassy, Paris, on June 8, 1960, advised he interviewed
Miss BAKER prior to the issuance of her H-1 visa on February 8,
1960. He stated that the issuance of this visa was considered
a routine matter and did not entail any hearings.

This document contains neither
recommendations nor conclusions of
the FBI. It is the property of
the FBI and is loaned to your agency;
it and its contents are not to be
distributed outside your agency.

62 95834 84

076

LA 105-5862

On May 24, 1960, ████████████████ Investigator, District Office, Immigration and Naturalization Service, Los Angeles, telephonically advised SA ████████████████ that ██████████ bearing French Passport number 161409, who was born on July 22, 1898, arrived in Los Angeles early in the morning of May 24, 1960, and departed that same day via United Air Lines for San Francisco where he could be reached at 322 Geary Street.

According to ██████████ his investigation regarding JOSEPHINE BAKER, aka Josephine Baker Bouillon, has established that she recently entered the United States as an H-1 visitor pursuant to a petition that was filed at New York, New York. From about April 27, 1960, until Sunday evening, May 22, 1960, BAKER resided at the Chateau Marmount, 8221 Sunset Boulevard, Los Angeles. On May 22, 1960, she left Los Angeles for San Francisco where she was to appear at the Alcazar Theater. Miss BAKER opened on April 29, 1960, at the Huntington-Hartford Theater, 1615 North Vine Street, Los Angeles, and closed with her final performance on May 14, 1960. In this production there were four other acts besides Miss BAKER's appearance. The producer was ██████████ and the stage manager was ██████████

b7C

b7C

b7C

- 8 -

NY. 100-4931

The article said that there were five hundred delegates to this meeting which was held under the auspices of the National Council of the Arts, Sciences and Professions. According to the article, EARL B. DICKERSON, President of the National Lawyers Guild, was the keynote speaker, while among the other speakers were PAUL ROBESON, Professor GOODWIN WATSON, of Columbia University, and Professor EDWARD BERRY BURGUM, of New York University.

The National Council of the Arts, Sciences, and Professions has been cited as a Communist front by the Congressional Committee on Un-American Activities in House Report No. 1954, dated April 6, 1950, Page 2.

Some of the measures adopted at the afore-mentioned conference, according to the "Daily Worker" of November 14, 1951, Page 7, Column 1, included:

A call to President TRUMAN to appoint a fact finding committee of cultural and professional leaders to conduct an investigation of said Jim Crow in the arts, sciences and professions, and recommend appropriate action in Congress.

A resolution supporting the Humphrey Bill for a permanent Fair Employment Practices Commission.

A call to the major radio and television networks to enforce their publicized statements in regard to utilizing and integrating negroes into all levels of the industry.

A request that the Federal Communications Commission withdraw and withhold radio and television channels from these institutions and companies which perpetrate stereotypes and job discrimination.

- 85 -

NY 100-4931

Federal Theatre was an era in which America saw the fullest flowering of the American theatres. She said that the Committee For the Negro in the Arts wants for America a real negro theatre about negroes, by negroes, and for negroes with the plays performed in negro neighborhoods near the ordinary people.

At the meeting, special mention was made of the contributions of JOSEPHINE BAKER in the field of opportunities for negroes in the theatre.

Awards were presented by HILDA HAYNES, who last appeared in "A Street Car Named Desire", and by ERNEST CRITCHLOW, Chairman of the CNA. They were presented to HARRY BELAFONTE, Singer; MARGARET BURROUGHS, Poet, Painter, and Director of the Chicago Negro Arts Council; LAZLO HALASZ, Director of the New York City Opera Company; PETER LAWRENCE, Producer of "Peter Pan"; posthumously to HUDDY LEDBETTER, better known as "Lead Belly", Folk Singer; CARLTON MOSS, Co-Author of the Biography of LENA HORNE; SIDNEY POITIER, Actor; PEARL PRIMUS, Dancer; WILLIAM WARFIELD, Baritone; PERRY WATKINS, Theatrical Designer; MARGARET WEBSTER, Producer; and the companies of "Just a Little Simple", and "NAT TURNER".

b7C

FBI Secret Files

SUMMARY FROM FRENCH

This communication from Josephine Baker is concerned with her efforts to preserve "Les Milandes," a children's village which was about to be disbanded because of insolvency.

As a matter of fact, foreclosure proceedings took place when Miss Baker was in the United States and, apparently, Miss Baker had a chance to discuss the situation with Mr. Robert F. Kennedy.

Miss Baker rushed back home and started a publicity campaign to appeal for financial help enabling her to save the village.

This letter is intended to give Mr. Robert F. Kennedy a report on how things are coming along. A list of countries from which contributions have come is provided along with a statement that "we already have about 80 million old francs out of the 200 million needed."

Miss Baker describes the touching messages of sympathy she has been receiving from many parts of the world, but feels that Les Milandes is not too well-known in the U. S. A. She mentions receiving a telephone call from CBS in which it was inquired whether the July 3 sale of the village had taken place, to which question, thank goodness, she was able to answer that for the time being the worst had been staved off.

After describing the noble motives and ideals which inspire the community of the village, the three-page letter concludes with a plea for help to have Les Milandes officially recognized "in the section of the United Nations."

Miss Baker feels that Les Milandes is a "pilot village of world fraternity and will always stand as a symbol for all those who struggle with so much fervor for equality and rights of man."

Enclosed with the letter is a mimeographed note in which Miss Baker introduces the also attached brochure which is a description of the village, its ideals, present status, history, etc.

Finally, Miss Baker also encloses a reprint of a press conference she held at Les Milandes on June 1 (1964).

TRANSLATED BY:

July 8, 1964

BUFILE 62-1077 (Translation and original material sent to Department 7/8/64, by Form 0-6, pursuant to their request).

REC- 15

UNITED STATES DEPARTMENT OF JUSTICE

FEDERAL BUREAU OF INVESTIGATION

In Reply, Please Refer to
File No. 157-2550

Chicago, Illinois
March 6, 1968

DECLASSIFIED BY SD-J GS/DSK
ON 9/8/82

CONFIDENTIAL

b2D

JOSEPHINE BAKER
INFORMATION CONCERNING

On February 2, 1968, a meeting was held at the
offices of the West Side Organization (WSO), Chicago, Illinois,
for the purpose of affording Martin Luther King, Jr., an
opportunity to solicit support from WSO members for the
Washington Spring Project (WSP), being promoted and organized
by King's Southern Christian Leadership Conference (SCLC).
A's publicly described by King, the WSP is an effort to
mobilize large numbers of persons in Washington, D.C., in
April, 1968, in protest of alleged United States Government
failure to solve the problems of the poor of this country.
King did not appear and it was announced that his wife was ill.
Approximately 95 persons were present.

Among the guest speakers was Josephine Baker,
described by source as a former well-known entertainer,
now residing in France. She stated she had experienced a
difficult time getting back into this country. She said she
had marched with King in his earlier march on Washington, and, as
a result, it appeared she was not wanted here. She described
the importance of the tent-in on the White House lawn and urged
all those present to participate. Her remarks, according to
source, were received by those present with no enthusiasm and no
apparent volunteers.

This document contains neither recommendations
nor conclusions of the FBI. It is the property
of the FBI and is loaned to your agency; it and
its contents are not to be distributed outside
your agency.

62- 95834 - 93

ENCLOSURE

CONFIDENTIAL
Group 1
Excluded from automatic
downgrading and
declassification

267

JOSEPHINE BAKER

Other speakers were Reverend Ralph Abernathy, SCLC official, representing King, and Reverend James Bevel of the Urban Training Center, Chicago, a former SCLC official.

Southern Christian Leadership Conference

The WSO is a small civil rights type group operating Chicago's near west side. It concerns itself principally with employment and welfare problems of Negro residents of this area.

Other Information Concerning Josephine Baker

The following articles appeared in the indicated editions of the Illinois Edition of "The Worker", an east coast communist newspaper:

April 22, 1951, page 8, column 5 - States in part that Josephine Baker insisted on singing at the Chicago Theater only before a mixed band and that she "also disturbed the composure of those who take the view that the real gains for the Negro people can come only after a long, long time. In her blunt, outspoken manner, she burst the 'progess' bubble which is used for hiding purposes by those who refuse to fight for liberation now. 'I can see no progress,' she said upon touring Chicago after 22 years."

July 22, 1951, page 1, column 5 - Article quoted statements by Josephine Baker as disclosed by Oscar C. Brown, Negro news commentator over Station WGES. Brown quoted Miss Baker as saying, "Support dynamic actions to save the life of Willie Mc Gee, like the protest parade being sponsored by the packinghouse workers. Wires and letters to the President to save Mc Gee are good but more forceful action is needed." The article further states that Miss Baker has previously interceded for the "Martinsville Seven" and that she recently visited the "Trenton Six" in their New Jersey prison where they face possible execution.

- 2 -

JOSEPHINE BAKER

July 22, 1951, page 1, column 3 - Article states that Josephine Baker, internationally celebrated Negro singer, was among the speakers invited to address a Chicago rally of the United Packinghouse Workers on April 29, 1951, to save the life of Willie Mc Gee, the Negro victim of a Mississippi "rape" indictment who was scheduled to die in Jackson, Mississippi, on May 8.

In its weekly edition dated February 24, 1968, the Chicago Defender, a Chicago newspaper, contained a number of photographs of Josephine Baker and others who attended a reception in her honor at the Fairfax House on Chicago's west side given by the WSO. It was stated that Miss Baker was in Chicago in an effort to get funds for a new international children's school in Paris, France.

- 3 -

Chapter IV

Bernstein: A Musical Genius Trapped In A Cultural Cage

In the 1930' s, 1940' s and 1950' s, Jews and Negroes were very close philosophically, because they were both victims of the racism that umbrellaed quota systems in the universities and excluded Jews and other ethnics from WASP (White Anglo- Saxon Protestant) controlled country clubs and many of the hotels and motels in Miami Beach and elsewhere in the United States.

It was during the same decades that great Negro musicians such as Eddie South, the Dark Angel of the Violin, had to play behind a screen when he accompanied a white artist. Teddy Wilson, the incomparable jazz pianist and member of the Benny Goodman Trio was relegated to use the freight elevator when he entered the Congress Hotel in Chicago where the trio and orchestra had a six month engagement in 1936. Renting a hotel room to a Negro in a downtown hotel until the 1950' s at the dawn of the civil rights struggle was unthinkable.

In the 1930' s and 1940' s, Bernstein was involved in all kinds of political left- wing and civil rights activities before and after graduating from Harvard University in 1939 at the age of twenty- one. As a young man, his temperament was in tune and compatible with Blacks who were still trying to scratch their way out of

President Herbert Hoover's Depression. In spite of the reality of the time, Hoover's 1931 campaign theme was "There would be a chicken in every pot and a car in every garage" if he was reelected in 1932.

Bernstein's working philosophy changed in the sunshine days of 1958 when he became the conductor of the New York Philharmonic Symphony Orchestra. He was in fact an employee of an ultra right-wing organization that had absolutely no concern about the plight of the Negro. Thus, he tiptoed to the beat of a muffled drum.

The case for Black musicians was articulated by T. J. Anderson, a top flight Black classical composer and Chairman of the Music Department at Tufts University in Medford, Massachusetts. He said:

> The keepers of the keys for classical music are not ready to accept a Black composer outside of a jazz milieu. How else can you account for the fact that they offered George Gershwin a platform, but not Scott Joplin. They welcomed Charles Edward Ives as a conductor of a symphony orchestra but not George Walker, William Levi Dawson or William Grant Still. Leopold Stokowski wrote, in 1945: 'Still is one of our greatest American classical composers.'

> Black composers are not on that list of musicians who receive commissions to write operas, symphonies and chamber music. Therefore, I personally feel that I have been blessed to have patrons like Richard Hunt another Black man who supports my efforts. When I tell him I want to write a chamber concerto for two violins and orchestra, he encourages me to go forward. He then puts icing on the cake by inviting me to present my work in concert at his studio. If it were not for Richard Hunt and others like him my career would have been minimized.

In May 1958 the New York chapter of the Urban League released a 21 page survey which described the rampant discrimination in everything musical from symphony orchestras to studio bands in radio and television. The report further pointed out that the stench of racism was overpowering in New York's five major orchestras. The Philharmonic Society of New York had never employed a Negro professional musician. The Metropolitan Opera Orchestra had never employed or even interviewed a Negro professional musician.

The report further condemned angels and entrepreneurs of Broadway musicals because in the 1956-58 seasons they employed 650 musicians but only 14 of whom were Negro. The 14 that were hired were employed under pressure when the principal stars of the shows were celebrated persons of color, such as Lena Horne, or Sammy Davis, Jr. They both insisted on integrated orchestras.

Douglas Pugh, who headed the Jim Crow music investigation for the New York Chapter of the Urban League hit a home run when he stated the following in the report:

> "Red baiting or using the Communist smear technique is one of the most onerous means used against liberal white conductors who are willing to employ qualified musicians in pit orchestras of Broadway musicals. The Industrial Relations Department of the Urban League interviewed several white conductors who stated that this red smear campaign ensued with vigor after they hired Negro musicians."

The communism by osmosis strategy was meant to scare the pants off of the musical conductors, and it did. A maestro would have to think twice before hiring a Negro musician for fear of jeopardizing his career.

The liberal wings of Bernstein's racial sensitivity were abridged from 1958 to 1964. However, when he got his first sabbatical from the New York Philharmonic Symphony Orchestra in July 1964, he instantly began spreading his wings for democracy in music. His first act was to give a fund raising party for the Legal Defense Fund of the National Association for the Advancement of Colored People. Some 600 people came to the jazz concert on the lawn of his Dunham Road estate in Fairfield, Connecticut. Dizzy Gillespie played as did John Megehan, a jazz musician who taught at Juilliard, and had been a friend of Bernstein since the mid 1940's.

On March 25, 1965 while still on his sabbatical, he spoke before Dr. Martin Luther King and 10,000 civil rights marchers in Montgomery, Alabama. Others who appeared on the same platform that night were Sammy Davis Jr., Harry Belafonte, Ossie Davis, Billy Eckstine, Shelly Winters, Mike Nichols, Elaine May, Peter Paul, and Mary who sang "Blowing in the Wind".

Following his sabbatical Bernstein's liberal ideals were forced to wrestle with his career demands. His career demands won.

Federal Bureau of Investigation

Freedom of Information/Privacy Acts Section

Subject: <u>Leonard Bernstein</u>

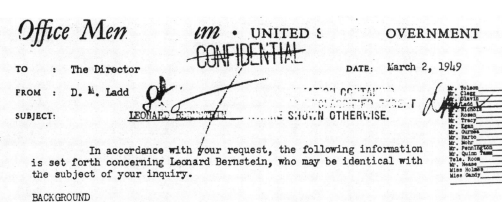

Office Men *im* · UNITED S OVERNMENT

~~CONFIDENTIAL~~

TO : The Director

DATE: March 2, 1949

FROM : D. M. Ladd

SUBJECT: LEONARD BERNSTEIN

... SHOWN OTHERWISE.

Mr. Tolson
Mr. Clegg
Mr. Glavin
Mr. Ladd
Mr. Nichols
Mr. Rosen
Mr. Tracy
Mr. Egan
Mr. Gurnea
Mr. Harbo
Mr. Mohr
Mr. Pennington
Mr. Quinn Tamm
Tele. Room
Mr. Nease
Miss Holmes
Miss Gandy

In accordance with your request, the following information is set forth concerning Leonard Bernstein, who may be identical with the subject of your inquiry.

BACKGROUND

The following information appears in "Who's Who in America, 1946-1947":

"Bernstein, Leonard, conductor, pianist, composer; b. Lawrence, Mass., Aug. 25, 1918; s. Samuel Joseph and Jennie (Resnick) B.; A.B., Harvard, 1939; attended Curtis Inst. of Music, 1939-41; studied conducting with Serge Koussevitzky and Fritz Reiner; studied piano with Helen Coates, Heinrich Gebhard and Mme. Isabella Vengerova; unmarried. Asst. to Serge Koussevitzky at Bershire Music Center, 1942; composer under contract to Music Publishers' Holding Corp., 1943; asst. conductor The Philharmonic Symphony Soc. of New York for season 1943-44. Premiere of Song Cycle, I Hate Music, on Nov. 13, 1943, at Town Hall, N.Y. and Symphony No. 1 in Pittsburg, Jan. 28, 1944. Composer: Clarinet Sonata, 1942; Song Cycle, I Hate Music, 1943; Piano Pieces, Seven Anniversaries, 1943; Symphony No. 1 (Jeremiah), 1942. Office: care Columbia Concerts, 113 W. 57th St., New York 19, N.Y."

This Bureau has never conducted any investigation of Leonard Bernstein.

CONNECTIONS WITH ORGANIZATIONS UNDER EXECUTIVE ORDER 9835

Leonard Bernstein has been connected, affiliated, or in some manner associated with the following organizations, which have been cited by the Attorney General as coming within the purview of Executive Order No. 9835:

American Committee for Yugoslav Relief
American Council for a Democratic Greece
American Youth for Democracy
Civil Rights Congress
Council on African Affairs
Joint Anti-Fascist Refugee Committee
National Council of American-Soviet Friendship
National Negro Congress
Southern Negro Youth Congress
Veterans of Abraham Lincoln Brigade

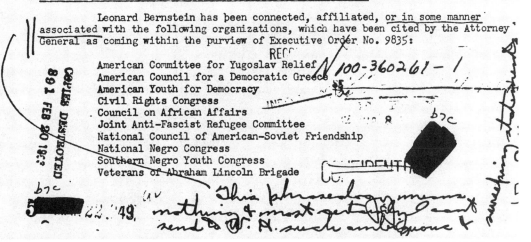

During October and November, 1947, articles appeared in the "Daily Worker" publicizing the national conference of the CRC scheduled to be held in Chicago November 21-23, 1947. The name of "Leonard Bernstein" appeared on a composite list of sponsors of that national conference; the list was prepared by the Chicago Office from three printed lists of sponsors made available by Confidential Informants ▮▮▮▮ (Lieutenant, Cambridge Auxiliary Police, P. D., Cambridge, Massachusetts) and ▮▮▮▮ (active, paid, reliable, Communist Party member). (61-10149-642)

b7C
b7D

The name of "Leonard Bernstein" appears on a list of signatures to an open letter to Congress demanding defeat of the Mundt Bill. This list appeared in a political advertisement of the CRC in the New York "Post and Home News" of May 10, 1948. The advertisement urged readers to send a protest to Speaker Joe Martin of the House of Representatives demanding that he "lead the House in rejecting the Bill in its entirety".

(61-10149-A, Sec. 2)

COUNCIL ON AFRICAN AFFAIRS (CAA)

A letterhead of the CAA listed "Leonard Bernstein" in 1947 as a member of the Council. No other identifying data appeared on the list of members. (100-69266-157, p. 2)

By letter to the Attorney General dated October 7, 1948, Max Yergan (former Executive Director of the CAA) transmitted a copy of a letter which he had sent to those members and former members of the CAA who supported him (Yergan) in the organizational conflict which he had had with the Paul Robeson Communist-led group. He attached a list of present and former Council members indicating those who supported Yergan and those who supported the Robeson-led Communist group. The name of "Leonard Bernstein, New York, New York" appears on the list of "Supporters of Paul Robeson-Communist-Led Group." (100-210026-236, Enclosure)

SOUTHERN NEGRO YOUTH CONGRESS (SNYC)

In a report dated May 4, 1948, at Birmingham it was reflected that Confidential Informants ▮▮▮▮ and ▮▮▮▮ made available a list of persons described by ▮▮▮▮ as members. Leonard Bernstein, 1239 Broadway, New York, New York, was listed under the caption "Sponsors or Contributors." (100-6548-337 pg 114)

b7C
b7D

SECRET

- 3 -

CONFIDENTIAL

THE AMERICAN YOUTH FOR DEMOCRACY

The American Youth for Democracy is the successor organization of the Young Communist League. The Young Communist League called a convention which was held in New York City from October 15 - 17, 1943, at which time the Young Communist League was dissolved and the American Youth for Democracy was formed. (X) (u)

The first Empire State Conference of the New York State American Youth for Democracy was held at the McAlpin Hotel in New York City, on December 19, 1943. This meeting was covered by microphone surveillances. David Livingston, co-chairman of this conference, announced during the course of the meeting that greetings to the conference had been received from several individuals which included the name Leonard Bernstein, who was described as a young assistant director of the New York Philharmonic Orchestra. (X) (u)   (61-777-34-106 p 27)

On October 16, 1944, the AYD held a "Salute To Young America" dinner at the Hotel Commodore, New York City, which resulted in pledges of $6700.00 to support the work of the AYD. According to the program, the Salute To Young America Committee was composed of numerous individuals including Leonard Bernstein.   (61-777-34-138)

On ████████████████ there was a meeting of the AYD Inter-
Collegiate Group at ██████████████ St. Louis, Missouri. St. Louis
Informant ████████████████ reported that everyone present at
this meeting attended a reception at the home of ████████████
████████████████ Missouri, in honor of Leonard
Bernstein, noted symphonic conductor and a national sponsor of the AYD.
This reception, according to the informant, was sponsored by the AYD for the purpose of raising money for the American Youth Orchestra. (X) (u)
            (66-2542-3-42-267)

The Second Annual dinner to "Salute Young America" was planned by the AYD for the evening of December 12, 1945, at the Hotel Roosevelt, New York City, to pay tribute to the average G.I. and to dramatize the postwar problems of youth. According to a technical surveillance on the Headquarters of the AYD it was learned that Leonard Bernstein was to be carried as chairman of the sponsoring committee for this Second Annual dinner. This Leonard Bernstein was described as a New York Philharmonic Orchestra Conductor. (X) (u)   (61-777-721x p 41)

SECRET

- 4 -

CONNECTIONS WITH OTHER ORGANIZATIONS REPORTEDLY HAVING A COMMUNIST INFLUENCE

Leonard Bernstein has been connected with the following organizations which have been cited as Communist fronts by the Tenney Committee of the California State Legislature in 1948:

Independent Citizens Committee of the Arts, Sciences and
    Professions
Hollywood Committee for the First Amendment
Young Progressive Citizens of America (Youth Group of
    Progressive Citizens of America)

Leonard Bernstein has also been connected with the organization, Peoples Songs, an organization which has been reported to be a Communist-dominated organization.

A complete summary of information in the Bureau's files is being prepared on Leonard Bernstein and will be available to you in the morning.

- 2 -

ACTIVITIES

No investigation of Leonard Bernstein has been conducted by the FBI.

CONNECTIONS WITH ORGANIZATIONS CITED BY ATTORNEY GENERAL AS COMING WITHIN THE PURVIEW OF EXECUTIVE ORDER 9835

AMERICAN COMMITTEE FOR YUGOSLAV RELIEF (ACYR)

The East Coast Communist newspaper, "Daily Worker," announced in its January 2, 1946, edition that the ACYR had opened its activities for 1946 with a Town Hall benefit concert the previous night. Among those named as sponsors of the concert was "Leonard Bernstein". (100-212169-A)

AMERICAN COUNCIL FOR DEMOCRATIC GREECE (ACDG)

A technical surveillance on Alfred K. Stern reflected on March 2, 1948, that ███████████████ of the ACDG, was making efforts to obtain sponsors for that organization prior to its national conference. In response to an inquiry made by Martha Stern concerning the identities of members of the National Board of the ACDG, ████████ named "Leonard Bernstein," among others. She gave no further identifying data concerning Bernstein. (X)(u)

(100-57453-278, pgs. 16 & 17)

CIVIL RIGHTS CONGRESS (CRC)

Confidential Informants ██████████ (active, reliable, not paid) and ████████████ (trash coverage on Communist Party headquarters in Bronx, New York City; paid, reliable) made available to the New York Office of this Bureau certain literature distributed by the National Committee to Oust Bilbo sponsored by the Civil Rights Congress, New York City, during October-December, 1946. This material particularly concerned charges made by the CRC against Senator Bilbo alleging that he was anti-Semitic, anti-Negro and anti-democratic. A letter dated December 6, 1946, requesting support of the drive to remove Bilbo, signed by Quentin Reynolds and Vincent Sheean on the stationery of the National Committee to Oust Bilbo, contains a partial list of the officers and members of this Committee. The name of "Leonard Bernstein" appeared on the list of Committee members. There were no additional identifying data. (X)(u)

(61-10149-517, p. 4)

SECRET

HQ 100-360261-2

CONFIDENTIAL

- 2 -

Investigation revealed that this "Welcome Home Joe" dinner, sponsored by the AYD, was held on December 12, 1945. According to New York Informant ██████████████████████ Leonard Bernstein and Reverend William H. Melish were co-chairmen at this dinner. (X)(u) (61-777-34-182 p 5)

Boston Informant ████████████████████ furnished Special Agent ████████ of the Boston Office with a copy of an invitation received from the AYD to attend a reception which was given for Leonard Bernstein and Donald Ogden Stewart at the Hotel Lincolnshire, 84 Beacon Street, Boston, Massachusetts, on March 24, 1946. The informant did not attend this reception but was subsequently advised that approximately 200 people were present. Bernstein played several selections on the piano and Stewart made a short and somewhat facetious speech in which he urged those present to support the AYD because it was an organization dedicated to the people and working to advance their interests. (X)(u) (100-18610-130)

On April 16, 1946, Detroit Informant ████████ (a technical surveillance on the AYD Headquarters) advised that Phil Schatz, Executive Secretary of the AYD in Detroit, arranged an interracial reception for Leonard Bernstein following the latter's direction of the Detroit Symphonic Orchestra. Schatz explained that the purpose of the reception was to explain to persons not familiar the purposes of the AYD. (X)(u) (100-58699-20)

Detroit Informant ████████████████████████████ advised that on April 21, 1946, the AYD held a musicale at the home of ██████████ ████████████████ Detroit, with Leonard Bernstein as the guest of honor. Tickets were sold for $2.50 each and about 100 or more people attended the musicale. The proceeds from this musicale, which amounted to about $200.00, were donated to the AYD. (X)(u) (61-777-15-306 p 11)

On December 20, 1946, there was a "Salute To Young America" rally held at Manhattan Center, New York City. This meeting was the commencement of the Second State Convention of the AYD. The "Salute To Young America" rally was open to the public. However, the convention scheduled a series of closed meetings on December 21 and 22, 1946, at the Tom Mooney Hall, 13 Astor Place, New York City. The co-chairmen at the "Salute To Young America" rally on December 20, 1946, were Leonard Bernstein and Ferdinand C. Smith, who was then an official of the National Maritime Union. (X)(u) (61-777-34-220)

The October, 1947 issue of "Youth", Fourth Anniversary issue published by the AYD, New York City, page 16, carries a plea for a $50,000 fund drive on behalf of the AYD. Leonard Bernstein was one of the individuals whose names appeared as assisting in this fund drive. (61-777-34-248)

SECRET

- 5 -

SECRET

NATIONAL COUNCIL OF AMERICAN SOVIET FRIENDSHIP

The "Worker", which is the Sunday edition of the "Daily Worker", Communist newspaper, for November 11, 1945, page 14, carried an article concerning the first conference on American Soviet cultural cooperation which was to be held at the Engineering Society's Building, New York City, on November 18, 1945. This conference was to be sponsored by the National Council of American Soviet Friendship and it was indicated that Leonard Bernstein would take part in the panel session in regard to music.
(100-146964-A)

b7C
b7D

▓▓▓▓▓▓▓▓ an active paid reliable informant of the New York Office, advised that the above-mentioned conference was held on November 18, 1945, and consisted of a series of panel discussions including one on music. The informant advised that Leonard Bernstein was scheduled to speak on the subject of Soviet influence in American music. (100-146964-744)
(u)

A technical surveillance on the National Council of American Soviet Friendship offices in New York City, on July 24, 1946, reflected that ▓▓▓▓▓

b7C ▓▓▓ of the National Council stated that Leonard Bernstein was assisting the NCASF in preparing a tour for two Russian violinists in the United States. It was indicated that Bernstein was then in the Soviet Union but that the NCASF had contacted him by cable when he was in Prague, Czechoslovakia. It

b7C was reported that Bernstein and ▓▓▓▓▓▓▓▓▓▓▓ had submitted the invitations to the Russian violinists for the trip to the United States. (u)
(100-146964-899)

An article appeared in the New York "Journal American" newspaper on April 17, 1948, written by Howard Rushmore captioned "Red Fronters Hit United States Italy Policy". It was stated that Leonard Bernstein, conductor, and a member or sponsor of Communist front groups, including the NCASF, was among the signers of a protest sent to President Truman asking for "an end to all outside interference with democratic electoral procedure" in Italy.
(94-8-113-A)

SECRET

- 7 -

The "Daily Worker" of December 17, 1947, reflected that Leonard Bernstein was one of the individuals signing a petition directed to Attorney General Tom C. Clark urging that the deportation proceedings against Hanns Eisler be dropped. It is noted that action was being taken against Hanns Eisler for deportation on the charges of misrepresentation and failure to state that he had been a member of the Communist Party. (100-195220)

C
7D
Confidential informant ██████████ on February 17, 1948, made available from a trash cover of the International Workers Order Headquarters, New York City, a letterhead from the "Committee For Justice For Hanns Eisler". The cochairman of this organization was shown to be Leonard Bernstein. Informants have indicated that many of the sponsors of this organization have been active in varying degrees in Communist front organizations in the cultural field. (U) (100-195220-181-5) pg.3

C
7D
Discontinued confidential informant ██████████ made available a press release dated January 5, 1945, issued by the "Committee For Equal Justice For Mrs. Recy Taylor". Among the sponsors listed on this press release for this organization was the name Leonard Bernstein, composer. Recy Taylor is a Negro woman who allegedly was raped by six white men in Abbeville, Alabama. The Grand Jury which heard the case refused to issue an indictment. Subsequently the "Daily Worker" and the Communist Party made much of the affair and were active in pushing the committee. (U) (100-341902-2)

CONNECTIONS WITH ORGANIZATIONS CITED BY ATTORNEY GENERAL AS COMING WITHIN THE PURVIEW OF EXECUTIVE ORDER 9835

NATIONAL COUNCIL OF AMERICAN SOVIET FRIENDSHIP

The "Worker," which is the Sunday edition of the "Daily Worker," Communist newspaper, for November 11, 1945, page 14, carried an article concerning the "First Conference on American Soviet Cultural Cooperation" which was to be held at the Engineering Society's Building, New York City, on November 18, 1945. This conference was to be sponsored by the National Council of American Soviet Friendship and it was indicated that Leonard Bernstein would take part in the panel session in regard to music. (100-146964-A) (u)

b7c
b7D

A confidential informant advised that in regard to the above-mentioned panel session, Leonard Bernstein was scheduled to speak on the subject of Soviet influence in American music. ██████████ active paid Inf. of NYC; 100-146964-744) (X)(u)

It was reported by a confidential source on July 24, 1946, that Leonard Bernstein, the composer, was assisting the NCASF in preparing a tour for two Russian violinists in the United States. It was reported by b7c this source that Bernstein and ██████████████ had gone to the Soviet Union and had submitted invitations to the Russian violinists for the trip to the United States. (Tech.Surv. on NCASF, NYC; 100-146964-899) (X)(u)

An article appeared in the New York "Journal American" newspaper on April 17, 1948, written by Howard Rushmore captioned "Red Fronters Hit United States Italy Policy." It was stated that Leonard Bernstein, conductor, and a member or sponsor of Communist front groups, including the NCASF, was among the signers of a protest sent to President Truman asking for "an end to all outside interference with democratic electoral procedure" in Italy. (u)
(94-8-113-A)

JOINT ANTI-FASCIST REFUGEE COMMITTEE

The May 15, 1944, edition of "The Worker" reported that the Boston Chapter of the above organization, together with the Council on African Affairs, was sponsoring "an evening with Paul Robeson, Leonard Bernstein and Muriel Smith" to be presented at the Boston Opera House on May 15, 1944. This article stated that Mr. Bernstein "will play selections by Liszt and Brahms, as well as his own suite, Seven Anniversaries." (u)
(100-7061-A)

SECRET

- 2 -

CONFIDENTIAL

The "Daily Worker" of January 10, 1949, referred to a peace conference to be held in March of 1949 in New York City under the auspices of the National Council of the Arts, Sciences and Professions and listed several of the "200 artists, scientists, educators, and clergymen" who had signed the invitation to the conference. This list included "composer and conductor Leonard Bernstein." The National Council of the Arts, Sciences, and Professions was formed in June, 1948, when the Arts, Sciences and Professions Council of the Progressive Citizens of America decided to withdraw from the Progressive Citizens of America and form an independent cultural-political organization.   (100-356137-21) (U)

MISCELLANEOUS AFFILIATIONS AND ACTIVITIES

A press release dated January 5, 1945, was issued by the "Committee For Equal Justice For Mrs. Recy Taylor". Among the sponsors listed on this release was Leonard Bernstein, composer. Recy Taylor is a Negro woman who allegedly was raped by six white men in Abbeville, Alabama. The Grand Jury which heard the case refused to issue an indictment. Subsequently the "Daily Worker" and the Communist Party made much of the affair and were active in pushing the committee. (100-341902-2 Discontinued Conf. Infmt

The name of Leonard Bernstein, composer, was identified on a letterhead of the American Youth for a Free World organization dated January 6, 1945, as being on the initial list of sponsors of the World Youth Week meeting to be held March 21 at Carnegie Hall. The California Joint Fact-Finding Committee has stated that "American Youth for a Free World was linked directly to the international Communist dominated youth organization World Youth Council, with headquarters at London, England. (Tenney Com (1948 Report, pg. 54; Letterhead made availably by former Pitts. Inft.

In December of 1946, a confidential source identified Leonard Bernstein with the Communist faction of the American Federation of Musicians, A. F. of L.   (62-52493-39, Conf. Inft   NY Office)(X)(U)

Office Me ...andum · UNITED STATES GOVERNMENT

TO : THE DIRECTOR

FROM : D. M. Ladd

SUBJECT: LEONARD BERNSTEIN
SPECIAL INQUIRY - WHITE HOUSE

ALL INFORMATION CONTAINED March 15, 1949
HEREIN IS UNCLASSIFIED
DATE 2-8-80 BY SL4
AGREE 9803

Mr. Tolson
Mr. Clegg
Mr. Glavin
Mr. Ladd
Mr. Nichols
Mr. Rosen
Mr. Tracy
Mr. Egan
Mr. Gurnea
Mr. Harbo
Mr. Mohr
Mr. Pennington
Mr. Quinn Tamm
Tele. Room
Mr. Nease
Miss Holmes
Miss Gandy

Pursuant to instructions, Mr. Roach called on Mr. David K. Niles of the White House this morning in compliance with his request to discuss the Bureau letter we prepared on Bernstein. Mr. Niles informed Mr. Roach that he was greatly disturbed by the fact that Bernstein was undoubtedly mixed up in a lot of Communist and Liberal Movements, but on the other hand was a renown musician and someone that the White House could not push off at the forthcoming musical reception to be given by the President of Israel and President Truman. He desired to know if you or Mr. Roach would give him an opinion as to what action the White House should take concerning Bernstein and his presence at the musical reception. He stated that a "stinging" letter of protest had been received from the publication "Counterattack" and he was fearful that other complications would arise if Bernstein were permitted to appear on the program.

After listening to Mr. Niles very patiently for some time, Mr. Roach informed him that the Director could not, under the circumstances, make a recommendation one way or another, that we merely supplied to him (Niles) at his request such data as appeared in our files. Further that the Bureau had not conducted an investigation of Bernstein and certainly could not be called upon for a recommendation of any sort in this case.

It was suggested to Mr. Niles that he may desire to take into consideration any other information that he may have received in arriving at a decision, that such a decision was totally within the province of the White House. Mr. Niles inquired whether to the Bureau's knowledge Bernstein had ever criticized the President or any other Government official. In this regard, Mr. Roach referred him to paragraphs in the memorandum submitted by the Bureau wherein Bernstein had signed a letter of protest to the President and the Attorney General.

After considering this for a while, Mr. Niles stated he believed it would be necessary to ask the Committee handling the affair to ask that Bernstein be replaced, but that before doing so, he intended to discuss the matter with the Attorney General or Peyton Ford, as well as with Mr. Clark Clifford (Special Counsel to the President).

RECORDED - 14 EX-47 100-360261-6

Mr. Niles thanked Mr. Roach for calling and stated he understood the Bureau's position quite clearly but did desire to talk to you or Mr. Roach before considering the matter further.

1 - Mr. DeLoach
1 - Mr. W. C. Sullivan
1 - Mr. Bishop
1 - Mr. G. C. Moore
May 18, 1970

b7C

1 - ████████████ (Mass media)
1 - ████████████

BLACK PANTHER PARTY and
LEONARD BERNSTEIN'S BENEFIT   1 - ████████████

Among the representatives of the black extremist
violence-prone Black Panther Party who attended the fund-
raising party on January 14, 1970, at the New York City
home of the well-known music conductor Leonard Bernstein,
was the Black Panther Party Field Marshal Donald Lee Cox.
According to a well-informed source, the Black Panther
Party realized over $10,000 from this affair which was
attended by a number of socially prominent individuals.

Donald Lee Cox, with whom these elite socialites
were rubbing shoulders, is the same Donald Lee Cox currently
being sought by the Baltimore, Maryland, Police Department.
A warrant for his arrest was issued April 30, 1970, in
Baltimore charging him with conspiracy to commit murder.
This charge grew out of his involvement in the gruesome
torture and murder of Eugene Leroy Anderson in Baltimore
during July, 1969.

Cox was the author of an article which appeared in
the January 3, 1970, issue of the Black Panther Party newspaper,
"The Black Panther." This article was a vitriolic attack on the
"Zionist fascist state of Israel" and clearly shows the pro-
Arab posture of the Black Panther Party.

Prior to Bernstein and his misguided friends contribu-
ting additional funds for the alleged protection of the constitutional rights of such a group, shouldn't there first be given
consideration to the establishment of a fund to aid the surviving
members of the victim's family?

b7C ████████ (9)

(C)

105-90959-258 p.6
~~(11)~~

On 4/7/70, CIA advised that Leonard Bernstein, former conductor was reported to have been a strong supporter of ███████████████. (Comment: Although there was no clarification of Bernstein's support, it was presumed his opinions were directed toward ███████ professional ability.) (Locality not given.)

105-192802-12 p.1
~~(13)~~

In the "Los Angeles Times", dated 1/21/70, in a column of William F. Buckley, Jr., (not identified), he expressed his concern regarding a rece fund raising affair* given by Leonard Bernstein for the benefit of the Black Panthers. During the affair a Black Panther had announced that if business did not provide full employment, then the Panthers would take over the means of production and put them in the hands of the people. Bernstein's reply was "I dig absolutely".

(4)

The serial indicated that the SCEF grew out of the Southern Christian Human Welfare organization, and was concerned with racial segregation and oppression of black people, academic freedom, and movement for world peace.

100-340922-518 p.24,39
~~(7)~~

*1/14/70

100-36026-79

-13-

CONFIDENTIAL

, 2   in October, 1970, advised that Meir D. Kahane
(105-207795) advised ████████████████ in the Jewish Defense
League (JDL), that he finally got Lenny Bernstein's home address and
that soon they were going to ask JDL members to "take over the entire
building, sit in it, and see how much pressure Bernstein can take".
This sit-in at Bernstein's home, in NYC, was scheduled for 10/20/70,
according to this informant. (X) (u)

The serial indicated that the JDL had in the past opposed
Bernstein because of a party held in his home (date not given) which
included members of the Black Panther Party.   (Source not given) (Y)

105-207795-16 p.4
(13,19)

"The New York Times", a daily NYC newspaper, issue of 5/12/71,
contained an article captioned "Bernsteins Raise $35,000 for the Berrigan
Defense." The article in substance reported that Mr. and Mrs. Leonard
Bernstein gave a civil liberties gathering in behalf of the Reverend
Philip F. Berrigan and his five co-defendants.

According to the article, Berrigan, a Josephite priest, and
five others were charged with conspiracy to kidnap Henry A. Kissinger,
President Nixon's national security advisor.

100-446997-70-110 p.8
(10)

The "New York Times", 5/27/71, contained an article captioned
"Bernstein Incurs J.D.L.'s Wrath". The article related that Leonard
Bernstein, who was severely criticized for having held a fund-raising
gala* for the Black Panthers, was now the target of a group he had not
supported, the Jewish Defense League (JDL)(62-112767). The JDL picketed
the home of Bernstein in NYC and declared that Bernstein had remained
silent about Jewish civil rights. A photograph of Bernstein was included
with the article.

62-112767-A "New York Times" 5/27/71
(4)

*1/14/70

-14-

b7c 1 - ███████

July 11, 1974

LEONARD BERNSTEIN *SUMMARY*
Born: August 25, 1918
Lawrence, Massachusetts

In response to your name check request concerning the captioned individual, attached hereto is a memorandum dated April 21, 1964, entitled "Leonard Bernstein" which may relate to the subject of your inquiry.

In addition, you are advised information was developed indicating Bernstein was active in the civil rights movement; namely, in 1965, Harry Belafonte, well-known entertainer, organized a group of musical and literary artists to take part in the march from Selma to Montgomery, Alabama. Mr. Bernstein was one of the artists included in this group.

(100-360261-67)

You are also referred to memorandum dated April 4, 1966, at New York, New York, captioned "Leonard Berstein, which was forwarded to your agency on April 14, 1966.

(100-360261-65)

On May 12, 1971, Leonard Bernstein and his wife hosted a fund-raising party in support of Reverend Philip F. Berrigan and five codefendants charged with conspiring to kidnap Henry A. Kissinger, and blow up heating systems in Federal buildings in Washington. The party reportedly raised $35,000.

(100-460495-3692 p. 26)

Enclosure

Original and 1 - State Department
Request received 6-25-74

b7c

REC-52 *100 - 360261-7*

(4)

1 JUL 16 1974

b7c EX-109

AGREE 9803
ALL INFORMATION CONTAINED
HEREIN IS UNCLASSIFIED
DATE 2-10-80 BY ██

b7c

MAIL ROOM ☐   TELETYPE UNIT ☐

147

Chapter V

The Flamboyant Reverend
Adam Clayton Powell, Jr.

Adam Clayton Powell Jr. was born in New Haven, Connecticut on November 29, 1908. Shortly after his birth, the senior Adam Clayton Powell moved his family to New York City where he had been called to be the pastor of the Abyssinian Baptist Church which was reputed to be the oldest Negro Congregation in the North. In the late 1890's, it was located on Worth Street, between Church Street and Broadway. In 1923 the church moved with its Negro parishioners uptown to Harlem where "White flight" was in high gear. The location of the new church was on its present site at 132 West 138th Street which is an area that gained fame in the 1920's as the cradle of the Harlem Renaissance.

As the only boy child and heir-apparent in a highly respected church family, young Powell was reared as the spoiled brat of a relatively prosperous family as measured by Negro standards during that period. At the age of five, his mother was combing his shoulder length blond hair into ringlets and looking into his blue eyes and constantly reminding him that he was a blessed child.

Some twelve years later as a teenager at Colgate University in Hamilton, New York, he tried for a fleeting moment to avoid the identification of being Black in as much as his skin pigment was white enough to permit him to cross the color line in a heartbeat. As a matter of fact, he attempted to join an all-White fraternity. As was the custom, they checked out his family background and discovered he was the son of a Negro preacher. Hence, he was blackballed by the membership committee. There were fewer than five acknowledged Black students on the campus among the 1,000 at the all-male university. Prior to his ethnicity being discovered, he was housed in the freshman dormitory with a white roommate. The White boy that he shared a room with became chagrined, embarrassed, and demanded that Powell move posthaste. The crossover caper became the talk of the campus; thus, Adam Clayton Powell Jr. was ostracized by most of his White and Negro classmates. According to the best sources, this was the last time that Adam overtly attempted to cross the color line. Although his family was white skinned enough to have passed for white, they opted to live in Harlem on the border of Strivers Row which was Negro heaven for the Black elite who lived between 137th and 139th Street. His neighbors on Strivers Row were mostly light skin Negroes, like Fletcher Henderson, the great orchestra leader, composer, and arranger Noble Sissle, the musician, Dr. Louis T. Wright, M. D. who was fourth in his class at Harvard Medical School and A'Lelia Walker, daughter of Madame C. J. Walker, America's first Black millionairess. Both the daughter and mother were the Powell family's neighbors.

Before he graduated from Colgate, he was appointed Assistant Pastor under his father in 1929. After graduating from Colgate University in 1930, he enrolled at the Union Theological Seminary in New York City. The curriculum at the divinity school to him was void in that it did not accommodate his playboy, whiskey drinking and woman chasing lifestyle. He did not believe in heaven and hell as places you go after death. He believed that heaven and hell were right here on earth where you spent your time between birth and death. He accepted only the words of Jesus Christ as recorded in the chapters of the New Testament in Matthew, Mark, Luke and John.

After dropping out of the divinity school, he enrolled as a part-time student at Columbia University Teachers College where he received a Masters Degree in Religious Education in 1932. His handpicked curriculum enabled him to stand in the worlds of both anthropologist Margaret Mead and the great educator John Dewey.

In 1938 a honorary degree of Doctor of Divinity was conferred upon Powell by Shaw University, a Negro institution of higher learning in Raleigh, North Carolina. Although he accepted the honor, he was not grateful because he later openly stated that he did not want to prepare children to enter Negro colleges. He also became an ardent opponent of the Negro College Fund and proudly shouted from the pulpits of the nation that he was an Ivy League Colgate man. He would point out this fact to Black leaders such as Dr. Martin Luther King who did his undergraduate work at Morehouse College in Atlanta, Georgia. He frequently said that he did not look upon Black alma maters with the same warmth that he had for the Ivy League.

On March 8, 1933, Powell married the beautiful Isabel Washington, a native of Savannah, Georgia and dancer in the chorus line at the famed Harlem Cotton Club in New York City. The senior Powell did not approve of his son marrying a night club entertainer. As a concession to her father-in-law, she agreed to be baptized in Abyssinian Baptist Church (she was Catholic) before the marriage took place. The senior Clayton Powell and two other ministers officiated with gusto at the wedding ceremony. His daughter-in-law's sister Fredi Washington, was also a Cotton Club dancer and in 1934 was selected because of her light skin to play the role of Peola in a movie entitled Imitation of Life. Her role in the film was to wrestle with one of racist America's oldest dilemmas, the decision to "pass" across the color line from Black to White. As a matter of fact at DuSable High School in Chicago where the author attended in 1935, light skin girls formed a Peola Club. They announced their membership in the group with great pride. The motto was; "if you are yellow you are mellow, if you are brown stick around, and if you are black get back."

In the fall of 1932 Adam Clayton Powell Jr. became involved in a number of civic, business, and political activities. His oratorical and organizational skills made him an instant Harlem Leader. In 1939 at the age of twenty-four, he was appointed a member of Local School Board District 12 for a five year period. In November 1941, he was elected to the New York City Council. On January 3, 1945 Congressman William L. Dawson of Illinois escorted Congressman Clayton Powell Jr. to his seat in the historic Seventy-Ninth Congress of the United States. The day was significant in that it was the first time in the twentieth century that two Black men occupied seats in the hall of Congress.

Adam Clayton Powell Jr. came to the attention of FBI director J. Edgar Hoover in 1941 when he started rattling the civil rights cage as a member of the New York Council. Hence, Hoover sent a letter to the bureau's special agent in charge of New York City asking for a background check on the councilman because of what appeared to be his connections with the political left wing. From 1941 forward, the FBI collected information in many forms such as transcripts of conversations caught on electronic surveillance, memos from the U. S. Attorney's office, newspaper and magazine clippings and summaries of interviews on Adam Clayton Powell for the next thirty-one years.

Attending his funeral at the Abyssinian Baptist Church in 1972 a FBI observer noted that among the throng present were his second wife Hazel Scott, the talented Café Society, piano player and her son, Adam III. His third wife Yvette Diago, a Puerto Rican along with her son Adam IV occupied a front row center seat. Powell was living with his mistress in Bimini when he was stricken. Powell's first wife Isabel did not attend the funeral.

Adam Clayton Powell with Malcom X and Dick Gregory in 1962.

Powell meeting with President Lyndon B. Johnson at the White House in 1965.

Dr. Martin Luther King, Jr. and Powell who greets a stranger.

Federal Bureau of Investigation

Freedom of Information/Privacy Acts Section

Subject: <u>Adam Clayton Powell, Jr.</u>

- 2 -

On June 21, 1941, Powell wrote a letter to the Director requesting information regarding the number of youths arrested annually in the United States. He advised that this information was desired for work in connection with juvenile delinquency being conducted by the Abyssinian Baptist Church.

LABOR ACTIVITIES

The Daily Worker for January 7, 1937, comments that Powell was speaker at the Workers Alliance demonstration held in New York City to protest the layoffs in the W.P.A. (61-7559-1045X42)

Available information reflects that Powell was one of the signers of a letter sent to the National Convention of Railway Employees Department of A.F. of L. who were meeting at Chicago in 1938. This letter appealed that action be taken to eliminate from the constitutions of affiliated unions clauses discriminating against Negroes. (61-7563-58X; Daily Worker for 4-9-38)

It is reported that during April, 1941, he was the Chairman of the Strike Committee which called a strike against the Fifth Avenue Coach Company and the New York City Omnibus Corporation to force employment of Negroes as mechanics and bus drivers. The Daily Worker for April 11, 1941, states that 2,000 people attended a mass meeting at the Abyssinian Baptist Church in connection with this strike. The article further states that Powell, speaking before 5,000 at the Golden Gate Ballroom on April 7, 1941, said that all promises from the Coach Company and Omnibus Corporation must be in writing and in proper legal form. (61-7563-Sub A)

The New York Times on April 29, 1938, comments that the Co-ordinating Committee for Employment was headed by Powell and that its purpose was to picket and boycott companies discriminating against the Negroes. (61-7563-60X2)

The Daily Worker for May 23, 1938, hails the victory of the Coordinating Committee for Employment in forcing the Consolidated Edison Company to backdown from "its notorious anti-Negro employment policy." (61-7563-58X1)

The Daily Worker for September 24, 1938, states that Powell is a champion of labor and commends his victories over discrimination against Negroes by the New York Utility Companies. (61-7563-57X9)

The Daily Worker for April 9, 1939, states that Powell would lead the mass picket line outside Governor Whalen's World's Fair Building in protest against Negro discrimination by the World's Fair Corporation. (61-7563-254X1; 61-7563-71X)

It is reported that the Trade Unions Committee of New York City held a rally on behalf of Powell on October 29, 1941, and endorsed his candidacy at this time. (100-18264-112, Circular of the Rally)

ATTITUDE TOWARD WAR PRIOR TO JUNE 1941

CONFIDENTIAL

Testimony given before the Dies Committee reflects that in 1934 Powell was a member of the National Executive Committee of the American League Against War and Fascism and that in 1935 he was a member of the National Bureau of the American League for Peace and Democracy. (Dies Comm. p. 27, Testimony of Dr. Ward, Chairman of Amer.League Agst. War & Fascism, 61-

Available information reflects that on April 22, 1938, Powell sent a letter to House Chairman Sam McReynolds protesting the decision not to have open hearings on the Neutrality Act. This source advises that the letter was sent by Powell in the name of his congregation and stated that peace-loving Americans should have the opportunity to express themselves on such a vital matter. (61-7561-203X, Daily Worker for 4-22-38)

7569-40
62;
61-7566
743;

The Daily Worker for March 24, 1939, announces a meeting of the New York City Conference of the American League for Peace and Democracy and that one of the organizers is Powell. The alleged purpose of the meeting was to act for peace. (61-7559-4075X50; 61-7559-3629X34)

It has been reported that Powell was on the New York Council of Keep America Out of War as of September 25, 1940. (61-10123-18, Letterhead of the Congress)

In the Daily Worker for May 27, 1941, 160 leading Negro Americans flayed the defense program as a sham and accused the Administration of fostering a war drive. This article cited discrimination against Negroes in the defense program and stated that the Negroes of America wanted peace and equality. Powell was one of those signing as the initiating group. (61-7563-Sub A)

(100-38965-9; conf. inft.)

ATTITUDE TOWARD WAR SUBSEQUENT TO JUNE 1941

67D

(100-6548-42, p. 33;

62
67D

(61-8381-329,

(61-106-89, Conf. Inft.)

3

CONFIDENTIAL

In a release by the Russian War Relief, Incorporated, to all newspapers on March 25, 1942, it was stated that Powell would speak at the New York City Conference of the Russian War Relief, Incorporated, on April 11, 1942. (100-37226-96; 100-37226-Sub A)

Available information reflects that Powell was a speaker at the Rally held by the Japanese-American Committee for Democracy held on April 15, 1942, at the Hotel Diplomat, New York. (100-102326-1 & 61-10123-241)

The News Letter published by the Japanese-American Committee for Democracy on May 5, 1942, states that Powell was the opening speaker at the Mass Victory Rally sponsored by the Japanese-American Committee for Democracy on April 15, 1942. It is reported that at this rally Powell said, "This is a people's war and must be a people's victory. The pattern should be that set by the Russian Army, a democratic army of all Russia." (100-105197-0; 100-71226-12)

(100-7046-139)

The Daily Worker for May 16, 1942, reflects that Powell was a speaker at a Mass Victory Rally which took place at New York University during May, 1942. He is quoted as follows: "We are waging a people's war with a people's army for a people's peace and the key to victory can be learned from the Chinese people, who are fighting a people's war, and from the glorious Red Army, which is fighting a people's war. Let us demand a regiment of American people, Negroes and white, alike, fighting a people's war, so that democracy the world over shall become a reality." (100-89688-A; Daily Worker for May 16, 1942

The Sunday Worker for June 14, 1942, states that Powell was a speaker at an anti-discrimination mass meeting held on June 12, 1942, in Park Palace, New York City. He is quoted as follows: "Despite efforts of certain people, the common people may win this anti-Hitler war this year. The death blow to the old world ended with the accord signed by the United States, the Soviet Union and Great Britain." (100-28126-Sub A)

(100-74861-4?)

NFXENTIAL

Powell is reported to have been a sponsor for the American Rescue Ship Mission to Spain. The purpose of this mission allegedly was to save Spanish refugees. (61-7562-Sub-A) (61-9894-98, p. 41; 100-7058X-61; 100-7061-Sub A; 100-7061-50 & 69; 100-7061-115 p. 11)

b7D

(100-1170-110, p. 5; 100-1170-22, p. 7)

Available information reflects that Powell was a member of the Executive Committee of the New York Conference for Inalienable Rights and was a sponsor of the Emergency Meeting called in February, 1941, to combat legislation against free speech and the rights of labor. The New York Conference for Inalienable Rights reportedly had Communist affiliations. (100-10117-3)

Testimony given before the Dies Committee listed Powell on the National Advisory Board of the American Youth Congress which was reported to be dominated by the Communist Party. (100-3587-123 & Dies Committee Rpt. Vol. I, p. 875; testimony of J. B. Matthews)

The candidacy of Powell for the New York City Council was endorsed by the Daily Worker on October 30, 1941, and by the Sunday Worker on November 2, 1941. (100-13758-Sub A & 61-7563-Sub A)

James W. Ford, writing in the Daily Worker of November 23, 1941, hailed the election of Powell as a victory for democracy and for anti-Hitler forces. (61-7563-Sub A)

The Daily Worker for November 15, 1941, editorially commented on the election of Powell as a victory for the anti-Fascist coalition.

b2
b7D

(100-5095-13;

It is reported that Powell is a Vice President of the National Association for the Advancement of the Colored People. (61-3176-18X5, p. 2; 61-3176-18X26).

Information was received that Powell spoke at the opening meeting of the National Negro Youth Congress held on November 14, 1941, at Washington, D. C. At this time, he is reported to have said that Negroes should rise up and fight for their rights and that the present condition of the country was a fine opportunity for Negroes to achieve their objective. (100-50256-2, p. 4, & Serial 3)

b7D

(61-6728-235, p. 11)

(61-6728-49, p. 6)

b7D

CON☒DENTIAL

NY 100-22864

The Daily Worker for September 24, 1937, states that POWELL would be a speaker at a meeting to be held at Madison Square Garden October 1, 1937, under the auspices of the American League Against War and Fascism, and the American Friends of the Chinese People.

The Daily Worker for January 15, 1937, announces a mass trial to be held January 15, 1937, at the Abyssinian Baptist Church, to present first-hand evidence of brutality in the Harlem Public Schols. It was stated that POWELL would act as Judge at this trial.

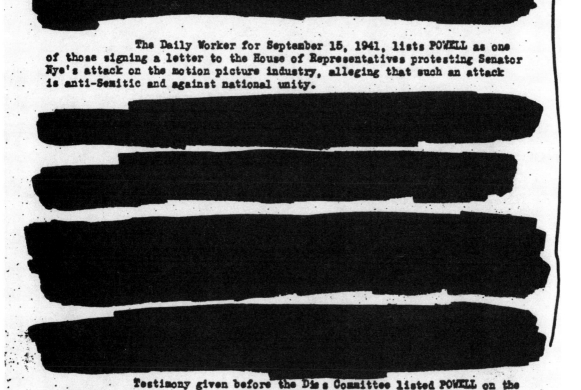

The Daily Worker for September 15, 1941, lists POWELL as one of those signing a letter to the House of Representatives protesting Senator Nye's attack on the motion picture industry, alleging that such an attack is anti-Semitic and against national unity.

Testimony given before the Dies Committee listed POWELL on the National Advisory Board of the American Youth Congress, which was reported to be dominated by the Communist Party.

- 15 -

NY 100-22864

The Daily Worker for February 18, 1942, states that POWELL introduced a resolution in the New York City Council against Negro Discrimination in the colleges of the City of New York. The Daily Worker for May 5, 1942, states that POWELL would be a speaker at a mass meeting at Carnegie Hall on May 4, 1942, that this meeting is sponsored by the Protestant Digest, Inc., and that a speech by Dr. HEWLETT JOHNSON, Dean of Canterbury, England, would be re-broadcast from London. Dr. JOHNSON was described as the author of "Soviet Power".

The Sunday Worker for March 22, 1942, quoted POWELL as follows:

"As long as we can put EARL BROWDER in prison then the entire basis of civil liberties is threatened. This travesty of justice has gone on long enough, and an end should be put to it speedily -- in fact, immediately."

POWELL, writing editorially in "The People's Voice", stated that BROWDER is a victim of un-Americanism, just as TOM MOONEY, SACCO and VANZETTI, The Scottsboro Boys and ANGELO HERNDON were. He further wrote as follows: "I make no brief for the Communist Party. They have much more able prophets than I ever would claim to be".

- 17 - CONFIDENTIAL

NY 100-23864

     The candidacy of POWELL for the New York City Council was endorsed by the Daily Worker on October 30, 1941, and by the Sunday Worker on November 2, 1941.

     JAMES W. FORD, writing in The Daily Worker of November 23, 1941, hailed the election of POWELL as a victory for democracy and for anti-Hitler forces.

     The Daily Worker for November 15, 1941 editorially commented on the election of POWELL as a victory for the anti-Fascist collation.

- 16 -

FBI Secret Files

NY 100-22864

for this years political campaign is LOYLE LAYNE and BENJAMIN DAVIS, JR. In regard to BENJAMIN DAVIS, JR., who ran on the Communist Party ticket for the office of Congressman at Large for the State of New York, POWELL stated: "Ben Davis deserves the vote of every Negro. He comes from a great Georgia family. His education left him head and shoulders above the usual run-of-the-mill Congressmen". He further stated, "The Negro vote is so important that major political parties nominate a Negro for the position of Congressman at Large, instead of nonentities that are running. My vote goes to Ben Davis, Jr." In another section of this editorial, POWELL states as follows: "It is time that the Negroes participated in the political scene as members of the democracy, not just as Negroes. This is the one reason I have always given credit to the Communist Party, because they have had the courage to run Negro people in national, state and county elections".

An editorial in the "People's Voice", dated November 28, 1942, states in large headlines as follows: "They put us out with guns, after the anti-poll tax bill was killed". The article states that five Negro ministers leading a delegation of over 100 from all over the country, to fight for passage of the Pepper-Geyer anti-poll tax bill, had guns pulled on them in the corridor of the United States Senate, and that the guns were brandished by two Senate police officers almost immediately following the 41 to 37 vote against the bill, and climaxed a day in which the clergymen had undergone various forms of democratic brush-off, including threats of physical violence. The article further reflects that the ministers referred to were the delegation lead by POWELL that had gone to Washington to aid the National Committee to Abolish the Poll Tax.

It should also be noted that the entire front page of the "People's Voice" for November 28, 1942, is devoted to the announcement, in large letters, that Negro preachers, naming them, were put out of the Senate at gun-point.

The "People's Voice", dated December 5, 1942, carries an editorial signed by POWELL, in which he states, "Democracy is fast waning at home. Whether you view democracy as an ideal or a realization, it is vanishing from the American scene. We may be extending democracy abroad, but we are surely losing it at home. When a fish decays it begins to stink at the head. Today Washington is beginning to stink. Unless the death grip on our nation's capitol is broken, and the ideals of democracy, if not the practices, are restored, the future of the Sweet Land of Liberty is far from promising".

- 23 -    CONFIDENTIAL

NY 100-22864

Part of this article is devoted to criticism of the government for failure to take action against the capitol policemen as soon as the delegates were reported to have been put out of the Capitol, and that the Capitol authorities had taken no steps even to investigate the situation. In the last paragraph of his article, POWELL states as follows:-

"Washington stinks. It stinks with Jim Crow discrimination, prejudice and hatred. It stinks on the street. It smells in the corridors of the government buildings. Now the stink and decay has reached into the Capitol itself. If democracy is going to be saved at home, it is going to be saved only by Negroes fighting for democracy."

"The People's Voice" of January 16, 1943, carries an article relative to the postponement of the hearings before the F.E.P.C. on discriminatory practices of Southern railroads against Negro fireman. This article reflects that in New York City the cancellation resulted in a meeting early on Monday, apparently January 11, 1943, of WARREN BANNER, Research Director of the National Urban League; EDWARD LEWIS, Executive Secretary of the New York Urban League; MAX YERGAN, President of the National Negro Congress; FERDINAND SMITH, Secretary and Vice President of the National Maritime Union; JOSEPH FORD, Executive Secretary of "The People's Voice", and ADAM CLAYTON POWELL, JR., Editor of "The People's Voice", with WENDELL WILLKIE. The article states that plans were discussed at this meeting, but that details were withheld temporarily.

"The People's Voice" dated January 23, 1943, carried an article by ADAM CLAYTON POWELL, JR., relative to the use of Hunter College by the WAVES and the SPARS, in which he stated that the City of New York would not dare to enter into a contract with any private agency, company or individual known to discriminate against any race. During 1942 the City Council passed a law prohibiting such contracts and agreements. POWELL went on to state, "We have a very exact Civil Rights Code in Albany on our staff books. The Constitution of the United States specifically is against second class citizens, but more than all these is the fundamental spirit of the people of our town. It is here in New York that the great spirit of democracy has reached the highest heights. Our city would render an inestimable service to the war effort if by conference it would be able to break down the barriers against Negro women in the WAVES and SPARS. It was just a short time ago that Hunter campus and its buildings echoed to the footsteps of young women of all races. Today, unless the situation is changed immediately, no Negro women may train on that campus, regardless of her love for her country. Such conditions will not hurt too much the prosecution of the war, but they will delay somewhat the day of victory, and they will surely endanger the day of peace."

- 24 -

NY 100-22864

sent to vote for the anti-poll tax bill, and further advised the audience,
"We want to know who is against us and who is for us". He praised the
magnificent resistance of the Russians and Chinese against aggression and
urged full support of the Freedom for India movement. He pointed out that
the Negroes were denied their rightful place after the last war, but if they
would all unite and demand their equal rights they would come into their own
upon the victorious conclusion of the present conflict.

Among other things, POWELL spoke of certain elements of Congress who were not cooperating with the Presidential war program, and made
several derogatory remarks concerning Congressman Dies and his committee.
In conclusion, POWELL referred to certain high ranking members of their race
who seemed to have forgotten their colored brothers and no longer furnished
the leadership which was expected of them. He stated, however, that the
colored masses were rising and on the march, and they were inviting all their
colored brothers to join them, but if they did not want to, then all they
asked was that they step aside, because, "Brothers and sisters, we're going
through".

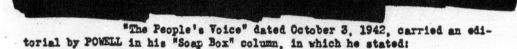

"The People's Voice" dated October 3, 1942, carried an editorial by POWELL in his "Soap Box" column, in which he stated:

"The attack by Martin Dies on Mary McLeod Bethune is the
last straw. Dies has already won infamy as an international jack-
ass, but today, with your permission, let us omit the jack. Any
low cracker scum like Dies who will dare to point his finger at
a great American woman like Dr. Bethune deserves to be publicly
purged. Dies is no good, never has been any good, and never will
be any good. The sooner he is buried the better. He is one of
the few people in history whose body has begun to stink before it
dies. Dies is Public Skunk #1. There is only one place fit for
him to live and that is Hitler's outhouse."

The article goes on to relate that the National Federation
for Constitutional Liberties has a 64 page booklet on Martin Dies which everyone should read; that Dies works hand-in-glove with the Nazi Fifth Column in
the United States and that his tactics are the same as Goebbels'. In the last
paragraph of this editorial, POWELL states as follows:-

"We demand that Congress impeach him and that the F.B.I.
investigate him, and that the President of the United States have
him arrested immediately as an enemy agent. There is not and

- 26 -

CONFIDENTIAL

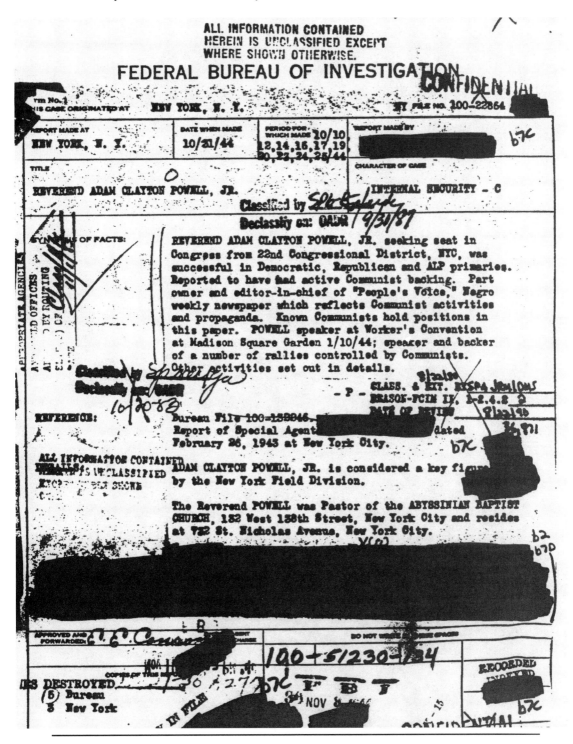

ALL INFORMATION CONTAINED
HEREIN IS UNCLASSIFIED EXCEPT
WHERE SHOWN OTHERWISE.

FEDERAL BUREAU OF INVESTIGATION

CONFIDENTIAL

THIS CASE ORIGINATED AT NEW YORK, N. Y.   FILE NO. 100-22864

REPORT MADE AT	DATE WHEN MADE	PERIOD FOR WHICH MADE	REPORT MADE BY
NEW YORK, N. Y.	10/31/44	10/10 12,14,16,17,19 20,22,24,25/44	

TITLE

REVEREND ADAM CLAYTON POWELL, JR.

CHARACTER OF CASE

INTERNAL SECURITY - C

Classified by ____
Declassify on: OADR 9/30/87

SYNOPSIS OF FACTS:

REVEREND ADAM CLAYTON POWELL, JR. seeking seat in Congress from 22nd Congressional District, NYC, was successful in Democratic, Republican and ALP primaries. Reported to have had active Communist backing. Part owner and editor-in-chief of "People's Voice," Negro weekly newspaper which reflects Communist activities and propaganda. Known Communists hold positions in this paper. POWELL speaker at Worker's Convention at Madison Square Garden 1/10/44; speaker and backer of a number of rallies controlled by Communists. Other activities set out in details.

- P -

CLASS. & EXT. ____
REASON-FCIM II, ____
DATE OF REVIEW ____

REFERENCE: Bureau File 100-138945.
                 Report of Special Agent ____ dated
                 February 26, 1943 at New York City.

ALL INFORMATION CONTAINED
HEREIN IS UNCLASSIFIED
EXCEPT WHERE SHOWN

ADAM CLAYTON POWELL, JR. is considered a key figure by the New York Field Division.

The Reverend POWELL was Pastor of the ABYSSINIAN BAPTIST CHURCH, 132 West 138th Street, New York City and resides at 722 St. Nicholas Avenue, New York City.

APPROVED AND FORWARDED:

100-51230-124

IS DESTROYED ____
(5) Bureau
5 New York

NOV ____ FBI

CONFIDENTIAL

NY 100-22854

670

The "People's Voice," Negro newspaper, dated February 5, 1944, carried an article entitled "Leaders Back Powell; Church Gives $10,000." The article stated in part that the ABYSSINIAN BAPTIST CHURCH of which POWELL is the Pastor, voted to take an active part in his election to Congress. It stated that authorization from the official board of the church gave practically carte blanc to marshal the entire resources of the church behind the efforts to give the largest Negro community in the world representation in the nation's representative body. Specifically, $10,000 was pledged to POWELL, payable on demand on or before April 1, the money to be contributed to whatever committee is set up to conduct the campaign on a non-partisan basis; that the non-partisan committee is already placing letters in the mails to over 2000 leaders of all phases of Harlem life and these letters would invite these leaders to serve as members of the non-partisan committee; that the campaign would be directed by JOSEPH FORD, POWELL's personal secretary.

The "New York Amsterdam News," Negro newspaper dated March 25, 1944 carried an article entitled "Four Candidates Battling for Congress Seat." This article stated in part that ADAM C. POWELL, WILLIAM T. ANDREWS, HARDLEE JOHN and GEORGE HARRIS were seeking the nomination for Congress. The article stated that WILLIAM T. ANDREWS was opposed to POWELL for the Democratic nomination and that JOHN and HARRIS were seeking the Republican nomination.

The "People's Voice" on April 1, 1944 carried an article entitled "NY Democrats Back Powell for Congress." The article stated that the New York County Democratic Committee in the New 22nd District has come out to back the Reverend POWELL for Congress and that the Honorable EDWARD LAUGHLIN, Chairman of the Committee, made the announcement. The article further stated that in accepting the nomination POWELL said:

"I wish to thank Harlem leaders of the New York Democratic County Committee for nominating me for Congress. While it is true that I am a registered Democrat, I have always been an independent. I want to assure my friends of all political faiths and races that I will continue to consistently maintain that independence. I value that above all else. I, therefore, am asking the continued support of members of the Republican party and the American Labor Party in helping me preserve my independence.

-2-

X

NY 100-22864

"On the other hand, I will cooperate with the local
Democratic party in so far as such cooperation does not lessen
that independence. I will assist whenever called upon in my
limited way to help make this party truly representative of the
best interests of all people.

"I believe that under the new, dignified leadership of
the Honorable EDWARD LOUGHLIN, and the present elected leaders of
Harlem, such a goal can be attained this year.

"I pledge to my people in the Harlem area and to all people
everywhere, vigorous all-out support in winning the war and the
peace, fighting every form of injustice, abolishing every form of
discrimination and guaranteeing the post-war world equality of
opportunity for everyone."

The April 8, 1944 issue of the "People's Voice" carried an
article concerning the candidacy for Congress of Mr. POWELL and stated
in part that the platform on which he would run was to be run by the
people themselves, that it will be arrived at by screening and condensing
the recommendations of the 212 delegates who recently attended the
annual PEOPLE'S COMMITTEE CONFERENCE and that these delegates who represent
over 178,000 people of every walk of life and organizational affiliation
in the community came to the conference fully instructed of the wishes and
recommendations of their several groups, churches, social, and fraternal
organizations. It was stated that a meeting had been held by twenty-six
unnamed citizens of the community who spent a full hour evolving a series
of proposals which along with those of the PEOPLE'S COMMITTEE would form
the foundation for the comprehensive platform on which POWELL would run.

The "New York Amsterdam News" on the same day carried an
article in which it stated that a move to draft A. PHILLIP RANDOLPH, head
of the March on Washington movement, as a candidate for Congress in
opposition to POWELL had started; that Harlem's non-partisan committee of
which MACK D. BOWE is chairman announced a conference for Saturday, April
15, and that the sponsors at this gathering were to be Dr. CHANNING H.
TOBIAS, ROY WILKINS, GEORGE S. SCHUYLER, ELMER CARTER, Mrs. ROBA BLOCKER,
NOAH WALTERS, A. A. AUSTIN, and LUDLOW V. WERNER. It was stated that a
definite attempt was being made to have RANDOLPH oppose POWELL for the
Congressional seat. It was reported that a meeting had been held at the
YWCA in Harlem when a group met to discuss the following questions:

-3-

UNITED STATES DEPARTMENT OF JUSTICE

FEDERAL BUREAU OF INVESTIGATION

In Reply, Please Refer to
File No.

Los Angeles, California
January 11, 1968

Mr. Tolson
Mr. DeLoach
Mr. Mohr
Mr. Bishop
Mr. Casper
Mr. Callahan
Mr. Conrad
Mr. Felt
Mr. Gale
Mr. Rosen
Mr. Sullivan
Mr. Tavel
Mr. Trotter
Tele. Room
Miss Holmes
Miss Gandy

<u>ADAM CLAYTON POWELL</u>

The "Los Angeles Times", a large, metropolitan, morning Los Angeles newspaper, on December 30, 1967, published an article which disclosed that Adam Clayton Powell, the Harlem Congressman who had been expelled from the House of Representatives, would leave his self-exile in the Bahamas to speak in behalf of the Speakers Bureau of the Associated Students, University of California at Los Angeles, West Los Angeles, California, on January 10, 1968. The article noted that an invitation had been extended to Powell in September, 1967 by Associated Student Chairman Aaron Grunfeld and the invitation was accepted during the early part of December, 1967. The article noted the Speakers Bureau reserved the Student Union, two thousand seat Grand Ballroom and the thirteen thousand seat Pauley Pavilion for Powell's talk.

The "Los Angeles Herald-Examiner", a large, daily, evening Los Angeles newspaper, on January 9, 1968, disclosed Powell arrived in Los Angeles via National Airlines on January 8, 1968. Powell told the approximately 50 newsmen greeting his arrival that he would speak at the University of California at Los Angeles on Wednesday, January 10, 1968, and his speech would deal with "A second civil war - the black revolution." He also indicated he was concerned about his personal problems and said that if two New York Grand Juries investigating him returned criminal indictments, that he would "blow the whistle...I'll blow it loud and long."

The "Los Angeles Times", on January 9, 1968, stated that Powell was greeted at the airport by an old friend who was identified as Mrs. Mable Howard, 2748 Glasell Street, who grew up with Powell in Harlem. Powell told the press that he has 14 speaking engagements at universities throughout the country and added that he did not plan to visit New York.

ALL INFORMATION CONTAINED
HEREIN IS UNCLASSIFIED
DATE 8/5/82 BY SP3 Clefork   IND-51230-348X

ADAM CLAYTON POWELL

Source One, who has furnished reliable information in the past, on January 9, 1968, advised Powell, following his press conference, proceeded to South Central Los Angeles where he walked in the vicinity of Vernon and Central Avenues, 45th and Central Avenue, Manchester Boulevard and Broadway, where he talked to approximately two to three hundred people in all. The source advised there were no incidents or arrests to mar his appearance in the predominately Negro section of Los Angeles. The source noted that Powell received extensive coverage by all phases of the local news media.

The "Los Angeles Times", on January 11, 1968, reported that Powell addressed approximately six thousand students at the University of California at Los Angeles on Wednesday, January 10, 1968, at the Pauley Pavilion. The audience, which was predominately white, gave Powell a standing ovation when he declared, "One day you are going to say this man (himself) is our man and he doesn't belong with those senile people in Washington." He said, "I challenge you bright young people to break from the cult of mediocrity. I challenge you to join the black revolution." Powell was accompanied by the University of California at Los Angeles basketball star Lew Alcindor and Arthur Ivie, a member of the Black Students Union (BSU) at the University of California at Los Angeles. The BSU has been publicly identified as a black nationalist organization with chapters at California State College at Los Angeles and Los Angeles City College.

The "Los Angeles Times" article noted that Powell told the students, "If you young white people don't develop leadership like we have, you have lost your confidence in your country and parents. We're a new breed of cats. We're finished with 400 years of deprivation. We're insisting on full equality now. In this day of the highest form of living, I can show you one million people who are starving." He told the students, "The trouble with you young people is you don't have leadership", and he said black power is "the saving grace of the United States." He compared the black power movement with religion and said, "If other people have have their religions than black people have the right to black power. Black power is merely an equality of purpose. We are proud we are black. We are the same as you are. And in a sense we are better than you."

- 2 -

ADAM CLAYTON POWELL

According to the "Los Angeles Times", Powell called President Johnson's Great Society a failure and said, "L.B.J. has tired, the poor old fellow. There is no leadership in our land. This is not a great society. It is a sick society. The society has a cancer which is eating the heart out of democracy." He noted that in an apparent reference to acts of disobedience in the black revolution, that whenever the law of the land conflicts with the law of man, it must give in to the law of man.

The "Los Angeles Times" article said that Powell stressed the fact that he is a pacifist and does not believe in black nationalism. He told the audience in part that he thought that his Harlem district was being properly taken care of by his office which is staffed by 66 people.

Copies of this memorandum are being furnished to Region II, 115th MI, U. S. Army, Pasadena; Office of Special Investigations, Norton Air Force Base; Naval Investigative Service, San Diego; U. S. Attorney, Los Angeles; and U. S. Secret Service, Los Angeles.

This document contains neither recommendations nor conclusions of the FBI. It is the property of the FBI and is loaned to your agency; it and its contents are not to be distributed outside your agency.

- 3* -

Chapter VI

Tennessee Williams: An American Original

Williams was born in Columbus, Mississippi on March 26, 1914. His parents Comelius Coffin and Edwina Dokin Williams draped him with two first names Thomas and Lanier. He renamed himself Tennessee because the name to him had a true ring of southern masculinity.

Williams aspired to be a writer long before he reached his teenage years. However, he did not come center stage on Broadway until 1945 at age 31 when his *The Glass Menagerie* won the New York Drama Critics Circle Award for that season.

The skeleton for *The Glass Menagerie* came out of a St. Louis experience which he had when he was thirteen years old and his father was forced to move the family north in search of employment. The Williams's lived in a crowded tenement apartment. His sister's space was a dark closet-like room which he helped make livable by painting the walls and furniture white. He also placed in her room a collection of tiny glass animals, that he found while junking in an alley. They made the room white and crystal in the midst of darkness. Williams was psychologically affected deeply by this territorial transition. Some years later, he put the memory of that St. Louis experience on paper and produced a classic stage play which he entitled, *The Glass Menagerie.*

Tennessee did not make J. Edgar Hoover's most watched surveillance list until 1946 when he revealed his liberal ideas by praising the *Sixty Million Jobs* book written by Henry A. Wallace, the Vice President under Franklin Delano Roosevelt from 1941 to 1945. In 1946 Tennessee Williams also became one of thirty-three other members of the Dramatists' Guild who agreed that they would not present their works in Washington, D. C. as long as racial segregation and discrimination were "practiced on either side of the footlights".

Hoover monitored and kept files on Tennessee Williams and other writers, such as Arthur Miller, Truman Capote and Nero Wolfe, who conveyed in their work the sordid and poverty-stricken side of life in America.

Joseph Kennedy the father of John F. Kennedy was never one to shun the spotlight. However, when Cardinal Spellman blasted the Tennessee Williams Elia Kazan film *Baby Doll* in 1957, he banned the movie from the Kennedy Theaters, because he was hellbent on projecting a public reputation as a family man with ten children as opposed to his after dark role as a Hollywood womanizer.

Tennessee Williams was inducted into "the class of people to watch" along with Einstein one of the world's great physicists. J. Edgar Hoover started collecting information on Albert Einstein in 1940, when it was learned that he attended pacifist meetings and occasionally occupied a seat next to a Communist Party member.

It was not until after World War II that Einstein realized that he was being spied on. In his disgust over Hoover's fascist tactics he said: "*I came to America because of the great, freedom which I was told existed in this country. I made a mistake in selecting America as a land of freedom, a mistake I cannot repair in the balance of my lifetime*". At the time of his death in 1955 the FBI dossier on Einstein had grown like "Topsy" to several thousand pages.

As far as J. Edgar Hoover was concerned, Tennessee Williams never had a chance although he left a body of work that has stood the test of time. The question is, should a democratic society be more concerned about who Tennessee Williams sat or slept with as opposed to the contribution he made to western civilization?

Federal Bureau of Investigation

Freedom of Information/Privacy Acts Section

Subject: Thomas "Tennessee" Williams

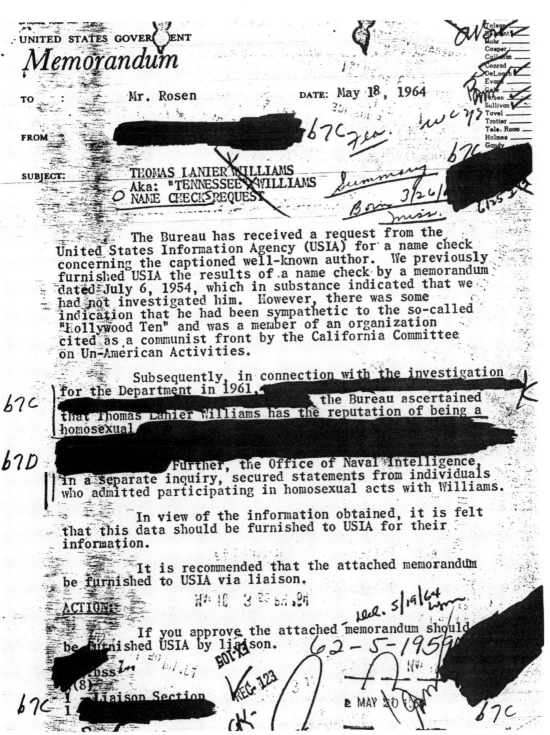

UNITED STATES GOVERNMENT

Memorandum

TO : Mr. Rosen   DATE: May 18, 1964

FROM :

SUBJECT: THOMAS LANIER WILLIAMS
Aka: "TENNESSEE WILLIAMS
NAME CHECK REQUEST

The Bureau has received a request from the United States Information Agency (USIA) for a name check concerning the captioned well-known author. We previously furnished USIA the results of a name check by a memorandum dated July 6, 1954, which in substance indicated that we had not investigated him. However, there was some indication that he had been sympathetic to the so-called "Hollywood Ten" and was a member of an organization cited as a communist front by the California Committee on Un-American Activities.

Subsequently, in connection with the investigation for the Department in 1961, the Bureau ascertained that Thomas Lanier Williams has the reputation of being a homosexual

Further, the Office of Naval Intelligence, in a separate inquiry, secured statements from individuals who admitted participating in homosexual acts with Williams.

In view of the information obtained, it is felt that this data should be furnished to USIA for their information.

It is recommended that the attached memorandum be furnished to USIA via liaison.

ACTION:

If you approve the attached memorandum should be furnished USIA by liaison.

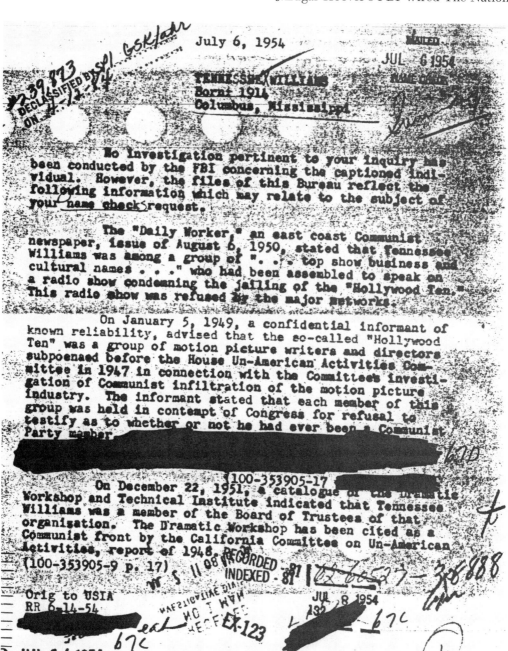

July 6, 1954

MAILED
JUL 6 1954

TENNESSEE WILLIAMS
Born 1914
Columbus, Mississippi

No investigation pertinent to your inquiry has been conducted by the FBI concerning the captioned individual. However, the files of this Bureau reflect the following information which may relate to the subject of your name check request.

The "Daily Worker," an east coast Communist newspaper, issue of August 6, 1950, stated that Tennessee Williams was among a group of ". . . top show business and cultural names . . ." who had been assembled to speak on a radio show condemning the jailing of the "Hollywood Ten." This radio show was refused by the major networks.

On January 5, 1949, a confidential informant of known reliability, advised that the so-called "Hollywood Ten" was a group of motion picture writers and directors subpoenaed before the House Un-American Activities Committee in 1947 in connection with the Committee's investigation of Communist infiltration of the motion picture industry. The informant stated that each member of this group was held in contempt of Congress for refusal to testify as to whether or not he had ever been a Communist Party member.

100-353905-17

On December 22, 1951, a catalogue of the Dramatic Workshop and Technical Institute indicated that Tennessee Williams was a member of the Board of Trustees of that organization. The Dramatic Workshop has been cited as a Communist front by the California Committee on Un-American Activities, report of 1948.
(100-353905-9 p. 17)

RECORDED
INDEXED - 81

Orig to USIA
RR 6-14-54

EX-123
JUL 8 1954

3-JUL 14 1954
F 819

CONFIDENTIAL

62-60527-38885

The foregoing information is furnished to you
as a result of your request for an FBI file check and is
not to be construed as a clearance or a nonclearance of
the individual involved. This information is furnished
for your use and should not be disseminated outside of
your agency.

Note: Information concerning receipt of name check and
data disseminated made available to ████████ prior
to transmitting to USIA.

-2-

CONFIDENTIAL

FBI Secret Files

SECURITY INFORMATION - CONFIDENTIAL

#239,873
DECLASSIFIED BY SPI GSK/ahr
ON 7-12-84

December 23, 1952

TENNESSEE WILLIAMS - Summary
Aka Thomas Lanier
Born March 26, 1914
Columbus, Mississippi

No investigation has been conducted by the FBI
pertinent to your inquiry concerning the above-named
individual.

However, a review of the files of this Bureau
reflects the following information which is believed
pertinent to your request.

The "Daily Worker", an east coast Communist newspaper, issue of August 6, 1950, stated that Tennessee
Williams was among a group of ". . . top show business and
cultural names . . ." who had been assembled to speak on
a radio show condemning the jailing of the "Hollywood Ten".
This radio show was refused by the major networks.

On January 5, 1949, a confidential informant of
known reliability, advised that the so-called "Hollywood Ten"
was a group of motion picture writers and directors subpoenaed
before the House Un-American Activities Committee in 1947
in connection with the Committees investigation of Communist
infiltration of the motion picture industry. The informant
stated that each member of this group was held in contempt
of Congress for refusal to testify as to whether or not he
had ever been a Communist Party member.

b7D

(100-353905-17)
On December 22, 1951, a catalogue of the Dramatic
Workshop and Technical Institute indicated that Tennessee
Williams was a member of the Board of Trustees of that
organization.
(100-353905-9 page 17)

RECORDED

The Dramatic Workshop has been cited as a Communist
front by the California Committee on Un-American Activities,
report of 1948.

INDEXED

DEC 24 1952

62-60527-32180

Orig. to Department of State

SECURITY INFORMATION - CONFIDENTIAL

b7C

JAN 7 - 1953

SECURITY INFORMATION — CONFIDENTIAL

The foregoing information which may relate to the subject of your inquiry is being furnished as the result of your request for an FBI file check only and does not constitute a clearance or nonclearance of the individual involved. It is furnished for your confidential information only and should not be disseminated outside of your agency.

FBI Secret Files

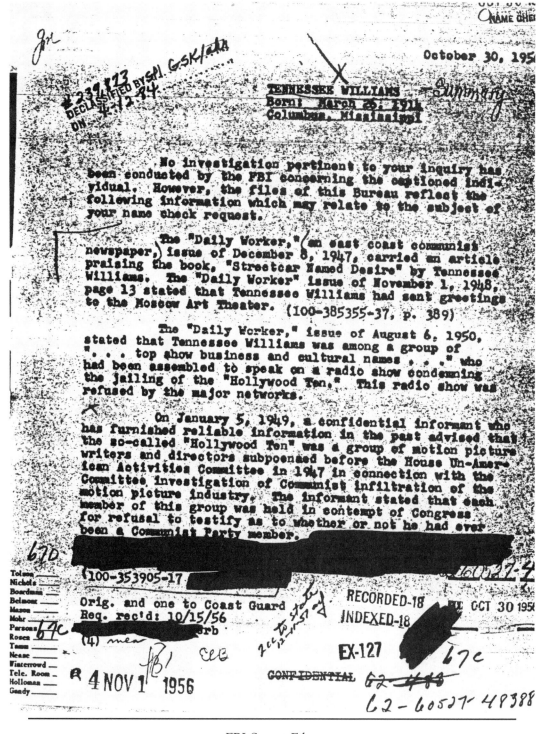

October 30, 1956

TENNESSEE WILLIAMS — Summary
Born: March 26, 1914
Columbus, Mississippi

No investigation pertinent to your inquiry has
been conducted by the FBI concerning the captioned individual. However, the files of this Bureau reflect the
following information which may relate to the subject of
your name check request.

The "Daily Worker," an east coast communist
newspaper, issue of December 8, 1947, carried an article
praising the book, "Streetcar Named Desire" by Tennessee
Williams. The "Daily Worker" issue of November 1, 1948,
page 13 stated that Tennessee Williams had sent greetings
to the Moscow Art Theater. (100-385355-37, p. 389)

The "Daily Worker," issue of August 6, 1950,
stated that Tennessee Williams was among a group of
". . . top show business and cultural names . . ." who
had been assembled to speak on a radio show condemning
the jailing of the "Hollywood Ten." This radio show was
refused by the major networks.

On January 5, 1949, a confidential informant who
has furnished reliable information in the past advised that
the so-called "Hollywood Ten" was a group of motion picture
writers and directors subpoenaed before the House Un-American Activities Committee in 1947 in connection with the
Committee investigation of Communist infiltration of the
motion picture industry. The informant stated that each
member of this group was held in contempt of Congress
for refusal to testify as to whether or not he had ever
been a Communist Party member.

100-353905-17

Orig. and one to Coast Guard
Req. rec'd: 10/15/56

RECORDED-18
INDEXED-18

OCT 30 1956

EX-127

CONFIDENTIAL

Tolson
Nichols
Boardman
Belmont
Mason
Mohr
Parsons
Rosen
Tamm
Nease
Winterrowd
Tele. Room
Holloman
Gandy

4 NOV 1 1956

CONFIDENTIAL

Tennessee Williams   October 30, 1956

On December 22, 1951, a catalogue of the Dramatic Workshop and Technical Institute indicated that Tennessee Williams was a member of the Board of Trustees of that organization. The Dramatic Workshop has been cited as a Communist front by the California Committee on Un-American Activities, report of 1948. (100-353905-9 p. 17)

You may also desire to consult the Public Hearings of the House Committee regarding Communist Infiltration of Hollywood Motion Picture Industry, Part 2, April and May, 1951, pages 331 and 2413. (100-385355-37, p. 389)

The foregoing information is furnished to you as a result of your request for an FBI file check and is not to be construed as a clearance or a nonclearance of the individual involved. This information is furnished for your use and should not be disseminated outside of your agency.

Some selected works by Tennessee Williams, who won his first Pulitzer Prize in 1948 for "*A Street Car Name Desire*".

Plays:

*27 Wagons Full of Cotton, and Other One Act Plays.
Norfolk: New Directions, 1945.*
*American Blues. New York: New York Dramatists Play
Service, 1948.*
Camino Real. Norfolk: New Directions, 1953.
Cat on a Hot Tin Roof. New American Library, 1955.
*Clothes for a Summer Hotel: A Ghost Play, New York:
New Directions, 1983.*
Battle of Ages. Murray, Utah: 1945.
*Dragon Counting, A Book of Plays. New York: New
Directions, 1970.*
*The Eccentricities of a Nightingale. New York: New
Directions, 1964.*
Five Plays. London: Secker & Warburg, 1962.
The Fugitive Kind. New York: New Directions, 1945.
Garden District. London: Secker & Warburg, 1959.
The Glass Menagerie. New York: New Directions, 1945.
Grand. New York: House of Book, 1964.
*I Rise a Flame, Cried the Phoenix. Norfolk: J. Laughlin,
1951.*
*In the Bar of a Tokyo Hotel. New York: Dramatists Play
Service, 1969.*
Kingdom of the Earth. New York: New Directions, 1968.
*A Lovely Sunday for Creve Coer. New York: New
Directions, 1980.*

The Milk Train Doesn't Stop Here Anymore. New York: New Directions, 1964.

The Mutilated. New York: New York Dramatists Play Service, 1967.

The Night of the Iguana. New York: New Directions, 1961.

Not About Nightingales. New York: New Directions, 1998.

Orpheus Descending. London: Secker & Warburg, 1958.

A Perfect Analysis is Given by a Parrot. New York: New York Dramatists Play Service, 1958.

Period of Adjustment. New York: New Directions, 1960.

The Red Devil Battery Sign. New York: New Directions, 1988.

The Remarkable Rooming-House of Mme. LeMonde. New York: Albondocani Press, 1984.

The Rose Tattoo. New York: New Directions, 1951.

Small Craft Warnings. London: Secker & Warburg, 1973.

Something Cloudy, Something Clear. New York: New Directions, 1995.

Steps Must Be Gentle. New York: Targ, 1980.

Stopped Rocking and Other Screenplays. New York: New Directions: 1984.

A Streetcar Named Desire. New York: New Directions, 1947.

Suddenly Last Summer. New York: New Directions, 1958.

Summer and Smoke. New York: New Directions, 1948.

Sweet Bird of Youth. New York: New Directions, 1959.

The Two-Character Play. New York: New Directions, 1979.

Vieux Carre. New York: New Directions, 1979.

You Touched Me! New York: S. French, 1947.

Fiction:

Eight Moral Ladies Possessed. New York: New
Directions, 1974.
Hard Candy. New York: New Directions, 1959.
It Happened the Day the Sun Rose. Los Angeles:
Sylvester and Orphanos, 1981.
The Knightly Quest. New York: New Directions, 1966.
Moise and the World of Reason. New York: Simon &
Schuster, 1975.
One Arm, and Other Stories. New York: New
Directions, 1967.
The Roman Spring of Mrs. Stone. London: J.
Lechmann, 1950.
Short Stories. New York: Ballentine, 1986.
Three Players of a Summer Game. London: Secker &
Warburg, 1960.

Poetry:

Androgyne, Mon Amour. New York: New Directions,
1977.
Five Young American Poets. Norfolk: New Directions,
1944.
In the Winter of Cities. Norfolk: New Directions, 1956.

Other:

Baby Doll: The Script for the Film. New American Library, 1956.
Blue Mountain Ballads. New York: Schlimer, 1946.
Five O' Clock Angel: Letters of Tennessee Williams to Maria St. Just, 1948-1982. New York: Knopf, 1990.
Letters to Donald Windham. New York: Holt, Rinehart, 1977.
Lord Byron's Love Letter. New York: Ricodi, 1955. (Libretto by TW).
Memoirs. Garden City: Doubleday, 1975.
The Notebook of Trigorin: A Free Adaptation of Anton Chekhov's The Sea Gull. New Directions, 1997.
Where I Live. New York: New Directions, 1978.

Stage Productions:

Cairo, Shanghai, Bombay, Memphis, 1935.
Candles to the Sun, St. Louis, 1937.
The Fugitive Kind, St. Louis, 1937.
Battle of Angels, Boston, 1940.
The Glass Menagerie, Chicago, 1944.
The Glass Menagerie, Broadway, 1945.
A Streetcar Named Desire, Broadway, 1947.
Summer and Smoke, Broadway, 1948.
The Rose Tattoo, Broadway, 1951.
Camino Real, Broadway, 1953.
Cat on a Hot Tin Roof, Broadway, 1955.
Orpheus Descending, Broadway, 1957.
Garden District, off-Broadway, 1958.
Sweet Bird of Youth, Broadway, 1959.
Period of Adjustment, Broadway, 1960.
Night of the Iguana, Broadway, 1961.
The Milk Train Doesn't Stop Here Anymore, Broadway, 1963.

Slapstick Tragedy, Broadway, 1966.
The Two Character Play, London, 1967.
The Seven Descents of Myrtle, Broadway, 1968.
In the Bar of a Tokyo Hotel, Broadway, 1969.
Small Craft Warnings, off-Broadway, 1972.
Out Cry, Broadway, 1973.
Red Devil Battery Sign, Boston, 1975.
This Is (An Entertainment), San Francisco, 1976.
Vieux Carre, Broadway, 1977.
A Lonely Sunday for Creve Coeur, off-Broadway, 1979.
A House Not Meant to Stand, Chicago, 1980.
Something Cloudy, Something Clear, off-Broadway, 1980.

Tennessee Williams accepts the Drama Critics' Circle Award from Howard Barnes for the Best Play of 1945.

Chapter VII

Richard Wright: The Black Boy Who Wouldn't Bend

Richard Wright was born on September 4, 1908, on a plantation 25 miles south of Natchez, Mississippi. His father Nathaniel Wright was an illiterate cotton picker, who was described by those who knew him as a six foot one hundred and ninety pound handsome, jovial stud, with coffee colored skin and a quick pearly grin. The poor guy scarcely made enough money to support a family of four. His mother Ellan Wilson Wright was from a tight corset wearing mulatto group of Seventh Day Adventist sisters who looked upon any natural pleasure such as sex, Sunday baseball or card playing as a cardinal sin. Hence, she put forth her best effort to save her husband from the ultimate hell of brimstone and fire. Wright's maternal grandmother had straight sandy hair and bright hazel eyes and skin as white as any (WASP) White Anglo Saxon Protestant.

As a small boy when Richard Wright heard that a "Black Boy" had been severely beaten by a "White" man, he naively felt that the man had the right to do it because the "White" man must have been the Black Boy's "father".

Richard Wright's daddy rejected his wife's domineering and overbearing demeanor the same as he had fought against her seven day a week Adventist religious doctrine. She insisted on opening the Sabbath in their home just before sun-down on Friday, and she always closed the Sabbath after sundown on Saturday. The entire Sabbath day was spent in church praying, listening to the elders and singing such hymns as "Don't Forget The Sabbath". She used the sunset table in the "Morning Watch" to determine the exact time that the sun would go down. In addition, there was a mandatory Sunday evening service where they showed Christian slides because movie theaters were off limits. Also forbidden by the Adventist Doctrine was the adornment of one's body with worldly dress and cosmetics of any kind such as lipstick and face powder. Adventism not only dictated the type of clothes one wore, but it also restricted the kind of food that dressed the lining of the stomach. No pork or shellfish was ever served in the home. Since cooking was not permitted on the Sabbath, the meals for Saturday were prepared before sundown on Friday.

Food was something of which young Richard Wright never got his fill. Wright made the following observation in his autobiography Black Boy. "Hunger had always been more or less at my elbow when I played, but now I began to awake at night to find hunger standing at my bedside, staring at me gauntly. The hunger I had known before this had been no grim hostile stranger".

During his daily waking hours, Richard Wright was both hostile and rebellious against his mother and the other domineering women in the family. His mother nearly whipped him to death when he was four years old because he accidentally set a fire in his grandmother's bedroom and burned her when she was ill in bed. Despite the beating, he refused to bend like a twig to her wishes. His grandmother frequently rained blows to the steeple of his head without rhyme or reason; and his maternal grandfather threatened to get his guns if necessary to enforce their sadomasochistic morality. Addie Wilson, his aunt and grade school teacher, was out of control in that she kicked all doors open before she entered a room and then shut them behind her so she could kick them wide open again.

Young Wright, at the age of six, was a world-beater in that he survived and succeeded in spite of his dysfunctional family. To make bad matters worse, old men encouraged him to become a drunk when he was hustling pennies for food in Beal Street bars in Memphis, Tennessee.

Richard Wright had been gifted by God with a survival kit loaded with antidotes for handling anger and hate. He was able to overcome most of his rage by successfully transforming it into a powerful competitive drive. It was his positive attitude and steadfast discipline that enabled him to walk barefoot across the burning sands of time. How else could one explain the evolution of a Black boy from Mississippi who attended the sharecroppers school 5 months a year through ninth grade and become a world class literary giant at age 32. He rejected a graduation speech prepared by the principal of the Jackson, Mississippi Smith Robinson public school in 1925 at the age of seventeen. He insisted on writing and delivering his own. A streak of Richard's Choctaw Indian blood from his paternal side must have surfaced because the principal acquiesced.

Richard Wright's, classic "Native Son" was selected in March 1940 by the Book Of The Month Club; it was his first full-length novel. That work put Richard Wright in the class of the best one hundred writers of the twentieth century.

Richard Wright with Vivian Harsh, Chief Librarian at Cleveland Hall Branch of the Chicago Public Library. This picture was taken in the Fall of 1937.

Federal Bureau of Investigation

Freedom of Information/Privacy Acts Section

Subject: <u>Richard Wright</u>

100-157464 -1

Date: December 9, 1942

To: SAC, New York

From: J. Edgar Hoover - Director, Federal Bureau of Investigation

Subject: RICHARD WRIGHT
                INTERNAL SECURITY - SEDITION

        Transmitted herewith are copies of a communication addressed by ▮▮▮▮▮▮▮▮ to the Honorable Henry L. Stimson, Secretary of War, at Washington, D. C., under date of October 13, 1942. The Bureau of course received this communication by reference from the Military Intelligence Service.

        In view of ▮▮▮▮▮▮ specific allegations as to certain writings of subject, it is desired that your office make inquiry of sources available to you for the purpose of determining whether the book entitled "Twelve Million Black Voices" or other publications of subject are in fact given to the expression of statements having significance under the Sedition Statutes. If possible, you should secure a copy of this publication as well as other writings of subject and review the same for the possible presence of such material.

        If your inquiry develops information of an affirmative nature, you should of course cause an investigation to be undertaken as to subject's background, inclinations, and current activities.

Mr. Tolson_____
Mr. E. A. Tamm__
Mr. Clegg_____
Mr. Glavin__Enclosures
Mr. Ladd_____
Mr. Nichols__|COMMUNICATIONS SECTION
Mr. Rosen___|
Mr. Tracy___| MAILED 10
Mr. Carson__| ★ DEC 10 1942 P.M.
Mr. Coffey__|
Mr. Hendon__|
Mr. Kramer__| FEDERAL BUREAU OF INVESTIGATION
Mr. McGuire_| U. S. DEPARTMENT OF JUSTICE
Mr. Quinn Tamm__
Mr. Nease_____

ALL INFORMATION CONTAINED
HEREIN IS UNCLASSIFIED
DATE 8-26-87 BY ▮▮▮▮▮▮

FEDERAL BUREAU OF INVESTIGATION

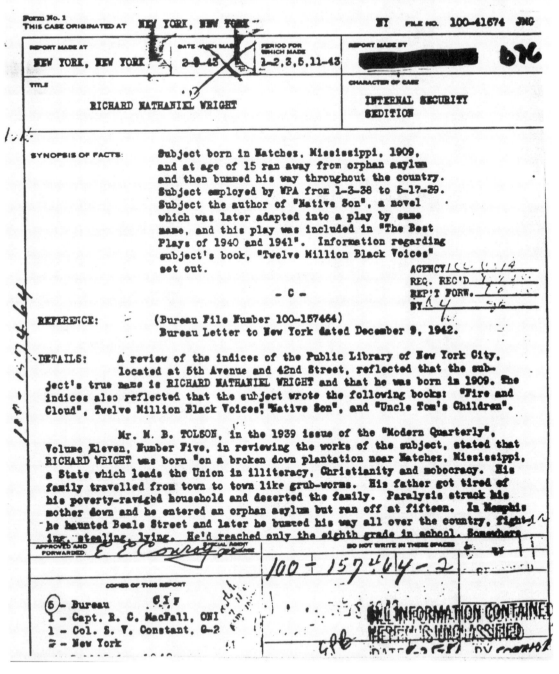

FORM No. 1
THIS CASE ORIGINATED AT **NEW YORK, NEW YORK**   NY   FILE NO. 100-41574 JMG

REPORT MADE AT	DATE WHEN MADE	PERIOD FOR WHICH MADE	REPORT MADE BY
NEW YORK, NEW YORK	2-9-43	1-2,3,5,11-43	▓▓▓▓▓▓▓▓

TITLE

RICHARD NATHANIEL WRIGHT

CHARACTER OF CASE

**INTERNAL SECURITY
SEDITION**

SYNOPSIS OF FACTS: Subject born in Natchez, Mississippi, 1909,
and at age of 15 ran away from orphan asylum
and then bummed his way throughout the country.
Subject employed by WPA from 1-3-38 to 5-17-39.
Subject the author of "Native Son", a novel
which was later adapted into a play by same
name, and this play was included in "The Best
Plays of 1940 and 1941". Information regarding
subject's book, "Twelve Million Black Voices"
set out.

AGENCY ▓▓▓▓▓
REQ. REC'D ▓▓▓▓
– C –   REP'T FORW. ▓▓▓▓
BY ▓▓▓▓

REFERENCE: (Bureau File Number 100-157464)
Bureau Letter to New York dated December 9, 1942.

DETAILS: A review of the indices of the Public Library of New York City,
located at 5th Avenue and 42nd Street, reflected that the subject's true name is RICHARD NATHANIEL WRIGHT and that he was born in 1909. The
indices also reflected that the subject wrote the following books: "Fire and
Cloud", Twelve Million Black Voices; "Native Son", and "Uncle Tom's Children".

Mr. M. B. TOLSON, in the 1939 issue of the "Modern Quarterly",
Volume Eleven, Number Five, in reviewing the works of the subject, stated that
RICHARD WRIGHT was born "on a broken down plantation near Natchez, Mississippi,
a State which leads the Union in illiteracy, Christianity and mobocracy. His
family travelled from town to town like grub-worms. His father got tired of
his poverty-ravaged household and deserted the family. Paralysis struck his
mother down and he entered an orphan asylum but ran off at fifteen. In Memphis
he haunted Beale Street and later he bummed his way all over the country, fighting, stealing, lying. He'd reached only the eighth grade in school. Somewhere

APPROVED AND FORWARDED ▓ E E Conroy SPECIAL AGENT IN CHARGE   DO NOT WRITE IN THESE SPACES

100 - 157464 - 2

COPIES OF THIS REPORT

5 – Bureau
1 – Capt. R. C. MacFall, ONI
1 – Col. S. V. Constant, G-2
2 – New York

ALL INFORMATION CONTAINED
HEREIN IS UNCLASSIFIED
DATE ▓▓▓ BY ▓▓▓▓

NY 100-41674

along the gutted road it dawned upon him that he needed an education. And then, whether digging ditches or clerking in the post office, he devoured the contents of newspapers and magazines as well as books that came his way."

████████████████████ advised the writer that the subject had been employed by the WPA on a Federal Writers' Project from January 3, 1938, to May 17, 1939, when he resigned to accept private employment. At this time subject was residing at 809 Saint Nicholas Avenue, New York City.

"The Best Plays of 1940 and 1941" by BURNS MANTLE included the subject's play, "Native Son", which was produced from the subject's novel by the same name.

Mr. BROOKS ATKINSON in the New York Times had the following to say about the subject's play, "Native Son": "In the drama Mr. GREEN and Mr. WRIGHT work in a more objective style. Without the subjective background their defense of Bigger Thomas's ghastly crime in the court scene sounds like generalized pleading. It lacks the stinging enlightment of the last third of Mr. WRIGHT's novel. But that completes this column's bill of exceptions to the biggest American drama of the season."

The novel, "Twelve Million Black Voices", which was written by the subject, was published by the Viking Press in New York City in October, 1941, and this book is divided into four parts: (1) Our Strange Birth; (2) Inheritors of Slavery; (3) Death on the City Pavements; and (4) Men in the Making. In the foreword, Mr. WRIGHT states "while this novel purports to render a broad picture of the processes of negro life in the United States, intentionally it does not include in its considerations those areas of negro life which comprise the so-called 'talented tenth' or the isolated islands of mulatto leadership which are still to be found in many parts of the South or the growing and influential negro middle class professional and business men of the North who have, for the past twenty years or more, formed a sort of liaison corps between the whites and the blacks".

The reference letter reflected that on Page 145 of the above-mentioned novel, there was material that appeared to be seditious in nature; and for the benefit of the Bureau, the above-mentioned page is being quoted in full:

"There are millions of us and we are moving in all directions. All our lives we have been catapulted into arenas where, had we thought consciously of invading them, we would have hung back. A sense of constant change has stolen silently into our lives and has become operative in our personalities as a law of living.

NY 100-41674

"There are some of us who feel our hurts so deeply that we find it impossible to work with whites; we feel that it is futile to hope or dream in terms of American life. Our distrust is so great that we form intensely racial and nationalistic organizations and advocate the establishment of a separate state, a forty-ninth state, in which we black folk would live.

"There are even today among us groups that forlornly plan a return to Africa."

"There are others of us who feel the need of the protection of a strong nation so keenly that we admire the harsh and imperialistic policies of Japan and ardently hope that the Japanese will assume the leadership of the 'darker races'.

"As our consciousness changes, as we come of age, as we shed our folk swaddling clothes, so run our lives in a hundred directions.

"Today, all of us black folk are not poor. A few of us have money. We make it as the white folk make theirs, but our money-making is restricted to our own people. Many of us black folk have managed to send our children to school, and a few of our children are now professional and business men whose standards of living approximate those of middle-class whites. Some of us own small businesses; others devote their lives to law and medicine.

"But the majority of us still toil on the plantations, work in heavy industry, and labor in the kitchens of the Lords of the Land and the Bosses of the Buildings.

"The general dislocation of life during the depression caused many white workers to learn through chronic privation that they could not protect their standard of living so long as we blacks were excluded from their unions. Many hundreds of thousands of them found that they could not fight successfully for increased wages and union recognition unless we stood shoulder to shoulder with them. As a consequence, many of us have recently become members of steel, automobile, packing and tobacco unions."

The following quotations are found on Page 146 of the same book and is the last page of the novel:

"The differences between black folk and white folk are not blood or color, and the ties that bind us are deeper than those that separate us. The common road of hope which we all have travelled has brought us into a stronger Kinship than any words, laws or legal claims."

"What do we black folk want? We want what others have, the right to share in the upward march of American life, the only life we remember or have

- 3 -

6

NY 100-41674

ever known. The Lord of the Land say: 'We will not grant this!' We answer: 'We
ask you to grant us nothing. We are winning our heritage though our toll in suffering is great!' The Bosses of the Buildings say: 'Your problem is beyond solution!'
We answer: 'Our problem is being solved. We are crossing the line you dared us to
cross though we pay in the coin of death!' "

"The seasons of the plantation no longer dictate the lives of many of us;
hundreds of thousands of us are moving into the sphere of conscious history."

"We are with the new tide. We stand at the crossroads. We watch each new
procession. The hot wires carrying urgent appeals. Print compels us. Voices are
speaking. Men are moving! And we shall be with them."

- CLOSED -

- 4 -

Federal Bureau of Investigation
United States Department of Justice
New York, N.Y.

EMC
100-41674

March 3, 1943

Director, FBI

RE: RICHARD WRIGHT
INTERNAL SECURITY
SEDITION

Dear Sir:

In reference to Bureau letter of January 20, 1943, (Bureau file 160-157464) requesting the status of the above entitled matter, this is to advise this case has been reassigned and placed in line for immediate investigation.

Very truly yours,

E. E. CONROY
SAC

ALL INFORMATION CONTAINED
HEREIN IS UNCLASSIFIED
DATE 8-25-81 BY 888IJLu

COPIES DESTROYED
153 AUG 10 1960

RECORDED

157464

MAR 5 1943

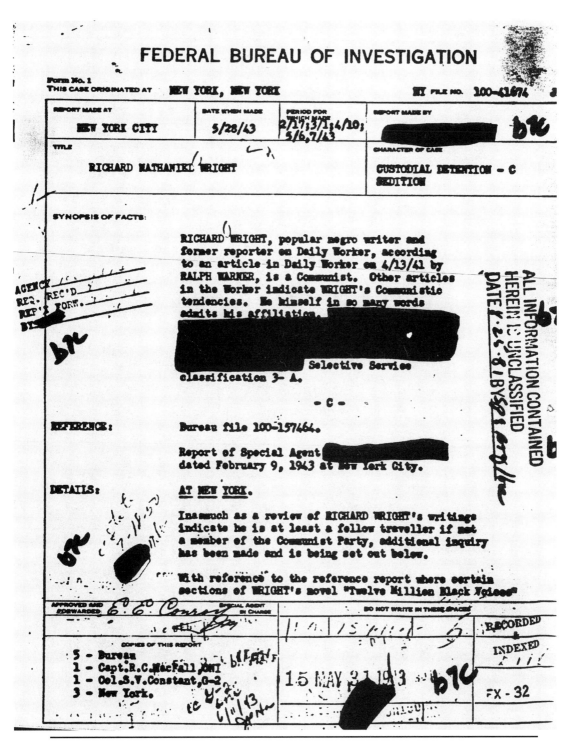

FEDERAL BUREAU OF INVESTIGATION

Form No. 1
THIS CASE ORIGINATED AT **NEW YORK, NEW YORK**   NY FILE NO. **100-61674**

REPORT MADE AT	DATE WHEN MADE	PERIOD FOR WHICH MADE	REPORT MADE BY
NEW YORK CITY	**5/28/43**	**2/1,13/1;4/10; 5/6,7/43**	**b7c**

TITLE	CHARACTER OF CASE
RICHARD NATHANIEL WRIGHT	**CUSTODIAL DETENTION - C SEDITION**

SYNOPSIS OF FACTS:

RICHARD WRIGHT, popular negro writer and former reporter on Daily Worker, according to an article in Daily Worker on 4/13/41 by RALPH WARNER, is a Communist. Other articles in the Worker indicate WRIGHT's Communistic tendencies. He himself in so many words admits his affiliation. ▮▮▮▮▮▮▮▮▮▮ Selective Service classification 3-A.

- C -

REFERENCE: Bureau file 100-157464.

Report of Special Agent ▮▮▮▮▮▮ dated February 9, 1943 at New York City.

DETAILS: AT NEW YORK.

Inasmuch as a review of RICHARD WRIGHT's writings indicate he is at least a fellow traveller if not a member of the Communist Party, additional inquiry has been made and is being set out below.

With reference to the reference report where certain sections of WRIGHT's novel "Twelve Million Black Voices"

APPROVED AND FORWARDED **E. C. Conroy**   SPECIAL AGENT IN CHARGE   DO NOT WRITE IN THESE SPACES

COPIES OF THIS REPORT
5 - Bureau
1 - Capt. R.C. MacFall, ONI
1 - Col. S.V. Constant, G-2
3 - New York.

RECORDED & INDEXED

15 MAY 31 1943

FX - 32

NY file
100-41674

were set out as possibly falling within the violation of the sedition
statute, a brief review of this book does not indicate that any other
portion of the novel is of an sedition nature.

"Twelve Million Black Voices" is a fictitious story
of the social conditions of the Negro in the United States from the first
slave days to the present in which he discusses the progress of the Negro.

WRIGHT was also the author of the popular novel
"Native Son" and when questioned by writers and critics why he created
such a character as "Bigger", he explained same in an article which was
published in "The Saturday Review" of June 1, 1940, page 18. He discussed pro and con what prompted him to write such a novel and to create
such a character as "Bigger" from which, among other things, is taken
the following excerpt:

> "Another thought kept me from writing. What would
> my own white and black comrades in the Communist
> Party say."

From such a published statement, one would assume
WRIGHT to be a member of the Party or at least a fellow traveller.

The American-Journal, New York daily newspaper of
February 15, 1943 states that RICHARD WRIGHT was a former reporter on
the Daily Worker. WRIGHT's picture appears in the "Negroes and the
War", published and distributed by the Office of War Information.

The files of the New York office also reflect that
RICHARD WRIGHT's name appears on the "Committee to Free Earl Browder",
which list was published in the People's Voice, a New York Negro weekly
newspaper issued March 21, 1942.

_____ advised that on March 6,
1942 WRIGHT's name appeared on the "American Committee to Save Refugees,"
and on September 18, 1942 was listed as one of the officers of the
League of American Writers, advocating a second front in Europe.

NY file
100-41674

It is noted that WRIGHT's name appeared frequently in the Daily Worker during 1941 and 1942. In an issue dated February 25, 1941, page 4, column 1, it is noted that RICHARD WRIGHT was listed along with EARL BROWDER, BEN GOLD and JOE NORTH as one of the speakers at which time the Daily Worker celebrated MIKE GOLD's 25th anniversary, in the labor movement.

In an issue dated February 28, 1941 WRIGHT was listed as one of the writers who would greet THEODORE DREISER at a testimonial luncheon attended March 1, 1941 at the Commodore Hotel under the auspices of the American Council on Soviet Relations. Others to be present were JESSICA SMITH, editor of "Soviet Russia Today", CLIFFORD ODETS, Dr. JOHN A. KINGSBURY and others.

In an issue of March 19, 1941, page 5, column 7, WRIGHT greeted WILLIAM Z. FOSTER, National Chairman of the Communist Party on his 60th Birthday.

In an issue dated March 22, 1941 WRIGHT along with RUTH McKENNEY, was reported to have accepted to serve on the Board of Honorary Chairmen of the May Day Committee.

In an issue of April 5, 1941, page 7, column 2, RICHARD WRIGHT's name appeared with other writers in what was known as the "Call to the 4th Congress of the League of America" to be held in New York City on June 6 and 8, 1941 to discuss how best writers can resist the trend toward war, what to do to restore the WPA and what to do in defense of culture.

In an issue dated April 13, 1941, the Sunday Worker, page 7, column 1, RALPH WARNER discussed the play "Native Son" and among other things admits that "Max", one of the characters in the play is symbolic of a Communist. "However, that nowhere in the play is he called a Communist but he is clearly a sympathiser." WARNER states however, that RICHARD WRIGHT is a Communist and the conception of Max and of his entire play is.

NY file
100-41674

In an issue of April 21, 1941, page 1, there is an editorial which speaks about WRIGHT's stirring condemnation of the imprisonment of EARL BROWDER and of a long forward by JAMES W. FORD contained in WRIGHT's "Bright the Morning Star", a short story in pamphlet form printed by the International Publishers. FORD highly endorsed WRIGHT and the article also pertains to a part of a letter to the International Publishers by WRIGHT in which he says he wants no royalty for this work and those that are received are to accrue to the "Earl Browder Defense Fund."

In an issue dated June 9, 1941, page 1, WRIGHT's name appears among those of the Writers Congress who adopted a firm anti-war program.

In an issue dated July 24, 1941, page 7, column 3, it is noted that WRIGHT's name appears among the American writers who pledged full support to Great Britain and the Soviet Union.

A change of attitude of RICHARD WRIGHT and other writers is pointed out in that in early June they adopted a firm anti-war program and in July they advocated full support to the Soviet Union. Further, that Germany declared war on Russia on June 22, 1941.

In an issue dated August 18, 1941 WRIGHT appears on the Citizen's Committee to Free Earl Browder and in an issue dated August 11, 1941, page 9, WRIGHT states that HARRY BRIDGES is a friend of America and has become a symbol in America and that those who fight against him are enemies of America.

In an issue dated October 22, 1941, page 1, paragraph 1, WRIGHT's name appears as one of the members of a group of citizens calling for a release of EARL BROWDER.

On November 19, 1941, page 3, in the Sunday Worker, RICHARD WRIGHT was declared winner of the Spingaro medal for the writing of "Native Son." Also in this issue WRIGHT along with A. W. BERRY, Secretary of the Communist Party, Reverend ADAM CLAYTON, POWELL, Jr., and HORACE MARSHALL, Vice-President of the National Negro Congress, protested against police brutality and general economic conditions existent in Harlem.

In an issue dated February 13, 1942, page 7, column 4, a letter of WRIGHT's was published dealing with the controversy on music which letter is dated February 10, 1942 and begins as follows:

"Dear Comrade Sender Garlin:"

WRIGHT complimented the Daily Worker and among other

NY file
100-41674

things states that he would like to see letters from the public on
"how can recruitment of negroes to the Communist Party be increased."
This letter also stated that "The Communist Party is the only political
party in America vitally concerned about culture and its problems."

It is also noted that in JAMES W. FORD's book "The
Negro and the Democratic Front", on page 193, FORD states that he
wants to "express publically the high appreciation of our Negro comrades
and Negro people for the splendid contributions of RICHARD WRIGHT,
LANGSTON HUGHES and other artists and musicians of our people."

On October 14, 1942 ████████████████████████
advised that RICHARD WRIGHT, a former known Communist Party member,
had split with the Party because of his dissatisfaction with the way
the Party handled the Negro question.

████████████████████████████████████

327 Lafayette Street, Brooklyn, furnished the following information as
reflected in the files of that board concerning WRIGHT.

He advised that WRIGHT's questionnaire was returned
May 9, 1941 at which time WRIGHT resided at 473 West 104th Street, New
York City. However, he presently resides at 7 Middagh Street, Brooklyn,
New York. On May 28, 1941 WRIGHT was placed in 3-A classification
because of collateral dependents. On July 1, 1942 his collateral
dependency was removed and he was placed in classification 1-A.

On July 6, 1942 he was about to be inducted into
the Army and he asked for a 90 day extention, which was granted. On
November 2, 1942 a continuation of this extension was granted. On
November 16, 1942 he was placed in 3-A in order to permit him an
opportunity to take Volunteer Candidate Training, but was subsequently
rejected.

The questionnaire reflects that WRIGHT was born
September 4, 1908 at Natchez, Mississippi. His education was given
as eight years of elementary school. He states his employment experience
is that of a novelist, playwright, poet and newspaper reporter. He did
not set forth his place of employment but advised that he was engaged
as a writer of political and labor news from 1937 to 1938. This might
possibly be the period that he was a reporter for the Daily Worker.

WRIGHT furnished a list of his writings to the Local
Board. It was noted that "Uncle Tom's Children" according to WRIGHT was
written by him and was later translated into Russian by the U.S.S.R. and
issued in international literature.

- 5 -

NY 100-41674

It appeared from Subject's contacts with his Local Board that his interest in the problem of the Negro has become almost an obsession and it was said that he apparently overlooks the fact that his own rise to success refutes many of his own statements regarding the impossibility of the Negro's improving his personal position.

From all the information concerning Subject in publications and according to information from Informants in the New York Office, Subject is continuing his activities as a writer. In addition to his better known books he has also been engaged in the writing of skits and stories, most of which concern the Negro. The publicity which has been received by Subject WRIGHT is typified by the rather lengthy review of his life appearing in the volume "Current Biography, 1940" published by the H. W. Wilson Company. This volume states that RICHARD WRIGHT, Author, was born September 4, 1908 and his present address is care of HARPER & BROTHERS, 49 East 33rd Street, New York City. It refers to him as a brilliant young Negro writer whose collection of short stories "Uncle Tom's Children" won a $500 prize competition in 1938 and whose book "Native Son" was the March, 1940 selection of the Book-of-the-Month Club. Much of the article contains a review of the character and theme of that book.

The life of RICHARD WRIGHT, beginning with his birth, September 4, 1908, on a plantation 25 miles from Natchez, Mississippi, is summarized, as follows:

His father, NATHAN WRIGHT, was a mill worker and his mother, ELLEN WRIGHT, a country school teacher. The family was continually on the move so his education was very much neglected. When his mother was stricken with paralysis during the first world war, the Subject was sent to an uncle's house to live. WRIGHT is quoted as having stated that he did so much fighting, lying and school-cutting that he was sent back to his grandmother who predicted that he would end on the gallows. He was put in a 7th Day Adventist

3

27

WASH FROM NEW YORK 2 28 1-14P

DIRECTOR   URGENT

GAIN. RICHARD NATHANIEL WRIGHT, IS-C. FOR THE BUREAUS INFO ARTICLE :

TODAYS NY HERALD TRIBUNE ENTITLED "NEGRO AUTHOR CRITICIZES REDS AS IN-

TOLERANT", STATES THAT RICHARD WRIGHT, AUTHOR OF "NATIVE SON" IN DIS-

CUSSING HIS OWN BREAK WITH COMMUNIST PARTY SAYS PARTY FEARS NEW IDEAS

AND THAT COMMUNIST POSITION ON AMERICAN NEGRO HAS UNDERGONE A "DISTIN(

AND LAMENTABLE REGRESSION" IN RECENT YEARS. WRIGHT WAS FURTHER CRE-

DITED WITH DESCRIBING COMMUNISTS AS "NARROW MINDED, BIGOTED, INTOLERA!

AND FRIGHTENED OF NEW IDEAS WHICH DONT FIT INTO THEIR OWN." THE HERAI

TRIBUNE FURTHER STATES THAT MR WRIGHTS REMARKS WERE PROMPTED BY QUEST

GROWING OUT OF AN ARTICLE WHICH HE HAS WRITTEN FOR THE ATLANTIC MONT!

FOR AUGUST UNDER THE TITLE OF "I TRIED TO BE A COMMUNIST." THE TRIBU!

FURTHER STATES THAT IN THE ATLANTIC MONTHLY ARTICLE THE AUTHOR OF NAT:

SON DISCUSSES HIS EARLIEST EXPERIENCES AS A CP MEMBER IN CHICAGO TOUC!

ING ON THE PROBLEMS HE FACED IN TRYING TO PRESENT HIS OWN IDEAS TO THI

PARTY. FURTHERMORE THE AUGUST ATLANTIC MONTHLY DESCRIBES THE ARTICLE

AS THE FIRST OF TWO INSTALLMENTS AND MR WRIGHT ADVISED THE TRIBUNE RE-

PRESENTATIVE YESTERDAY THAT HE WOULD NOT DISCUSS THE SPECIFIC DETAILS

END PAGE ONE   COPIES DESTROYED

153 AUG 10 1950

NY2 PAGE 2

OF THE CHICAGO BREAK WITH THE COMMUNISTS BECAUSE THESE WILL BE COVERED
IN THE SECOND MAGAZINE ARTICLE. WRIGHT FURTHER ADVISED THE TRIBUNE
THAT HIS CP MEMBERSHIP COVERED THE PERIOD, ROUGHLY, FROM THE LATTER
PART OF NINETEEN THIRTYTWO TO NINETEEN FORTY AND THAT HIS EARLY ASSO-
CIATION WITH THE COMMUNISTS IN CHICAGO HAS BEEN BROKEN IN NINETEEN
THIRTYSEVEN WHEN HE WAS EJECTED FROM THE SAME. WRIGHT FURTHER ADVISED
THAT HE WAS ON THE OUTS WITH THE PARTY FROM MAY UNTIL AUGUST THIRTY
SEVEN AND THAT HE WAS REINSTATED IN NY IN SUCH YEAR AND "MAINTAINED
A RELATIONSHIP" WITH THE PARTY UNTIL FORTY WHEN HE SAID HE LEFT THE
SAME. THE TRIBUNE ARTICLE DISCUSSING WRIGHTS COMMENTS ABOUT THE LAMEN-
TABLE REGRESSION OF THE CP POSITION ON THE AMERICAN NEGRO CREDITED MR.
WRIGHT WITH STATING "PUBLICLY COMMUNISTS WILL DENY THAT THERE IS ANY
SUBSTANTIAL CHANGE IN THEIR MILITANCY, BUT PRIVATELY THEY OFFER ANY
HANDY EXCUSE. THE MILITANCY OF THE NEGRO QUESTION HAS PASSED INTO THE
HANDS OF RIGHT WING NEGROES. THAT WAS NOT TRUE EIGHT YEARS AGO. MOST
OF THE BATTLES THEN WERE LED BY COMMUNISTS." THE ARTICLE FURTHER STA-
TED THAT IN ANSWER TO THE QUESTION AS TO WHAT CAUSED THE CHICAGO RIFT
BETWEEN HIM AND THE COMMUNISTS WRIGHT HAD STATED "IT WAS AN ACCUMULATIC
OF MANY THINGS — NOT SO MUCH A LEAVING AS AN EJECTION OF A DIFFERENCE
OF OPINION. I HAD MY WAY OF EXPRESSING MY CONCEPTION OF NEGRO EXPER-
END PAGE TWO

NY2 PAGE THREE

IENCE IN WRITING. I THOUGHT IT WOULD BE OF VALUE TO THEM. THEY HAD
THEIR IDEAS OF HOW I SHOULD REACT AS A COMMUNIST. THERE WAS AN IRRE-
CONCILABLE GAP BETWEEN OUR ATTITUDES. I DO NOT REGARD THE COMMUNISTS·
TODAY AS EFFECTIVE INSTRUMENTS FOR SOCIAL CHANGE." WRIGHT FURTHER
ADVISED THE TRIBUNE THAT THE COMMUNISTS HAVE A TERRIBLE LOT TO LEARN
ABOUT PEOPLE. COMMUNISTS PECULIARLY ARE TOO MUCH THE VICTIMS OF THE
VERY SOCIETY THEY ARE TRYING TO CHANGE. THIS TOO OFTEN FINDS EXPRESSI
IN INTOLERANCE AND NARROWNESS." AT THE PRESENT TIME THE NY OFFICE HAS
UNDER CONSIDERATION THE ADVISABILITY OF INTERVIEWING MR WRIGHT.

CONROY

HOLD

35

LVO
100-157464 —))

SAC – New York City   August 4, 1944

John Edgar Hoover – Director, Federal Bureau of Investigation

RICHARD NATHANIEL WRIGHT
INTERNAL SECURITY – C

     Reference is made to your teletype of July 28, 1944, concerning the reported disaffiliation on the part of the subject with the Communist Political Association. It is noted in your teletype that you have under consideration the advisability of interviewing Wright.

     In connection with any interview you might undertake with Wright, it is suggested that you consider obtaining from him specific information concerning exploitation of the Negro race by the Communist Political Association. Furthermore, if the interview actually takes place a previous study should be made of Wright's articles and particularly pertinent comments he makes with regard to the Communist Political Association.

     Any interview with Wright must, of course, be most discreet, particularly in light of his reported comments in which he laments the "regression" of the Communist Political Association's position with respect to the American Negro. From a review of the teletype you submitted in this regard, it would seem that Wright does not think the Communist Political Association revolutionary enough at the present time with respect to the advancement of the Negro. This should be considered seriously prior to any action on your part.

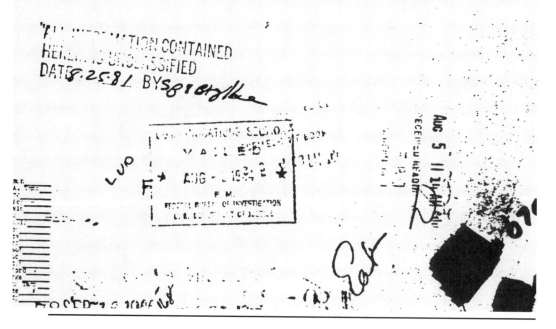

Chapter VIII

Walt Disney: The Father of Mickey Mouse And A Spy for Hoover

Walter Elias Disney was born in Chicago, Illinois on December 5, 1901. He was the fourth son of Elias and Flora Disney. Elias Disney a carpenter came to Chicago in the early 1890's to work as a carpenter on the World's Fair Building at the forthcoming Columbian Exposition, which was held in Jackson Park on the Southeast side of Chicago near Lake Michigan in 1893. The Disney family lived on Tripp Avenue, which is located on the West Side of the city.

In 1908 the family moved to Marceline, Missouri where Elias Disney bought a farm. Walt became fascinated with the farm animals and within a short period of time he was drawing them. While his teachers at Marceline's brand new Park School were drilling the students on mathematics and spelling, Walt was doodling pictures of farm animals.

The Elder Disney's hopes for his farm in 1910 faded quickly when he became bedridden with typhoid fever, a virus that was killing thousands of Americans each year. Medicine during that period was just coming out of the dark ages. When Elias got back on his feet he sold the farm for $5, 175 and moved his family into a rented house in Kansas City, Missouri.

While attending Benton Elementary school in Kansas City, Walt Disney got his first commercial assignment from one of the Kansas City barbershops. The barber gave the kid a free haircut each week in exchange for a weekly sketch which he showcased on the barbershop wall. In addition to drawing, he busied himself after school delivering newspapers and carrying groceries for the corner merchant. At age 16 he found himself back in Chicago attending McKinley High School on the West Side during the day and taking a night course in cartooning at the Academy of Fine Arts in downtown Chicago.

In 1917 when World War I broke out in Europe, he tried to join the army, but was rejected because he was under age(16). However, in spite of his age he managed to get overseas as a driver of a Red Cross ambulance for the American Expeditionary Forces in France. After the war, he returned to Kansas City and got a job with an advertising firm sketching illustrations for a farm journal. At the same time, he was making cartoon slides for a film company in his private studio which was located over his father's garage. He called the cartoons "Laugh-O-Grams", and had some success with them, as he did with other free-lance cartoons during that period.

Walt Disney Productions' history from 1919 to 1957 was as follows: Commercial artist, 1919; cartoonist Kansas City film Ad. 1920-22; prod. Alice Comedies, a combination of a live girl and animated cartoons, for M. J. Winkler, New York, 1923-26; prod. Oswald, The Rabbit, for Universal, 1926-28; ehmn. bd. , exec Walt Disney Prodns. , Ltd. , producers Mickey Mouse, Silly Symphony Cartoons since 1928; Three Little Pigs, 1933 (certificate from Acad. Motion Picture Arts); also Snow White and Seven Dwarfs (Acad. Motion Picture Arts and Science award), 1938; Ferdinand the Bull, 1939, Fantasia (awarded plaque Dowling Foundation of Plymouth, Mich, scroll New York Critics, N. Y. City; medal N. Y. Sohs. Music), also Pinocchio, 1940; The Reluctant Dragon, also Dumbo, 1941; Bambi, 1942; Saludos Amigos, 1942; Victory Through Air Power, 1943; The Three Caballeros, 1944; Make Mine Music, also Song of the South, 1946; Fun and Fancy Free, 1947; Melody Time, 1948; So Dear To My Heart, 1949; Ichabod and Mr. Toad, 1949; Cinderella, also Treasure Island, 1950; Alice in Wonderland, 1951; The Story of Robin Hood, 1952; Peter Pan, 1953; Sword and Rose, 1953; Rob Roy, 1954; 20,000 Leagues Under the Sea, 1954; Siam, 1954; Lady and the Tramp, 1955. Producer True Life Adventure Nature films. Elaborated true-life adventures to full features with The Living Desert, 1953; The Vanishing Prairie, 1954; The African Lion, 1955; Secrets of Life, 1956. Producer Live action features, Littlest Outlaw, 1955; Johnny Tremain. Old Yeller, Westward Ho, the Wagons, 1957; Lapland, Blue Man of Morocco, of the People and Places series, released to 1957.

As a very wealthy, successful Hollywood producer, Walt Disney was called as a friendly witness to testify before the House Un-American Activities Committee. He testified that Communists at his studio were trying to use Mickey Mouse to spread Communist propaganda.

Disney was in Hoover's pocket as a name namer the same as former President Ronald Reagan. Disney as a namer operated undercover. The people who he had named as Communist were under constant surveillance by FBI agents. Disney was so comfortable with Hoover that he gave him permission to review his work before it was released. Hoover was not bashful about expanding his authority; hence, he tested Disney with an outright request to make some changes in an episode of "The Mickey Mouse Club". This statement is validated in the following Walt Disney FBI files.

Snow White And The Seven Dwarfs was released by the Disney Studio in 1937 and earned well over 22,000,000 dollars at a time when theater tickets were selling for 25 cents.

Federal Bureau of Investigation

Freedom of Information/Privacy Acts Section

Subject: <u>Walt Disney</u>

RE: WALT DISNEY

BACKGROUND

WALT DISNEY was born in Chicago, Illinois, on December 5, 1901. He received his elementary and high school education in the schools of that city and became a commercial artist in 1919. Between 1919 and 1922 he produced a number of cartoons and in 1928 created Mickey Mouse, his most famous cartoon.

Mr. DISNEY has been associated with his brother, ROY O. DISNEY, in the management and operation of the Walt Disney Productions since the establishment of the company by the brothers in the early 1930's. Mr. DISNEY resides with his wife and family in the Holmby Hills section of Los Angeles.

DEROGATORY INFORMATION

No derogatory information concerning this individual appears in the files of this office.

SAC RECOMMENDATION

Because of Mr. DISNEY's position as the foremost producer of cartoon films in the motion picture industry and his prominence and wide acquaintanceship in film production matters, it is believed that he can be of valuable assistance to this office and therefore it is my recommendation that he be approved as an SAC contact.

with the Bureau.

    III.   Disney appears to be a very reliable individual and has been quite friendly with the FBI. He is an approved SAC Contact. His television programs have been very popular and educational and have been conducted on a high plane. The Disney- land Amusement Park appears to have been popularly received.

    Disney's two proposals at this stage seem rather vague and it might be desirable to have him furnish more facts so that each can be considered.

RECO***ENDATION:

    Mr. Nichols consider this matter and offer his recommendations to the Director and carry on through with notifica- tion to SAC Malone at Los Angeles.

I don't see how we can do anything

I agree

3/8

I concur

Office Memorandum • UNITED STATES GOVERNMENT

TO : DIRECTOR, FBI (94-4-4667) DATE: 10/31/56

FROM : SAC, LOS ANGELES (80-294) ATTENTION: TRAINING
AND INSPECTION DIVISION

SUBJECT: WALT DISNEY
SAC CONTACT
LOS ANGELES DIVISION

     For the information of the Bureau, it was announced on
October 24, 1956 that the above captioned motion picture producer,
who is an SAC contact of this office, has been selected to receive
the annual Milestone Award of the Screen Producers Guild at an
award banquet scheduled for February 3, 1957 in the Beverly Hilton
Hotel. This announcement was made by SAMUEL G. ENGEL, President
of the Screen Producers Guild and also an SAC contact of this office.

     The award recognizes DISNEY'S contribution to motion
pictures during his 33 years in Hollywood, contributions which
have also brought him a total of 25 Academy Awards.

2 - Bureau
1 - Los Angeles
JMC:pas
(3)

RECORDED - 10

INDEXED - 10 94-4-4667-6

21 NOV 5 1956

RECORDED - 10

94 - 4 - 4467 - 6

EX-127

November 9, 1956

PERSONAL

Mr. Walt Disney
2400 Alameda Avenue
Burbank, California

Dear Mr. Disney:

Mr. John F. Malone, Special Agent in Charge of
our Los Angeles Office, has advised me of the annual Milestone
Award of the Screen Producers Guild which is to be presented to
you on February 3, 1957.

You must derive great satisfaction from this
recognition, and I want to be among the many persons in this
country who will extend congratulations to you on this occasion.
Your work in the past has been a credit not only to the motion
picture industry but to the entire Nation, and I want to assure you
of my every good wish for continuing success.

Sincerely yours,

J. Edgar Hoover

cc - Los Angeles, Reurlet 10-31-56

NOTE: The Bureau has had cordial relations with Disney who is an
SAC contact of the Los Angeles Office. There is no derogatory data in
Bufiles on the Screen Producers Guild. Samuel G. Engel, a producer
20th Century-Fox and an SAC contact of the Los Angeles Office, was
president of the Guild in 1955.

Tolson
Nichols
Boardman
Belmont
Mason
Mohr
Parsons
Rosen
Tamm
Nease
Winterrowd
Tele. Room
Holloman
Gandy

FJH:pjj
(4)

1 00

7 1 NOV 20 1956

MAILED 5
NOV 9 1956
COMM-FBI

REC'D-READING ROOM
FBI
Nov 9   3 54 PM '56

WALT DISNEY

January 20, 1961

Dear Mr. Hoover -

Mr. William Simon, agent in charge of the Los Angeles F.B.I. office, came in to see me yesterday and presented me with a copy of your book, MASTERS OF DECEIT. I sincerely appreciate this personally inscribed copy which will be a welcome addition to my collection of autographed books for my personal library.

I wish to take this opportunity to express my appreciation as a citizen for what you have done and the fight which you are continually waging for the protection of our way of life.

With deepest respect and admiration, and again, many thanks.

Sincerely,

Walt Disney

Walt Disney

Mr. J. Edgar Hoover
Federal Bureau of Investigation
Washington, D. C.

WD:mc

REC- 35

94 - 4 - 4667 - 32

17 JAN 24 1961

3/16/61

airtel

REC-9 94-4-4667-36

To: SAC, Los Angeles (94-761)

From: Director, FBI

"MOON PILOT"
MOTION PICTURE BY WALT DISNEY
RESEARCH (CRIME RECORDS)

Reurairtel dated 3/1/61.

You should arrange to personally confer with Walt Disney concerning his proposed filming of the story "Moon Pilot." Tactfully point out to him the uncomplimentary manner in which FBI Agents are depicted. Advise him that the Bureau will strongly object to any portrayal of the FBI in this film. As you will note from the story, FBI action basically involves guarding of the Air Force officer who is to make the first flight to the moon. Suggest to Mr. Disney that since FBI jurisdiction does not extend to the guarding of individuals that this action can be better represented by another Government agency. Handle diplomatically.

MAR 17 1961

1 - Mr. DeLoach
Follow-up made for 3/29/61.
killed on faais
dated 3-27-61

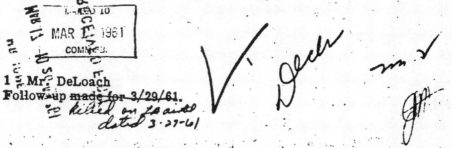

NOTE: See Jones to DeLoach memorandum captioned "Motion Picture 'Moon Pilot,' Robert Buckner, Author, Walt Disney Productions, Inc.," dated 3/13/61.

66 APR 4 1961 763

JCFM:eah (6)

MAIL ROOM ☐   TELETYPE UNIT ☐

lson
rsons
hr
mont
llahan
arad
Loach
ns
lane
sen
vel
tter
C. Sullivan
le. Room
ram
ndy

1 - Mr. Belmont
1 - Mr. Evans
1 - Mr. Rosen
1 - Name Check Section
August 31, 1961
1 - Mr. Stefansson

WALTER E. DISNEY

No investigation has been conducted by the FBI concerning the captioned individual. However, this Bureau's files reveal the receipt of a flier issued by the Council for Pan-American Democracy advertising the "Night of the Americas" to be held at the Martin Beck Theater on February 14, 1943, in New York City. The flier carried a partial list of sponsors and guests of honor which included the name of "Walt Disney."

The Council for Pan-American Democracy has been designated pursuant to Executive Order 10450.

The "People's Voice," issue of January 15, 1944, contained an article captioned "New Masses Sponsors Tribute to Art Young." The article set forth that "New Masses" was sponsoring a mass meeting to pay tribute to Art Young, Dean of American Cartoonists who had died recently. It was indicated that the meeting would be held on January 27, 1944, at Manhattan Center, 34th Street and 8th Avenue, in New York City. Among the individuals sponsoring the meeting was listed the name "Walt Disney."

According to the Special Committee on Un-American Activities in its report dated March 29, 1944, "New Masses" is a "nationally circulated weekly journal of the Communist Party." (62-60527-25375; 94-4-4667-4)

Enclosure to letter to White House 9-1-61 DRR:fjb.

KLS:fjb
(7)

J-11167

7/16/63

EX-108 airtel

REC-22 94-4-4667-40

To: SAC, Los Angeles

From: Director, FBI

"THAT DARNED CAT"
PROPOSED WALT DISNEY PRODUCTION
RESEARCH (CRIME RECORDS)

Reurairtel 7/11/63.

For your information, Gordon Gordon's new novel on
which captioned motion picture is to be based is scheduled for publication
9/6/63. The title will be "Undercover Cat." You should determine if
copies of this novel and proposed movie script are available. If so, you
should attempt to obtain copies of them and forward same to the Bureau
as soon as possible for review. Follow this matter closely and keep
Bureau advised.

MAILED 8
JUL 16 1963
COMM-FBI

V

1 - Mr. DeLoach - (sent direct with cover memo)

NOTE: See M. A. Jones to DeLoach memorandum, dated 7/15/63, captioned
"'That Darned Cat,' Proposed Motion Picture."

olson
elmont
ohr
asper
allahan
onrad
eLoach
vans
ale
osen

b.7c

Threaten film folk with jail terms in 'red' hunt

Leo Carillo, cowboy, and Mickey Mouse's maker, Walt Disney, were standing staunchly by the House Un-American committee this week as four (and maybe more to come) screen writers were cited for contempt.

Ava Gardner Benny Goodman Kath. Hepburn Eddie Cantor

Hollywood answers attack on freedom

HOLLYWOOD—The top talent of the movie industry this week threw its strength behind the nation's fight for civil rights, forming the Committee for the First Amendment and issuing the following statement:

"We, the undersigned, as American citizens who believe in constitutional democratic government, are disgusted and outraged by the continuing attempt of the House committee on un-American activities to smear the motion picture industry.

"We hold that these hearings are morally wrong because:

"Any investigation into the political beliefs of the individual is contrary to the basic principles of our democracy;

"Any attempt to curb freedom of expression and to set arbitrary standards of Americanism is in itself disloyal to both the spirit and the letter of our Constitution."

Richard Brooks	Benny Goodman	Myrna Loy
Eddie Cantor	Van Heflin	Dorothy McGuire
Richard Conte	Paul Henreid	Burgess Meredith
Norman Corwin	Katharine Hepburn	Gregory Peck
Phillip Dunne	John Houseman	Vincent Price
Henry Fonda	Marsha Hunt	Barry Sullivan
Ava Gardner	John Huston	Cornel Wilde
Sheridan Gibney	Norman Krasna	Billy Wilder
Paulette Goddard	Anatole Litvak	William Wyler

First group of screen writers cited was Dalton Trumbo, Alvah Bessie, Albert Maltz and John Howard Lawson.

In the heat of the kleig lights, bald, round and resolute Chairman Thomas (R., N.J.) addressed the hearing last week, saying:

"This committee has found no field where communism is more firmly entrenched than in Hollywood."

• • •

THE CITATIONS met with the indignant roar of the movie-going public, angered by the persecution of the screen writers, whose scripts are known to be devoid of any calls to the barricades.

"What is this communism stuff in the movies—and WHERE is it?"

At the same time, Leo Carillo filed a telegram with the committee congratulating it on its work; Walt Disney likewise. Disney, however, belatedly stated that he had not intended to leave the "impression," when he testified concerning "Red infiltration" in Hollywood, that the League of Women Voters was a "communist front" organization.

• • •

THE UN-AMERICAN committee threatened to prosecute the film writers' attorney, Robert W. Kenny, former California Attorney General, on the charge of an alleged "conspiracy" against the United States," saying that he had advised his clients not to testify.

When Kenny stated that communications between lawyer and client were constitutionally sacred

RECORDED & INDEXED

100 138754

The Chicago Star
November 1, 1947
Pg. 3

ALL INFORMATION CONTAINED HEREIN IS UNCLASSIFIED
DATE 1/23/84 BY SPR TPP/EWW b.7c

88 DEC 1

Chairman Thomas said grimly: "You've squirmed out of this one."

* *

AFTER referring to the committee Chief Investigator Robert E. Stripling as "Mr. Quisling," screen writer Albert Maltz testified:

"I claim and insist upon my right to join the Republican party of the Communist Party, Democratic, or Prohibition Party, no matter what certain legislators may think of them."

All four of the screen writers insisted the committee had no right to inquire into a man's political beliefs. Alvah Bessie declared that even Gen. Dwight D. Eisenhower hasn't disclosed his political beliefs, "and what is good enough for Gen. Eisenhower is good enough for me."

A group of 26 film stars, headed by Humphrey Bogart, June Havoc, Gene Kelly and Lauren Bacall, have filed a formal protest against the committee and demanded a "redress of grievances."

The petition went to the clerk of the House and it was indicated it will be used as a basis for a floor fight against the committee soon after Congress reassembles next month.

'Thou shalt not wear red flannels'

WASHINGTON. — (FP) — Larry Parks, screen star subpoenaed by the House un-American committee in its Hollywood p r o b e, suggested this week that if the Thomas committee succeeds in dictating what shall be in films, some day the Bible may be revised.

The Ten Commandments may reappear, he said, in this altered form:

"Thou shalt have no other Gods before Taft and Hartley!

"Thou shalt not covet a higher wage!

"Thou shalt not take the name of thy Congress in vain!

"Honor they NAM and thy DAR"

To Moe Jack
Best Wishes

Nat King Cole

Chapter IX

Nat "King" Cole: The Unforgettable

Nathaniel Adam Coles was born on March 17, 1917 in a frame house at 1524 St. Johns Street in Montgomery, Alabama. His father James Coles was a skilled butcher at a local grocery store and a church deacon at the Beulah Baptist Church. His mother Perlina Adam Coles played the piano for the choir at the 10:30 A. M. Sunday service.

In 1923 Deacon James Coles was called by the Lord early one Sunday morning before daybreak to go North to Abraham Lincoln's City by the Lake and preach. Shortly after arriving at the Illinois Central Railroad Station in Chicago with his wife and four children, he immediately rented a small two bedroom unfurnished apartment in the 4200 block on Prairie Avenue. His second move was to find a job as a butcher in the stockyards at either the Wilson or Swift meatpacking companies where several of his Alabama home boys worked.

Reverend Edward Coles was only in Chicago for approximately two months when he organized the Second Progressive Baptist Church in a State Street store-front several blocks from his apartment. His fame as a preacher of the Gospel began to spread like the flames of a forest wild fire. Thus, in 1924 he was invited by the board of Deacons to replace the retiring minister of the Truelight Baptist Church, a corner edifice which could seat over two hundred parishioners at 45th and Dearborn.

At age eleven, Nat began sharing the piano chores with his mother at the church. Although he could not read music, he could play anything that he heard once. Some years later Evelyn Cole who was the writer's next door neighbor in the Chatham community on the South East Side of Chicago said: "The first song that Nat learned to play was not a religious hymn but a popular song written in 1923 by Frank Silver and Irving Cohn entitled *Yes We Have No Bananas.*"

The writer first met Nat Cole on Easter Sunday in 1934. He was leading a Teenage Orchestra at a Matinee dance being held at the Warwick Dance Hall located at 543 East 47th Street in Chicago. At that time he had dropped the (s) from Coles. The dropping of the (s) was further noted in February 1935 by the writer in a Spanish class where they were both students at the New Phillips / DuSable High School located at 4934 South Wabash Ave.

Henry E. Fort a mutual friend of both Nat Cole and Dempsey Travis, made the following observation during an interview for <u>An Autobiography of Black Jazz</u> written by the author in 1983:

> In January of 1934, Henry Fort, a young bass player and child-hood friend of Nat Cole's, received a telephone call from Cole asking him to join a teenaged band he was organizing. Henry went to the first rehearsal of the new twelve-piece band in the home of Nat's parents, the Reverend Edward and Mrs. Perlina Cole in the 4200 block on South Prairie Avenue in Chicago. Cole had called together four saxophone players, three trumpet players, a trombone player and a full rhythm section including guitar, bass, drums and piano.
>
> Nat seemed much older than seventeen, Fort says. He was serious and so intense and nervous that he frequently bit his fingernails. He was authoritative without being dictatorial, and he was able to whip a bunch of undisciplined teenagers into a music unit in less than sixty

days. His objective was to make us sound like Earl 'Fatha' Hines' band; Earl was Nat's idol.

Nat lived within four blocks of the old Grand Terrace where Hines' orchestra played and Nat used to hang out in the gangway next to the Terrace and listen to Hines. Nat's musical memory was almost perfect. He could hear something and repeat it note by note without a mistake. This was a great asset to our young group. Nat lifted so much of the Hines material intact that at first other musician called our group the Rogues of Rhythm.

Nat's father objected to young Cole's intense interest in jazz piano. But his mother, Perlina, had a different opinion. Finally the family reached a compromise: Nat could play jazz on Sunday afternoons as long as he played organ for the morning service at his father's True Light Baptist Church. Nat's mother made our first uniforms, Cossack shirts, to give the band a professional look.

Malcolm Smith made an arrangement for us to play at the Warwick Hall on East 47th Street every Sunday afternoon. Consequently we began to get a lot of press, especially when we did a battle of the bands with Tony Fambro and his Jungle Rhythm Orchestra, another teenaged group. By early 1935, the band had become so popular among South Side youth that Malcolm Smith arranged a tour of Illinois for us. I recall our first trip took us down to Aurora, Joliet and then Kankakee, where we suffered our first casualty. A trumpet player named "Rail" became caught in the undertow while he was swimming in the Kankakee River, and was never seen again. That incident disturbed Nat's mother so that she decided that Nat's eldest brother, Eddie, should leave Noble Sissle's band, one of the top bands of the period, and come back to Chicago to give Nat the benefit of his mature wisdom. Nat had three brothers and one sister, Evelyn, and Eddie was a good ten years older than Nat. He was one of the best musicians Chicago produced: a master bass player, but he could play any number of instruments, including the piano. All the Cole boys were musically inclined. On the other hand, none had the style of Nat "King" Cole. Nat played like Earl Hines and sat at the piano like Earl Hines, but he bore himself like Duke Ellington. Nat was proud. Even when he couldn't afford a new suit, he was always neat and he was always professional on the stage. It was just in him, and in his whole family.

"Nat could sit down at a piano, from the very beginning, and tell the horn player to play a B-flat here or a C there and believe it or not, it came out perfect. But I never saw Nat read a piece of music the whole time I was with him. If he heard something once, he could play it as if he had been playing it all his life. If someone hummed a tune around Nat, before the last sixteen bars were finished, he would pick up the tune and play it as if it were his own. He could play anything he heard. At rehearsal when the band played a number Nat hadn't heard yet, he usually got up and directed. Then he could sit down at the piano and play that number a second time around as if he had written the arrangement, which was phenomenal. I'm certain that Nat couldn't read music during our early years, but I'm equally certain that he must have learned how to read later on after I left the band.

"In 1936 after Nat finished a six-month engagement at the Panama Café at 58th and Prairie in Chicago, he organized a big band to go on the road with Miller and Lyles, the producers of a show called Shuffle Along. Our first stops were in Michigan, where we toured five cities, including Ann Arbor. We played the University auditorium there, and Nat got married to a chorus girl in the show named Nadine Robinson. I was his best man.

"After we completed the Michigan tour, we headed West, our final destination being Los Angeles. When we reached Long Beach, California, we found out that the show had to fold because it was running out of money. We decided to go on strike in Los Angeles. But Miller and Lyles got to the union before we did. The union consequently would not permit a strike and ordered us to work even though we were not going to get paid. At that point some of the guys decided to return to Chicago, but several of us agreed to stay on the West Coast with Nat and form a smaller group.

We used an old Chicago trick to get a job. Six or seven of us went separately into a nightclub. Of course Nat was a star attraction, and the bandleader asked him to come up and play a number on the piano. Nat did that, and after about ten or fifteen minutes, I went up and told the bass player that I would relieve him. A little later somebody else from our group relieved the sax man, and before the set was over the entire Cole ensemble was on the bandstand. We outplayed the house band. Management approached us and offered us the job if we would work below scale. Scale at that time was thirty-five to forty dollars in California, but they offered us twenty-five dollars. We obviously could-n't accept that offer and remain in the union, so at that point I left Nat.

Nat decided that he would stay on the West Coast and work as a single. Bob Lewis of Swanee Inn suggested that Nat add a bass guitar and a drum. The first person Nat contacted was Oscar Miller, a gui-tarist, who jumped at the chance to get a steady job. Next he called bassist Wesley Prince and then a drummer, who did not show up for the first night. The drummer was not needed on the second night because the King Cole Trio had been born. It had been accepted overwhelming-ly by the clientele of the Swanee Inn.

Nat's personality took a 180 degree turn towards his old friends after he divorced Nadine Robinson and married Maria Ellington. Some people attributed the change in him to his new marriage. I recall in 1958 I took my family to Hawaii and stopped off in Los Angeles. I called Nat and left a message with his answering service, but he never called me back. Shortly after I got back to Chicago, I received a call from Ralph Edwards, of the television show This Is Your Life. Nat had told him that I was one of the original members of his band, and Edwards wanted me to come back to California and appear on the show for Nat. My first inclination was to refuse, because Nat had not returned my call. But we all did appear on the show in 1958.

Marty Faye, Chicago TV and radio star, remembers that Nat always used to stay at the Ambassador East Hotel whenever he was in town.

Nat made the transition from 42nd and Prairie to the Gold Coast without any sweat, Faye recalls. *He was comfortable with opulence. He was very smooth and warm and very businesslike. He always knew what he was doing, how he was doing it and when he was doing it. He always demanded the best.*

Nat was the only celebrity ever to appear on my TV show who would not perform there. I could interview him, and that was all. He was such a perfectionist that he never wanted to do anything unless he was absolutely certain that it was right in every detail. He had to be sure the piano was tuned, that the acoustics were good in the room or the studio and that the lighting was properly adjusted. Only his people could set things up for him, otherwise he would not perform. I was satisfied just to interview him because he was very amusing. He could tell funny stories and he was glib. He was a great human being.

Baldwin "Sparky" Tavares was hired as a valet by Nat Cole at the Blue Note Club in Chicago in 1949.

I had met Nat earlier in New York through my brother-in-law Ervin Ashby, who played bass for Nat, Sparky Tavares said: "*The valet work was actually too much for one man because Nat always carried big trunks filled with a full wardrobe, so he had to hire an ex-railroad man to help me. If Nat was going to do six shows a day, he would have nine or ten changes of clothing. That meant everyone in the trio had to have nine uniforms. They were all single or double-breasted suits, not one tuxedo. Nat was a perfectionist and a slavemaster. He worked the hell out of me. By the time I got to California several months later, I had dropped from one hundred twenty-seven to one hundred nine pounds. But I was stuck, I was his man. Around strangers he was very shy and quiet, but with his friends he acted like just another one of the cats. He liked to sit around and have a taste, argue sports and joke. He loved* comedy and had a great sense of humor. He had the loudest laugh I ever heard.

He could laugh at himself. I remember one afternoon in Chicago we were coming out of the stage door of the Regal Theater and found ourselves facing a big group of kids in the alley. I asked them what they wanted, an autograph? One kid said, "No, he wanted a hat." Another kid said, 'I want to see the show and you better let me in that door. I am Nat Cole's brother.'

I said, 'What's your name?'

He said, 'My name is Charcoal.'

Nat laughed louder than anyone in that alley. The boy apologized to Nat when he recognized him. And Nat said, 'Come on over here, son, and tell me your name.' When the kid told him his name, Nat told him not to tell lies like that again. Then he said to me, 'Take those kids out front and tell Ken Blewett to give them good seats.'

A good way to wipe the smile off Nat's face was to mention the NAACP. The only time I've seen Nat really upset was after he sent a telegram to Roy Wilkins of the NAACP which read:

I will not join the NAACP in speech making, but I am willing to do everything within my efforts in any way I can to further our cause.

Wilkins immediately issued a press release paraphrasing the telegram and implying that Nat had refused to join the NAACP. A legal official of that organization phoned and had the nerve to call Nat a sort of handkerchief-head. The son-of-a-bitch that called him wasn't even married to a black woman. One ironic thing about the whole episode was that Nat had been doing benefits for the NAACP since Day One, probably as many if not more than most entertainers-and yet he was being publicly insulted just because he didn't want to make speeches or be a card-carrying member. The thing came to a head in Detroit when civic leaders there asked Nat why he wouldn't join the NAACP.

Nat said, 'I have done more benefits for you people than anyone else you have mentioned.'

"The Detroit officials said, 'Well, join anyway.'

"Nat finally joined on his wife's advice and the advice of his manager Collis Gastell and others he respected. But that incident really hurt him and he carried the bruise to his grave.

"He was hurt again in 1950 when we played the Thunderbird Hotel in Las Vegas. We had a congo player at the time named Jack Coustanza, an Italian boy from Chicago. He was working for Nat, but since he was white he could get a room in the Thunderbird and Nat and the rest of us couldn't: we had to stay at Mrs. Shaw's on the west side of town, known as Darkie City. On top of that, although our name was on the marquee, we had to enter the hotel through a side door and stay in our dressing rooms until we went on stage, and our food was brought up and served buffet style every night. We refused to eat it. We did the show, returned to the dressing rooms to change our clothes and then left, because there was nothing they could do for us. When Nat finished that engagement, he told Collis, 'I don't want to play this town anymore until I can walk through the front door.' Collis agreed.

"We did not go back to Vegas again until 1953, when we played at a place called El Rancho Vegas. It was managed by Jack Entrotter, former head man of the Copacabana in New York. He had an unwritten rule that all facilities must be open to all entertainers who worked in the hotel. Nat was given a large cabin and I also had a cabin. They told Nat he could use all facilities and they meant it. Nat was the first to break the color barrier for black entertainers in Las Vegas and for black people in general there. Shortly afterward, the Sands Hotel brought in Lena Horne and opened the entire place up to her. She could have guests and do whatever she pleased.

"We had a strange experience at the Sahara Hotel. Bill Miller, the manager from New York, called Nat and invited our group over to see the show, and we were treated royally. We had good food and drinks, and everything was beautiful. The next night we decided to go back on our own and see the show. But when we got to the Sahara,

the security man stopped us at the door. Nat got on the telephone and called Miller who said he was sorry but his hands were tied and he couldn't do a thing about it. We were their guests one night and turned away from the door the next. Strange things happen in America.

Life is full of peaks and valleys and one of the peaks for Nat occurred at the Brown Derby in Hollywood. We were sitting around having drinks and talking, when Hoagy Carmichael came over and joined us. After a few minutes of general conversation Hoagy said to Nat, 'You know, the prettiest vocal version I ever heard of my song Stardust was by you. I have felt more honored by your version than any other I know.' Nat bubbled for the rest of the evening; Stardust was one of his favorite songs, but he had no idea that Hoagy felt that way about his version.

Nat's mother was the leader of that family. She had an incredibly strong influence over her daughter and her sons. They all respected her. Although she was not educated, she was articulate and she spoke as crisply and distinctly as Nat sang. She treated all her children equally, and made no bigger fuss over one that was a star than over the others. When she died, it hit Nat hard. He fainted at the funeral services, which were held at a church pastored by the Reverend Rawls, Lou Rawls' uncle, at 42nd and Indiana.

In October, 1964, we were working a club in Lake Tahoe, doing two shows a night and flying to Hollywood every day to do a picture called Cat Ballou with Lee Marvin. One evening after we returned from Hollywood, we napped for an hour and went over to the club for dinner. While we were sitting around, I noticed that one of Nat's valets was making extra holes in Nat's belt. I asked him what the hell he was doing. He told me that the belt had gotten too large for Nat.

I turned to Nat and said, 'What's wrong?'

'I'm losing weight,' Nat said. He never weighed more than one hundred seventy-four pounds.

I looked at him and said, 'Yeah, I guess you are losing a little weight, Dick.' I always called him Dick. When I handed him his *clothes that night I asked him when he had started losing weight.*

" 'I don't know,' he said. 'Maybe I've been working too hard. I should probably take a few days off. I seem to stay tired. '

"After we left Lake Tahoe, we went to Vegas to play an engagement at The Sands and one night Nat got dizzy there, and that's when he knew he was really sick and it was more than just fatigue. We called a doctor and they sent us a 'Feel Good' doctor who gave him a shot and said he would be all right. The doctors down there will do anything to stay in good with the hotels. They come in and treat entertainers, but the treatment mostly consists of making the entertainers feel good.

"In November of 1963, Nat saw a doctor in Chicago and that's when he found out he had lung cancer. He had no idea before that that there was anything seriously wrong with him. We finished an engagement at the Fairmont Hotel in San Francisco on December tenth and on the twelfth Nat went back to Los Angeles and checked into a hospital. While we were driving to the hospital, Nat leaned over to me in the car and asked for a cigarette.

"On the morning of February fifteenth, 1965, when I was in Miami Beach working with Nancy Wilson at the Diplomat Hotel, the clerk called me and asked me if I had heard the news that morning. I hadn't. 'Nat Cole is dead,' he said. I called Nancy and told her I had to go home. I took a flight back to Los Angeles and went directly to the funeral parlor. When I saw Nat's body lying there on a table I walked up and lifted him and held him in my arms. He was as cold as an ice cube, but I just had to hold him. "

Federal Bureau of Investigation

Freedom of Information/Privacy Acts Section

Subject: <u>Nat "King" Cole</u>

Office Memorandum • UNITED STATES GOVERNMENT

TO : DIRECTOR, FBI

FROM : SAC, LOS ANGELES

SUBJECT: NAT KING COLE
SECURITY MATTER - C

DATE: 4/20/51

On March 27, 1951 ███████████████████████
of Los Angeles, was interviewed by SAS ████████
and ████████████ during which ████ recalled NAT KING COLE
as an old friend and contact of CP member ████████
████ said that he had recently seen KING COLE and talked with
him briefly; that he, ████████ feels positive COLE would be
amenable to discussing his CP membership and activities with
a Bureau agent. ████████ recalled that sometime in the early 1940's
████████ and one ████████ (phonetic) brought COLE to
████ and talked with him regarding receiving instruction
from ████ in the subject of Marxism. It was decided, however,
that ████ should not be the one to give COLE such instruction
because ████ is colored. NAT KING COLE himself is also colored,
although according to ████ he was at that time, and still is,
associating almost exclusively with white "progressives".

For the Bureau's information, NAT KING COLE is the well
known Negro musician who lives in Los Angeles and who recently
received considerable mention in the press due to income tax
difficulties with the Internal Revenue Department, which seized
COLE's home for payment of back taxes due the Government. It
has been since reported in the press, however, that COLE has
recovered his property by making some sort of an arrangement for
the payment of these taxes.

From information furnished this office in 1945 by
████████ it appears that COLE ████████████████ were
members of the Communist Party and the Communist Political
Association during that period, probably attached to the cultural
groups in Hollywood. Our files indicate, however, that COLE was
on tour a considerable part of the time and no particular Communist
activity on his part has been reported.

It is possible that COLE may have dropped out of the
CP movement since that period and, as indicated by ████████
above, might be willing to discuss his past affiliation with
representatives of this Bureau. If so, he might be able to

MMB:WAB
100-29226

RECORDED · 53
SE 23
INDEXED · 53

APR 24 1951
1C

COPIES DESTROYED

b7C
b7D

6

b2,
b7C,
b7D

b7C
b7D

INFORMATION CONTAINED
THEREIN IS UNCLASSIFIED
DATE 5-28-77 BY SP3BTJC
365 844

LA 100-29226

furnish pertinent information, depending upon the length of the period of his affiliation and the degree of activity on his part.

It is suggested that the Bureau might deem it desirable to arrange such an interview with COLE. However, no such step is being taken unless the Bureau authorizes it.

SAC, Los Angeles   May 21, 1951

Director, FBI

NAT KING COLE
SECURITY MATTER - C
Your file 100-29226
Bureau file 100-379380 ___ |

RECORDED - 57

01 - 10/1
#3

Reurlet dated April 20, 1951.

Before further consideration will be given to allow- b7
ing your Office to contact Cole, the Bureau would like to have
the benefit of your reasons why ▇▇▇▇▇▇▇▇ believed that Cole b7.
would be receptive to an interview by this Bureau. If you do
not have this information available, you should recontact ▇▇▇▇▇
for such and thereafter advise the Bureau.

For your information, Bureau files reflect several
references to Cole's activities in the Communist Party;
however, all of these references have been furnished to the
Bureau by your Office.

JLQ:ban

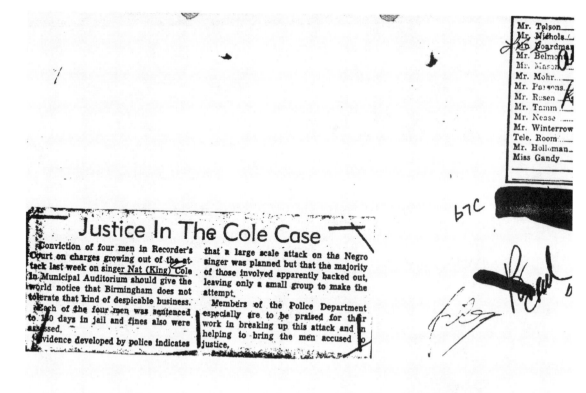

Mr. Tolson
Mr. Nichols
Mr. Boardman
Mr. Belmont
Mr. Mason
Mr. Mohr
Mr. Parsons
Mr. Rosen
Mr. Tamm
Mr. Nease
Mr. Winterrow
Tele. Room
Mr. Holloman
Miss Gandy

b7C

Justice In The Cole Case

Conviction of four men in Recorder's Court on charges growing out of the attack last week on singer Nat (King) Cole in Municipal Auditorium should give the world notice that Birmingham does not tolerate that kind of despicable business.

Each of the four men was sentenced to 180 days in jail and fines also were assessed.

Evidence developed by police indicates that a large scale attack on the Negro singer was planned but that the majority of those involved apparently backed out, leaving only a small group to make the attempt.

Members of the Police Department especially are to be praised for their work in breaking up this attack and in helping to bring the men accused to justice.

BIRMINGHAM POST-HERALD
Birmingham, Alabama
April 19, 1956
Final Edition
Editorial
JAMES E. MILLS - Editor.

RACON.

ALL INFORMATION CONTAINED
HEREIN IS UNCLASSIFIED
DATE 5-28-7 BY SP3BTJ/rw

RDED
1 1956

Resumes Monday

Four go on trial, attack details told

The slow-moving trial of four men accused in an assault on Negro Singer Nat (King) Cole resumes in Recorder's Court Monday morning.

Only one witness testified after the proceeding got under way Friday in Judge Ralph Parker's court. Fifteen were sworn in.

POLICE OFFICER H. E. Schatz, first to reach the Negro entertainer when he was felled on the stage of Municipal Auditorium last Tuesday night, told the court how police dragged two men forcibly out of the building after the assault.

Schatz testified he and Officer A. A. Norman knocked the two men into the orchestra pit when one tried to drag Cole off the stage.

Schatz's testimony mainly concerned two men not yet on trial. The four being tried are accused of a variety of misdemeanors in connection with the assault.

JUDGE PARKER ordered the trial to begin over vigorous defense objections. He overruled motions by Defense Atty. Roderick Beddow for a two-week continuance and separate trials for the four defendants.

Beddow contended the four were "dissasociated from each other."

Police investigators have charged that the assault was a conspiracy in which 150 men were to take part.

Another delay of more than an hour came when Judge Parker ordered the prosecution to prepare separate warrants in each case. He pointed out that the defendants could be found guilty of only one charge contained in a warrant.

OFFICER H. E. SCHATZ
First witness

THE BIRMINGHAM NEWS
Birmingham, Alabama
April 14, 1956
(Front Page)

RACON;
IS-X.

ALL INFORMATION CONTAINED
HEREIN IS UNCLASSIFIED
DATE 5-28-97 BY SP3BT/kw

191 APR 20 1956

One charge against each of three of the defendants was dropped in the proceedings.

ALL SIX MEN, the four now on trial and the two facing preliminary hearing on felony counts, are members of the North Alabama Citizens Council, a strongly pro-segregation organization.

The defendants and the charges against them now are:

Mike Fox, 36, conspiracy to commit a breach of the peace and conspiracy to commit assault and battery (one warrant).

Edgar Leo Vinson, 25, disorderly conduct and conspiracy to commit assault and battery.

Orliss Wade Clevenger, 18, disorderly conduct, carrying a concealed weapon and conspiracy to commit assault and battery.

Jesse W. Mabry, 43, disorderly conduct, refusal to obey the lawful command of an officer and conspiracy to commit a breach of the peace.

All but Mabry are from Anniston. Mabry, who lives at 960 West-blvd, Roebuck, is associate editor of The Southerner, a publication of the North Alabama Citizens Council.

OFFICER SCHATZ said he was at the east end of the Auditorium stage about 8:50 p.m. Tuesday night when he saw Willie Robert Vinson, 23, and Kenneth Adams, 35, running down the east aisle.

W. R. Vinson and Adams, also of Anniston, face preliminary hearing April 20 on charges of assault with intent to murder. Adams is an official of the Anniston White Citizens Council.

Schatz testified W. R. Vinson dived on stage and grabbed Cole by his legs, dragging him down, Adams dived over Vinson's shoulders, the witness said.

"I went over and knocked Vinson from his hold. About that time Officer A. A. Norman grabbed Adams. Adams jerked like he was going to run and I knocked him off the stage. Norman went with him. We arrested Vinson and Adams," Schatz said.

SCHATZ SAID he saw Mabry, who followed the officers out, asking, "why we had the white boys under arrest when we ought to be in the Auditorium beating the _____ Negro."

UNITED STATES DEPARTMENT OF JUSTICE

FEDERAL BUREAU OF INVESTIGATION

301 Continental Bank Building
Salt Lake City 1, Utah
October 8, 1957

In Reply, Please Refer to
File No.

Mr. J. Edgar Hoover, Director
Federal Bureau of Investigation
U. S. Department of Justice
Washington, D. C.

PERSONAL

b7C

Dear Mr. Hoover:

b7C   While in Las Vegas, Nevada, last week, I had
lunch with ▮▮▮▮▮▮▮▮▮▮▮▮
He said his most pressing problem at the moment is Nat
King Cole, who is presently the featured attraction at
the Sands Hotel.

b7C   By way of background, traditionally the "Strip"
hotels have been strictly segregated so far as colored
persons are concerned. Recently, however, top flight
colored entertainers have been allowed to stay at the
hotel where they were performing. These performers
include Cole, ▮▮▮▮▮▮▮▮▮▮▮▮▮▮▮▮ and Pearl
Bailey.

b7C

FX-131   INDEXED - 54   100-377580-6

b7C

1957

b7C   The problem for ▮▮▮▮▮▮ is complaints have
been received concerning Cole's actions. One citizen
insists the Sands Hotel be closed for permitting such

ALL INFORMATION CONTAINED
HEREIN IS UNCLASSIFIED
DATE 5-28-77 BY SP3 BTJ/RW

activity. This individual personally called at all "Strip" hotels to inquire whether they would accept colored guests. The Sands, Flamingo and Riviera Hotels all stated they would register any presentable person, regardless of color. All other hotels said they would refuse to register colored persons. ▮▮▮▮▮▮ said he would keep me advised of developments in this matter.

b7c

In Reno the newest hotel is the Holiday. It is an extremely modern building and was built by the Dollar Steamship family. The Hotel had slot machines but was losing money until recently purchased by a syndicate headed by ▮▮▮▮▮▮▮▮▮▮▮▮▮

b7c

is a close personal friend of Bing Crosby.

Under ▮▮▮▮▮ a casino with all types of gambling was placed in the Hotel. To stimulate business they have instituted a contest called "In 80 Days, Around the World." Each jackpot winner receives a chance on a nightly drawing, and the winner of each nightly drawing is entitled to a chance during the final drawing. Needless to say, the grand prize is a first class trip for two around the world. To feature this contest, a large replica of the balloon used in the motion picture of a similar name has been placed in front of the Hotel.

I have insisted to the Agents at both Las Vegas and Reno that materially increased informant coverage is necessary, and you can be sure I will personally follow this important matter.

Respectfully,

W. MARK FELT
Special Agent in Charge

-2-

Memorandum

TO : Mr. DeLoach

DATE: January 18, 1961

FROM : ▮▮▮▮▮▮ b7C

SUBJECT: NAT "KING" COLE

Callahan
DeLoach
Malone
McGuire
Rosen
Tamm
Trotter
W.C. Sullivan
Tele. Room
Ingram
Gandy

b7C

PURPOSE:

Mr. Tolson requested a file check on Nat "King" Cole the singer. It is pointed out that we have a main file on Cole as well as approximately 100 See references. In the interest of expediency review has been limited to a review of Cole's main file and recent See references.

BACKGROUND DATA:

Nat "King" Cole was born Nathaniel Adams Coles on March 17, 1919 in Montgomery, Alabama. He began his career as a pianist and in 1939 formed a trio and while playing the piano in a California club started to sing and is now better known as a singer of popular jazz music. He has capitalized on his voice and now earns approximately $400,000 a year from records. Cole was the first Negro to host his own TV show staring in 1957. In 1937 Cole married ▮▮▮▮▮▮ but this marriage ended in divorce. In 1948 he wed singer ▮▮▮▮▮▮ He has two daughters and is active in the fight for equal rights for Negroes. Cole is a member of the National Association for the Advancement of Colored People (NAACP). He resides in Hollywood, California. (Celebrity Register)

INFORMATION IN BUREAU FILES:

No investigation has been conducted by the Bureau concerning Cole, however, files reflect the following salient information.

A confidential informant who has furnished reliable information in the past advised in 1945 that Nat "King" Cole ▮▮▮▮▮▮ were then members of the Communist Political Association in Hollywood.

A confidential informant who has furnished reliable information in the past advised in August, 1949, that "King" Cole was a member of the music division of the Southern California Chapter of the Arts, Sciences, and Professio Council (Hollywood Arts, Sciences, and Professions Council)

ALL INFORMATION CONTAINED
HEREIN IS UNCLASSIFIED
DATE 2-29-97 BY SP3BTJ/RW

62- ▮▮▮▮▮ Mr. DeLoach b7C

DGH:dau (7)

JAN 26 1961

(Continued, next page) CORRESPONDENC

Re: NAT "KING" COLE

The National Council of Arts, Sciences, and Professions has been cited as a communist front by the Congressional Committee on Un-American Activities.

A Salt Lake City criminal informant advised Bureau Agents on February 21, 1955, that ███████████████████████ Las Vegas, Nevada, informed him, the informant, that ██████████

██████████████████████████ Nat King Cole was appearing

███ at the hotel in the Copa Room as the star ██████████████

██████████████████████████████████████ Nat King Cole discontinued his engagement at the Sands for personal reasons. █

It will be recalled that in April, 1956, while appearing in Birmingham, Alabama, Cole was attacked by a group of men, reportedly members of the North Alabama Citizens Council. The attack took place in Municipal Auditorium and the assailants were prosecuted in local court and sentenced to one hundred eighty days in jail.

By personal letter to the Director dated October 8, 1957, SAC Salt Lake City advised as follows.

Nat King Cole is presently performing at the Sands ██

██

█████████████████████ there were many complaints received from citizens and suggestions that The Sands be closed. (100-379380)

The "New York Herald Tribune" of May 4, 1960, contained a story concerning the "Committee to Defend Martin Luther King." The committee was described as a group formed to raise money to help Dr. King fight an income tax evasion indictment in the state of Alabama. A pretext telephone call by Agents of the New York Office ascertained that this committee was at 372 West 125 Street and that Nat King Cole was the treasurer. (100-40377-326)

RECOMMENDATION:

None. For information.

CONFIDENTIAL

expected to leave Los Angeles by Pan American Airways,
May 5, 1961, for a trip of three to four weeks to Japan,
Phillipines, and Hong Kong for business and pleasure. His
address is given as 401 Muirfield Road, Los Angeles, his
date and place of birth as March 17, 1919, at Montgomery,
Alabama.

In 1945, a confidential source furnished
information to the effect that NAT COLE ████████████
██████ were affiliated with the Communist Party (CP) or
Communist Political Association (CPA) at Los Angeles during
the period 1944 - 1945, probably attached to one of the
CP's so-called cultural groups in Hollywood. However,
it was also indicated that COLE was on tour a considerable
part of the time; and no particular CP activity on his part
was known to informant.

In 1951, another source, now deceased, who was
once personally acquainted with COLE, recalled that sometime
during the early 1940s, NAT KING COLE was brought around to
see the source by a motion picture actor who was known to the
source as an old time CP member. The purpose of the visit
was to arrange for COLE to receive instruction in Marxism.
The arrangement was not carried through, however, for the
reason that it was decided that the source who was to be
the instructor was colored, and NAT KING COLE, although
himself colored, was at the time associating almost
exclusively with white "progressives".

Confidential sources who are currently connected
with the Professional-Cultural Section of the CP and who
have some information regarding their membership and
activities, advise they have no information that NAT KING
COLE is affiliated with the CP organization at Los Angeles,
nor have they heard him referred to in any CP meeting as
though he might be a member or even sympathetic to the Party.

A physical description of COLE as noted from the
passport record of the State Department is as follows:

Name	NATHANIEL ADAMS COLE
Also known as	Nat King Cole
Date of birth	March 17, 1919
Place of birth	Montgomery, Alabama

CONFIDENTIAL

An informant who has furnished reliable information
in the past reported on February 21, 1955, that an employee of
the Sands Hotel, Las Vegas, Nevada, who was a gambler from the
east coast, had advised the informant that Jack Entratter, part
owner of the Sands Hotel and who was in charge of the Sands'
Copa Room, found Nat King Cole and Dorothy Dandridge together
in Cole's room at the hotel. Cole was appearing as a star in
the Copa Room at the time. The informant stated that Entratter
became furious with Cole for having an "affair" with Dorothy
Dandridge and threatened him. Dandridge reportedly told

Entratter to forget the whole matter as she was Cole's color,
too. The informant further advised that Entratter was formerly
manager and part owner of the Copacabana in New York City and
has reportedly spent a great deal of time and money promoting
Dandridge's career and that Entratter considered her his girl
friend. (CI SU-273-C; 62-75147-44-591)

President Harry S. Truman at the 1952 Chicago Democratic National Convention fingers Governor Adlai Stevenson as his man for Presidential Candidate. Stevenson of Illinois, was a dark-horse candidate for the Presidency, strong in the party's ruling council and in his own pivotal State of Illinois. As such, he was a natural choice to make the Convention's welcoming address, which turned out to be a brilliant exercise both in political philosophy and phrase-making.

Chapter X

Adlai E. Stevenson II: The Man Who Should Have Been President

Adlai Ewing Stevenson II was born in Los Angeles on February 5, 1900. He was the grandson and namesake of the vice-president in President Grover Cleveland's second term and became the father of United States Senator Adlai Stevenson III of Illinois.

His grandfather Adlai Stevenson I was known as "The Headsman" because he fired forty thousand Republican postmasters during President Cleveland's first term. Young Adlai Stevenson II attended the public elementary schools of Bloomington, Illinois which are located 126 miles southeast of Chicago. Following the completion of eighth grade, he prepared for college at the exclusive Choate Prep School in Wallingford, Connecticut. Upon finishing Choate, he went to Princeton

University where he graduated in 1922 with a B. A. degree and he subsequently matriculated at Northwestern University Law School in Chicago where he received a Juris Prudence degree in 1926 and passed the Illinois bar in the same year. He went on to serve in many government appointed posts from 1933 to 1965 with distinction. In 1948 he won the governorship of Illinois from Dwight Green, a two term Governor, with the widest vote margin in the history of the state. Illinoisans loved him.

Within days after taking office as the new Illinois governor, Stevenson in an aside to a <u>Chicago Sun</u> reporter, said that he probably wouldn't pick a FBI man to head the Illinois State Police because "FBI agents are not renowned administrators". His off the cuff observation appeared in the morning edition of the January 14, 1949 <u>Chicago Sun</u>.

When the governor's statement reached the ears of J. Edgar Hoover, he became enraged enough to throw the full force of the FBI into Stevenson's every path. Evidence of Hoover's towering rage over Stevenson's remarks can best be measured by the thickness of Stevenson's FBI file. At the last count, it was more than 900 pages. The file was compiled over a period of twenty years dating back to 1940 when the Chicago Civil Liberty Committee gave him an award. The Civil Liberal Committee was considered a Communist front organization; hence, Hoover declared that Stevenson was an enemy of the people and, therefore, warranted being kept under close surveillance.

Early in 1949 within a few months after taking office, Governor Stevenson was able to get a bill through the State House and Senate that enabled him to depoliticize the Illinois State Police Department. Stevenson, by a letter dated July 12, 1949 invited FBI Director J. Edgar Hoover to Illinois to witness the signing of the bill "removing the Illinois State Police from politics. " The Director ignored the invitation.

On December 21, 1950 via letter, Governor Stevenson sent a second invitation to his 'closet' enemy Director J. Edgar Hoover for a dedicatory program in Springfield, Illinois. It was the graduation ceremony involving the first training class under the new police system. The second invitation was acknowledged, but the Director declined, due to other alleged pressing matters.

Director Hoover's initial personal slights heaped upon Stevenson were minuscule compared to things to come. The first massive boulder aimed at Stevenson rolled down the mountainside when the former governor entered the 1952 Presidential Campaign against the World War II hero General Dwight David Eisenhower and Congressman Richard Milhouse Nixon of California. The three Red baiters who worked overtime on Stevenson were J. Edgar Hoover, Senator Joseph McCarthy and Congressman Richard M. Nixon, they all served as Ike's hatchet men. They were all experts at their craft. Poor Adlai did not even have eye water to cry with. As a matter of a fact after Stevenson lost the 1952 and the 1956 campaign to Ike, he said: "It hurt too much to laugh and I am too old to cry."

Nixon was the kind of politician who would cut down a California redwood tree, and then mount the stump and make a speech declaring he was for conservation. He also said that "Stevenson was a weakling, a waster, and a small - calibered President Harry Truman" a president who owed his career to Tom Pendergast's boss of the political machine in Kansas City, MO. The Pendergast machine was infested with "mobsters, gangsters, and remnants of the old Al Capone gang."

McCarthy was cruder than Nixon. At the end of the campaign, the Senator from Wisconsin planned to smear "Ad- Ad- Ad- Lie (Adlai) as a member of the State Department's "pinks and pansies." The Democratic National Committee cut him off at the path when they threatened to release a letter obtained from the Pentagon files exposing Eisenhower's apparent intention to divorce his wife Mamie at the end of World War II and marry his English jeep driver Kay Summersby.

J. Edgar Hoover was playing dirty pool with Adlai Stevenson's manhood when he permitted his agents to spread rumors that Stevenson was a homosexual. Ellen Borden Stevenson, Adlai's ex- wife and the heir to the Borden Milk Company fortune added fuel to the fire when she announced that she would "expose" her husband in a book of poems entitled "The Egg and I."

In this writer's opinion, Stevenson was a great American statesman. He possessed the high qualities of past Presidents Abraham Lincoln and Franklin Delano Roosevelt. His service would have benefited the country.

Adlai Ewing Stevenson
February 5, 1900   July 14, 1965

Federal Bureau of Investigation

Freedom of Information/Privacy Acts Section

Subject: <u>Adlai E. Stevenson II</u>

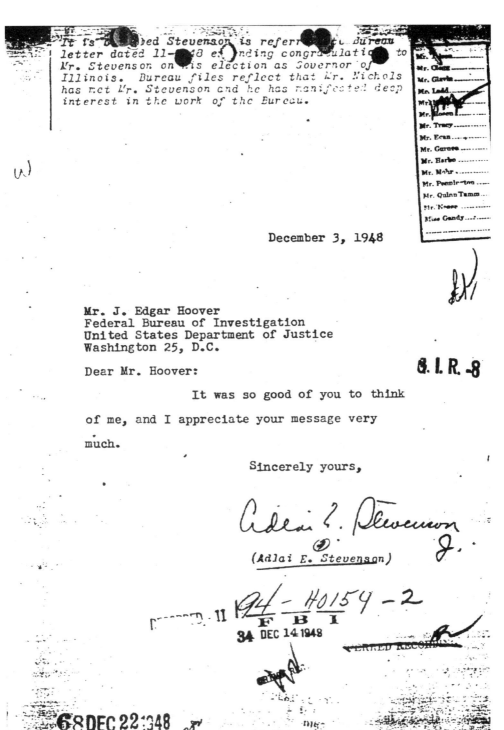

It is described Stevenson is referred to Bureau
letter dated 11-__48 extending congratulations to
Mr. Stevenson on his election as Governor of
Illinois. Bureau files reflect that Mr. Nichols
has met Mr. Stevenson and he has manifested deep
interest in the work of the Bureau.

Mr. Clegg
Mr. Glavin
Mr. Ladd
Mr. Rosen
Mr. Tracy
Mr. Egan
Mr. Gurnea
Mr. Harbo
Mr. Mohr
Mr. Pennington
Mr. Quinn Tamm
Mr. Nease
Miss Gandy

December 3, 1948

Mr. J. Edgar Hoover
Federal Bureau of Investigation
United States Department of Justice
Washington 25, D.C.

Dear Mr. Hoover:

&. I. R. -8

It was so good of you to think

of me, and I appreciate your message very

much.

Sincerely yours,

(Adlai E. Stevenson)

November 8, 1948

Honorable Adlai E. Stevenson
Libertyville, Illinois

My dear Mr. Stevenson:

I wanted to take this opportunity
of joining with your many friends in congratulating you on your election as Governor of
Illinois. If at any time we of the FBI can
be of assistance to you please do not hesitate
to let us know.

With best wishes,

Sincerely yours,

Mailed by the Director

CC - Chicago
CC - Springfield

NOTE: Mr. Nichols has met Mr. Stevenson and he
has manifested deep interest in the work of the
Bureau. It is felt that a letter of congratulations is in order. According to the Associated
Press today Stevenson won the election.

ECK:eab

RECORDED - 42

ADLAI E. STEVENSON
SEVEN SOUTH DEARBORN STREET
CHICAGO 3, ILLINOIS

December 21, 1948

Dear Mr. Hoover:

I was sorry to miss you but I had a
profitable and informative talk with Mr. Ladd.
You were very good to send me the model Police
Act. As Mr. Ladd doubtless told you, I am
very anxious to reform the State Police administration in Illinois with a view to removing it
from politics, and I am in search of people
qualified by experience and conviction to do
that job.

Sincerely yours,

Adlai E. Stevenson

Honorable J. Edgar Hoover
Federal Bureau of Investigation
United States Department of Justice
Washington 25, D. C.

December 15, 1948

Honorable Adlai E. Stevenson
Libertyville
Illinois

62-37713-77

My dear Mr. Stevenson:

Reference is made to your recent conversation with Assistant Director D. M. Ladd, and the interest which you expressed in statutes concerning the establishment of state police agencies.

I am very pleased to enclose herewith a copy of a proposed model State Police Act which was sponsored by the International Association of Chiefs of Police. I find that we have exhausted our supply of statutes establishing and maintaining the state police forces of specific states which were discussed by you with Mr. Ladd, but I am endeavoring to obtain additional copies of these permanent statutes. I will be glad to forward them to you just as soon as they become available to us.

Your interest, I assure you, is deeply appreciated, and I would like for you to understand that it would be a pleasure to cooperate with you and the law enforcement organizations of your state in all matters of mutual interest. The services of this Bureau in fingerprint identification, uniform crime reporting, technical laboratory and police training will be made freely available in keeping with your wishes and the wishes of the law enforcement officers of your state. Please do not hesitate to let me know whenever I may be of service.

With best wishes and kindest regards,

Sincerely yours,

J. Edgar Hoover

Enclosure

cc: Chicago

HHC:dgh

COMMUNICATIONS SECTION
MAILED 7
DEC 15 1948 P.M.
FEDERAL BUREAU OF INVESTIGATION
U. S DEPARTMENT OF JUSTICE

Mr. Tolson
Mr. Clegg
Mr. Glavin
Mr. Ladd
Mr. Nichols
Mr. Rosen
Mr. Tracy
Mr. Egan
Mr. Gurnea
Mr. Harbo
Mr. Mohr
Mr. Pennington
Mr. Quinn Tamm
Tele. Room
Mr. Nease
Miss Gandy

49 DEC 28 1948

Memo to Mr. Nichols   *April 3, 1952*

In a memo dated March 4, 1952, from Mr. Rosen to Mr. Ladd concerning the roundup of gambling devices, it was noted the SAC at Springfield had advised that two of the machines for which seizure had been authorized were located at the Bloomington Country Club, Bloomington, Illinois, of which Governor Stevenson was a member, his sister being a member of the Club's Board of Directors. *(71-3380-79)*

F. ALGER HISS CASE

    1. *Past Association with Alger Hiss*

A confidential informant*advised the Washington Field Office in January, 1946, that Mrs. Pricilla Hiss mentioned to John C. Ross, Director of the Office of Departmental Administration, State Department, that on January 1 the overseas operator in New York called their home asking for Alger Hiss. She indicated her belief it might have been from Adlai Stevenson, then a Special Assistant to the Secretary of State. *(65-58402-1-131)* It was further confidentially learned*that on August 15, 1946, Alger Hiss had a luncheon engagement with Adlai Stevenson, believed identical with instant Stevenson. *(74-1333-2450-30)*

    2. *Interview of Stevenson in Hiss Investigation*

Walter Schaefer of the Northwestern University Law School in January, 1949, advised that as Stevenson's representative, he had partially arranged to have Alger Hiss lecture before the Law School in November of 1946. He said Governor Stevenson had several letters from Hiss concerning this. In January, 1949, Governor Stevenson made available his personal file containing all correspondence in connection with assistance he had rendered Northwestern University in obtaining an appearance by Alger Hiss and other State Department officials to lecture at the Law School. The file contained a typewritten letter to him from Alger Hiss concerning the University appearance, the letter beginning "Dear Adlai." *(74-1333-1217, 1385, 2338)*

    3. *Character Deposition by Stevenson for Hiss' Defense*

On June 22, 1949, a deposition by Governor Adlai Stevenson was read into the record by Defense Counsel Lloyd Paul

- 6 -

* *Technical surveillances*

Memo to Mr. Nichols   April 3, 1952

Adlai E. Stevenson appeared as a member of its Executive
Committee. (61-7560-3036)

An annual report (1940) of the Chicago Civil Liberties
Committee, Inc., of which one Ira Latimer was Executive Secretary, reflected that in March (1940) among awards for meritorious
service on behalf of civil rights was one to the Civil Rights
Committee of the Chicago Bar Association. The award was accepted
by Adlai Stevenson "first chairman of that Committee." Bureau
investigation of the Chicago Civil Liberties Committee reflected
that its program and policies closely paralleled those of the
Communist Party with respect to the issues of race discrimination,
election laws, and poll taxes. (100-6805-4-6)

In September or October, 1941, a highly confidential
informant advised the Chicago Office that the names of Mr. and Mrs.
Adlai Stevenson of Libertyville, Illinois, appeared in a list of
names on file in the offices occupied jointly by the Veterans of
the Abraham Lincoln Brigade and the United Spanish Aid Committee,
Chicago. The purpose of the list was not known to the informant.
Another Chicago informant* advised on December 27, 1944, that
William Card, Executive Secretary of the Chicago Council of
American-Soviet Friendship had discussed the possibility of approaching Adlai Stevenson to accept the position of Chairman of
the CCASF Executive Board. Informant said it was indicated in
the discussion that Stevenson had a good government record and
was a good progressive-thinking fellow. It was further reported
that on January 10, 1945, the name of Stevenson was again discussed as to the possibility of securing him as Board Chairman.
One Harland Allen, according to the informant, indicated he had
succeeded Stevenson as Chairman of the Committee to Defend America.
The Chicago Office noted that in 1944 the Committee to Defend
America by Keeping out of War had been cited as a Communist front
organization. The Chicago Office further advised that on
December 21, 1948, Ira A. Latimer, Executive Secretary of the
Chicago Civil Liberties Committee and a former member of the CP
who broke with the Party in 1945, had confidentially furnished
a leaflet announcing a dinner to be held at the Continental Hotel,
Chicago, May 1, 1948, sponsored by the Southern Congress on Human
Welfare. Latimer stated that in his opinion this organization
was controlled by the Communist Party. The leaflet listed among
sponsors for the dinner the name Adlai E. Stevenson. It is noted
that the Southern Conference for Human Welfare was cited on
March 29, 1944, as a Communist front. (74-1333-3282)

- 8 -

* Technical surveillance

Memo to Mr. Nichols   April 3, 1952

     The former Premier of Italy, Ferruccio Parri, in 1947
an invitation of the American Society for Cultural Relations
with Italy, New York City, toured the United States to raise
funds for the Society which purported to be a cultural and
relief organization. One high light of the visit was a meeting
in Chicago on April 25, 1947, at which Adlai E. Stevenson was
among the scheduled speakers. A highly confidential source
advised the Chicago Office that Mr. and Mrs. Adlai E. Stevenson
were among some of the first persons to accept sponsorship of
the events in Chicago of this Society during visit of Ferruccio
Parri. Frederick Woltman of the New York World Telegram
characterized the ASCRI as a Communist front group. A reliable
informant in New York City reported that Bella V. Dodd of the
Communist Party National Committee had been instrumental in
setting up the organization which was formed in New York in
1946. A public relations firm in New York City, which had acted
as Agent for the ASCRI, withdrew, stating the ASCRI tended to
swing the Italian-American group to the left. (105-9929-8, 11)

     A brochure of the American Association for the United
Nations, Inc., (AAUN) circulated in June, 1951, at New York
listed Adlai Stevenson as a member of its Board of Directors.
As of August, 1950, Sumner Welles was Honorary President. Its
stated aims were to carry on educational work designed to
promote international cooperation by the United States. It
was not connected with the UN. A New York Office informant
in February, 1951, advised he was of the opinion there is
"probably not too much Communist infiltration into the AAUN"
(100-377086)

- 9 -

Memo to Mr. Nichols   *April 3, 1952*

**H. ATTITUDE OF GOVERNOR STEVENSON TOWARD STATE LEGISLATION
AFFECTING THE COMMUNIST PARTY**

>   *Governor Stevenson telephoned the Director on
February 20, 1951, suggesting the Director see two representatives
of the American Legion, Illinois. The men intended to discuss
various subversive bills under consideration there. Governor
Stevenson said he hoped the Director could talk to them in a
sobering way. The Director by letter to the Governor March 1,
1951, expressed his regret at not having been able to see the men
due to a sudden commitment elsewhere. The Governor by letter
3-7-51 expressed his disappointment in this and mentioned he
suspected that a bill would pass setting up a subversive committee
in Illinois. (94-1-18258-21, 23, 24 and 94-40154-7)*

>   *The Springfield Office forwarded the Bureau in
February, 1951, copies of four state bills introduced in January
of 1951 by Illinois State Senator Paul V. Broyles. The bills
would define Communism and prohibit its advocacy; would declare
ineligible for public office persons advocating the unlawful
overthrow of the government; and would create a seditious
activities investigating commission. Senator Broyles confidentially advised the Springfield Office he expected the Governor
to veto the legislation. (100-3-70-1110)*

>   *The Daily Worker, New York, issue of 3-15-49, page 6,
reported opposition to the "Six Broyles Police-State Bills" by
the National Lawyers' Guild, the Progressive Party, and other
organizations. (100-3-70-A)*

>   *The Washington Post issue of 6-27-51 reported that
Governor Stevenson on 6-26-51 vetoed the Broyles bills which
sought to outlaw Communism in Illinois. The article said the
Governor did so because they were "wholly unnecessary" due to
existing Federal and Illinois laws on subversive activity. (100-
3-70-A)*

I. MISCELLANEOUS ORGANIZATIONAL ACTIVITY

>   *Governor Stevenson was listed as a member of the
national committee of "Americans United for World Government,
Inc." in material distributed by that organization during the
years 1944-1946. The organization's chief aim was to secure
acceptance by the American people of the UN. (100-90431-164,
193 and 100-343001-20-8)*

>   *The name Adlai E. Stevenson, Navy Department, appeared
in 1942-1944 as a sponsor on letterheads of the "Appreciate
America, Inc.," a nonprofit organization which purported to promote Americanism through leaflets and posters. (94-1-22773)*

- 10 -

FBI Secret Files

ec - Mr. Belmont

June 24, 1952

THE DIRECTOR

D. M. Ladd

ADLAI EWING STEVENSON
GOVERNOR OF ILLINOIS

     Pursuant to your request, there is attached hereto a blind memorandum concerning Governor Stevenson, who, it has been alleged, is a known homosexual. SAC Scheidt sent to you a personal memorandum dated April 17, 1952, in which he stated that ████████████████████████████ *had gone to Peoria, Illinois, to return Bradley basketball players who were under indictment for a basketball fix. According to this note, the Peoria Police Department and one of the basketball players told* ██████████████ *that David B. Owen, President of Bradley University, and Governor Stevenson were two of the best-known homosexuals in the State of Illinois.*

Attachment

ABF:lw

ADLAI EWING STEVENSON

An official of the City of New York
ascertained from an individual, as well as from
a public official, both from the State of
Illinois, that Governor Adlai Ewing Stevenson
was one of the best-known homosexuals in the
State of Illinois. Stevenson was allegedly well-
known as "Adeline." Because of Stevenson's being
a homosexual, it was the opinion of the individuals
who made this statement that he would not run for
President in 1952.

A. B. FIPP:lw

MR. A. H. BELMONT   April 12, 1960

MR. G. H. SCATTERDAY

DAVID BLAIR OWEN
INFORMATION CONCERNING

       The Director has asked for a summary on D. B. Owen,
51, former President of Bradley University, Peoria, Illinois,
who was found strangled to death on Thursday, 4-7-60, in a
third-floor room of the Alton Hotel, a walk-up hostelry at
1007 E Street, N.W., Washington, D. C.

       No investigation has been conducted of Owen by the
Bureau who at the time of his demise was in Washington to
testify before congressional committees on small boat harbor
improvements as a representative of the Greater Santa Cruz
(California) Chamber of Commerce. Owen was a graduate of
Bradley University (1929) and from 1936 to 1942 was Director
of Public Relations and a member of the University's English
Department. He served as President from 1946 to 1952 when his
resignation for health reasons was accepted by the Board of
Trustees.

       Bureau files reveal that on 11-25-52, Senator Everett
Dirksen (R-Illinois) advised that the trustees at Bradley
University had learned that Owen was a homosexual and were
endeavoring to place Owen on an extended leave of absence and
then relieve him of his position as President in order to avoid
as much publicity as possible. Senator Dirksen furnished
allegations concerning Bradley faculty members to the extent
that Owen was being exploited by ████████████████ reportedly
a communist, and ████████████████████████ in
exploiting Owen. The Senator related his contacts with Owen
and furnished unfounded information concerning Communist Party
activities and the possible existence of an espionage apparatus
at the University, the widespread use of narcotics on the
campus, and the purchasing of grades by students.

       A preliminary inquiry into these allegations revealed
that rumors of Owen's homosexuality were reportedly initiated
by Gene Melchoris, a former Bradley basketball star involved in the
fixed-games scandal, in order to pressurize the Bradley staff

b6
b7C

1 - Mr. Parsons   F B I   1 - Mr. Belmont
1 - Mr. DeLoach RECD DE LOACH   1 - Name Check Section
WFW:dm   1 - Mr. Woods
(6)

Adlai E. Stevenson Quotes

During his 1956 presidential campaign, a woman called out to Adlai E. Stevenson "Senator, you have the vote of every thinking person!" Stevenson called back "That's not enough, madam, we need a majority!"

"My definition of a free society is a society where it is safe to be unpopular."

"In America, anyone can become president. That's one of the risks you take."

I believe that if we really want human brotherhood to spread and increase until it makes life safe and sane, we must also be certain that there is no one true faith or path by which it may spread.

It is often easier to fight for one's principles that to live up to them.

"America is much more than a geographical fact. It is a political and moral fact - the first community in which men set out in principle to institutional-ize freedom, responsible government, and human equality." - Adlai Stevenson

Accuracy is to a newspaper what virtue is to a lady, but a newspaper can always print a retraction.

Eggheads unite! You have nothing to lose but your yolks.

Flattery is all right - if you don't inhale.

That which seems the height of absurdity in one generation often becomes the height of wisdom in another.

Chapter XI

Duke Ellington: The Master Maestro

On April 29, 1899, in a middle class home located in the Negro section of northwest Washington, D. C. at 2129 Ward Place, Daisy Kennedy Ellington gave birth to a baby who was delivered by a midwife named Eliza Jane Johnson. The baby boy was given the Christian name Edward, the second name of his father, James Edward Ellington. His middle name would be Kennedy, in honor of his maternal grandparents, James William Kennedy and Alice Kennedy, who owned the house in which he was born.

Edward Kennedy Ellington's mother treated her baby like a prized jewel. She did not want his little toes to touch the floor. Her sparkling and penetrating brown eyes and long, thin, queenly fingers were never more than a few feet from her copper-colored prince until he reached the age of four.

On Edward's first day of liberation, in the summer of 1903, Mrs. Ellington's precious child wandered onto the front yard of his grandmother's house and stumbled over a lawn mower bruising the fourth finger of his left hand. The scratch on his pinkie was treated as a major emergency by Daisy Ellington, who called the entire family into conference to decide what to do about a mishap that could ordinarily be healed by a mother's kiss.

The strength of his mother's obsessive devotion must have permeated young Edward's psyche with the notion that he was somebody special. She constantly instilled in him the values that gave him high self-esteem. She frequently reminded him that he was a blessed child who could accomplish anything in the world that he wanted.

When little Edward Ellington was 5 years old, his mother raised his age to 6 so that he could skip kindergarten and enter grammar school at the first grade level. She dressed her little darling like a young prince and sent him off to Garnet Public School, the same one she had attended, just a couple of blocks away from her mother's home. Every morning, rain or shine, she secretly followed him right up to the school playground and watched as he disappeared behind the schoolhouse door. Daisy Ellington never suspected that her son was very much aware of her Sherlockian sleuthing. At 3:15 p. m. every day she could be found waiting at the front door of the school or nervously standing on the sidewalk in front of their house awaiting his arrival.

Ellington started taking private piano lessons when he was 7 years old from music teacher Marietta Clinkscales (her real name). Mrs. Clinkscales came to the Kennedy house twice a week to give him instructions for 25 cents per session and rap his knuckles when he made a mistake. Nevertheless, Edward's interest in baseball and art overshadowed his interest in music. His artistic talents must be credited to the Kennedy side of the family because several of his uncles produced works of exhibit quality. Edward Kennedy Ellington dreamed of someday being a great artist like them.

James Edward Ellington, the Duke's dad, never completed elementary school but carried himself with the demeanor of a Harvard graduate as he performed his daily tasks as a butler. His handsome good looks complimented his elegant manner. Moreover, James Edward had excellent language skills, which served him well as an employee of Dr. Middleton F. Cuthbert, a prominent white physician, who lived in the big house at 1467 Rhode Island Avenue. Mr. Ellington's household authority was limited to supervising the cook and the maid as well as graciously opening and closing the front door for members of the family and their guests. He comported himself like the chief executive officer of a major business and talked like a man who had plenty of money. Mr. Ellington treated his wife Daisy and son Edward as though he was a millionaire, though he did not earn enough money to move them out of his mother-in-law's home.

Edward Kennedy Ellington was greatly influenced by the way his father dressed and talked. And his good manners were also affected by his mother Daisy, a graduate of the "M" Street High School, predecessor to the classic Dunbar Public High School, one of only two secondary schools for colored students in the District of Columbia.

Ellington worshiped his mother and admired his father, who agreed that he should pursue his dream and become an artist. Hence, piano lessons were allowed to fade faster than sundown on December 21st .

The summer before graduating from grammar school, young Ellington visited his mother's brother, John Kennedy, an accomplished artist who lived on Catherine Street in Philadelphia. During his visit to the "City of Brotherly Love", he heard a piano player that was a year older than himself whip the piano keys until they figuratively "smoked. " That young musician's name was Harvey O. Brooks, who had a tremendous left-hand keyboard swing like Eubie Blake, Willie "The Lion" Smith and "Fats" Waller.

When Edward returned to Washington, he was stricken with a severe case of the flu that was threatening to turn into pneumonia; thus, he was confined to the house for two weeks. During Ellington's convalescence, the piano performance of young Brooks continued to bubble and boil in Ellington's consciousness to the point that it rekindled his interest in the piano. While tinkering around on the piano, Ellington wrote his first musical composition "Soda Fountain Rag. " The title arose from Ellington's weekend gig as a soda jerk at the Poodle Dog Cafe on Georgia Avenue in the Negro section of the District of Columbia. "Soda Fountain Rag," though it was never recorded or copyrighted, was played by Ellington around Garnet Elementary School whenever the opportunity presented itself. His playing drew much attention from the blossoming young girls.

Young Edgar McEntree, Ellington's wealthy friend became a party crasher and a hawker for the Duke, a nickname, he had hung on him because of his physical appearance and style of dress. As an advance man, Edgar milled around among party goers and bragged about how well Ellington could play the piano. When Duke made his grand entrance at a party, he was a sought-after commodity who never objected to playing the piano. Ellington typified a sheltered mama's boy, eager to display his newly discovered talent.

Duke repeatedly played his second composition, "What You Gonna Do When The Bed Breaks Down?" which was a big hit with the belly rubbing, tight hugging, and slow-drag dancing bunch. Luckily for Duke, the kids liked his song and requested it over and over again. Duke had only one other song in his musical repertory, and that was his "Soda Fountain Rag." He could play the two compositions in a number of dance tempo variations from 2/4 time (Charleston), to 3/4 (waltz), and 4/4 (fox trot). This technique he employed with many of his compositions throughout the balance of his long career. He would also change titles to old songs. "Never No Lament" and "Concerto for Cootie" later became very popular songs under new names: "Don't Get Around Much Anymore" and "Do Nothing 'Till You Hear From Me." The Duke's classic "Mood Indigo" was once known as the "Dreamy Blues."

On the party circuit, Duke discovered that there was always some pretty girls anxious to stand at the side and back of the piano player whenever he played. He was delighted with the admiration and attention he was getting from the ladies; thus, he buried the notion of ever becoming a professional athlete or artist.

At 15, Ellington started hanging out at Frank Holliday's Poolroom on "T" Street between Sixth and Seventh, next door to the Howard Theater. Frank's place was not an ordinary neighborhood poolroom, but a top-of-the-line billiard parlor where high school and college kids from all over Washington, D. C. gathered to watch the great pool sharks. Players crawled out of the corner pockets of every pool den in the District to shoot pool at Frank Holliday's.

Duke, was fascinated by the pool hustlers and their hip braggadocio behavior. He also enjoyed listening to the conversations among the Pullman porters and dining-car waiters who also hung out at Holliday's. They were always "fish bone" clean from the top of their heads to the soles of their shoes. They dressed as sharply as dancers preparing to perform in a main event. In addition, these fellows had a lot to say about their travels and the women they had known in far-flung cities. Duke's toes tingled with excitement when he would overhear them say, "I was in Chicago last night," or "I am going out to San Francisco tomorrow." Unlike the Duke's own father, these men had been to some big towns and heard some big talk. Duke wanted to emulate the railroad men because in the colored community, they represented both "cool" and respectability.

Not generally known outside of the Negro community was that Pullman porters and waiters were often college graduates stuck in service jobs which were considered the best a racist job market could offer men of color who had rub their heads against a book.

In August of 1930, the Duke Ellington Orchestra traveled from the jazz slave masters Cotton Club in New York City to the West Coast by train to do some guest shots in <u>Check and Double Check</u>, a film featuring the popular radio team of Amos 'N' Andy. Duke termed his appearance in the film a "crowning point." His Negro fans and many white liberals did not share his opinion because they felt that the enormously talented and articulate musician deserved more than a few brief flashes across the big screen. Moreover, his presence in the film was blacked out of the news releases and on all the theater marquees in the country except those in the most sophisticated Northern urban areas. The RKO Studio executives feared that spotlighting a Negro would offend Southern movie goers.

As the swing era reached its peak in the mid-30's, Hollywood developed a separate platform for Negro performers in keeping with the Jim Crow mind-set for presenting popular Negro entertainers without making them a part of the plot. Moreover, there was an absence of intelligent dialogue written in movie scripts for Negroes. That is, unless they were wearing a maid's apron or a coachman's cap. There was also a special language for sharecroppers whose bodies were always draped in blue denim overalls or colorful gingham dresses, complimented with red or blue bandannas around their necks or on their heads. Duke Ellington and members of his band were not forced to dress down from their customary elegance, a compromise that gave artistic dignity to the Ellington musician. In that sense, Duke was right in calling it a "crowning point. "

It was in the early summer of 1941 that Duke reached his theatrical "Pikes Peak" in that he and Billy Strayhorn wrote the entire music score for a Sun- Tanned Revu- sical entitled Jump For Joy featuring Dorothy Dandridge, Ivie Anderson, Herb Jeffries and the Duke as both actor and musician. The spirited title song contained these lines:

"Don't you grieve, Little Eve,

All the hounds, I do believe

Have been killed, ain't you thrilled,

Jump for joy. "

The idea for the Jump For Joy production was a collaborative effort of 15 Hollywood screen writers, including Mickey Rooney, the movie star, and Langston Hughes, the great Negro poet. Some members of the group were on J. Edgar Hoover's list of persons belonging to Communist front organizations such as the NAACP and the Urban League. It was decided that they would attempt to elimi- nate racism in America from a platform of theatrical propaganda. The original script had Uncle Tom a symbol of Jim Crow on his deathbed with all of his children danc- ing around him singing, "He lived to a ripe old age. Let him go, God bless him! " At the same time, there was a Hollywood producer on the left side of the bed and a Broadway producer on the right side, both trying to keep Uncle Tom alive by inject- ing adrenaline into the veins of his arms.

The opening act was entitled "Sun Tan Tenth of a Nation! " and the finale of the first act was "Uncle Tom's Cabin Is a Drive- In Now! " The first eight bars of the lyrics were:

"There used to be a chicken shack in Caroline,

But now they've moved it to Hollywood and Vine;

They paid off the mortgage - nobody knows how

And Uncle Tom's Cabin is a drive- in now! "

`Ellington said that the "angels" (investors) made them take out the origi- nal second act of the show because it had more fishbones than America was willing to swallow. The title of that act was " I've Got A Passport From Georgia (And I'm

Going to the U. S. A.) "

The Jump For Joy revue opened July 10, 1941, at the Mayan Theater in Los Angeles and closed 12 weeks later on September 27 following a highly successful run. The initial objective was to take the show across the country from Los Angeles to San Francisco, Chicago, Boston and then to Broadway. The message was too strong for Jim Crow pre-World War II America. Therefore, financing for the show dried up like a grape in the sun. The show never played anywhere outside of Los Angeles, except for a three-week aborted revival in 1958 in Miami.

AMERICAN REVUE THEATRE
(WALTER JURMANN, Chairman)

PRESENTS

DUKE ELLINGTON

in

A Sun-Tanned Revu-sical

"JUMP FOR JOY"

with

DOROTHY DANDRIDGE

IVY ANDERSON

HERB JEFFRIES

Music by
Duke Ellington and Hal Borne

Lyrics by
Paul Webster

Sketches by
Sid Kuller   Hal Fimberg

Staged by
Nick Castle

Costumes, Scenery, Lighting
Rene Hubert

Sketches Directed by
Sid Kuller   Everett Wile

Additional Lyrics and Music
Sid Kuller, Otis Rene, Langston Hughes, Charles Leonard, Mickey Rooney,
Sidney Miller, Ray Golden, Richard Weil

Entire Production Supervised by
Henry Blankfort

Jimmy Blanton and Duke Ellington look on as Herb Jefferies sings one of the "Jump For Joy" title songs from the orchestra pit of the Mayan Theater in Los Angeles.

Federal Bureau of Investigation

Freedom of Information/Privacy Acts Section

Subject: <u>Duke Ellington</u>

MAILED
JUL 25 1955
NAME CHECK

July 22, 1955

DUKE ELLINGTON *Summary*
also known as Edward Kennedy Ellington
Born: April 29, 1899
Washington, D. C.

No investigation has been conducted by the FBI pertinent to your inquiry concerning the above-named individual.

However, the files of this Bureau contain the following information concerning Ellington developed during the course of other security-type investigations:

The May 12, 1938, issue of the "Daily Worker," an east coast Communist newspaper, contained an article captioned "Harlem Youth Parley Rallies for Jobs, Peace." This article listed Duke Ellington among the prominent endorsers of the first All-Harlem Youth Conference which was to convene on May 13, 1938, in New York City. The All-Harlem Youth Conference has been described as "among the more conspicuous Communist-front groups in the Racial---subclassification" by the California Committee on Un-American Activities in a report issued by that group in 1948 (pages 73 and 75).
(61-7563-60X6)

The "West Coast Volunteer" for June and July, 1941, a monthly news bulletin published by the Henry Eaton Post of the Abraham Lincoln Brigade at Los Angeles, California, reflected that the Hollywood Chapter of the Veterans of the Abraham Lincoln Brigade on July 26, 1941, gave a barn dance to raise funds. The publication related that Duke Ellington had appeared at the dance with a portion of his band. The Veterans of the Abraham Lincoln Brigade has been cited by the Attorney General of the United States as within the purview of Executive Order 10450. (100-7060-9)

Orig. and one to USIA
Req Rec'd: 7-1-55

Tolson
B. Emm.
Nichols
Belmont
Harbo
Mohr
Parsons _____ (4)
Rosen _____ NOTE: Copy of memo furnished State 4-21-53.
Tamm
Sizoo
Winterrowd
Tele. Room
Holloman
Gandy

CONFIDENTIAL

RE: EDWARD KENNEDY (DUKE) ELLINGTON (S-1) (C) 61

*sinister stirring of antagonisms of one racial group against
another..... Among the more conspicuous Communist-front groups
in the Racial...subclassification...(is) All Harlem Youth
Conference."* (61-7563-60X6)

The June-July, 1941, issue of the "West Coast
Volunteer," a publication of the Henry Eaton Post of the
Abraham Lincoln Brigade, Los Angeles, California, reflected
that on July 26, 1941, the Hollywood Chapter of the Veterans
of the Abraham Lincoln Brigade had given a barn dance to raise
funds. The article reflected that Duke Ellington had appeared
at the dance. The Veterans of the Abraham Lincoln Brigade has
been designated ~~by the Attorney General~~ pursuant to Executive
Order 10450. (100-7060-97 page 4)

On November 10, 1941, a dinner was given at Ciro's
Restaurant, Hollywood, California, under the auspices of the
American Committee to Save Refugees, the Exiled Writers
Committee, and the United American Spanish Aid Committee.
The program for the dinner listed one Duke Ellington as being
on the Committee of Sponsors for the dinner. The American
Committee to Save Refugees was cited as a communist front by
the Special Committee on Un-American Activities in a report
dated March 29, 1944. The California Committee on Un-American
Activities in 1948 described the Exiled Writers Committee as
an organization established by the communist League of American
Writers to bolster the communist front, the American Committee
to Save Refugees. The Exiled Writers Committee was further
reported as having worked with other communist fronts and in
1942 merged into the Joint Anti-Fascist Refugee Committee. The
United American Spanish Aid Committee has been designated ~~by
the Attorney General~~ pursuant to Executive Order 10450.
(100-7061-115)
The report of the Special Committee on Un-American
Activities, United States House of Representatives, published
in 1944, reflected that the Artists' Front to Win the War
made its debut at a mass meeting at Carnegie Hall, New York,
New York, on October 16, 1942. Exhibit Number 1, set out in the
report, which appears to be a program of the above-described
mass meeting, reflected Duke Ellington as one of the sponsors.
The Artists' Front to Win the War was cited as a communist front
by the Special Committee on Un-American Activities in a report
dated March 29, 1944. (61-7582-1298 page 576)

CONFIDENTIAL
SECRET

RE: EDWARD KENNEDY (DUKE) ELLINGTON

On June 23, 1943, the "Daily Worker" contained an article captioned "Negro Tribute to Hit Back at Axis Plot Here" which reflected that a "Tribute to Negro Servicemen" was to be held on June 27, 1943, in New York, New York. The article reflected Duke Ellington was one of the artists who would be presented. The tribute was supported by the Negro Labor Victory Committee and the National Negro Congress among other organizations. The Negro Labor Victory Committee and the National Negro Congress have been designated by the Attorney General pursuant to Executive Order 10450. (61-6728-A)

On October 7, 1943, the "Daily Worker" contained an article captioned "Civic Leaders Endorse Davis." The article concerned Benjamin J. Davis, Jr., the Communist Party candidate for city councilman in New York City. The article reflected a "Davis Victory Show" was to be held on October 24, 1943, at the Golden Gate Ballroom in New York, New York. Duke Ellington was mentioned as one of the artists "who will pay tribute to the Communist leader." On October 10, 1943, "The Worker," the Sunday edition of the "Daily Worker," contained an article captioned "Ben Davis Candidacy Arouses Nat'l Interest." The article reflected: "From the world of art this week came backing from...Duke Ellington...." (100-149163-A)

A confidential informant who has furnished reliable information in the past, advised in 1944, that Duke Ellington had mailed out approximately 1500 letters on behalf of the National Committee to Abolish the Poll Tax and that the committee had been receiving money from the people he had contacted. The California Committee on Un-American Activities in 1947 described the National Committee to Abolish the Poll Tax as being among the communist front organizations for racial agitation which also served as "money-collecting media." (100-11507-204; ▯)

At the national convention of the American Youth for Democracy held in New York, New York, in 1946, the report of the National Board was presented on June 15, 1946. The report, in reviewing activities of the American Youth for Democracy, reflected that the "Tribute to Fats Waller" held at Carnegie Hall, New York, New York, in April, 1944, had been sponsored by the American Youth for Democracy. The report stated that

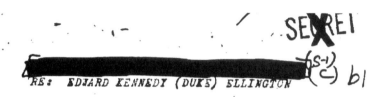

SECRET (S-1) (C) b1

RE: EDWARD KENNEDY (DUKE) ELLINGTON

the meeting had turned into a "tremendous, spontaneous demonstration of inter-racial unity." The report further reflected that Duke Ellington was among those individuals who joined with the American Youth for Democracy in this event. The American Youth for Democracy has been designated by the Attorney General pursuant to Executive Order 10450. (61-777-742-page 41)

A confidential informant who has furnished reliable information in the past, advised in 1944 that on May 14, 1944, a concert was held at Carnegie Hall in New York, New York, under the sponsorship of the Joint Anti-Fascist Refugee Committee. The informant advised that Duke Ellington was among the persons who volunteered their professional services for the concert. The Joint Anti-Fascist Refugee Committee has been designated by the Attorney General pursuant to Executive Order 10450. (100-7061-631)

On August 7, 1944, the "Daily Worker" contained an article captioned "Stars Lead Coast Dem. Committee," which reflected that bandmaster-composer Duke Ellington was a member of the executive board of the Hollywood Democratic Committee. The report of the California Committee on Un-American Activities in 1948 described the Hollywood Democratic Committee as a communist front organized in 1942. (100-138754-A)

On January 2, 1946, the "Daily Worker" contained an article captioned "Yugoslav Relief Opens 1946 Drive." The article reflected that the American Committee for Yugoslav Relief opened its 1946 activities with a concert the preceding evening in New York, New York. Duke Ellington was listed as one of the sponsors of the concert. The American Committee for Yugoslav Relief, Incorporated, has been designated by the Attorney General pursuant to Executive Order 10450. (100-212469-A)

On March 11, 1946, the "Washington Daily News" contained an article captioned "Politicians Eye Ickes New Role of Prophet for 10 Million Voters." The article reflected former Secretary of the Interior Harold L. Ickes had become executive chairman of the Independent Citizens Committee of the Arts, Sciences, and Professions. The article reflected "some notable Negro artists and authors are on his committee's nation__ board of directors or are vice-chairmen. Among them are Duke Ellington, band leader,...." The Independent Citizens

CONFIDENTIAL SECRET   SECRET

RE: EDWARD KENNEDY (DUKE) ELLINGTON

Committee of the Arts, Sciences, and Professions was cited as
a communist front by the Congressional Committee on Un-American
Activities, House Report Number 1954. (100-338892-41)

On May 5, 1947, the "Brooklyn Eagle," a daily newspaper published in Brooklyn, New York, reflected that a bazaar
sponsored by the National Council of American-Soviet Friendship
had opened with a variety concert on May 4, 1947, at City
Center Casino Ballroom, New York, New York. The article
reflected that Duke Ellington was one of the persons starring
in the concert. The National Council of American-Soviet
Friendship has been designated by the Attorney General
pursuant to Executive Order 10450. (100-146964-1301 page 17)

On September 30, 1950, "The New Leader," a weekly
magazine, contained an article captioned "No Red Songs For Me"
by Duke Ellington. A foreword by the editors indicated that
the "Daily Worker," on May 27, 1950, had first reported that
Ellington had signed the Stockholm Peace Petition and that on
August 25 and 27, 1950, additional stories had been published
repeating the same false claim. It was also stated that
Ellington, upon his return from a European tour, had repudiated
the allegations. In the article, Ellington denied signing the
petition and told of his efforts to get his name removed. The
Stockholm Peace Petition was "Cited as Communist" by the
Congressional Committee on Un-American Activities in a statement
issued July 13, 1950. (100-370500-A)

The foregoing information is furnished as a result
of your request and is not to be construed as a clearance or
nonclearance of the individual involved. It is furnished for
your confidential information and is not to be disseminated
outside of your agency.

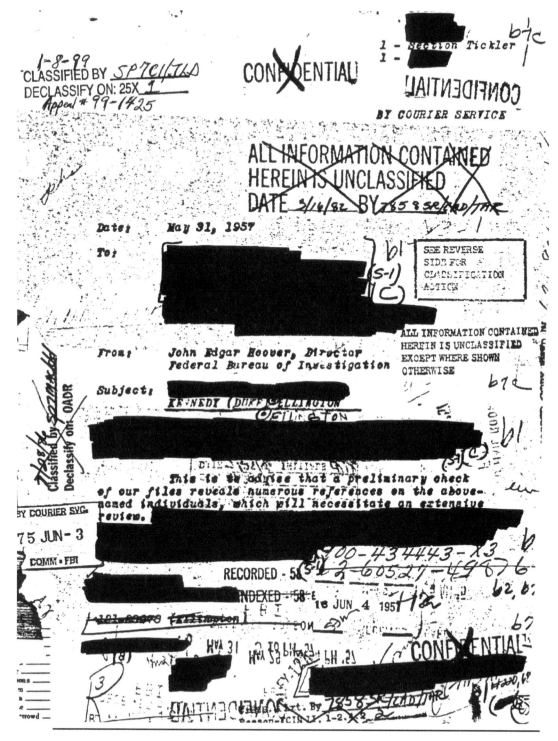

CONFIDENTIAL

1 - Liaison Section
1 - _____ b7C

CLASSIFIED BY _SP7C1/TLO_
DECLASSIFY ON: 25X _1_
_1-8-99_ to _99-1425_

SEE REVERSE
SIDE FOR
CLASSIFICATION
ACTION

Date: December 29, 1960

To:

From: John Edgar Hoover, Director

Subject: EDWARD KENNEDY ELLINGTON
SECURITY MATTER - C

This matter is being referred to the Legal Attache
in Paris for his information in the event Ellington's activities
while in France come to his attention.

Classified by _spzmacldd_
Declassify on: OADR

134443

1 - Office of Security
Department of State

1 - New York (See Note, Page Two)
1 - Paris (See Note, Page Two)

REC- 35

15 DEC 30 1960

ENCLOSURE

1 - Foreign Liaison Unit

SEE NOTE ON YELLOW, PAGE TWO   EX-113

Tolson
Mohr
Parsons
Belmont
Callahan
DeLoach
Malone
McGuire
Rosen
Tamm
Trotter
W.C. Sullivan
Tele. Room
Ingram
Gandy

(9)

MAIL ROOM [ ]   TELETYPE UNIT [ ]   CONFIDENTIAL

BY COURIER SVC.
10 DEC 30
COMM-FBI

ATTENTION: SAC, NEW YORK, AND LEGAL ATTACHE, PARIS

For the information of the Legal Attache, subject was never the subject of a main case file. However, Bureau files indicate that Ellington has had some affiliation with numerous communist front groups such as the All-Harlem Youth Conference, the Hollywood Chapter of the Veterans of the Abraham Lincoln Brigade, the American Committee to Save Refugees, the Artists' Front to Win the War and the National Committee to Abolish the Poll Tax. Furthermore, Ellington reportedly volunteered his professional services for a concert held in 1944 in Carnegie Hall, New York, sponsored by the Joint Anti-Fascist Refugee Committee. He appeared at another concert in 1947 sponsored by the National Council of American-Soviet Friendship. He also, according to an article in the October 10, 1943, issue of "The Worker," sponsored the candidacy of Benjamin J. Davis, Jr., Communist Party candidate for city councilman in New York. Ellington was born 4/29/99 at Washington, D. C.

NOTE ON YELLOW: Subject not on SI. He is well-known Negro musician who is presently traveling abroad, according to information received by Bureau from State Department in memorandum received 12/21/60.

Deleted in the file.
Not FOIA deletion.

- 2 -

CONFIDENTIAL

CONFIDENTIAL

UNITED STATES GOVERNMENT

Memorandum

TO : President, FBIRA   DATE: May 23, 1962

FROM : Activity Promoter

SEE REVERSE
SIDE FOR
CLASSIFICATION
ACTION

SUBJECT: THE FIRST INTERNATIONAL JAZZ FESTIVAL, WASHINGTON, D. C.
5/31 - 6/3/62

CLASSIFIED BY:
DECLASSIFY ON: 25X 1

Enclosed circular is one of a number received from the Department of Justice Recreation Association for possible distribution among our employees. The circular announces sponsorship of captioned festival by the President's Committee of the People to People Program listing Gunther Schuller as Musical Director and Duke Ellington as Musical Host.

    Bureau indices are negative as to ███████. However, Bufile contains the name ███████ as an ex-crew member of "Graf Spee," married to ███████ 31 years of age, Paraguayan citizen. Letter 3-12-46 from Legat, Montevideo, Uruguay, placed ███████ name among 24 individuals, all former crew members of the "Graf Spee" or "Tacoma" who were not repatriated to Germany on 2-16-46. Letter also advised the State Department's secret instruction dated 12-18-48 specified that case histories be prepared concerning individuals suggested for repatriation.

    Concerning Duke Ellington, Bufile 100-434443 contains a Bureau communication to ███████ that this individual as Edward Kennedy Ellington had never been investigated by the Bureau but the following substance of the information was furnished from Bufile. Ellington has had some affiliation with numerous communist front groups such as the All-Harlem Youth Conference, the Hollywood Chapter of the Veterans of the Abraham Lincoln Brigade, the American Committee to Save Refugees, the Artists' Front to Win the War and the National Committee to Abolish the Poll Tax. Furthermore, Ellington reportedly volunteered his professional services for a concert held in 1944 in Carnegie Hall, New York, sponsored by the Joint Anti-Fascist Refugee Committee. He appeared at another concert in 1947 sponsored by the National Council of American-Soviet Friendship. He also, according to an article in the October 10, 1943, issue of "The Worker," sponsored the candidacy of Benjamin J. Davis, Jr., Communist Party candidate for city councilman in New York. Ellington was born 4/29/99 at Washington, D. C.

LDH:sas
(2)
Enclosure

100-434443

NOT RECORDED
102 JUN 4 1962
(OVER)

MAY 25 1964

May 22, 1964

Summary ✗

DUKE ELLINGTON
400 Central Pk West
New York City

SEE REVERSE SIDE FOR
ADD. DISSEMINATION.

No investigation pertinent to your inquiry has been conducted by the FBI concerning the captioned individual. However, the files of this Bureau reveal the following information which may relate to the subject of your name check request.

On May 12, 1938, the "Daily Worker," an east coast communist newspaper, contained an article captioned "Harlem Youth Parley Rallies for Jobs, Peace." The article reflected that the first All Harlem Youth Conference would convene on May 13, 1938. Duke Ellington was listed as one of the prominent endorsers of the conference. In connection with the All Harlem Youth Conference, the 1948 Report of the California Committee on Un-American Activities reflected: "Nothing more plainly reveals the fraud and dishonesty of the Communists than the sinister stirring of antagonisms of one racial group against another..... Among the more conspicuous Communist-front groups in the Racial...subclassification...(is) All Harlem Youth Conference."
(61-7563-60X6)

The June-July, 1941, issue of the "West Coast Volunteer," a publication of the Henry Eaton Post of the Abraham Lincoln Brigade, Los Angeles, California, reflected that on July 26, 1941, the Hollywood Chapter of the Veterans funds. The article reflected that Duke Ellington had appeared at the dance. The Veterans of the Abraham Lincoln Brigade has been designated pursuant to Executive Order 10450.
(100-7060-97 page 4)

On November 10, 1941, a dinner was given at Ciro's Restaurant, Hollywood, California, under the auspices of the American Committee to Save Refugees, the Exile Writers Committee, and the United American Spanish Aid Committee. The program for the dinner listed one Duke Ellington as being

REC Z *100-43443-3*

Original & 1 SECRET SERVICE
Request Received-5/21/64

10 MAY 26 1964

ALL INFORMATION CONTAINED
HEREIN IS UNCLASSIFIED
DATE 3-16-92 BY 7553 SR/CAP/TAR

58 JUN 4 1964

Duke Ellington

on the Committee of Sponsors for the dinner. The American
Committee to Save Refugees was cited as a communist front by
the Special Committee on Un-American Activities in a report
dated March 29, 1944. The California Committee on Un-American
Activities in 1948 described the Exiled Writers Committee as
an organization established by the communist League of American
Writers to bolster the communist front, the American Committee
to Save Refugees. The Exiled Writers Committee was further
reported as having worked with other communist fronts and in
1942 merged into the Joint Anti-Fascist Refugee Committee. The
United American Spanish Aid Committee has been designated
pursuant to Executive Order 10450.

(100-7061-115

    The report of the Special Committee on Un-American
Activities, United States House of Representatives, published
in 1944, reflected that the Artists' Front to Win the War
made its debut at a mass meeting at Carnegie Hall, New York,
New York, on October 16, 1942. Exhibit Number 1, set out in the
report, which appears to be a program of the above-described
mass meeting, reflected Duke Ellington as one of the sponsors.
The Artists' Front to Win the War was cited as a communist front
by the Special Committee on Un-American Activities in a report
dated March 29, 1944.

(61-7582-1298 page 576)

    On June 23, 1943, the "Daily Worker" contained an
article captioned "Negro Tribute to Hit Back at Axis Plot Here"
which reflected that a "Tribute to Negro Servicemen" was to be
held on June 27, 1943, in New York, New York. The article
reflected Duke Ellington was one of the artists who would be
presented. The tribute was supported by the Negro Labor Victory
Committee and the National Negro Congress among other organizations. The Negro Labor Victory Committee and the National
Negro Congress have been designated pursuant to Executive
Order 10450

(61-6728-A)

    On October 7, 1943, the "Daily Worker" contained
an article captioned "Civic Leaders Endorse Davis." The
article concerned Benjamin J. Davis, Jr., the Communist Party
candidate for city councilman in New York City. The article
reflected a "Davis Victory Show" was to be held on October 24,
1943, at the Golden Gate Ballroom in New York, New York.
Duke Ellington was mentioned as one of the artists "who will
pay tribute to the Communist leader." On October 10, 1943,
"The Worker," the Sunday edition of the "Daily Worker," contained an article captioned "Ben Davis Candidacy Arouses Nat'l
Interest." The article reflected: "From the world of art
this week came backing from...Duke Ellington..."

(100-149163-A)

- 2 -

28

Duke Ellington

A confidential informant who has furnished reliable information in the past, advised in 1944, that Duke Ellington had mailed out approximately 1500 letters on behalf of the National Committee to Abolish the Poll Tax and that the committee had been receiving money from the people he had contacted. The California Committee on Un-American Activities in 1947 described the National Committee to Abolish the Poll Tax as being among the communist front organizations for racial agitation which also served as "money-collecting media." *b2 b7D* (00-11507-204;

At the national convention of the American Youth for Democracy held in New York, New York, in 1946, the report of the National Board was presented on June 15, 1946. The report, in reviewing activities of the American Youth for Democracy, reflected that the "Tribute to Fats Waller" held at Carnegie Hall, New York, New York, in April, 1944, had been sponsored by the American Youth for Democracy. The report stated that the meeting had turned into a "tremendous, spontaneous demonstration of inter-racial unity." The report further reflected that Duke Ellington was among those individuals who joined with the American Youth for Democracy in this event. The American Youth for Democracy has been designated pursuant to Executive Order 1045 (61-777-742-page 41)

A confidential informant who has furnished reliable information in the past, advised in 1944 that on May 14, 1944, a concert was held at Carnegie Hall in New York, New York, under the sponsorship of the Joint Anti-Fascist Refugee Committee. The informant advised that Duke Ellington was among the persons who volunteered their professional services for the concert. The Joint Anti-Fascist Refugee Committee has been designated pursuant to Executive Order 10450. (100-7061-631)

On August 7, 1944, the "Daily Worker" contained an article captioned "Stars Lead Coast Dem. Committee," which reflected that bandmaster-composer Duke Ellington was a member of the executive board of the Hollywood Democratic Committee. The report of the California Committee on Un-American Activities in 1948 described the Hollywood Democratic Committee as a communist front organized in 1942 (100-138754-A)

On January 2, 1946, the "Daily Worker" contained an article captioned "Yugoslav Relief Opens 1946 Drive." The article reflected that the American Committee for Yugoslav Relief opened its 1946 activities with a concert the preceding evening in New York, New York. Duke Ellington was listed as one of the sponsors of the concert. The American Committee for Yugoslav Relief, Incorporated, has been designated pursuant to Executive Order 10450. (100-212169-A)

- 3 -

19

February 19, 1968

BY LIAISON

Mrs. Mildred Stegall
The White House
Washington, D. C.

DECLASSIFIED BY 7858 SE/CAB/TAR
3-17-82

Dear Mrs. Stegall:

Set forth herein is data relating to a number of
entertainers which may be of interest to you.

The central files of the FBI reveal no pertinent
derogatory information concerning the Marlboro Vermont Orchestra
and ▮▮▮▮▮▮▮▮▮▮▮▮▮▮▮▮▮▮▮▮ The fingerprint files
of the Identification Division of the FBI contain no arrest data identifiable with ▮▮▮▮▮▮▮▮ based upon background information available.

Attached are separate memoranda regarding the Robert
Joffrey Ballet Company, Mitch Miller Men's Chorus and the following
individuals:

Duke Ellington

A copy of this communication has not been sent to the
Attorney General. This letter of transmittal may be declassified when
the enclosures bearing a classification are removed.

Sincerely yours,

Delivered to Mildred Stegall
on 2/14/65

Enclosures (12)
1 - Mr. DeLoach (sent direct) - Enclosures
1 - ▮▮▮▮ (sent direct) - Enclosures

TOP SECRET

EX 101
REC 55
100-434143
NOT RECORDED
176 FEB 20 1968

February 19, 1968

DUKE ELLINGTON *Summary*

A summary memorandum containing information from our files regarding captioned individual was furnished to the White House on May 26, 1965.

Since that time, information has been received that bandleader Duke Ellington would appear with James Forman, Student Non-Violent Coordinating Committee, on a program sponsored by the United Ministers on the Texas Southern University campus in October, 1966. Forman was to speak on the theme, "Black Power: A New Religion?"

The fingerprint files of the Identification Division of the FBI contain no arrest data identifiable with Duke Ellington based upon background information submitted in connection with this name check request.

ALL INFORMATION CONTAINED
HEREIN IS UNCLASSIFIED
DATE 3-17-82 BY 7858/CAD/TAP
7/28/86   sp7mmc/dcl

olson _____
eLoach _____
ohr _____
ishop _____
asper _____
allahan _____
onrad _____
elt _____
ale _____
osen _____
illivan _____
avel _____
rotter _____
ele. Room _____
oimes _____
andy _____

NOTE: Per request of Mrs. Mildred Stegall, White House Staff.

MAIL ROOM ☐   TELETYPE UNIT ☐

100- 4341143- 4   b7c

ENCLOSURE

32

MAILED

DEC 31 1969

NAME CHECK

December 31, 1969

N 3-1

EDWARD KENNEDY ELLINGTON
Also Known As: "DUKE"
Born: April 29, 1899
Washington, D. C.

In response to your name check request, refer to a summary memorandum captioned "Duke Ellington," dated May 22, 1964, and sent to State (CU/CP) on March 30, 1966. (100-434443-3)

Since that time, information has been received that bandleader Duke Ellington would appear with James Forman, Student Non-Violent Coordinating Committee, on a program sponsored by the United Ministers on the Texas Southern University campus in October, 1966. Forman was to speak on the theme, "Black Power: A New Religion?" (100-434443-4)

Original and 1 - STATE (CP)
Request Received - December 11, 1969

_____ (4)

b7c

REC-35

ALL INFORMATION CONTAINED
HEREIN IS UNCLASSIFIED
DATE 3-16-82 BY 7458 SR/CAD/TAR
7/28/06 SP7MAC/dd

100 - 434443 - 6

JAN 6 1970

FBI Secret Files

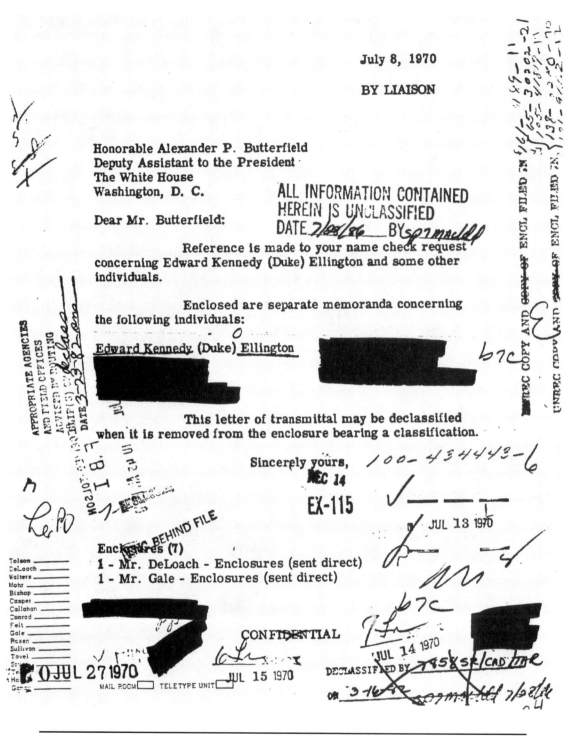

July 8, 1970

BY LIAISON

Honorable Alexander P. Butterfield
Deputy Assistant to the President
The White House
Washington, D. C.

ALL INFORMATION CONTAINED
HEREIN IS UNCLASSIFIED
DATE 7/28/86 BY sp7macldl

Dear Mr. Butterfield:

Reference is made to your name check request concerning Edward Kennedy (Duke) Ellington and some other individuals.

Enclosed are separate memoranda concerning the following individuals:

Edward Kennedy (Duke) Ellington

This letter of transmittal may be declassified when it is removed from the enclosure bearing a classification.

Sincerely yours,

EX-115

Enclosures (7)
1 - Mr. DeLoach - Enclosures (sent direct)
1 - Mr. Gale - Enclosures (sent direct)

CONFIDENTIAL

Tolson
DeLoach
Walters
Mohr
Bishop
Casper
Callahan
Conrad
Felt
Gale
Rosen
Sullivan
Tavel
Soy..
Tel..
Ho..
Gan..

MAIL ROOM   TELETYPE UNIT

Chapter XII

John Lennon: A Beatle In Protest

John Winston Lennon was born on October 9, 1940 in Liverpool, England several months before the battle at Dunkirk and the day of shame when Hitler's army pushed the French and British forces into the English Channel. John's father, Alfred, deserted the family during World War II when John was only three. His mother, Julia Stanley Lennon, was killed in an automobile accident eleven years later when he was fourteen. A maternal aunt who was a gifted musician became his guardian and gave him music lessons. However, his musical blues and jazz inspiration came in the 1950's from the Black recordings and also the Elvis Presley records which were really takeoffs from race (Negro) works.

Lennon attended Liverpool College for two years. It was there that he met Paul McCartney, his co-musical composer and rhythm guitar player. During that period, John was a triple threat in that he played the piano, guitar, harmonica, and also sang.   John and Paul were fifteen years old at the time of their initial meeting.

John, the tall skinny sixteen year old kid from Liverpool, organized their first musical group which he named the Quarryman (after the Quarryman School) in Liverpool. Liverpool is the fourth largest city behind London in the United Kingdom, both cities are important seaports.

In 1958 he changed the name of the original group from the Quarryman to Johnny and the Moondogs, and a short time later they became known as the Silver Beatles and subsequently the Beatles in that order.   The four musicians were emulating the styles of Black American artists Chuck Berry and Little Richard.

The Beatle name was inspired by African-American musical "Bird Groups" such as the Crows, the Flamingos, and the Ravens. Lennon decided to name their band after an insect.   They spelled their name BEATLE with "ea" instead of the traditional spelling with "ee".   This was to reinforce the fact that their musical group was unique.

Shortly after the Beatles: John Lennon, Paul McCartney, George Harrison, Stuart Sutcliffe and Peter Best made some recordings in Germany under the Beatle banner, Brian Epstein, the owner of a Liverpool record shop received an order for a Beatle recording.   Epstein had heard of the Beatles but had never seen them perform; thus, he ventured out to the Cavern Club where they were the house band and heard them jump.   The music was good, but the players were an untidy looking group of guys.   In spite of their appearance, he was fascinated by the band and felt certain that they could become big time if he could fence them in without interfering with their infectuous wild spirit.   He also had to deal with their habit of turning their backs on the audience in Miles Davis style, in addition to eating, smoking talking among themselves and drinking on the bandstand.

When Brian Epstein assumed the management of the group in 1962, he worked on giving them a fresh and presentable image.   He had them adopt an earlier period dress fashion.   The new dress code included a four button black jacket, tight stovepipe pants and ankle boots.   This gave them a look that was different but wore well with their 15th century hair style.

Their new image enabled Epstein to secure better bookings in Hamburg, Germany and increase their number of gigs throughout England.   He arranged for them to make their television debut in London on October 4, 1962 and to make recordings for EMI (Electrical and Musical Industries) whose European label was Parlaphone, and their American Label was, Capitol in Los Angeles, California. Capitol refused to handle their records; therefore, the first USA issues were on Vee Jay Records, a Black owned company located in Chicago on 22nd block on South Michigan, an area known during that period as Record Row.

Their first English single was "Love Me Do" backed by "P. S. I Love You" both songs written by Lennon and McCartney. The personnel on the record were John Lennon, Paul McCartney, George Harrison and Ringo Starr. Ringo's real name was Richard Starkey. The nickname Ringo was tagged on him because of his passion for rings.

The Beatles were unique enough for Miles Davis the great American trumpet player from East St. Louis, Illinois to riff on Beatle tunes because of their harmonic structure and lyrics. Louis Armstrong was very fascinated with their soulful lyrics to "Let It Be, Let It Be" which is unmistakenly Black Gospel. Among Black American musicians, the opinion of the Beatles varied for example Randy Weston said: "I have been told by people that the Beatles have produced some very beautiful things, but when the white man starts singing the blues I just have to cut him out, because I know that all he can do is imitate. "

John Lennon married Cynthia Powell in England on August 23, 1962 and divorced her on November 2, 1968. He married Yoko Ono of Tokyo, Japan. She was his senior by seven years. Their wedding took place in Gibraltar on March 20, 1969, approximately one year after he filed for his divorce from Powell.

The event of the marriage of Yoko and John was a major news story and also anticlimactic in that Yoko and John had been living together as soul mates for some time before the wedding. John and Yoko were an artistic two-some which is evident by the release of their first album collaboration, Two Virgin. The record was issued by Apple Records on November 1, 1968 one day before John's divorce from Cynthia was finalized. The album was the first individual record release by a Beatle and was the foreboding forecast of the ultimate breaking up of the group.

Federal Bureau of Investigation

Freedom of Information/Privacy Acts Section

Subject: <u>John Lennon</u>

b (CIA)

RECEIVED FROM

FEB 0 1972

CIA VIA COURIER

I- 360
3 FEB 1972

SUBJECT: John LENNON;
Allamuchy Tribe (NL)

1. Reference is made to your teletype 003, dated
24 January 1972, Subject: Protest Activity and Civil
Disturbances, reporting that former Beatles singer
John LENNON had contributed a large sum of money to
the "Allamuchy Tribe", headed by Rennie DAVIS. (u)

2. It is requested that you furnish this office
with any additional pertinent information concerning
LENNON's relationship with the "Allamuchy Tribe" and any
indications that DAVIS has received other funds for
his activities from foreign sources. (u)

Please transmit reply via [CACTUS] channel

REC-30 222166

100-469910 - X
16 FEB 10 1972

FEB 14 1972

51 FEB 24 1972

b3
(CIA)

Election Year Strategy
Information Center (EYSIC)

NOTE: 4 Per CIA letter dtd. 1/16/84 and affidavit 12/12/83 SA w/my 1-25-84

Classified "Secret – No Foreign Dissemination/No
Dissemination Abroad" since information being furnished in
CACTUS channel and CIA has requested that all such information
be so classified. CIA has requested details of information we
furnished in daily summary teletype captioned "Protest Activities
and Civil Disturbances," dated 1/24/72, reporting that John
Lennon contributed large sum of money to captioned organization.
CIA also requested any details that other foreign sources have
contributed funds to captioned organization. First source
referred to in LHM is ▓▓▓▓▓ second source is ▓▓▓▓▓

b2
b7D

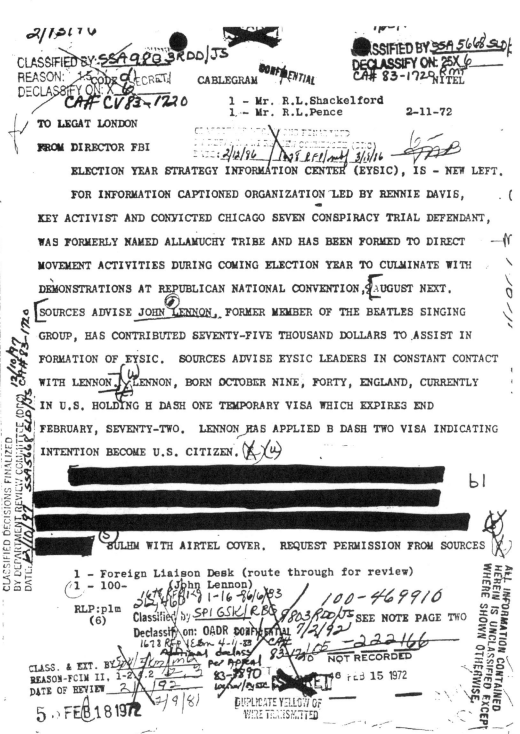

CABLEGRAM

1 - Mr. R.L.Shackelford
1 - Mr. R.L.Pence   2-11-72

TO LEGAT LONDON

FROM DIRECTOR FBI

ELECTION YEAR STRATEGY INFORMATION CENTER (EYSIC), IS - NEW LEFT.

FOR INFORMATION CAPTIONED ORGANIZATION LED BY RENNIE DAVIS,

KEY ACTIVIST AND CONVICTED CHICAGO SEVEN CONSPIRACY TRIAL DEFENDANT,

WAS FORMERLY NAMED ALLAMUCHY TRIBE AND HAS BEEN FORMED TO DIRECT

MOVEMENT ACTIVITIES DURING COMING ELECTION YEAR TO CULMINATE WITH

DEMONSTRATIONS AT REPUBLICAN NATIONAL CONVENTION, AUGUST NEXT.

SOURCES ADVISE JOHN LENNON, FORMER MEMBER OF THE BEATLES SINGING

GROUP, HAS CONTRIBUTED SEVENTY-FIVE THOUSAND DOLLARS TO ASSIST IN

FORMATION OF EYSIC. SOURCES ADVISE EYSIC LEADERS IN CONSTANT CONTACT

WITH LENNON. LENNON, BORN OCTOBER NINE, FORTY, ENGLAND, CURRENTLY

IN U.S. HOLDING H DASH ONE TEMPORARY VISA WHICH EXPIRES END

FEBRUARY, SEVENTY-TWO. LENNON HAS APPLIED B DASH TWO VISA INDICATING

INTENTION BECOME U.S. CITIZEN.

BULHM WITH AIRTEL COVER. REQUEST PERMISSION FROM SOURCES

1 - Foreign Liaison Desk (route through for review)
1 - 100- (John Lennon)
RLP:plm
(6)   SEE NOTE PAGE TWO

NOT RECORDED
46 FEB 15 1972

CLASS. & EXT. BY
REASON-FCIM II, 1-2.2.2
DATE OF REVIEW

5 FEB 18 1972

DUPLICATE YELLOW OF
WIRE TRANSMITTED

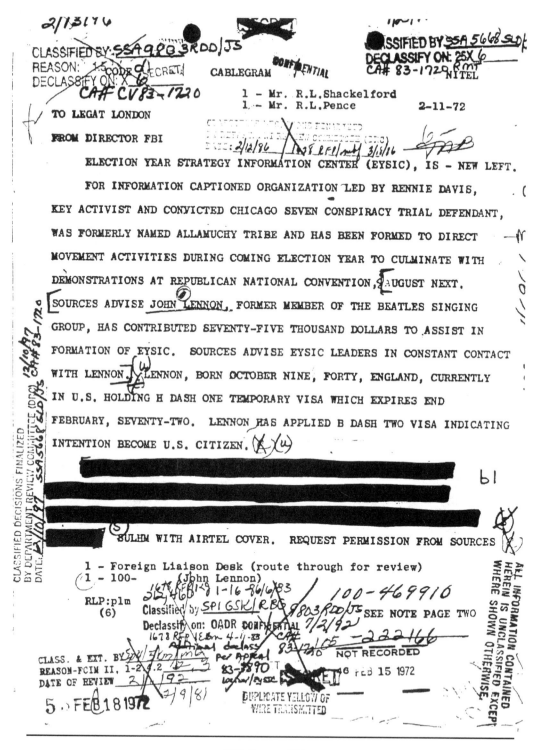

CABLEGRAM

1 - Mr. R.L. Shackelford
1 - Mr. R.L. Pence   2-11-72

TO LEGAT LONDON

FROM DIRECTOR FBI

ELECTION YEAR STRATEGY INFORMATION CENTER (EYSIC), IS - NEW LEFT.

FOR INFORMATION CAPTIONED ORGANIZATION LED BY RENNIE DAVIS,

KEY ACTIVIST AND CONVICTED CHICAGO SEVEN CONSPIRACY TRIAL DEFENDANT,

WAS FORMERLY NAMED ALLAMUCHY TRIBE AND HAS BEEN FORMED TO DIRECT

MOVEMENT ACTIVITIES DURING COMING ELECTION YEAR TO CULMINATE WITH

DEMONSTRATIONS AT REPUBLICAN NATIONAL CONVENTION, AUGUST NEXT.

SOURCES ADVISE JOHN LENNON, FORMER MEMBER OF THE BEATLES SINGING

GROUP, HAS CONTRIBUTED SEVENTY-FIVE THOUSAND DOLLARS TO ASSIST IN

FORMATION OF EYSIC. SOURCES ADVISE EYSIC LEADERS IN CONSTANT CONTACT

WITH LENNON. LENNON, BORN OCTOBER NINE, FORTY, ENGLAND, CURRENTLY

IN U.S. HOLDING H DASH ONE TEMPORARY VISA WHICH EXPIRES END

FEBRUARY, SEVENTY-TWO. LENNON HAS APPLIED B DASH TWO VISA INDICATING

INTENTION BECOME U.S. CITIZEN.

BULHM WITH AIRTEL COVER. REQUEST PERMISSION FROM SOURCES

1 - Foreign Liaison Desk (route through for review)
1 - 100-   (John Lennon)
RLP:plm
(6)   Classified by
                 Declassify on: OADR   SEE NOTE PAGE TWO

CLASS. & EXT. BY
REASON-FCIM II, 1-2 4.2
DATE OF REVIEW

NOT RECORDED
46 FEB 15 1972

DUPLICATE YELLOW OF
WIRE TRANSMITTED

FEDERAL BUREAU OF INVESTIGATION
COMMUNICATIONS SECTION

MAR 16 1972

TELETYPE

ALL INFORMATION CONTAINED
HEREIN IS UNCLASSIFIED
DATE 2/9/81 BY SP4 3km/mc

NR 028 NY CODE

440 PM URGENT 3-16-72 BGW

TO DIRECTOR

ATTN: DID

FROM NEW YORK (100-175319) 2P

Security Matter
JOHN WINSTON LENNON; SM-NEW LEFT   OO:NY

ON MARCH SIXTEENTH INSTANT MR. VINCENT SCHIANO,
Immigration and Naturalization Service, New York City
CHIEF TRIAL ATTORNEY, INS, NYC, ADVISE THAT JOHN LENNON AND

HIS WIFE YOKO ONO APPEARED AT INS, NYC THIS DATE FOR

DEPORTATION PROCEEDINGS. BOTH INDIVIDUALS THRU THEIR ATTORNEY

WON DELAY OF HEARINGS. LENNON REQUESTED DELAY WHILE HE

ATTEMPTED TO FIGHT A NARCOTOCS CONVICTION IN ENGLAND. YOKO ONO

REQUESTED DELAY ON BASIS OF CHILD CUSTODY CASE IN WHICH SHE

IS INVOLVED.   ST-111   REC-36   MCT-1

100 - 469910 - 2

16 MAR 20 1972

MR. SCHIANO ADVISED THAT NEW HEARINGS WOULD BE

HELD ON APRIL EIGHTEEN NEXT. IF LENNON WINS OVERTHROW OF

BRITISH NARCOTIC CONVICTION, INS WILL RECONSIDER THEIR ATTEMPTS

END PAGE ONE

MAY 18 1972

MR. ROSEN FOR THE DIRECTOR

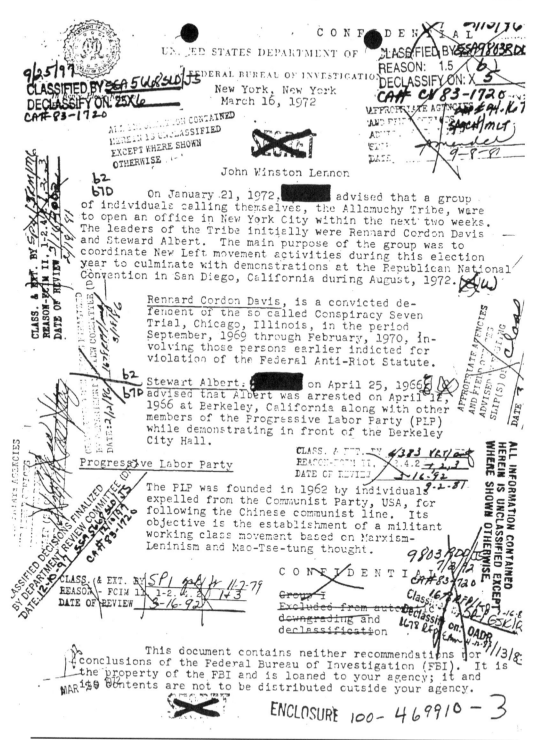

CONFIDENTIAL

UNITED STATES DEPARTMENT OF
FEDERAL BUREAU OF INVESTIGATION
New York, New York
March 16, 1972

ALL INFORMATION CONTAINED
HEREIN IS UNCLASSIFIED
EXCEPT WHERE SHOWN
OTHERWISE

John Winston Lennon

On January 21, 1972, ███████ advised that a group
of individuals calling themselves, the Allamuchy Tribe, were
to open an office in New York City within the next two weeks.
The leaders of the Tribe initially were Rennard Cordon Davis
and Steward Albert. The main purpose of the group was to
coordinate New Left movement activities during this election
year to culminate with demonstrations at the Republican National
Convention in San Diego, California during August, 1972.

Rennard Cordon Davis, is a convicted defendant of the so called Conspiracy Seven
Trial, Chicago, Illinois, in the period
September, 1969 through February, 1970, involving those persons earlier indicted for
violation of the Federal Anti-Riot Statute.

Stewart Albert, ███████ on April 25, 1966,
advised that Albert was arrested on April 12,
1966 at Berkeley, California along with other
members of the Progressive Labor Party (PLP)
while demonstrating in front of the Berkeley
City Hall.

Progressive Labor Party

The PLP was founded in 1962 by individuals
expelled from the Communist Party, USA, for
following the Chinese communist line. Its
objective is the establishment of a militant
working class movement based on Marxism-
Leninism and Mao-Tse-tung thought.

CONFIDENTIAL

Group I
Excluded from automatic
downgrading and
declassification

This document contains neither recommendations nor
conclusions of the Federal Bureau of Investigation (FBI). It is
the property of the FBI and is loaned to your agency; it and
its contents are not to be distributed outside your agency.

ENCLOSURE 100- 469910 - 3

C O N F I D E N T I A L

John Winston Lennon

b2
b7D
On February 15, 1972, ▮▮▮▮▮▮ advised that John Lennon on November 28, 1969, pled guilty in Marylebone Magistrates Court, London, England to possession of dangerous drugs (Cannabis). He was fined L150 and ordered to pay L21 in court cost.

b7C
John Winston Lennon. On February 2, 1972, ▮▮▮▮▮▮▮▮▮ Immigration Officer, Immigration and Naturalization Service, (INS) New York City advised that Lennon, Alien Registration Number A-17597321, first arrived in New York City on August 11, 1968 under a B-2 visitors visa. He subsequently departed the United States, and during his 1971 re-entry was granted another B-2 visa. His latest visa was due to expire on February 29, 1972.

b7C
Yoko Ono. ▮▮▮▮▮ advised that Ono, Alien Registration Number A-19489154 was born on February 18, 1933 in Japan. She entered the United States on August 13, 1971 along with Lennon after being granted a B-2 visa.

INS has a current address of the Saint Regis Hotel, 150 Bank Street, New York City for both Lennon and his wife.

During Lennon and his wife's current stay in the United States they made a public appearance along with Jerry Rubin, on the Mike Douglas Television Show which was aired on February 22, 1972 on Channel II, Columbia Broadcasting System, in New York City.

b2
b7D
During February, 1972, ▮▮▮▮▮ advised that Rennard Davis, Stewart Albert, Jerry Rubin and John Lennon are heavy users of narcotics. Source advised that Rubin and Davis are apparently at odds with Lennon due to his excessive use of drugs, which are referred to in the Vernacular as "Downers".

C O N F I D E N T I A L

- 3 -

Airtel

~~CONFIDENTIAL~~   4/10/72

To: SAC, New York (100-175319) (Enclosures - 2)

From: Director, FBI (100-469910)   1 - Mr. Horner
                                                    1 - Mr. Preusse
JOHN WINSTON LENNON   1 - Mr. Shackelford
SM - NEW LEFT   1 - Mr. Pence

          ReNYtel 3/16/72.

          Enclosed for information of New York are two copies of
Alexandria airtel dated 3/31/72 captioned "White Panther Party,
IS - WPP; CALREP; MIDEM," which contains information from Alexandria
source relating to current activities of subject.

          It appears from referenced New York teletype that subject
and wife might be preparing for lengthy delaying tactics to avert
their deportation in the near future. In the interim, very real
possibility exists that subject, as indicated in enclosed airtel,
might engage in activities in U.S. leading toward disruption of
Republican National Convention (RNC), San Diego, 8/72. For this
reason New York promptly initiate discreet efforts to locate subject
and remain aware of his activities and movements. Handle inquiries
only through established sources and discreet pretext inquiries.
Careful attention should be given to reports that subject is heavy
narcotics user and any information developed in this regard should be
furnished to narcotics authorities and immediately furnished to
Bureau in form suitable for dissemination.

1 - Alexandria
1 - San Diego   EX-105   REC-33

RLP:mcm (9)

CLASS. & EXT. BY
REASON-FCM II, 1-2 4.2
DATE OF REVIEW

100 - 469910 - 4

MAILED 21   SEE NOTE PAGE TWO   APR 10 1972
APR 7 - 1972

ALL INFORMATION CONTAINED
HEREIN IS UNCLASSIFIED
DATE 23/9/81 BY

Tolson
Felt
Campbell
Rosen
Mohr
Bishop
Miller. E.S.
Callahan
Casper
Conrad
Dalbey
Cleveland
Ponder
Bates
Walkart
Walters
Soyars
Tele
Holmes
Gandy

5 APR 12 1972

MAIL ROOM   TELETYPE UNIT

ALL INFORMATION CONTAINED
HEREIN IS UNCLASSIFIED EXCEPT
WHERE SHOWN OTHERWISE.

Airtel to New York
RE: John Winston Lennon
100-469910

In view of subject's avowed intention to engage in disruptive activities surrounding RNC, New York Office will be responsible for closely following his activities until time of actual deportation. Afford this matter close supervision and keep Bureau fully advised by most expeditious means warranted.

NOTE:

John Lennon, former member of Beatles singing group, is allegedly in U.S. to assist in organizing disruption of RNC. Due to narcotics conviction in England, he is being deported along with wife Yoko Ono. They appeared at Immigration and Naturalization Service, New York, 3/16/72, for deportation proceedings but won delay until 4/18/72 because subject fighting narcotics conviction and wife fighting custody child case in U.S. Strong possibility looms that subject will not be deported any time soon and will probably be in U.S. at least until RNC. Information developed by Alexandria source that subject continues to plan activities directed toward RNC and will soon initiate series of "rock concerts" to develop financial support with first concert to be held Ann Arbor, Michigan, in near future. New York Office covering subject's temporary residence and being instructed to intensify discreet investigation of subject to determine activities vis a vis RNC.

- 2 -

CONFIDENTIAL

The Acting Attorney General   CONFIDENTIAL

Lennon has been appointed to the National Commission on
Marijuana and Drug Abuse. A fourth confidential source in a
position to furnish reliable information advised that Lennon
has been offered a teaching position at New York University
for the Summer of 1972.

        This information is also being furnished to the
Honorable H. R. Haldeman, Assistant to the President, at The
White House. Pertinent information concerning Lennon is being
furnished to the Department of State and INS on a regular
basis.

1 - The Deputy Attorney General

1 - Assistant Attorney General
    Internal Security Division

NOTE:

        Classified "Confidential" since information is
contained from ▮▮▮▮▮▮▮▮▮▮▮▮▮▮▮▮▮▮▮▮▮
▮▮▮▮▮ first confidential source is ▮▮▮▮▮▮▮▮ second
confidential source is ▮▮▮▮▮▮▮ third confidential source is
pretext inquiry by WFO with ▮▮▮▮▮▮▮▮
▮▮▮▮▮▮▮, National Commission on Marijuana and Drug Abuse,
Washington, D. C.; and fourth confidential source is ▮▮▮▮
▮▮▮▮▮▮▮▮▮, New York University, New York,
New York.

        See memorandum R. L. Shackelford to Mr. E. S. Miller,
4/21/72, captioned as above, prepared by RLP:plm.

CONFIDENTIAL

- 2 -

CONFIDENTIAL

UNITED STATES GOVERNMENT

Memorandum

1 - Mr. A. Rosen
1 - Mr. T. E. Bishop

TO : Mr. E. S. Miller   DATE: 4-21-72

FROM : R. L. Shackelford

1 - Mr. E. S. Miller
1 - Mr. T. J. Smith (Horner)
1 - Mr. R. L. Shackelford
1 - Mr. R. L. Pence

SUBJECT: JOHN WINSTON LENNON
SECURITY MATTER - NEW LEFT

PURPOSE:

To advise of recent tactics of subject, New Left sympathizer already in U.S. illegally, to avoid deportation from the U.S.

BACKGROUND:

Lennon is former member of Beatles singing group in England who, despite clear ineligibility for U.S. visa due to conviction in London in 1968 for possession of dangerous drugs (marijuana), was allowed to re-enter U.S. during 1971 on visitors visa due to unexplained intervention by State Department with Immigration and Naturalization Service (INS). Visas of Lennon and wife Yoko Ono expired 2-29-72 and since that time INS has been attempting to deport the Lennons.

(C)He has come to our attention specifically during 2-72 when information developed he had donated $75,000 to organization named Election Year Strategy Information Center, organized to disrupt Republican National Convention.

On 3-1-72 INS notified Lennons to be out of U.S. by 3-15-72. On 3-16-72 Lennons appeared at INS, New York City, for deportation proceedings and, through their attorney, won delay of hearings based on subject's attempt to fight narcotics conviction in England and wife's attempt to regain custody of child who is now living in U.S. On 4-18-72 Lennons again appeared at INS, New York City, during which appearance attorney

100-469910
Enclosures sent 4-25-72 ST-114
RLP:plm
(7)

REC-70 100-469910-10
MAY 9 1972

CONTINUED - OVER

Memorandum to Mr. E. S. Miller
RE: John Winston Lennon
100-469910

commented that subject felt he was being deported due to his
outspoken remarks regarding U.S. policy in Southeast Asia.
Attorney requested delay so character witnesses could be
introduced to testify on behalf of subject. Attorney also
read into court record fact subject had been appointed to the
President's Council for Drug Abuse, correct name National
Commission on Marijuana and Drug Abuse (NCMDA), and to the
faculty of New York University, New York City. As a result of
these revelations, INS set new hearing date for 5-2-72, and
Lennons left INS to be met by throng of supporters and news
media reporters who listened to subject's press release
implying he was being deported due to his political ideas and
policy of the U.S. Government to deport aliens who speak out
against the Administration.

OBSERVATIONS:

        Irony of subject being appointed to President's Council
for Drug Abuse, if true, is overwhelming since subject is currently
reported heavy user of narcotics and frequently avoided by even
Rennie Davis and Jerry Rubin, convicted Chicago Seven Conspiracy
trial defendants, due to his excessive use of narcotics. New York
City Police Department currently attempting to develop enough
information to arrest both Lennons for narcotics use. WFO has
contacted NCMDA under pretext and determined no information
available indicating subject has been appointed to NCMDA.
New York Office has confirmed that Lennon has been offered
teaching position at New York University for Summer of 1972.
In view of successful delaying tactics to date, there exists real
possibility that subject will not be deported from U.S. in near
future and possibly not prior to Republican National Convention.
Subject's activities being closely followed and any information
developed indicating violation of Federal laws will be immediately
furnished to pertinent agencies in effort to neutralize any
disruptive activities of subject. Information developed to date
has been furnished as received to INS and State Department.
Information has also been furnished Internal Security Division
of the Department.

ACTION:
        Attached for approval are letters to Honorable H. R.
Haldeman at The White House and Acting Attorney General with copies
to the Deputy   Attorney General and Assistant Attorney
General, Internal Security Division, containing information
concerning Lennon.

John Winston Lennon

John Winston Lennon, a former member of the Beatles Rock Music Group is presently the subject of deportation hearing by the Immigration and Naturalization Service.

Lennon is described as follows:

Name: John Winston Lennon
Race: White
Date of Birth: October 9, 1940
Place of Birth: Liverpool, England
Hair: Brown to Blond
Weight: 160 pounds
Height: Approximately six feet
Build: Slender
Nationality: English
United States Residence: 105 Bank Street New York City
Arrest Record: 1968 Narcotics Arrest, in England for Possession of Dangerous Drugs (Cannabis) Pled Guilty

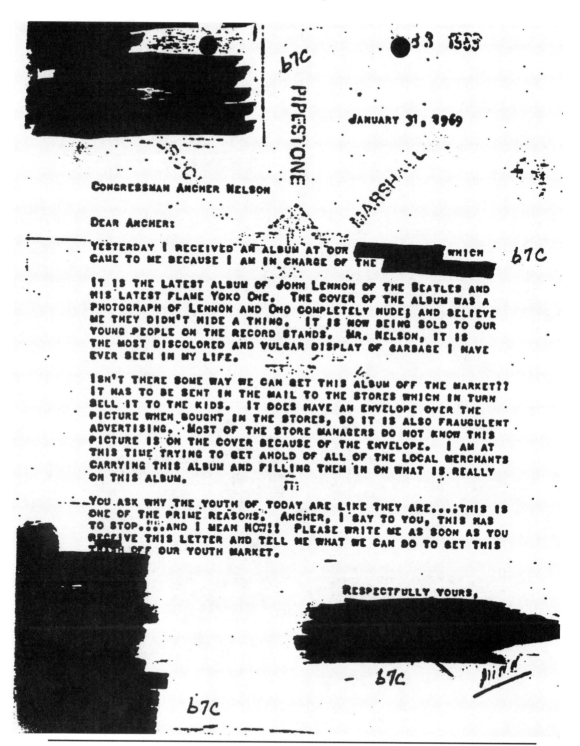

PIPESTONE

33 1969

JANUARY 31, 1969

MARSHALL

CONGRESSMAN ANCHER NELSON

DEAR ANCHER:

YESTERDAY I RECEIVED AN ALBUM AT OUR ▮▮▮▮▮ WHICH CAME TO ME BECAUSE I AM IN CHARGE OF THE ▮▮▮▮▮

IT IS THE LATEST ALBUM OF JOHN LENNON OF THE BEATLES AND HIS LATEST FLAME YOKO ONE. THE COVER OF THE ALBUM WAS A PHOTOGRAPH OF LENNON AND ONO COMPLETELY NUDE; AND BELIEVE ME THEY DIDN'T HIDE A THING. IT IS NOW BEING SOLD TO OUR YOUNG PEOPLE ON THE RECORD STANDS. MR. NELSON, IT IS THE MOST DISCOLORED AND VULGAR DISPLAY OF GARBAGE I HAVE EVER SEEN IN MY LIFE.

ISN'T THERE SOME WAY WE CAN GET THIS ALBUM OFF THE MARKET?? IT HAS TO BE SENT IN THE MAIL TO THE STORES WHICH IN TURN SELL IT TO THE KIDS. IT DOES HAVE AN ENVELOPE OVER THE PICTURE WHEN BOUGHT IN THE STORES, SO IT IS ALSO FRAUGULENT ADVERTISING. MOST OF THE STORE MANAGERS DO NOT KNOW THIS PICTURE IS ON THE COVER BECAUSE OF THE ENVELOPE. I AM AT THIS TIME TRYING TO GET AHOLD OF ALL OF THE LOCAL MERCHANTS CARRYING THIS ALBUM AND FILLING THEM IN ON WHAT IS REALLY ON THIS ALBUM.

YOU ASK WHY THE YOUTH OF TODAY ARE LIKE THEY ARE....THIS IS ONE OF THE PRIME REASONS. ANCHER, I SAY TO YOU, THIS HAS TO STOP.....AND I MEAN NOW!! PLEASE WRITE ME AS SOON AS YOU RECEIVE THIS LETTER AND TELL ME WHAT WE CAN DO TO GET THIS TRASH OFF OUR YOUTH MARKET.

RESPECTFULLY YOURS,

145_0 -1766

March 10, 1969

1 - Mr. McKinnon

Honorable Ancher Nelsen
House of Representatives
Washington, D. C. 20515

My dear Congressman:

I have received your communication dated March 5, 1969, along with its enclosure, a letter to you dated January 31, 1969, from ▮▮▮▮▮▮▮▮▮▮ b7C

A representative of the Department of Justice has advised that he is familiar with the photograph contained on the cover of an album by John Lennon. He stated that no violation with regard to obscenity exists concerning this photograph as it does not meet the criteria of obscenity from a legal standpoint.

Your bringing this to my attention is indeed appreciated. I am returning ▮▮▮▮▮▮▮▮ letter to you as requested.

b7C

Sincerely yours,

J. Edgar Hoover

MAILED 3
MAR 10 1969
COMM-FBI

Enclosure

1 - SAC, Minneapolis - Enclosure

NOTE TO SAC, MINNEAPOLIS:

b7C

Enclosed is a copy of a letter dated 1-31-69, from ▮▮▮▮▮ ▮▮▮▮to Congressman Ancher Nelsen for your information.

CRM:erg
(5)

SEE NOTE PAGE TWO

Tolson
DeLoach
Mohr
Bishop
Casper
Callahan
Conrad
Felt
Gale
Rosen
Sullivan
Tavel
Trotter
Tele. Room
Holmes
Gandy

5 MAR 17 1969   TELETYPE UNIT ☐

ALL INFORMATION CONTAINED
HEREIN IS UNCLASSIFIED
DATE 4-8-83

GC

John & Yoko Wait & Wait

A decision in the deportation proceedings against former Beatle John Lennon and his Japanese-born wife, Yoko Ono may not be reached until September, the U.S. Immigration and Naturalization Service said yesterday.

The government and the defense were to have submitted briefs by July 1, but they are still waiting for a transcript of the May 17 hearing.

Special inquiry officer Ira Fieldsteel, who is hearing the case, will be away in August, and so a decision is not expected until September.

The government wants to deny Lennon permanent residence here because of a 1968 marijuana conviction in England.

PacTel Appeals Refund

Pacific Telephone & Telegraph asked the U.S. Supreme Court yesterday to stop a $145 million refund to its customers which was ordered by the California Supreme Court Tuesday. The California court denied Pacific Tel's $143 million rate increase.

P. BL 30

7/14/72

DAILY NEWS

NEW YORK, N.Y.

100-175319 -
cc cc 46

ALL INFORMATION CONTAINED
HEREIN IS UNCLASSIFIED
DATE 4.9.82 BY
9269/3bd/alm/ng

263

Chapter XIII

Billie Holiday: The Motherless Child

There was never anyone in Billie Holiday's (Eleanora Fagan) life who pointed out to her that you don't cross the street against a red stoplight. Sadie Fagan, a 13 year old female, who gave birth to Billie was a child and so was Clarence Holiday the impregnator. It has been said that Billie Holiday was born in Baltimore, Maryland on April 17, 1915; however, no one has produced a birth certificate or any other document that would validate that statement.

Since education was not high on the agenda for the blossoming baby Holiday, she scrubbed floors, ran errands, and turned tricks at a neighborhood whorehouse. The only thing positive that came out of her brothel experience was the opportunity to lounge in the front parlor and listen to records over and over on the Victrola by her two idols, Louis "Dipper Mouth Blues" Armstrong and the great blues singer Bessie "Give Me A Pigfoot And A Bottle of Beer" Smith when she was not occupied turning tricks for four bits. Billie was an original baby doll. In every song she later sang, she paid an unannounced but obvious tribute to Armstrong and Smith.

Following the act of being brutally raped at age ten, by a "white" john, she was sent to a Catholic institution by the police and charged with "seducing" the rapist. The reformatory was run by Catholic nuns. The nuns never went outside of the four walls, but they managed to scare the hell out of the physically attractive Billie. The first night she was incarcerated they locked her up in a room with a dead girl who had been laid out on a long white table.

At age thirteen Billie Holiday, was jailed again for being a professional prostitute without a pimp. On the day that she was sprung from jail by her mother, she had a New York City frame of mind because her mother had sent her a ticket to come to Long Branch, New York and live with her. However, when her maternal grandfather put her on the train, she immediately ripped the big yellow tag that read Long Branch, New York from her chest because she had made up her mind that she was going to see what New York City's Harlem Renaissance was all about.

The year that Billie made her maiden trip to New York City must have been 1928 because Charles "Lucky Lindy" Lindbergh had made that solo nonstop flight across the Atlantic in "The Spirit of St. Louis" from Roosevelt Field in Long Island, New York to Paris, France the previous year.

When Billie and her mother finally got hooked up in Harlem, the mother arranged to rent her daughter a room in a fancy furnished apartment on 141st Street off of Seventh Avenue. The landlady was Florence Williams, one of the biggest madams in Harlem. Billie's mother asked Florence to take good care of her only child. Underneath her teenage facade Billie was a cocky hip chick from Baltimore's Pennsylvania Avenue and she felt streetwise enough to take care of Florence.

Billie Holiday found working on her back in the world's oldest profession boring. She wanted to dance like Bill "Bojangles" Robinson and Florence "Shuffle Along" Mills. She walked up and down Seventh Avenue looking for a gig but found no takers until she walked into Jerry Preston's Log Cabin and got his attention with her plea for a job as a dancer. Jerry sent her to the back of the room where the piano player was going over some numbers and shouted, "Piano player play something and let me see what she can do". She only knew two steps and they were the time step and the crossover. After watching her for a few minutes Jerry growled: "Young lady you are wasting my time". She continued pleading to Jerry for a trial. The piano player interrupted her plea and asked her if she could sing. She replied: "Yes! I have been singing all my life".

Billie asked the musician to play "Traveling All Alone". Her unique style of singing captured the mood that she was in that afternoon. When she finished singing, two choruses of that song everybody in the joint was openly weeping in their beer or wiping teardrops from their wet eyes. She netted $58. 00 in tips that day. During the 1930's Depression, $58. 00 was three weeks salary for a common laborer.

The rest of her story is history starting with her being discovered by a rich white boy named John Hammond who just happened to drop in at Monette Moore's place on 133rd and Seventh Avenue to hear Monette, a fine blues singer. That night, young Billie Holiday was substituting because Monette had gotten a part in a Broadway Show with the deft and debonair Clifton Webb. Webb later starred with Gene Tierney in the 1944 movie Laura. Billie's accompanist that night was Dot Hill, and among the first songs that Hammond heard her sing was "Wouldja For A Big Red Apple".

Billie was in luck that night because beside being rich Hammond was a member of the Commodore Vanderbilt family in addition to being a cheerleader for Black artists. He had become the wind under the wings of such stars as Count Basie, Lionel Hampton, Teddy Wilson and his brother-in-law Benny Goodman, the clarinet playing band leader, and many others.

In addition to being an impresario Hammond was a newspaper critic, talent scout and record producer. In the fall of 1933, Hammond arranged a record session with Columbia Records for Billie and Benny Goodman who assembled a small group of swinging musicians for the date. The titles that they recorded were "Riffin the Scotch" and "Your Mother's Son-In-Law" That was Billie's first recording session and also the first tune that Benny had recorded with a Negro musician, and that was Shirley Clay one of Don "Chant Of The Weed" Redman's trumpet players.

As Billie Holiday moved up the ladder in the jazz world, it was observed by some of the writer's older friends such as Zinky Cohn, the pianist for Ethel Waters, violinist Eddie South and Jimmie Noone that her beauty surpassed her disposition, which was like a revolving door. You never knew whether you were going to get the sometimes I am happy Billie or the Billie that was in a deep blue funk. Smoking marijuana, opium and drinking booze did not help her case.

Note: The difference between the way the F. B. I. profiled Billie Holiday on page 268 and Tallulah Bankhead on page 273.

Federal Bureau of Investigation

Freedom of Information/Privacy Acts Section

Subject: <u>Billie Holiday</u>

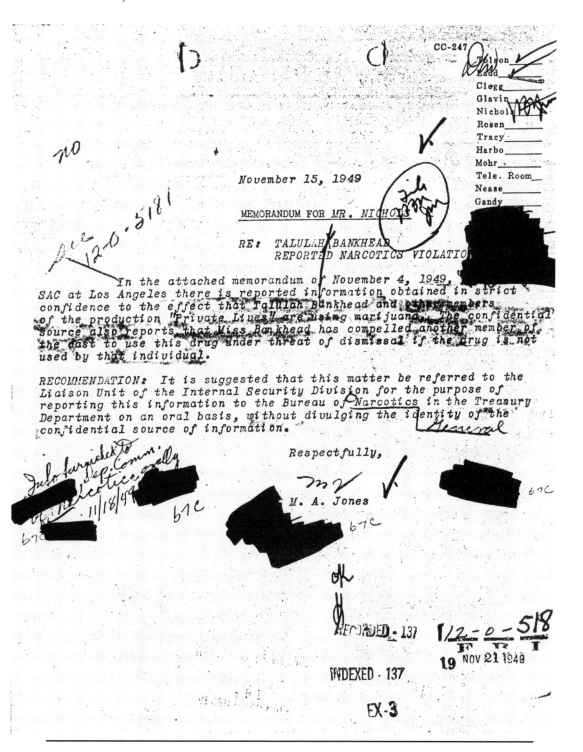

CC-247

Tolson ___
Ladd ___
Clegg ___
Glavin ___
Nichols ___
Rosen ___
Tracy ___
Harbo ___
Mohr ___
Tele. Room ___
Nease ___
Gandy ___

November 15, 1949

MEMORANDUM FOR MR. NICHOLS

RE: TALULAH BANKHEAD
REPORTED NARCOTICS VIOLATION

In the attached memorandum of November 4, 1949,
SAC at Los Angeles there is reported information obtained in strict
confidence to the effect that Talulah Bankhead and other members
of the production "Private Lives" are using marijuana. The confidential
source also reports that Miss Bankhead has compelled another member of
the cast to use this drug under threat of dismissal if the drug is not
used by that individual.

RECOMMENDATION: It is suggested that this matter be referred to the
Liaison Unit of the Internal Security Division for the purpose of
reporting this information to the Bureau of Narcotics in the Treasury
Department on an oral basis, without divulging the identity of the
confidential source of information.

Respectfully,

M. A. Jones

RECORDED - 137

INDEXED - 137

112-0-518
F B I
19 NOV 21 1949

EX-3

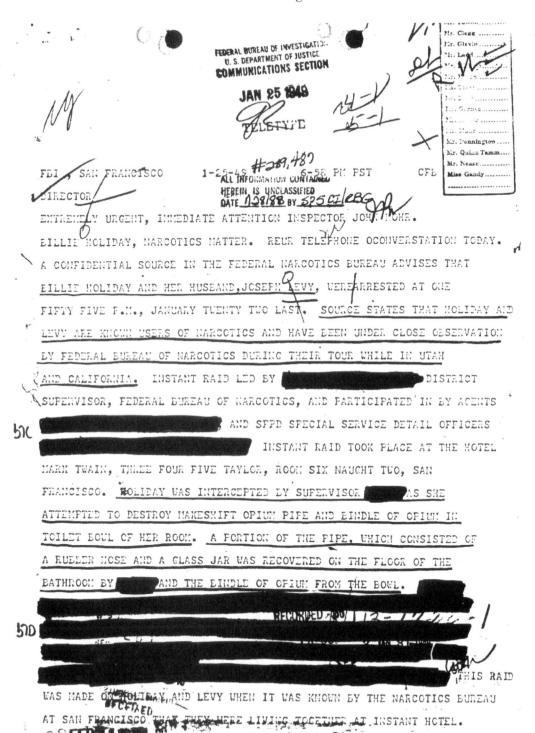

FEDERAL BUREAU OF INVESTIGATION
U. S. DEPARTMENT OF JUSTICE
COMMUNICATIONS SECTION

JAN 25 1948

TELETYPE

FBI SAN FRANCISCO   1-25-48 #289,489   6-58 PM PST   CFL

DIRECTOR

ALL INFORMATION CONTAINED
HEREIN IS UNCLASSIFIED
DATE 1/28/88 BY SPS CI/CBG

EXTREMELY URGENT, IMMEDIATE ATTENTION INSPECTOR JOHN MOHR.

BILLIE HOLIDAY, NARCOTICS MATTER. REUR TELEPHONE OCONVERSATION TODAY.

A CONFIDENTIAL SOURCE IN THE FEDERAL NARCOTICS BUREAU ADVISES THAT

BILLIE HOLIDAY AND HER HUSBAND, JOSEPH LEVY, WERE ARRESTED AT ONE

FIFTY FIVE P.M., JANUARY TWENTY TWO LAST. SOURCE STATES THAT HOLIDAY AND

LEVY ARE KNOWN USERS OF NARCOTICS AND HAVE BEEN UNDER CLOSE OBSERVATION

BY FEDERAL BUREAU OF NARCOTICS DURING THEIR TOUR WHILE IN UTAH

AND CALIFORNIA. INSTANT RAID LED BY ▓▓▓▓▓▓▓ DISTRICT

SUPERVISOR, FEDERAL BUREAU OF NARCOTICS, AND PARTICIPATED IN BY AGENTS

▓▓▓▓▓▓▓ AND SFPD SPECIAL SERVICE DETAIL OFFICERS

▓▓▓▓▓▓▓ INSTANT RAID TOOK PLACE AT THE HOTEL

MARK TWAIN, THREE FOUR FIVE TAYLOR, ROOM SIX NAUGHT TWO, SAN

FRANCISCO. HOLIDAY WAS INTERCEPTED BY SUPERVISOR ▓▓▓ AS SHE

ATTEMPTED TO DESTROY MAKESHIFT OPIUM PIPE AND BINDLE OF OPIUM IN

TOILET BOWL OF HER ROOM. A PORTION OF THE PIPE, WHICH CONSISTED OF

A RUBBER HOSE AND A GLASS JAR WAS RECOVERED ON THE FLOOR OF THE

BATHROOM BY ▓▓▓ AND THE BINDLE OF OPIUM FROM THE BOWL.

RECORDED

THIS RAID

WAS MADE ON HOLIDAY AND LEVY WHEN IT WAS KNOWN BY THE NARCOTICS BUREAU

AT SAN FRANCISCO THAT THEY WERE LIVING TOGETHER AT INSTANT HOTEL.

PAGE TWO

OF ANY NARCOTICS IN THEIR POSSESSION BUT PRESUMED THAT SINCE
THEY WERE TOGETHER THEY PROBABLY POSSESSED SOME NARCOTICS,
AND ACCORDINGLY THEY REQUESTED THE ASSISTANCE OF THE SAN FRANCISCO
POLICE DEPARTMENT IN CONDUCTING THIS RAID BECAUSE OF MORE LIBERAL
STATE LAWS COVERING SEARCHES AND SEIZURES. THE SOURCE STATES THAT
BECAUSE OF THE IMPORTANCE OF HOLIDAY IT HAS BEEN THE POLICY OF HIS
BUREAU TO DISCREDIT INDIVIDUALS OF THIS CALIBER USING NARCOTICS.
BECAUSE OF THEIR NOTORIETY IT OFFERED EXCUSES TO MINOR USERS. SOURCE
STATES THAT RAID WAS A LEGITIMATE RAID BASED ON ABOVE AND THAT CLAIMED
QUOTE FRAME UP UNQUOTE WAS AS MUCH FOR PUBLICITY PURPOSES AS IT
WAS TO AVERT THE SUSPICION OF GUILT FROM HER INASMUCH AS SHE WAS
CAUGHT IN POSSESSION OF THE MAKESHIFT PIPE. ▮▮▮▮▮▮▮▮▮▮, HEAD
OF SPECIAL SERVICES DETAIL, TOGETHER WITH OFFICER ▮▮▮▮▮▮▮▮▮▮
WERE CONTACTED AND THEY ADVISED SUBSTANTIALLY THE SAME INFORMATION
AS SET FORTH ABOVE. HOLIDAY IS CHARGED WITH POSSESSION OF OPIUM AND
IS BEING TRIED IN MUNICIPAL COURT. HER HEARING IS SET FOR FEBRUARY
TWO NEXT. NO FURTHER ACTION BEING TAKEN.

b7C

KIMBALL

END AND ACK PLS
1015PM OK FBI WA LS

cc Rosen

574

FEDERAL BUREAU OF INVESTIGATION
U. S. DEPARTMENT OF JUSTICE
COMMUNICATIONS SECTION

JAN 27 1949

TELEMETER

| Mr. Tolson |
| Mr. Clegg |
| Mr. Glavin |
| Mr. Ladd |
| Mr. Nich |
| Mr. Rosen |
| Mr. Tracy |
| Mr. Egan |
| Mr. Gurney |
| ...ington |
| Mr. Q....Tamm |
| Mr. Nease |
| Miss Gandy | RN |

WASHINGTON FROM SFRAN S2   1-27-49   12-33 PM

DIRECTOR   ROUTINE   -REPEAT-

ATTENTION - INSPECTOR JOHN MOHR

BILLIE HOLIDAY, NARCOTICS MATTER. REMYTEL JAN. TWENTY FIVE LAST.

A SQUIB APPEARING IN COLUMN OF HERB CAEN, LOCAL GOSSIP COLUMNIST

OF SAN FRANCISCO CHRONICLE, ISSUE OF JAN. TWENTY SEVEN READS

"CHANTOOSE BILLIE HOLIDAY, OUT ON BAIL AFTER BEING NABBED ON A

NARCOTICS CHARGE SAT., HAD A PACKED HOUSE AS USUAL AT CAFE

SOCIETY UPTOWN TUES. NIGHT -- BUT THE CUSTOMER WHO MUST-VE IN-

TRIGUED HER MOST WAS A GENT WHO SAT AT RINGSIDE THROUGH TWO

SHOWS AND EVEN MADE A COUPLE OF REQUESTS. ~~GO~~ COL. GEORGE

H. ~~WHITE~~ WHITE, BOSS OF THE FEDERAL NARCOTICS BUREAU HERE.."

                                                                KIMBALL

SE 28

RECORDED - 80   1/2 - 172... - 2

62 FEB 11 1949

EX-76

Hotel Elysee
60 East 54th Street
New York, N. Y.
February 9, 1949

J. Edgar Hoover
Federal Bureau of Investigation
Washington, D. C.

Dear Mr. Hoover:

I am ashamed of my unpardonable delay
in writing to thank you a thousand times for the kindness,
consideration and courtesy, in fact all the nicest
adjectives in the book, for the trouble you took re
our telephone conversation in connection with Billie Holiday.

I tremble when I think of my audacity
in approaching you at all with so little to recommend me
except the esteem, admiration and high regard my father
held for you.   I would never have dared to ask him or you
a favor for myself but knowing your true humanitarian spirit
it seemed quite natural at the time to go to the top man.
As my Negro mammy used to say - "When you pray you pray to
God don't you?".

I have met Billie Holiday but twice in
my life but admire her immensely as an artist and feel
the most profound compassion for her knowing as I do the
unfortunate circumstances of her background.   Although my
intention is not to condone her weaknesses I certainly
understand the eccentricities of her behaviour because she
is essentially a child at heart whose troubles have made her
psychologically unable to cope with the world in which she
finds herself.   Her vital need is more medical than the
confinement of four walls.

RECORDED - 92   12-17 ---- 3

However guilty she may be, whatever penalty
she may be required to pay for her frailties, poor thing,
you I know did everything within the law to lighten her
burden.   Bless you for this.

Kindest regards,

Tallulah Bankhead

Tallulah Bankhead

ack
2/11/49

February 11, 1949

12-1720-3

Miss Tallulah Bankhead
Hotel Elysee
60 East 54th Street
New York, New York

Dear Tallulah:

I have received your kind letter of February 9 and was very glad indeed to hear from you. Your kind comments are greatly appreciated, and I trust that you will not hesitate to call on me at any time you think I might be of assistance to you.

Hoping to see you in the not too distant future and with kindest regards,

Sincerely,

J. Edgar Hoover

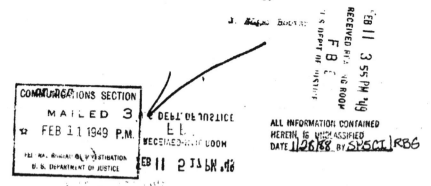

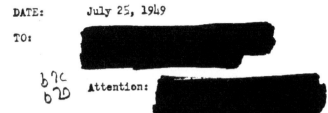

RECORDED - 4

EX-1

CONFIDENTIAL
AIR MAIL

DATE: July 25, 1949

TO:

b7C
b7D

Attention:

FROM: John Edgar Hoover – Director, Federal Bureau of Investigation

SUBJECT: BILLY HOLIDAY

        Reference is made to your letter dated June 28, 1949 requesting information regarding the above-captioned individual.

        Enclosed herewith are two copies of the Identification Record of Billie Holiday as it appears in the files of the Identification Division under FBI#-4855389.

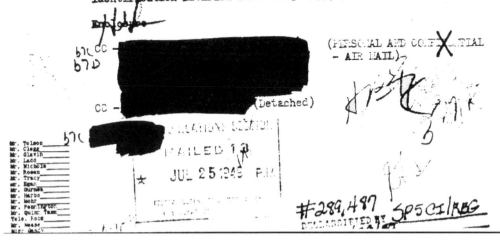

(PERSONAL AND CONFIDENTIAL
- AIR MAIL)

CC   (Detached)

CC

MAILED 12
JUL 25 1949 P.M.

#289,497

Billie Holiday, Singer, Held In Coast Dope Raid

SAN FRANCISCO, Jan. 22 (UP). Dusky blues singer Billie Holiday and her agent were arrested in a Tenderloin district hotel room in downtown San Francisco today and charged with possession of opium.

The 29-year-old star of radio, night clubs and recordings was booked at the Hall of Justice with John Levy, 40, of New York and Los Angeles, and both were released on $500 bail each.

Charge Opium Found

Police charged a vial of opium was found in her apartment. Both promptly denied they knew the opium was there.

A five-man squad of officers, including federal agent Gene White and four police from a special San Francisco detail, raided her apartment in the Mark Twain hotel in San Francisco's night life area.

White said the detail found the colored song enchantress in the bathroom, washing her hands beneath the medicine cabinet where they located a small vial of opium.

Took "Cure" in New York

Miss Holiday, only recently released from a federal institution at Alderson, W. Va., as "cured" of drug addiction, appeared at the city prison for fingerprinting and booking in a black dress beneath $7,000 blue mink coat.

She wore high heels and a perky hat and was flanked by Levy, hatless and coatless in the chill San Francisco weather. Throughout the proceedings Miss Holiday remained virtually silent. But Levy indignantly denied the charge.

"We both deny everything," he said, "She didn't even sleep in her room last night."

Claims Friend Used Room

Levy said Miss Holiday "lent" the room to a girl he knew only as "Mandy," a Negro girl friend of the singer.

He charged the officers "apparently were tipped" and said they went "directly to the bathroom and took the vial out of the chest."

Levy said he first got suspicious "something was up" when he got a call from the lobby downstairs that said: "Are you the Levy who is a stocking salesman?" He said "No", and hung up and a few minutes later the police knocked on the door and he admitted them.

Sang at Night Club

The chubby Negro songstress, whose record albums feature smoky, world-weary numbers, has been appearing at the Cafe Society Uptown in San Francisco's "Harlem" district along Fillmore Street.

Levy said he had just arrived in San Francisco on the Coaster, an overnight passenger train from Los Angeles, and that he had been in his client's room only about an hour before the law burst in. Immediately after the booking, the pair left for the cafe with the words, "The show must go on."

Since the death of her acknowledged model and mentor, Bessie Smith, the husky-voiced Miss Holiday has generally been rated tops in her line. Her albums are best-sellers and her recording of "Strange Fruit," the weird, minor-key lament of a Negro lynching, has become her virtual trademark.

SE 3, 17- A-
NOT RECORDED
44 MAR 11 10

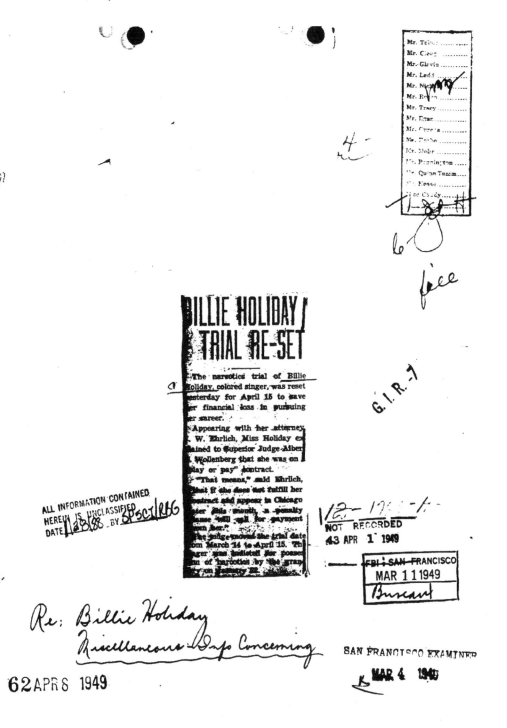

BILLIE HOLIDAY TRIAL RE-SET

The narcotics trial of Billie Holiday, colored singer, was reset yesterday for April 15 to save her financial loss in pursuing her career.

Appearing with her attorney, J. W. Ehrlich, Miss Holiday explained to Superior Judge Albert C. Wollenberg that she was on a "play or pay" contract.

"That means," said Ehrlich, "that if she does not fulfill her contract and appear in Chicago later this month, a penalty clause will call for payment from her."

The judge moved the trial date from March 14 to April 15. The singer was indicted for possession of narcotics by the grand jury on January 22.

ALL INFORMATION CONTAINED
HEREIN IS UNCLASSIFIED
DATE 10/13/08 BY SPSCT/RHG

G.I.R.-7

12 - 17 - 1
NOT RECORDED
43 APR 1 1949

FBI - SAN FRANCISCO
MAR 11 1949
Buscant

Re: Billie Holiday
Miscellaneous Info Concerning

62 APR 8 1949

SAN FRANCISCO EXAMINER
MAR 4 1949

Mr. Tolson_____
Mr. Clegg_____
Mr. Glavin_____
Mr. Ladd_____
Mr. Nichols_____
Mr. Rosen_____
Mr. Tracy_____
Mr. Egan_____
Mr. Gurnea_____
Mr. Harbo_____
Mr. Mohr_____
Mr. Pennington__
Mr. Quinn Tamm_
Mr. Nease_____
Miss Gandy_____

llie Holiday Cleared
f Opium Possession

San Francisco, June 4 (U.P).—
lie Holiday, blues singer, has
en declared innocent of charges
possessing opium.
A jury of six men and six women
turned a not guilty verdict yes-
day, after hearing Miss Holiday
fy that her manager, John
y, thrust a package of narcotics
to her hand just before her hotel
om was raided by federal agents.
The defense contended Levy
ned informer on Miss Holiday
avoid marriage.

83 JUL 12 1949

ALL INFORMATION CONTAINED
HEREIN IS UNCLASSIFIED
DATE 11 08 88 BY SP5 CI BBG

JUN 5 1949
WASHINGTON POST

Chapter XIV

Lorraine Hansberry: A Brilliant Playwright Who Died Too Soon

L orraine was born in Chicago, Illinois on May 19, 1930 at Provident Hospital located at 51st and Vincennes Avenue. Her parents Carl Augustus Hansberry and Nannie Perry Hansberry resided at 5330 South Calumet Avenue at the time of her birth. She was the fourth and the last of their children. Her other siblings were Mamie, Carl Jr. and Perry.

Mr. Hansberry Sr. was an intelligent high energy man from Gloster, Mississippi where he attended Alcorn College on a part-time basis from 1909 to 1915. He ultimately graduated from Chicago Technical College in 1927. One of his early jobs in Chicago was as a bank teller at Anthony Overton's Douglas National Bank located at 36th and South State Street. The Douglas Bank was founded in

1922 and was the first National Bank in the state of Illinois to be owned by Negroes.

Hansberry went into the real estate business in the roaring twenties before the stock market crash of October 1929. Carl Hansberry's first real estate office was located at 4250 South Evans Avenue and in the 1930's he was known as the "kitchenette king" because of the large number of old Grand Boulevard (King Drive) mansions and old apartment buildings that he had converted into mini apartments to accommodate the burgeoning Negro population that had migrated to Chicago, a city that was affectionately called Abraham Lincoln's City by the Lake. Following World War I, restrictive covenants were put in place by the Chicago Real Estate Board of Realtors. The covenants effectively barred Negroes from any of the housing stock that had not been redlined and specifically identified as the "Black Belt".

In 1936, Carl Hansberry and his wife Nannie Hansberry established a $10,000 trust fund. The income from the fund was to be used to fight housing segregation. It was from this fund that the National Association for the Advancement of Colored People obtained financial support to fight certain housing discrimination cases that came before the courts. He also used these funds to specifically fight housing restrictive covenants in Chicago. The Hansberry funds were certainly instrumental in hiring lawyers to take a restrictive covenant housing case before the United States Supreme Court where his lawyer succeeded in winning the first round. However, the knockout punch was not delivered until the fourth round when the United States Supreme Court ruled in Shelley vs. Kramer on Monday May 3, 1948, that racial restrictive covenants were unenforceable.

In addition to the Hansberry Foundation, Carl A. Hansberry was the President of the National Negro Program Association, Inc. In 1940 he was the recipient of the Arthur Schomburg award for his contribution to Negro Advancement.

Attorney Jewel Stratford Lafontant, a mutual friend of the Hansberrys', and the writer made the following observation during an interview for a book entitled "Autobiography of Black Chicago" by Dempsey J. Travis in 1981, she said:

> "My family was very friendly with the Carl Hansberry family. He was a real estate man in Chicago. He was very well-to-do. Hansberry bought a two-flat building at 6140 South Rhodes in

1941. He had been renting an apartment since May 1939 at 5936 South Park (Martin Luther King Drive) which was just a few blocks west of his new acquisitions. Blacks had not lived between 60th and 63rd between Vernon Avenue and Cottage Grove prior to the Hansberrys moving into the Washington Park subdivision. My father Attorney C. Francis Stratford represented him when he bought the building. I remember a short time after they moved into 6140 South Rhodes, we were sitting in the living room of their new apartment, when several bricks came flying through the first floor front window. The Whites were up in arms because a Negro family had moved into the Washington Park subdivision which in their mind-set was a lily-white domain.

The white neighborhood Improvement Association filed suit to get the Hansberrys out, and my father represented the family in the suit. My father brought in the Supreme Liberty Life Insurance Company lawyers as one of the defendants in the suit, the Supreme Liberty Life had made the mortgage for the Hansberrys. My father was the main lawyer for the defendants. The lawyers from the Supreme Liberty Life were Earl B. Dickerson, T. K. Gibson, Jr., Loring B. Moore and Irwin C. Mollison. Dickerson was the one who was finally selected to argue the case. My father was very unhappy about it, and the Hansberrys were unhappy about it. My father had labored with them through all the dramatic days in that the case had gone on for years. The Hansberrys knew my father had done most of the work and wanted him to get the credit.

When the United States Supreme Court decision came down, one of the newspapers said, "Attorneys C. Francis Stradford, Earl B. Dickerson, T. K. Gibson, Jr., Irwin B. Mollison, and Loring B. Moore, acting in concert for various clients, have gained a unanimous opinion from the United States Supreme Court upsetting a residential covenant barring Negroes from certain areas. It seems to have been the brief presented in the case of Mr. and Mrs. Carl Hansberry, prepared by Attorney C. Francis Stradford, which swung the court.

The Hansberrys were the real defendants, and my father prepared the brief. Having argued many cases in court myself, I know the person who argues the case, which is the glamorous part of the law, gets the credit. You are up there for a half hour or forty-five minutes, but the bulk of the work has been done before Judgment day.

I knew playwright Lorraine Hansberry. She was about four years younger than I. Her sister, Mamie, and I were about the same age, and we were good friends. Lorraine was considered spoiled. She was the only one in the family born into affluence; all the others could remember when they were poor. By the time Lorraine was born in 1930, the Hansberrys had a chauffeur, fur coats and several cars. Lorraine was very smart. She was very quiet and a little stand-offish. I was shocked when she turned out to be a brilliant playwright. She always wanted to be a doctor. I never thought of her in the theatre or being a writer.

After finishing Englewood High School on January 28, 1948, Lorraine enrolled at the University of Wisconsin, at Madison where racial and social obstacles were placed in her path thus impeding her road to success. In her second year, she enrolled in a theater class on set design. Her work in the course was considered by the professor to be above average but she was given a D for her final grade. The teacher explained that he gave her the low mark because he did not want to encourage a young Black woman to enter a white dominated field. Hansberry left the University and did some studying at Roosevelt College in Chicago during the 1950 summer semester. She moved to New York City in the fall of 1950 and enrolled in the New School for Social Science. She also studied African History, and culture with Dr. W. E. B. DuBois at the Jefferson School for Social Science.

In 1951, she became a staff writer for the Freedom periodical and in 1952 she was promoted to associate editor and without missing a beat in 1952 she also taught at the Frederick Douglass School in Harlem. In 1956, she became a full-time writer and completed the first draft of <u>A Raisin in the Sun</u>. Her works from that point forward are the following:

Nonfiction

The Movement: Documentary of a Struggle for Equality, Simon & Schuster, 1964.
To Be Young, Gifted and Black: Lorraine Hansberry in Her Own Words, introduction by James Baldwin, Prentice-Hall, 1969.

Plays

A Raisin in the Sun, opened in New Haven and Philadelphia, moved to Chicago, then produced on Broadway at the Ethel Barrymore Theatre, March 11, 1959; published by New American Library, 1961.
Les Blancs, single scene staged at Actors Studio Workshop, New York, 1963; two-act play produced at Longacre Theater, New York City, 1970.
The Sign in Sidney Brustein's Window, produced on Broadway, 1964; published by Random House, 1965.
Lorraine Hansberry's "A Raisin in the Sun" and "The Sign in Sidney Brustein's Window," New American Library, 1966.
To Be Young, Gifted and Black, adapted for the stage by Robert Nemiroff, first produced at the Cherry Lane Theater, January 2, 1969; acting edition published by Samuel French, 1971.
Les Blancs: The Collected Last Plays of Lorraine Hansberry, edited by Robert Nemiroff, introduction by Julius Lester, Random House, 1972, reprinted, New American Library, 1983.
Lorraine Hansberry: The Collected Last Plays (Les Blancs, The Drinking Gourd,

What Use Are Flowers?), *edited by Robert Nemiroff, New American Library, 1983.*

Other

A Raisin in the Sun: The Unfilmed Original Screenplay, edited by Robert Nemiroff, 1992.
All the Dark and Beautiful Warriors, an unfinished novel.

Author of about two dozen articles for Freedom, 1951-55, and over 25 essays for other publications, including the Village Voice, New York Times, New York Times Magazine, Freedomways, Mademoiselle, Ebony, Playbill, Show, Theatre Arts, Black Scholar, Monthly Review, and Annals of Psychotherapy.

Her New York Critics Award for the best play of 1959 was for <u>A Raisin in the Sun</u> which was autobiographic in that it mirrored many of the housing experiences of her father and the emotional effect that that period had on her life.

Federal Bureau of Investigation

Freedom of Information/Privacy Acts Section

Subject: <u>Lorraine Hansberry</u>

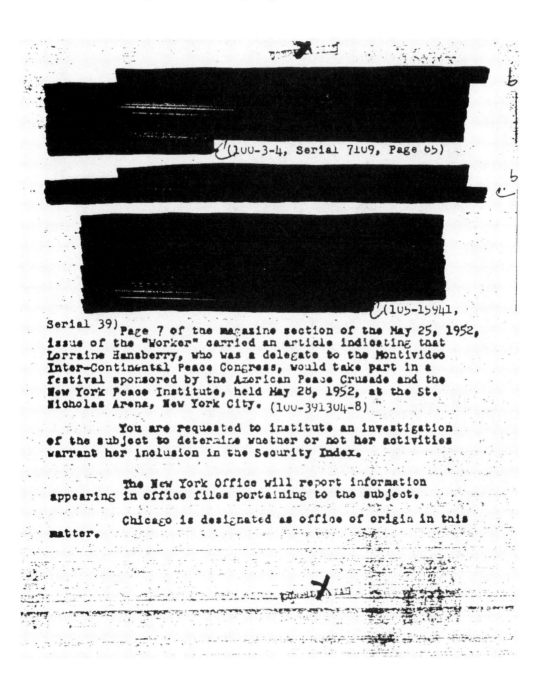

(100-3-4, Serial 7109, Page 65)

(105-15941,
Serial 39) Page 7 of the magazine section of the May 25, 1952,
issue of the "Worker" carried an article indicating that
Lorraine Hansberry, who was a delegate to the Montivideo
Inter-Continental Peace Congress, would take part in a
festival sponsored by the American Peace Crusade and the
New York Peace Institute, held May 28, 1952, at the St.
Nicholas Arena, New York City. (100-391304-8)

You are requested to institute an investigation
of the subject to determine whether or not her activities
warrant her inclusion in the Security Index.

The New York Office will report information
appearing in office files pertaining to the subject.

Chicago is designated as office of origin in this
matter.

Office Memorandum CONFIDENTIAL UNITED STATES GOVERNMENT

TO : Director, FBI　　　　　　　　　　　　DATE: 3/30/53

FROM : SAC, New York (100-107297)

SUBJECT: LORRAINE HANSBERRY
　　　　　　SM - C　　　　　　　　　　3 I. R. 9

"The Worker", dated April 13, 1952, reveals that the subject attended the "Inter-Continental Peace Conference" at Montivedeo, Uruguary, from March 12 to 16, 1952.

Washington Field Office is requested to examine the files of the Passport Division of the United States Department of State in an effort to obtain all available background material on the subject, any derogatory information contained therein, and a photograph and complete description of the subject.

The following description of the subject is furnished for the assistance of the Washington Field Office:

Name	LORRAINE HANSBERRY
Present Address	820 West 180th St., NYC
Previous Address	5936 South Park, Chicago, ILL.
Sex	Female
Age	21-24
Race	Negro
Weight	130
Height	5'4"
Hair	Black
Eyes	Brown
Relatives	Mother - IRMA HANSBERRY
	5936 South Parkway
	Chicago, Ill.
	Sister - MAMIE L. HANSBERRY
	Brother- CARL HANSBERRY

REGISTERED MAIL

2 - Washington Field (RM)

LSH:JR

Class. & Ext. By ___
Reason-FCIM II, 1-2.4.2
Date of Review 4/15/91

RECORDED - 9

INDEXED - 9　　　38 MAR 31 1953

EX-112

CONFIDENTIAL

FEDERAL BUREAU OF INVESTIGATION

SECURITY INFORMATION - CONFIDENTIAL

FORM No. 1
THIS CASE ORIGINATED AT NEW YORK

REPORT MADE AT	DATE WHEN MADE	PERIOD FOR WHICH MADE	REPORT MADE BY
WASHINGTON, D. C.	11/27/53	10/20,28;11/17,25/ 53	DL

TITLE CHANGED:
LORRAINE VIVIAN HANSBERRY,
was. Loraine Hansberry

CHARACTER OF CASE

SECURITY MATTER - C

DECLASSIFIED BY _Spietert berg_
ON _4/15/81_

SYNOPSIS OF FACTS:

Subject born 5/19/30, at Chicago, Illinois. Subject was
issued New York Series Passport #45060 on 3/11/52, for
proposed two months travel to England, Scotland, France and
Italy for vacation. Gave permanent residence as 5936 South
Parkway, Chicago, and mailing address as c/o Mrs. E. BERKOWITZ,
499 West 130th Street, New York City. Subject's passport
picked up by State Department in July, 1952, at which time
subject allegedly residing with a JONES family, Apartment 6-A,
504 West 143rd Street, NYC. Subject's passport reflects travel
to South America in March, 1952. Details and descriptive data
set out.

AGENCY _ICC-USIA_
REQ. REC'D _4-28-59_
REP'T FORW. _4-29-59_
BY _BVS_

- RUC -

DETAILS: AT WASHINGTON, D. C.:

The title of this case has been marked changed to show
the subject's full name as LORRAINE VIVIAN HANSBERRY and to
show as an alias LORAINE HANSBERRY, as evidenced by her
passport file.

The files of the Passport Office, Department of State,
disclose that LORRAINE VIVIAN HANSBERRY was issued New York
Series Passport #45060 on March 11, 1952, for proposed two
months travel to England, Scotland, France and Italy for the
purpose of vacation. In her passport application dated March 7,

APPROVED AND FORWARDED	SPECIAL AGENT IN CHARGE	DO NOT WRITE IN THESE SPACES
		100 - 393031 - SE 27

COPIES OF THIS REPORT
5 - Bureau
3 - New York (100-107297) (RM)
(ENCLS 6)
2 - Washington Field
(100-27468)

RECORDED · 50
INDEXED · 50

COPY IN FILE

PROPERTY OF FBI

SECURITY INFORMATION - CONFIDENTIAL

TJD:aeo
(2)

NY 100-107297

<u>American Labor Party</u>

The records of the Manhattan Board of Elections, as reviewed by SA ████████████████, on June 6, 1956, reflected that LORRAINE NEMIROFF registered a preference for the American Labor Party (ALP) in 1953 and for one of the two major political parties in 1955. There was no record for 1954.

b7C

61

<u>Committee to Restore PAUL ROBESON's Passport</u>

b7C
b7D

████████████████████ as reviewed on May 14, 1956 at the request of SA ████████████ reflected that LORRAINE HANSBERRY was a speaker and performer at a rally titled "A Salute to Paul Robeson" held by the Committee to Restore PAUL ROBESON's Passport on May 26, 1954, at the Renaissance Casino, 138th Street and 7th Avenue, New York City.

FD-263 (6-12-81)

CONFIDENTIAL

FEDERAL BUREAU OF INVESTIGATION

Reporting Office	Office of Origin	Date	Investigative Period
NEW YORK	NEW YORK	10/21/57	26;10/1,2,4,7/57 9/19,20

TITLE OF CASE	Report made by		Typed By:
		b7c	hj

LORRAINE VIVIAN HANSBERRY NEMIROFF, was.

CHARACTER OF CASE

SECURITY MATTER-C

Synopsis:

Subject resides 337 Bleecker Street, New York City, and is unemployed. ███████████████████

b7D

RA

ALP, 1954-1956 set forth. New York City informants negative, re subject.

-C-

ALL INFORMATION CONTAINED HEREIN IS UNCLASSIFIED EXCEPT WHERE SHOWN OTHERWISE

Class.& Ext. By Sec-Petersberg
Reason-FCIM II, 1-2.4.2
Date of Review 5/14/91

DETAILS:

BACKGROUND

Residence

A pretext call by a Special Agent of the Federal Bureau of Investigation to subject's residence on September 26, 1957, reflected that the subject presently resides at 337 Bleecker Street, New York City.

Approved _____ Special Agent in Charge _____ Do not write in spaces below

Copies made:

1-Bureau (100-393031) (RM)
3-New York (100-107297)

Agency _____
Req. Rec'd _____
Date Forw. _____
How Forw. _____
By _____

100-393031-19 RECORDED 19

8 OCT 24 1957

SUBV. CONTROL

AGENCY _____
REQ. REC'D _____
DATE FORW. _____
HOW FORW. _____
BY _____

AGENCY ICC-ZIS-1A
REP. FR'D 4-28-57
REP'D FORW. 4-29-57 b7c
BY _____
dissem. _____

NOV 5 1957 CONFIDENTIAL

NY 100-107297

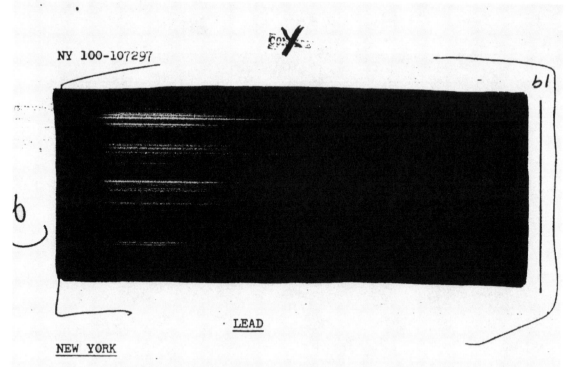

LEAD

NEW YORK

<u>At New York, New York</u>

Will continue investigation in an effort to determine
if the play subject has written is in any way controlled or
influenced by the CP and whether it in any way follows
the Communist line.

- 2 -

FBI

Date: 1/23/59

Transmit the following message via ___ **AIRTEL** ___

(Priority or Method of Mailing)

TO: DIRECTOR, FBI (100-393031)

FROM: SAC, NEW YORK (100-107297)

SUBJECT: LORRAINE VIVIAN HANSBERRY NEMIROFF, aka.
          SM-C

Re NY airtel, dated 1/22/59.

The "New York Herald Tribune," in its late city edition of 1/23/59, page 8, carried the following verbatim account of the play "A Raisin in the Sun" which opened in New Haven on 1/21/59:

"The New Haven audience and critics gave a warm reception Wednesday night to 'A Raisin in the Sun' starring Sidney Poitier and an all-Negro cast.

"The 'New Haven Journal-Courier' wrote: 'The combination of an engrossing story, a beautifully written play and superb direction by Lloyd Richards marks the production for certain success on Broadway.'

"The 'New Haven Register' wrote: "A new Negro play of exceptional warmth and discernment and a Negro cast of great charm and proficiency last night made 'A Raisin in the Sun' one of the dramatic high spots of the season at the Shubert."

"The play has yet to find a house in New York."

The above is being furnished for information purposes.

4- Bureau (100-393031)(RM)
2- New Haven (100-   )(RM)
2- Philadelphia (100-   )(RM)
1- New York (100-120148)
1- New York (100-107297)
CJG:mel
(11)

REC. 31

100-393031-27

JAN 24 1959

Special Agent in Charge   Sent ___

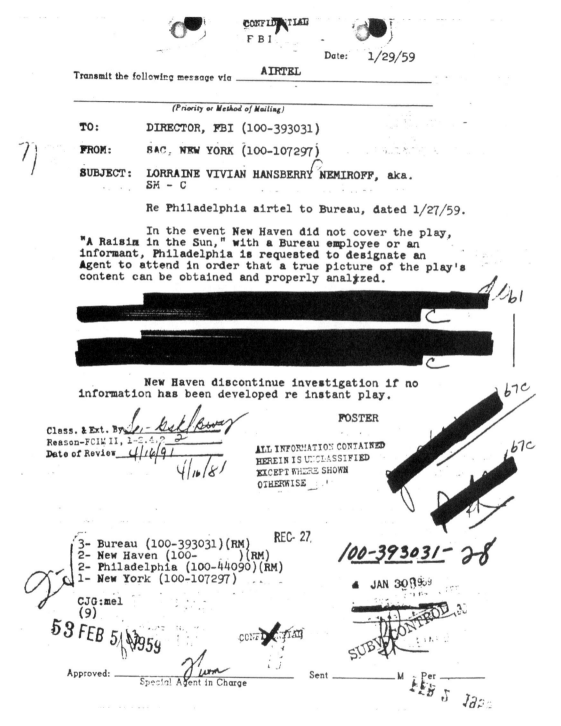

CONFIDENTIAL
F B I

Date: 1/29/59

Transmit the following message via _____ AIRTEL

(Priority or Method of Mailing)

TO: DIRECTOR, FBI (100-393031)

FROM: SAC, NEW YORK (100-107297)

SUBJECT: LORRAINE VIVIAN HANSBERRY NEMIROFF, aka.
           SM - C

Re Philadelphia airtel to Bureau, dated 1/27/59.

In the event New Haven did not cover the play, "A Raisin in the Sun," with a Bureau employee or an informant, Philadelphia is requested to designate an Agent to attend in order that a true picture of the play's content can be obtained and properly analyzed.

New Haven discontinue investigation if no information has been developed re instant play.

FOSTER

Class. & Ext. By _____
Reason-FCIM II, 1-2.4,2 2
Date of Review 4/16/91   4/16/81

ALL INFORMATION CONTAINED
HEREIN IS UNCLASSIFIED
EXCEPT WHERE SHOWN
OTHERWISE

3- Bureau (100-393031)(RM)   REC- 27
2- New Haven (100-   )(RM)
2- Philadelphia (100-44090)(RM)
1- New York (100-107297)

CJG:mel
(9)

53 FEB 5 1959

CONFIDENTIAL

Approved: _____   Sent _____ M Per _____
          Special Agent in Charge

100-393031- 28

JAN 30 1959

F B I

Date: 1/28/59

Transmit the following in _____
(Type in plain text or code)

Via **AIRTEL**   **REGULAR MAIL**
                          (Priority or Method of Mailing)

TO   : DIRECTOR, FBI (100-393031)

FROM   : SAC, PHILADELPHIA (100-44090)

SUBJECT: LORRAINE VIVIAN HANSBERRY NEMIROFF, Aka.
          SM - C .... **ALL INFORMATION CONTAINED**
                                    HEREIN IS ~~UNCLASSIFIED~~
          (00 - New York)   **DATE 4/16/8 BY S. Gelfan**

          Remyairtel 1/27/59.

          Enclosed for New York's information is one copy each
of the following newspaper clippings and one copy of the Playbill
of "A Raisin in the Sun," which opened in Philadelphia on 1/26/59.

          1. Clipping from the 1/25/59 issue of the Sunday
Bulletin captioned, "On the Stage."

          2. Clipping from the 1/25/59 issue of the Sunday
Inquirer, which is an announcement of the opening of "A Raisin
in the Sun" in Philadelphia.

          3. Clipping from the 1/27/59 Final Edition of the
Philadelphia Inquirer captioned, "POITIER in Timely Play on
Trials of Negroes," by HENRY T. MURDOCK. Excerpts from MURDOCK's
review were furnished in reairtel.

④ - Bureau (RM) (Encls. - 2) 67C
     3 - 100-393031 ██████████   EX-102
3 - New York (RM) (Encls. - 8)
     2 - 100-107297   100-393031-29
     1 - 100-120148
2 - Philadelphia   REC- 92   19 JAN 29 1959
     1 - 100-44090   67C
     1 - 100-19999 (AMERICAN JEWISH CONGRESS)

JES:KSK

(9)

Approved: _____   Sent _____ M Per _____
                  Special Agent in Charge
          52 FEB 8 1959

FD-36 (Rev. 12-13-56)

F B I

Date:

Transmit the following in _____
(Type in plain text or code)

Via _____   _____
(Priority or Method of Mailing)

PH 100-44090

    4. Clipping from the 1/25/59 Sunday Edition of the Philadelphia Inquirer captioned, "Footlight Fare Old and New" by BARBARA L. WILSON. This item announces the opaing of new plays in Philadelphia during the current week which includes "A Raisin in the Sun." According to this item, Miss HANSBERRY says that her play is "an effort to say a great deal about a large and important part of our contemporary situation. I believe one or two affirmative things are still left to be said about life and people." This item also contains a photograph of SIDNEY POITIER and RUBY DEE, playing his wife.

    5. Clipping from the 1/25/59 Sunday Bulletin captioned, "Family Life is Theme of Two Plays Bowing Here" by WAYNE ROBINSON. This item announced that on opening night a 27 year old Negro authoress from Chicago will be introduced to local playgoers with the drama, "A Raisin in the Sun," about a family in her own Windy City. The playwright is LORRAINE HANSBERRY and her play stars SIDNEY POITIER. POITIER in his first starring role for the Broadway stage will play the ambitious, restless elder son in a family of strong individualists. With one exception, JOHN FIEDLER, who plays the role of a lawyer, the cast is all Negro.

    6. Clipping from the 1/27/59 issue of the Evening Bulletin captioned, "Raisin in the Sun Opens at the Walnut," by ERNIE SCHIER. This item sets out SCHIER's review of the play, and one copy of this item is enclosed for the Bureau.

    7. This item is a clipping from the 1/27/59 issue of the Philadelphia Daily News captioned, "Raisin in Sun Warms Walnut," by JERRY GAGHAN. This item sets out GAGHAN's review of the opening night of the play and one copy of the article is enclosed for the Bureau. This review begins, "Explosive in content, topical as today and extraordinarily well performed, 'Raisin in the Sun' brings back the excitement of controversy to our stage season."

- 2 -

Approved: _____   Sent _____ M   Per _____
    Special Agent in Charge

FD-36 (Rev. 12-13-50)

FBI

Date:

Transmit the following in _____
(Type in plain text or code)

Via _____   _____
(Priority or Method of Mailing)

PH 100-44090

"The new play at the Walnut looks bleakly upon the
facts of integration. The action takes place in the North,
an area which piously prefers to segregate this problem to the
South.

"LORRAINE HANSBERRY . . . . is seething with
purpose, but never lets the preachment impede the progress of
the play. Underneath the ready racial humors are tensions
always about to erupt into violence, which adds the quality of
suspense. . . . .
The hero is a product of his environment, a muddled husband
bitter about his lack of education and his job as a chauffeur.
He is bursting with resentment also against the mother, who
refuses to finance him in the opening of a liquor store. . . . . .
. . . . Miss HANSBERRY's message seems to be that
the restrictions, repressions and segregations produce only half
a man, but that maturity must result when the victim finally
fights back." This article continues that the play is bright
with laugh lines, a lot of which are due to CLAUDIA McNEIL as
the matriarch of the family. It is her purchase of a house in
a white neighborhood which brings on the crisis. The item
concludes that IVAN DIXON employs the diction of HERBERT MARSHALL
in his role as a visiting African student. JOHN FIEDLER is
reasonableness itself as the white "villain" of the piece.

8. The Playbill.

Local Philadelphia Negro newspapers have been reviewed,
however, since these papers are not daily, no reviews were
located. It is noted that "The Pittsburgh Courier" of 1/31/59,
contained an announcement of the play. On Page 22 of this paper
an item was noted in a column captioned, "IZZY ROWE's Notebook."
This item stated that SIDNEY POITIER is scheduled to receive
the Stephen Wise Award from the Philadelphia Chapter of the
American Jewish Congress on 2/6/59, and the 369th Veterans Annual
Achievement Award in March. The article stated that in New

- 3 -

Approved: _____   Sent _____ M   Per _____
          Special Agent in Charge

FD-36 (Rev. 12-13-56)

FBI

Date:

Transmit the following in _____
(Type in plain text or code)

Via _____   _____
(Priority or Method of Mailing)

- -

PH 100-44090

Haven the talented actor received rave reviews for his role in
"A Raisin in the Sun." According to the item, another cast member
importance who held the eyes of the critics was CLAUDIA McNEILL
with her best dramatic role to date, and one which may be hers
in the star category when the vehicle reaches Broadway.

Copies of the above items not retained by Philadelphia.

Philadelphia will continue to follow.

HENNRICH

- 4 -

Approved: _____   Sent _____ M   Per _____
Special Agent in Charge

'Raisin in Sun' Warms Walnut

By JERRY GAGHAN

Explosive in content, topical as today and extraordinarily well performed, "Raisin in the Sun" brings back the excitement of controversy to our stage season.

The new play at the Walnut looks bleakly upon the facts of integration. The action takes place in the North, an area which piously prefers to segregate this problem to the South.

LORRAINE HANSBERRY, the playwright, has turned out a remarkably effective and workmanlike drama for a newcomer.

She is seething with purpose, but never lets the preachment impede the progress of the play. Underneath the ready racial humors are tensions always about to erupt into violence, which adds the quality of suspense.

The story concerns a Negro family on Chicago's South Side. They have just received a $10,000 settlement claim after the death of the father. The bickerings developed over the spending of this windfall. The daughter (Diane Sands) wants enough to pay her tuition in medical

ALL INFORMATION CONTAINED
HEREIN IS UNCLASSIFIED
DATE 4/16/81 BY

PHILADELPHIA, PA.

INQUIRER
BULLETIN
DAILY NEWS

DATE
EDITION
PAGE
COLUMN
EDITOR
TITLE OF CASE

100-393031-29

school.

THE CONFUSED SON of the household is Sidney Poitier. The hero is a product of his environment, a muddled husband bitter about his lack of education and his job as a chaffeur. He is bursting with resentment also against the mother, who refuses to finance him in the opening of a liquor store.

His targic ineptness with money, when he gets the fleeting chance to play the big shot, hastens the plot to its grim, if hopeful, conclusion. Miss Hansberry's message seems to be that the restrictions, repressions and segregations produce only half a man, but that maturity must result when the victim finally fights back.

IF THIS SOUNDS too much like a tract, let us add that "Raisin in the Sun" is bright with laugh lines and hilarious situations.

A lot of them are due to Claudia McNeil, as the matriarch of the family. It is her purchase of a house in a white neighborhood which brings on the crisis.

A figure of authority, Miss McNeil manages to be wholly sympathetic. Her interpolative timing is perfect. She can be uproariously funny without sacrificing dignity and in her big scenes, the discovery of the son's stupid loss of their precious hoard is most affecting.

RUBY DEE is cast as the hopeless daughter-in-law who has given up trying to understand what forces her husband to seek outside con-solations.

Louis Gossett contributes an engaging takeoff of a Negro collegiate on the make for the younger sister. Ivan Dixon employs the diction of Herbert Marshall in his role as a visiting African student. John Fiedler is reasonableness itself as the white "villain" of the piece.

The Living Theater
'Raisin in the Sun' Opens at the Walnut

Philip Rose and David J. Cogan present "A Raisin in the Sun," a new play by Lorraine Hansberry; directed by Lloyd Richards; designed and lighted by Ralph Alswang. At the Walnut.

Cast

Ruth Younger .... Ruby Dee
Travis Younger ...... Glynn Turman
Walter Lee Younger (Brother) ...... Sidney Poitier
Beneatha Younger ...... Diana Sands
Lena Younger (Mother) .. Claudia McNeil
Joseph Asagai ...... Ivan Dixon
George Murchison ...... Louis Gossett
Bobo .... Lonne Elder
Karl Lindner .. John Fielder
Moving Men .. Douglas Turner, Ed Hall

By ERNIE SCHIER

The ambitions and conflicts of a Chicago family have given Lorraine Hansberry the materials for the best play in a decade about Negro life. "A Raisin in the Sun," which opened last night at the Walnut is a human drama written with love and honesty.

In character and quality it has the same hearty appeal of a Sean O'Casey play and the rich, bitter humor of a people striving to make tomorrow a little better than today.

The playwright's talent is impressive for in writing about one family's drive to break into the middle class she has touched shrewdly on almost every phase of modern Negro life, from the cry for assimilation to the hol-

Sidney Poitier has starring role in new play, "A Raisin in the Sun," at the Walnut.

lowness of pursuing an empty dream.

In one uncomfortably accurate scene, Miss Hansberry has given devastating treatment to a one-man white "welcoming committee" who represents the community the family plans to move into.

PHILADELPHIA, PA.

INQUIRER _____
BULLETIN _____
DAILY NEWS _____

DATE, 1/27/59
EDITION Postscript
PAGE 54
COLUMN 2
EDITOR
TITLE OF CASE

100-393031- 29

Full of Life and Vitality

But "A Raisin in the Sun" is not a problem play, it is too full of life and vitality for that. Although the author has written knowingly about Negroes, her play could be applied to people anywhere who have their eyes on the future.

The warmth of "A Raisin in the Sun" is contagious and it is spread about generously by a winning cast of Negro actors, led by Sidney Poitier, the impressive young screen actor, and a motherly performer named Claudia McNeill. Beware, Miss McNeil will positively wring your heart.

The plot of the drama centers around the family dreams of what each will achieve when an insurance policy is paid to the mother, Miss McNeil.

To the son, played by Poitier, the money means a chance to buy into a liquor store and wheel and deal like any important white man. To a daughter, the money will buy her a degree in medicine. To Ruby Dee, Poitier's wife, it means a house in the sun for their young boy.

For the playwright the story is a dramatic means to examine the past, the present and the future of each character.

Play Moves Rapidly

Under the direction of Lloyd Richards the play moves rapidly through the changing moods to a heart-rending climax, when Poitier learns he has been deluded into throwing most of the money away, and on to an uplifting ending.

Miss McNeil is a sweet and dignified performer but also a powerful actress. Her anguish in a key scene shared with Poitier is nearly overwhelming.

Poitier is almost just as effective as the confused, ambitious husband and paces himself through a performance that requires frequent shifts in mood.

Fine Supporting Cast

Although "A Raisin in the Sun" runs past conventional theater time it can be brought under control by cutting that will not damage the structure of the play.

There are fine supporting performances from Ruby Dee, as Poitier's wife; Diana Sands, as the coed sister; and a youngster with a dazzling grin named Glynn Turman.

Ivan Dixon, as a visitor from Nigeria, and Louis Gosset as another collegian, are both good.

Ralph Alswang has designed the crowded apartment in which the family is fighting a losing battle against insect life.

Office Memorandum • UNITED STATES GOVERNMENT

TO : SAC (100-44090) DATE: 2/5/59

FROM : SA ~~███████████~~ b7c

SUBJECT: LORRAINE VIVIAN HANSBERRY NEMIROFF, aka
SM - C

At the request of the New York Office, the play "A Raisin in the Sun" was witnessed by the writer on 2/4/59. The plot is summarized generally in Ph airtel 1/28/59, pages 2 and 3, from a review by JERRY GAGHAN of the Philadelphia Daily News.

The program specifies that the action of the play is laid in Chicago, south side, sometime between World War II and the present. The play is in three acts and seven scenes, all utilizing the same set, a shabby tenement flat housing three generations; the widowed mother, her son, age 35, her daughter, age 20, the son's wife, and their son, age 11.

The play contains no comments of any nature about Communism as such but deals essentially with negro aspirations, the problems inherent in their efforts to advance themselves, and varied attempts at arriving at solutions. The contrasting proposals for solutions are set up through the character delineations of the widowed mother, her son, and her daughter. The specific bone of contention which is the central theme of the plot is the sum of $10,000 received by the widow as a result of the death of her late husband.

The mother is middle aged, hard working, religious, has a strong sense of right and wrong and what is fitting, is a firm-minded dominating matriarch with very strong feeling for family unity. She represents the fifth generation of her line in the United States and basically believes in negroes advancing themselves through a process of gradualism. She has lived in the same flat since her marriage. She and her late husband always wanted a house with conveniences, adequate room, and sunlight. She planned to use part of the insurance money for a house. She buys the house hastily in a desperate effort to hold the family together and to forestall a proposed abortion by the newly pregnant daughter-in-law. She buys the best house she can get for her money which happens to be in a white neighborhood since comparable houses in a negro development are twice as expensive. The other members of the family are appalled that she bought in a white neighborhood but are willing to accept

100-393031- 32
ENCLOSURE

MEMO, SAC
Ph File 100-44090)

the problems of moving since they are so afflicted with "ghetto-itis"
and have so great and so old a hunger for a house with adequate
bedrooms, space, and light.

The son lacks the education he wished for and works as a
chauffeur with the hope or plan for a better job. He wants to
be on an economic par with his employer, wants to make "big deals".
He has no qualms about the ethics or honesty of his deals but is
willing to sell liquor to other negroes against his mother's wishes.
He is also perfectly ready to bribe State officials in order to
expedite a liquor license since everyone knows this is the way
things are done. When thwarted, he seeks escape by going off by
himself and through drink. He is entrusted with the remaining
$6500 of the insurance money with instructions to set aside $3,000
for his sister's medical education and to put the balance in a
checking account which he will manage. Having been given a position
of trust, he promptly violates it by attempting to invest the money
in a liquor business and it is stolen from him. Thereafter, he
loses his self respect to the point where he expresses a willingness
to accept an offer to sell the house back to the white neighbors
at a profit. In the final scene, he regains his self respect and
the love of the family by rejecting the offer.

The daughter is a college girl of 20 who aspires to be a
doctor in an effort to fulfill a childhood ambition to help people,
to heal them, to put them together again. At this point she seeks
a means of self-expression and self-identification. She passes
from hobby to hobby, generally expensive, under the amused and
tolerant scrutiny of the other women. Her comments and her discussions with other characters produce such propaganda messages as
are included in the play:

To her mother she denies her belief in God and the existence
of God. God does not pay the tuition. Things are what people make
them, not God. Her mother by superior force of will forces her to
repeat, "in my mother's house there is still God", but the daughter
remains resentful and unconvinced.

When her brother has stolen from him the $6500 insurance money,
including her medical school tuition, she reviles him as an
"entrepreneur".

She has two suitors both of college status. One is the son
of a rich, successful business man. He is dressed in over narrow,
over emphatic ivy league clothes. He views his college work as the

- 2 -

MEMO, SAC
Ph File 100-44090

means of obtaining a few facts, passing the courses, and receiving
a degree. He is not interested in hearing of her ideas and her
struggle toward identifying herself but is primarily interested in
the girl from a physical standpoint.

The other suitor is a Nigerian studying in the United States
and Canada. He is highly urbane and wears his ivy league clothing
in good taste. He too is interested in the girl physically but is
obviously a man with a cause, he knows exactly what he wants and
is not inclined to waste time on trivia and side issues. His purpose is to educate himself so that he can return to teach and raise
the level of the people of his village. They must overthrow the
rule of European nations, find political freedom, improve themselves
economically and educationally, and make their own future. He
anticipates in the process there will be a period when people of
his country will do evil things even to each other, including
violence, swindling, and political self-aggrandizement but he is
willing to accept these things as an intermediate stage on the
path to the ultimate goal. As for himself, he assumes that he may
be assassinated in the process and is agreeable to this. If, on
the other hand, he should grow old and powerful and at that time
tries to hold his own power too long or refuse to give way to new
ideas so that young men waiting in the background should slit
his throat, that will be as it should be. He is mildly and
amusedly critical of negroes who straighten the kinks from their
hair and imitate other ways of the whites. These people are
"assimilationists". He comments upon, but is willing to accept
the girl's light skin since her profile remains negroid. He helps
to set up for her self-identification with the independence movement in Africa. (Africa, incidentally, is a matter which is only
dimly comprehended by the other members of the family except for
her brother who while drunk is carried away and imagines himself
a tribal chief). The Nigerian wants the girl to complete her
education, marry him, and return to Africa as a doctor. By the
end of the play this would appear to have become her goal.

There is one white man in the play who comes to the family
as the representative of a neighborhood improvement group. He tries
to explain to them plausibly that they are not wanted, that the
present residents fear for their investments and fear that the
neighborhood may deteriorate as a place in which to raise their

- 3 -

(̆ ˙()˙

MEMO, SAC
Ph File 100-44090

children. He offers to buy back the house at a substantial profit.
The family is insulted. The negro explanation for the white
rejection is that the whites are "afraid we will marry them".
Their attitude toward the offer of a deal is that the offer is
degrading and the acceptance would make them lower than human, or
as the daughter describes her brother when he is considering the
offer, a "toothless rat".

From the writer's observations of the plot and the dialogue,
nothing specific was found that is peculiar to a CP program.
Audience reaction varied considerably to different scenes and
lines. The quality of some of the acting was applauded, some of
the lines drew applause primarily on a racial basis, others
appeared to be applauded not only by negroes in the audience but
by a substantial number of whites. The play was well attended.
Comments overheard from whites appeared to indicate that they
appreciated the drama and the quality of the acting, especially on
the part of CLAUDIA Mc NEIL who handled the part of the mother.
Relatively few appeared to dwell on the propaganda messages.

CAST

(In order of appearance)

RUTH YOUNGER ....RUBY DEE

TRAVIS YOUNGER ....GLYNN TURMAN

WALTER LEE YOUNGER (BROTHER) ....SIDNEY POITIER

BENEATHA YOUNGER ....DIANA SANDS

LENA YOUNGER (MOTHER) ....CLAUDIA McNEIL

JOSEPH ASAGAI ....IVAN DIXON

GEORGE MURCHISON ....LOUIS GOSSETT

BOBO ....LONNE ELDER

KARL LINDNER ....JOHN FIEDLER

MOVING MEN ....DOUGLAS TURNER, ED HALL

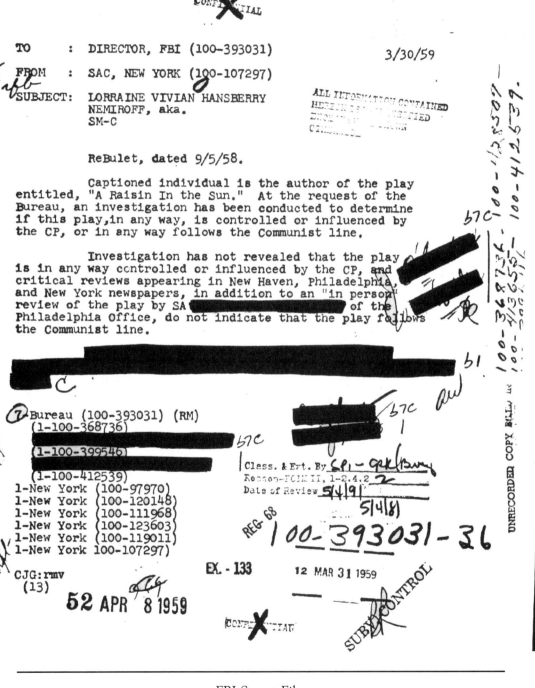

OFFICE MEMORANDUM   UNITED STATES GOVERNMENT

CONFIDENTIAL

TO   : DIRECTOR, FBI (100-393031)   3/30/59

FROM   : SAC, NEW YORK (100-107297)

SUBJECT: LORRAINE VIVIAN HANSBERRY   ALL INFORMATION CONTAINED
          NEMIROFF, aka.   HEREIN IS UNCLASSIFIED
          SM-C

        ReBulet, dated 9/5/58.

        Captioned individual is the author of the play
entitled, "A Raisin In the Sun." At the request of the
Bureau, an investigation has been conducted to determine
if this play, in any way, is controlled or influenced by
the CP, or in any way follows the Communist line.

        Investigation has not revealed that the play
is in any way controlled or influenced by the CP, and
critical reviews appearing in New Haven, Philadelphia,
and New York newspapers, in addition to an "in person"
review of the play by SA ████████████████████ of the
Philadelphia Office, do not indicate that the play follows
the Communist line.

⑦ Bureau (100-393031) (RM)
  (1-100-368736)
  (1-100-399546)
  (1-100-412539)
1-New York (100-97970)
1-New York (100-120148)
1-New York (100-111968)
1-New York (100-123603)
1-New York (100-119011)
1-New York 100-107297)
CJG:rmv
(13)
        52 APR 8 1959

EX - 133   12 MAR 31 1959

Class. & Ext. By ████████
Reason-FCIM II, 1-2.4.2
Date of Review 5/4/91

REG-68
100-393031-36

CONFIDENTIAL

Columbia Pays $300,000 For 'A Raisin in the Sun'

Motion picture rights to Lorraine Hansberry's Broadway hit play, "A Raisin in the Sun," have been purchased by Columbia, for $300,000, with David Susskind and Philip Rose set to co-produce.

Negotiations are under way for the services of Sidney Poitier and Claudie McNeil, co-stars of the stage vehicle, to repeat their roles. Miss Hansberry has been signed to write the screenplay.

CLIPPING FROM THE
N Y POST

N.Y. _____

EDITION ___ 7th. BLUE FINAL

DATE ___ 1 APR 1959

PAGE ___ 72

FORWARDED ___

RE: LORRAINE VIVIAN
HANSBERRY NEMIROFF
SM-C

BUFILE 100-

ALL INFORMATION CONTAINED
HEREIN IS UNCLASSIFIED
DATE 4/10/89 BY

67C

100 — 393031-A
NOT RECORDED
149 APR 10 1959

APR 13 1959

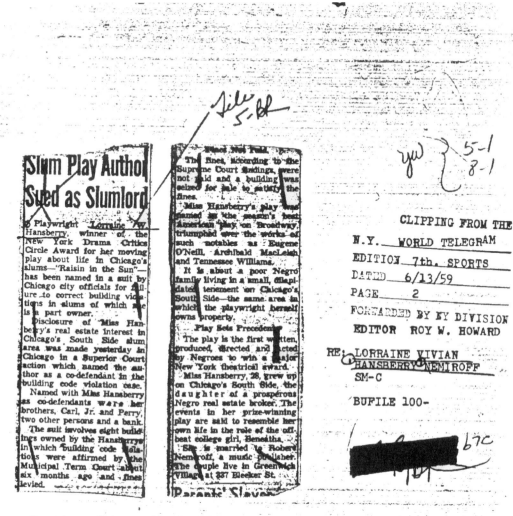

Slum Play Author Sued as Slumlord

Playwright Lorraine W. Hansberry, winner of the New York Drama Critics Circle Award for her moving play about life in Chicago's slums—"Raisin in the Sun"—has been named in a suit by Chicago city officials for failure to correct building violations in slums of which she is a part owner.

Disclosure of Miss Hansberry's real estate interest in Chicago's South Side slum area was made yesterday in Chicago in a Superior Court action which named the author as a co-defendant in the building code violation case.

Named with Miss Hansberry as co-defendants were her brothers, Carl, Jr. and Perry, two other persons and a bank.

The suit involves eight buildings owned by the Hansberrys in which building code violations were affirmed by the Municipal Term Court about six months ago and fines levied.

The fines, according to the Supreme Court findings, were not paid and a building was seized for sale to satisfy the fines.

Miss Hansberry's play was named as the season's best American play on Broadway, triumphed over the works of such notables as Eugene O'Neill, Archibald MacLeish and Tennessee Williams.

It is about a poor Negro family living in a small, dilapidated tenement on Chicago's South Side—the same area in which the playwright herself owns property.

Play Sets Precedent

The play is the first written, produced, directed and acted by Negroes to win a major New York theatrical award.

Miss Hansberry, 28, grew up on Chicago's South Side, the daughter of a prosperous Negro real estate broker. The events in her prize-winning play are said to resemble her own life in the role of the offbeat college girl, Beneatha.

She is married to Robert Nemeroff, a music publisher. The couple live in Greenwich Village at 337 Bleecker St.

CLIPPING FROM THE
N.Y. WORLD TELEGRAM
EDITION 7th. SPORTS
DATED 6/13/59
PAGE 2
FORWARDED BY NY DIVISION
EDITOR ROY W. HOWARD

RE: LORRAINE VIVIAN
HANSBERRY NEMIROFF
SM-C

BUFILE 100-

ALL INFORMATION CONTAINED
HEREIN IS UNCLASSIFIED
DATE 4/16/81 BY ___

100-393031-A-
NOT RECORDED
199 JUN 17 1959

MCT-25

53 JUN 22 1959

NY 100-107297

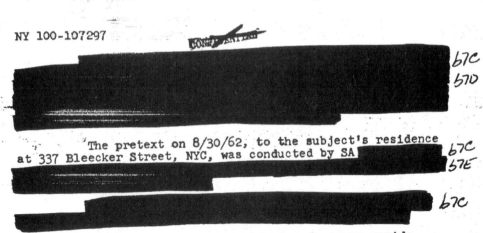

The pretext on 8/30/62, to the subject's residence at 337 Bleecker Street, NYC, was conducted by SA

It is noted that the subject and spouse reside at two different addresses, the wife living at 112 Waverly Place, NYC, and the husband residing at 337 Bleecker Street, NYC. It is believed that the purpose of these two addresses is for business reasons inasmuch as during the above mentioned pretext subject's spouse stated that his wife was unavailable and had "retreated" to her private residence at 112 Waverly Place, where she was unavailable for interview. The spouse mentioned that this was the customary practice of his wife whenever she was engaged in writing.

-B-
COVER PAGE

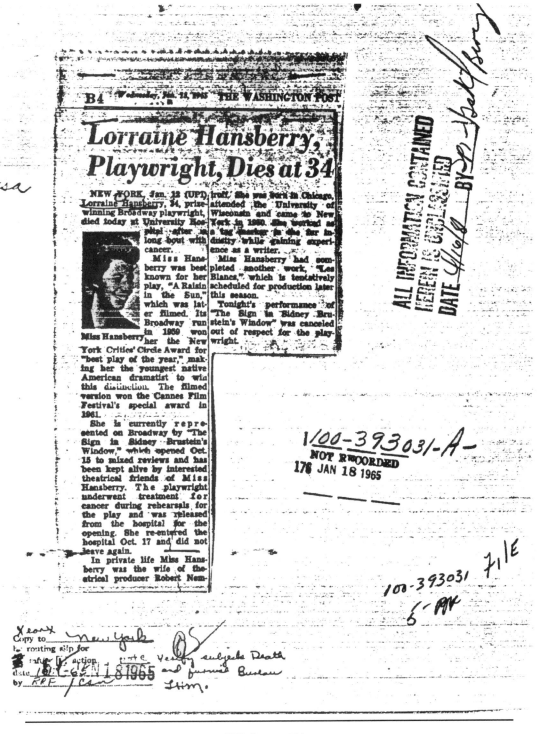

B4 Wednesday, Jan. 13, 1965 THE WASHINGTON POST

Lorraine Hansberry, Playwright, Dies at 34

NEW YORK, Jan. 12 (UPI) — Lorraine Hansberry, 34, prize-winning Broadway playwright, died today at University Hospital after a long bout with cancer.

Miss Hansberry was best known for her play, "A Raisin in the Sun," which was later filmed. Its Broadway run in 1959 won her the New York Critics' Circle Award for "best play of the year," making her the youngest native American dramatist to win this distinction. The filmed version won the Cannes Film Festival's special award in 1961.

She is currently represented on Broadway by "The Sign in Sidney Brustein's Window," which opened Oct. 15 to mixed reviews and has been kept alive by interested theatrical friends of Miss Hansberry. The playwright underwent treatment for cancer during rehearsals for the play and was released from the hospital for the opening. She re-entered the hospital Oct. 17 and did not leave again.

In private life Miss Hansberry was the wife of theatrical producer Robert Nem-

roff. She was born in Chicago, attended the University of Wisconsin and came to New York in 1950. She worked as a tag checker in the fur industry while gaining experience as a writer.

Miss Hansberry had completed another work, "Les Blancs," which is tentatively scheduled for production later this season.

Tonight's performance of "The Sign in Sidney Brustein's Window" was canceled out of respect for the playwright.

ALL INFORMATION CONTAINED HEREIN IS UNCLASSIFIED DATE _____ BY _____

100-39303I-A-
NOT RECORDED
176 JAN 18 1965

100-393031 71/E

Copy to ___ New York
routing slip for ___ action
date ___ JAN 18 1965
by RPF/csn

Chapter XV

Ernest Hemingway: An American Counterspy

E rnest Miller Hemingway, the son of Clarence Edmonds Hemingway, M. D. and Grace (Hall) Hemingway, was born on July 21, 1898, in Oak Park, Ill. His father, was an avid hunter and fisherman, and it was through him that Hemingway acquired a zeal for the wide open spaces that never faded. At the Oak Park High School, he played football, boxed, and wrote columns for the student newspaper. His literary mentor during his teenage years was Ringgold (Ring) Lardner, the American humorist, who authored <u>How to Write Short Stories</u> with samples.

In spite of his father and mother's desire for him to go downstate to the University of Illinois at Urbana after graduating from high school in 1917, Hemingway opted to become a cub reporter for the Kansas City Star in Missouri.

There he learned something from professionals about the craft of writing.

As news of World War I began blanketing Chicago's major newspapers, Hemingway's thirst for action in Europe pushed him into attempting to enlist in the Army and becoming a doughboy. His efforts to get into the service were in vain in that he was rejected because of an earlier sports injury to his left eye. Thus, his only chance of getting near the European battlefield was to become a Red Cross ambulance driver with the Italian Army. Shortly before his 19th birthday, he was seriously wounded at Fossalta di Piave, Italy. The Italians subsequently decorated him for bravery.

Hemingway recuperated from his war wounds in Italy and stateside in northern Michigan before signing on as a foreign correspondent for the Canadian Toronto Star. His first assignment in Europe was in Paris, France where he was aided in his efforts to become a writer by other American expatriates, notably Ezra Pound who became his tutor and Gertrude Stein whose works included Three Lives (1908) and The Autobiography of Alice B. Toklas (1933).

His first major publication, In Our Time (1925), combined short stories with long patternless but poetic paragraphs. It attracted much attention because of its unique lean style and brutal straight- through- the- heart- and- guts subject matter, both of which would remain his trademarks. His second important publication and first major novel, The Sun Also Rises (1926), depicted in colloquial, vivid terms the aimlessness of the postwar "lost generation" and it gained him fame during the roaring twenties that would become his signature for a lifetime.

In 1927 Hemingway married Pauline Pfeiffer a fashion writer in Paris, France. Two children, Patrick and Gregory, were born from that union, and the custody of the two boys was awarded to the mother following an uncontested divorce.

Hemingway's first marriage was destroyed because of a commonly known love affair with Martha Gellhorn who he subsequently married. It has been noted that his second wife, Martha, was also a journalist in her own right and a contributor to the Colliers magazine. Despite his multiple "I can't get enough of your love" theme that ran through all of his women, he still managed to stay put long enough to marry wives three and four in the following sequence: Hadley Richardson and

Mary Welsh.

At the age of 47, Hemingway made a loose attempt to relax for a spell with booze and broads on an estate called Finca Vigia near Havana, Cuba. He camped there until the Fidel Castro regime forced the ex-American counterspy to leave their country. For the next decade he continued to gallop at a much slower pace behind a mulitude of women and a few bullfights in Spain. At age 59, he was forced to settle down in Ketchum, Idaho because of his very poor health which had been accelerated by his "I don't give a damn" lifestyle. On top of his physical problem, he was inflicted with mental disorders that were reflected in bouts of acute depression and loss of memory. He was hospitalized twice within a short period of time at the Mayo Clinic in Rochester, Minnesota. On July 2, 1961, immediately following his second visit to Mayo, he stuck a shotgun in his mouth and blew his brains out at his home in Ketchum. He was 63 years old.

Hemingway's works mirrored his lifestyle which was filled with the ingredients of war, sports, drinking, brawling, traveling, and womanizing. Yet these preoccupations did not obscure his dedication to his craft. On the one hand, he was among the most colorful and most publicized men of his time; on the other hand, he was an artist, perhaps in some opinions the most influential American writer of prose in the first half of the 20th century.

Hemingway produced six novels and more than 50 short stories. Of his novels, The Sun Also Rises (1926) portrays the aimless expatriates of the 1920's, in Paris and at a fiesta in Pamplona, Spain. A Farewell to Arms (1929) is about a young American, disillusioned with World War I and the society that produced it, who is driven to desert the crumbling Italian Army and loses his mistress during childbirth. To Have and Have Not (1937) is a Depression novel, set in Cuba and Key West, Fla., about a man who is killed after becoming an outlaw to support his family. For Whom the Bell Tolls (1940), an epic work set in the Spanish Civil War, argues for the brotherhood of man and is Hemingway's first basically optimistic novel. The novelette The Old Man and the Sea (1952) chronicles the adventure of an old Cuban fisherman, Santiago, who sails out beyond sight of land, farther than he should, to catch a huge marlin, only to have it eaten by sharks. It is a paean to man's endurance, with the theme that a man can be destroyed but he cannot be defeated. This was Hemingway's last work to be published during his lifetime.

Ernest and his second wife, Martha Gellhorn, at the Stork Club in New York City in December 1940.

(John F. Kennedy Library)

Federal Bureau of Investigation

Freedom of Information/Privacy Acts Section

Subject: <u>Ernest Hemingway</u>

CONFIDENTIAL

ALL INFORMATION CONTAINED
HEREIN IS UNCLASSIFIED
EXCEPT WHERE SHOWN
OT...

Havana, Cuba
October 8, 1942

Director,
Federal Bureau of Investigation,
Washington, D. C.

Re: ERNEST HEMINGWAY

DECLASSIFIED BY 6383 VEP/AG
ON 5-26-81

Dear Sir:

The writer desires to acquaint the Bureau, in detail,
with a relationship that has developed under the direction of the
Ambassador with Mr. ERNEST HEMINGWAY.

As the Bureau is aware, HEMINGWAY has been resident in
Cuba almost continuously during the past two years, occupying his
private finca at San Francisco de Paula about 14 miles east of
Havana.

Mr. HEMINGWAY has been on friendly terms with Consul
KENNETH POTTER since the spring of 1941; recently he has become
very friendly with Mr. ROBERT P. JOYCE, Second Secretary of Embassy,
and through Mr. JOYCE has met the Ambassador on several occasions.
It is the writer's observation that the initiative in developing
these friendships has come from HEMINGWAY, but the opportunity of
association with him has been welcomed by Embassy officials.

At several conferences with the Ambassador and officers
of the Embassy late in August 1942, the topic of utilizing HEMINGWAY'S
services in intelligence activities was discussed. The Ambassador
pointed out that HEMINGWAY'S experiences during the Spanish Civil
War, his intimate acquaintances with Spanish Republican refugees
in Cuba, as well as his long experience on this island, seemed to
place him in a position of great usefulness to the Embassy's
intelligence program. While this program is inclusive of all
intelligence agencies and the Embassy's own sources of information,
the fact is that the Ambassador regards the Bureau representation
in the Embassy as the unit primarily concerned in this work. The
Ambassador further pointed out that HEMINGWAY had completed some
writing which had occupied him until that time, and was now ready
and anxious to be called upon.

RECORDED & INDEXED   64-23315-

The writer pointed out at these conferences that any
information which could be secured concerning the operations of the
Spanish Falange in Cuba would be of material assistance in our work,
and that if HEMINGWAY was willing to devote his time and abilities
to the gathering of such information, the results would be most
welcome to us. It was pointed out to Mr. JOYCE, who is designated

-X JAN 4 1943

CLASS. & EXT. BY SA DSK
...SON - FCIM 11, 1-2, 2
DATE OF REVIEW 10-24-89

CONFIDENTIAL

CONFIDENTIAL

Director,   Re: Ernest Hemingway

by the Ambassador as the Embassy's coordinator of intelligence activities, that some consideration should be given to the question of relationship between Mr. HEMINGWAY and the Bureau representatives directly.

This question existed in the writer's mind for two reasons: (1) It is recalled that when the Bureau was attacked early in 1940 as a result of the arrests in Detroit of certain individuals charged with Neutrality Act violations for fostering enlistments in the Spanish Republican forces, Mr. HEMINGWAY was among the signers of a declaration which severely criticized the Bureau in that case; (2) in attendance at a Jai Alai match with HEMINGWAY, the writer was introduced by him to a friend as a member of the Gestapo. On that occasion, I told HEMINGWAY that I did not appreciate the introduction, whereupon he promptly corrected himself and said I was one of the United States Consuls.

Mr. JOYCE made inquiries of HEMINGWAY concerning his attitude toward working with us, without disclosing the reasons therefor, and reported that his attitude appeared to be entirely favorable to the Bureau; that he was unable to remember any details of the Detroit incident of 1940, and that he regarded the Gestapo introduction as a jest.

It was decided, nevertheless, that HEMINGWAY would work directly in contact with Mr. JOYCE and not with the writer; this suggestion came from Mr. JOYCE, and no advantage was seen in making any different arrangements. It was also decided that the expenses he would incur would be paid by the Embassy directly out of special funds.

Consequently, early in September 1942, ERNEST HEMINGWAY began to engage directly in intelligence activities on behalf of the American Embassy in Havana. These activities he manages from his finca, with visits to Havana two or three times weekly. He is operating through Spanish Republicans whose identities have not been furnished but which we are assured are obtainable when desired. At a meeting with him at his finca on September 30, 1942, the writer was advised that he now has four men operating on a full time basis, and 14 more whose positions are barmen, waiters, and the like, operating on a part-time basis. The cost of this program is approximately $500 a month. Reports are submitted to HEMINGWAY, who dictates the material to a personal secretary and furnishes duplicate copies to Mr. JOYCE, one being for the Embassy and the other for our use. The material thus far submitted appears to be carefully prepared and set out, and the Ambassador has noted

CONFIDENTIAL

- 2 -

CONF**X**ITIAL

Director,   Re: Ernest Hemingway

on several memoranda that he likes HEMINGWAY'S approach, and wishes
to encourage him in the type of work that he is doing. HEMINGWAY
himself told me that he declined an offer from Hollywood to write
a script for a "March of Time" report on the "Flying Tigers" in
Burma, for which the compensation was to be $150,000, because he
considers the work he is now engaged in as of greater importance.

   One of the aspects of Mr. HEMINGWAY'S relationships with the
Embassy ▇▇▇▇▇▇▇▇▇▇▇▇▇▇▇▇▇▇▇▇▇▇▇▇ to utilize his services for certain
coastal patrol and investigative work on the south coast of Cuba.
HEMINGWAY, who has a wide reputation as a fisherman, knows the
coast line and waters of Cuba very intimately; he has also engaged
over a 12-year period in some scientific investigations concerning
the migration of Marlin on behalf of the Museum of Natural History,
New York City. ▇▇▇▇▇▇▇▇▇▇▇▇ has acceded to HEMINGWAY'S request for authorization to patrol certain areas where submarine activity has been
reported. ▇▇▇▇▇▇▇▇▇▇▇▇▇▇▇▇▇▇▇▇▇▇▇▇▇ and an allot-
ment of gasoline is now being obtained for his use. He has requested
▇▇▇▇▇▇▇▇▇▇▇▇▇▇▇ he has secured from the Ambassador a promise that his
crew members will be recognized as war casualties for purposes of
indemnification in the event any loss of life results from this
operation.

   With specific reference to the conducting of intelligence
investigations on the island of Cuba by Mr. HEMINGWAY, the writer
wishes to state that his interest thus far has not been limited to
the Spanish Falange and Spanish activities, but that he has included
numerous German suspects. His reports are promptly furnished and he
assures Mr. JOYCE that his only desire is to be of assistance on a
cooperative basis, without compensation to himself, and that he will
be guided at all times by our wishes. So far, no conflict has
developed between his work and that which Bureau personnel is handling
in Havana; and HEMINGWAY told me that he wishes to be told where to
limit his investigations whenever this is thought desirable.

   The Bureau will be continuously advised of pertinent
developments in this situation. Meanwhile, if there is any information or instructions for the guidance of the writer, I would
appreciate being advised.

                              Very truly yours,

                              R. G. Leddy

                              R. G. LEDDY
                              Legal Attache

RGL:RM

- 3 -   CONF**X**IDE...

'ALL INFORMATION CONTAINED
HEREIN IS UNCLASSIFIED
EXCEPT WHERE SHOWN
OTHERWISE

CONFIDENTIAL

Havana, Cuba
October 9, 1942

Director,
Federal Bureau of Investigation,
Washington, D. C.

PERSONAL AND CONFIDENTIAL

Attention Mr. C. H. Carson
Room 2266

Re: ERNEST HEMINGWAY

DECLASSIFIED BY 6383 VRT/A
ON 5-26-81

Dear Sir:

Reference is made to my letter dated October 8, 1942 in this matter. For the further information of the Bureau regarding Mr. HEMINGWAY'S participation in intelligence activities, under the auspices of the Embassy, it is now understood that one GUSTAVO DURAN is being sent from Washington for the special purpose of assisting Mr. HEMINGWAY in this work.

Mr. HEMINGWAY advised the Ambassador that DURAN had been active with him in intelligence work on the Republican side of the Spanish Civil War, and recommended his abilities very highly. DURAN, he said, held some position in the Department of State, the exact position being unknown. He was uncertain whether DURAN who was formerly a Spanish citizen had acquired American citizenship.

At the instance of Mr. HEMINGWAY, the Ambassador communicated with the Department of State which agreed to release DURAN on leave of absence in order that he might come to Cuba and work with Mr. HEMINGWAY as he did in Spain.

Of further interest in this matter is a visit of Mrs. ERNEST HEMINGWAY (the former MARTHA GELHORN) to Washington during the week commencing October 12, 1942. Mrs. HEMINGWAY is to be the personal guest of Mrs. ROOSEVELT during her stay in Washington, and the Ambassador outlined to her certain aspects of the intelligence situation in Cuba in order that she might convey the same, in personal conversation, to the President and Mrs. ROOSEVELT. This has specific reference to the Embassy's request for approval of financing by the American Government of internment and investigative program brought out by the Cuban authorities. To date, no action has resulted from Washington on this proposal and it is thought by the Ambassador that some results may be obtained through this form of personal contact.

COPIES DESTROYED
9 08 NOV 2 1951

RECORDED & INDEXED

64-23312-X1
FEDERAL BUREAU OF INVESTIGATION
OCT 14 1942
U. S. DEPARTMENT OF JUSTICE

70 FEB 15 1943   CONFIDENTIAL

CLASS. & EXT. BY SP7 05K/du
REASON - FCIM 11 - 24.2 (2)(3)
DATE OF REVIEW 10-24-79

Director   Re: ERNEST HEMINGWAY ~~CONFIDENTIAL~~ 10-9-42

    In view of the importance of this matter, you may
desire to bring this and reference letter to the personal
attention of the Director.

        Very truly yours,

        R. G. Leddy

        (R. /G. LEDDY
        Legal Attaché

-2- ~~CONFIDENTIAL~~

HOOVER

Federal Bureau of Investigation
United States Department of Justice
Washington, D. C.

December 17, 1942

CHC:LL   CONFIDENTIAL

Mr. Tolson
Mr. E. A. Tamm
Mr. Clegg
Mr. Glavin
Mr. Ladd
Mr. Nichols
Mr. Rosen
Mr. Tracy
Mr. Carson
Mr. Coffey
Mr. Hendon
Mr. Kramer
Mr. McGuire
Mr. Harbo
Mr. Quinn Tamm
Tele. Room
Mr. Nease
Miss Beahm
Miss Gandy

MEMORANDUM FOR THE DIRECTOR

Re: ERNEST HEMINGWAY   ALL INFORMATION CONTAINED
HEREIN IS UNCLASSIFIED
EXCEPT WHERE SHOWN
OTHERWISE

BACKGROUND

Mr. Ernest Hemingway, well-known American writer, recently
has been acting as personal informant of Ambassador Spruille Braden
in Havana, Cuba.

DETAILS

FBI Attache R. G. Leddy, stationed at the American Embassy in
Havana, Cuba, has recently advised that Ernest Hemingway, well-known American
writer, has been residing in Cuba, just outside Havana, for approximately
two years. Hemingway, it will be recalled, engaged actively on the side
of the Spanish Republic during the Spanish Civil War, and it is reported that
he is very well acquainted with a large number of Spanish refugees in Cuba
and elsewhere. Hemingway, it will be recalled, joined in attacking the Bureau
early in 1940, at the time of the "general smear campaign" following the
arrests of certain individuals in Detroit charged with violation of Federal
statutes in connection with their participation in Spanish Civil War activities.
It will be recalled that Hemingway signed a declaration, along with a number
of other individuals, severely criticizing the Bureau in connection with the
Detroit arrests. Hemingway has been accused of being of Communist sympathy,
although we are advised that he has denied and does vigorously deny any
Communist affiliation or sympathy. Hemingway is reported to be personally
friendly with Ambassador Braden, and he is reported to enjoy the Ambassador's
complete confidence. According to Agent Leddy, Hemingway is also on very
friendly terms with United States Consul Kenneth Potter, presently stationed
in Cuba, and with Mr. Robert P. Joyce, Second Secretary of the American
Embassy in Havana.

RECORDED & INDEXED   64-23312-X2

Mr. Leddy has advised that Hemingway has been acting as an informant of Ambassador Braden for the past several months and in this capacity
has been dealing closely with Ambassador Braden and Second Secretary Joyce.
Leddy stated that Ambassador Braden has made no secret of this connection,
in so far as Agent Leddy is concerned, and, further, that the Ambassador has
instructed that all of Hemingway's reports and any information furnished by him
must be turned over to Mr. Leddy.

FOR DEFENSE
BUY
UNITED
STATES
SAVINGS
BONDS
AND STAMPS

70 FEB 10 1943   CONFIDENTIAL

CONFIDENTIAL

Memorandum for the Director

CONFIDENTIAL

Page 2

Mr. Leddy has advised that the original arrangement whereby Mr. Hemingway would act as informant of Ambassador Braden was largely concerned with certain political matters, particularly as to the connection or alleged connection of certain Cuban political leaders with the Spanish Falange and the involvement of Cuban officials generally in local graft and corruption within Cuba. Ambassador Braden, as you will recall, is a very impulsive individual and he apparently has had a "bee in his bonnet" for some time concerning alleged graft and corruption on the part of certain Cuban officials. Agent Leddy has stated that Mr. Hemingway has apparently organized a number of informants among the Spanish refugee group, whose identities are not known to Leddy, and, according to the best of his information, their identities are not known to anyone except Hemingway.

Agent Leddy has advised that Hemingway's activities have branched out and that he and his informants are now engaged in reporting to the Embassy various types of information concerning subversive activities generally. Mr. Leddy stated that he has become quite concerned with respect to Hemingway's activities and that they are undoubtedly going to be very embarrassing unless something is done to put a stop to them. Mr. Leddy has advised that Hemingway is apparently undertaking a rather involved investigation with regard to Cuban officials prominently connected with the Cuban Government, including General Manuel Benitez y Valdes, head of the Cuban National Police; that he, Agent Leddy, is sure that the Cubans are eventually going to find out about this if Hemingway continues operating, and that serious trouble may result.

Mr. Leddy has advised that there is an individual attached to the Embassy by the name of Gustavo Duran, who is of Spanish descent and is employed by the Coordinator of Inter-American Affairs; that Duran is a very close friend of Hemingway and is apparently consulting and actually working with Hemingway in connection with the latter's activities.

This matter has been discussed at some length with Mr. Leddy, and he was asked just what objection, if any, he has ever personally or officially offered to the arrangement or whether he has discussed its possible bad effects with the Ambassador.

Leddy stated that he has not offered any objection whatsoever to this proposition; that the Ambassador has advised Leddy quite frankly and openly that Hemingway is the Ambassador's informant and that all information of any kind whatsoever furnished by Hemingway will be immediately

CONFIDENTIAL   CONFIDENTIAL

Memorandum for the Director   Page 3

turned over to Leddy, which, according to Leddy, is actually being
done. Leddy suggested that the Bureau take this matter up with Ambassador Braden while he is in the United States.

    It was pointed out to Leddy that the Bureau certainly cannot
take the matter up with Ambassador Braden and protest to him unless
Leddy has first made the Bureau's position quite plain to the Ambassador
himself. It was pointed out to Mr. Leddy that the Ambassador would
undoubtedly resent any complaint or protest concerning the arrangement
from the Bureau direct, which complaint and protest could only be based
upon Leddy's recommendations and information, unless Leddy has himself
first discussed the matter with the Ambassador and pointed out the
Bureau's position, this being particularly true inasmuch as Ambassador
Braden has apparently been quite frank with Agent Leddy about the
arrangement and has insisted that all information furnished by Hemingway
be immediately furnished to Agent Leddy.

(b1)

(C)

    Mr. Leddy stated that he can point out to the Ambassador that
he, Leddy, has not checked any reports from Hemingway concerning corruption
in the Cuban Government; that he does not feel that Bureau Agents should
become involved in any such investigations, it being entirely without our
jurisdiction and a matter in which the Cubans themselves alone are concerned and something that, if we get involved in it, is going to mean that
all of us will be thrown out of Cuba "bag and baggage."

    Agent Leddy stated he can point out to the Ambassador the
extreme danger of having some informant like Hemingway given free rein
to stir up trouble such as that which will undoubtedly ensue if this
situation continues. Mr. Leddy stated that despite the fact the

Memorandum for the Director

Memorandum for the Director   **CONFIDENTIAL** ~~CONFIDENTIAL~~ Page 4

Ambassador likes Hemingway and apparently has confidence in him, he is of the opinion that he, Leddy, can handle this situation with the Ambassador so that Hemingway's services as an informant will be completely discontinued. Mr. Leddy stated that he can point out to the Ambassador that Hemingway is going further than just an informant; that he is actually branching out into an investigative organization of his own which is not subject to any control whatsoever.

RECOMMENDATION

(C)

    Mr. Leddy, if you approve, will be told to advise the Bureau promptly and in detail as to the outcome of his negotiations with the Ambassador concerning this matter, at which time we should, it is believed, advise Mr. Berle for the Bureau's protection.

Respectfully,

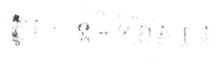

D. M. Ladd

CONFIDENTIAL

~~CONFIDENTIAL~~

CONFIDENTIAL

December 19, 1942

ALL INFORMATION CONTAINED
HEREIN IS UNCLASSIFIED
EXCEPT WHERE SHOWN
OTHERWISE

MEMORANDUM FOR MR. TAMM
MR. LADD CLASSIFIED BY 6383 VRT/AG
ON

In regard to Mr. Ladd's memorandum of the 17th instant concerning the use of Ernest Hemingway by the United States Ambassador to Cuba, I of course realize the complete undesirability of this sort of a connection or relationship. Certainly Hemingway is the last man, in my estimation, to be used in any such capacity. His judgment is not of the best, and if his sobriety is the same as it was some years ago, that is certainly questionable.

However, I do not think there is anything we should do in this matter, nor do I think our representative at Havana should do anything about it with the Ambassador. The Ambassador is somewhat hot-headed and I haven't the slightest doubt that he would immediately tell Hemingway of the objections being raised by the FBI. Hemingway has no particular love for the FBI and would no doubt embark upon a campaign of vilification.

In addition thereto, you will recall that in my conference recently with the President, he indicated that some message had been sent to him, the President, by Hemingway through a mutual friend, and Hemingway was insisting that one-half million dollars be granted to the Cuban authorities so that they could take care of internees.

I do not see that it is a matter that directly affects our relationship as long as Hemingway does not report directly to us or we deal directly with him. Anything which he gives to the Ambassador which the Ambassador in turn forwards to us, we can accept without any impropriety.

Mr. Tolson _____ I have no objection to Mr. Tamm informally talking with
Mr. E. A. Tamm Mr. Berle about this matter, but impress Mr. Berle with the fact that
Mr. Clegg we do not want to become involved in any controversies concerning the
Mr. Glavin
Mr. Ladd ✓✓
Mr. Nichols
Mr. Rosen   Very truly yours
Mr. Tracy   RECORDED & INDEXED
Mr. Carson
Mr. Coffey   SENT FROM   John Edgar Hoover
Mr. Hendon   Director
Mr. Kramer
Mr. McGuire
Mr. Harbo
Mr. Quinn Tamm
Mr. Nease
Miss Gandy

-X FEB 5 1943   CONFIDENTIAL

OFFICE OF THE LEGAL ATTACHE   CON~~FIDENTIAL~~

ALL INFORMATION CONTAINED
HEREIN IS UNCLASSIFIED
EXCEPT WHERE SHOWN
OTHERWISE

EMBASSY OF THE
UNITED STATES OF AMERICA
HABANA, CUBA

April 21, 1943

Director,
Federal Bureau of Investigation,
Washington, D. C.

Re: ERNEST HEMINGWAY

DECLASSIFIED BY L 383 VRT/AC
ON 5-24-77

Dear Sir:

The Bureau has previously been advised
of the activities of Mr. Ernest Hemingway in the
operation of an under cover "intelligence" organization in Cuba, under the auspices of the American
Embassy.

The writer has been advised in confidence
by an Embassy official that Hemingway's organization
was disbanded and its work terminated as of April 1,
1943. This action was taken by the American
Ambassador without any consultation or notice to
representatives of the Federal Bureau of Investigation.

A complete report on the activities of
Mr. Hemingway and the organization which he operated is now being prepared, and will be forwarded
to the Bureau in the immediate future.

10-24-79
CLASS. & EXT. BY SP-1
REASON - FCIM 11, 1-2.4.2 (2) (3)
DATE OF REVIEW 10-24-89

Very truly yours,

RGL:RM

CONF. INFT. S. I. S. # 396

RECORDED

64-2331-1
FEDERAL BUREAU OF INVESTIGATION
L - APR 24 1943
U. S. DEPARTMENT OF JUSTICE

CONFIDENTIAL

BRIEFED SIS

JOHN EDGAR HOOVER
DIRECTOR

CC-287

Mr. Tolson
Mr. E.A. Tamm
Mr. Clegg
Mr. Glavin
Mr. Ladd
Mr. Nichols
Mr. Rosen
Mr. Tracy
Mr. Carson
Mr. Coffee
Mr. Hendon
Mr. Kramer
Mr. McGuire
Mr. Harbo
Mr. Quinn Tamm
Mr. Room
Mr. Nease
Miss Beahm
Miss Gandy

Federal Bureau of Investigation
United States Department of Justice
Washington, D. C.

CONFIDENTIAL April 27, 1943

WHA:CSM:LNS

ALL INFORMATION CONTAINED
HEREIN IS UNCLASSIFIED
EXCEPT WHERE SHOWN
OTHERWISE

MEMORANDUM FOR THE DIRECTOR.

RE: ERNEST HEMINGWAY

DECLASSIFIED BY 6383 JKTAR
ON 5-26-81

In accordance with your request, there is attached a memorandum which summarizes the information in our files regarding Ernest Hemingway, the author.

Mr. Hemingway, it will be noted, has been connected with various so-called Communist front organizations and was active in aiding the Loyalist cause in Spain. In the latter connection he spent sometime in Spain during the Spanish revolution and reported the events transpiring there for the North American Newspaper Alliance.

Despite Hemingway's activities, no information has been received which would definitely tie him with the Communist Party or which would indicate that he is or has been a Party member. His actions, however, have indicated that his views are "liberal" and that he may be inclined favorably to Communist political philosophies.

Hemingway is now in Havana, Cuba where he has resided for over two years. For sometime he acted as an under-cover informant for American Ambassador Spruille Braden, and apparently enjoyed the Ambassador's complete confidence. You will recall that on December 17, 1942, there were set forth in a memorandum for you, the details of Hemingway's activities in Cuba, as well as the details of his association with the American Ambassador.

Briefly, Hemingway established what was termed "an amateur information service" and gathered alleged intelligence data which he turned over to Mr. Braden. In this work Hemingway developed his own confidential informants and was said to be friendly with a number of Spanish refugees in Cuba. His relationship with the Ambassador was quite friendly, but the Ambassador was perfectly frank with the Bureau representatives in Havana regarding this relationship and made all of the information which Hemingway furnished to him, available to the Bureau. These data, however, were almost without fail valueless.

CLASS. & EXT. BY SPN DJK/gW
REASON - FCIM 11, 1-2.4.2 (2)(3)
DATE OF REVIEW 10-25-77

RECORDED 64-23312-3

FOR VICTORY
BUY
UNITED STATES
SAVINGS
BONDS
AND
STAMPS

75 JUN 18 1943

CONFIDENTIAL

CONFIDENTIAL

MEMORANDUM FOR THE DIRECTOR

C.I. S.I.S.# 396

██████████ the Bureau representative stationed at the
American Embassy in Havana, Cuba has recently advised that the Ambassador
discontinued Hemingway's services effective April 1, 1943. At the present
time he is alleged to be performing a highly secret naval operation for
the Navy Department. In this connection, the Navy Department is said to
be paying the expenses for the operation of Hemingway's boat, furnishing
him with arms and charting courses in the Cuban area. (S)u

The Bureau has conducted no investigation of Hemingway, but his
name has been mentioned in connection with other Bureau investigations
and various data concerning him have been submitted voluntarily by a
number of different sources.

Respectfully,

D. M. Ladd

Enclosure

- 10 -

CONFIDENTIAL

to this informant, approximately 4,000 persons attended this meeting which had been previously advertised by the Communist press and at organizational meetings. Donald Ogden Stewart presided at the meeting and lauded Ernest Hemingway for donating an ambulance to the Spanish Loyalists.

Writers and Artists Ambulance Corps

The Daily Worker of January 12, 1938 described Hemingway as one of the sponsors of the Writers and Artists Ambulance Corps which was said to have sent ambulances to Spain. Hemingway was credited with having personally purchased the first two ambulances which were sent to that country in May, 1937.

Possible Connections with Communist Party

The following information was secured from a confidential source:

"Ernest Hemingway, New York specialty writer for New Masses and Daily Worker, page 1, Daily Worker, 9-13-35; wires greeting to Soviet Union, page 2, Daily Worker, 5-2-38."

A former letterhead of the Deutsches Volksecho, which bore the date of February 16, 1939, carried the name of Ernest Hemingway as one of the contributors to this group.

In the fall of 1940 Hemingway's name was included in a group of names of individuals who were said to be engaged in Communist activities. These individuals were reported to occupy positions on the "intellectual front" and were said to render valuable service as propagandists. According to the informant, those whose names were included on this list loaned their efforts politically as writers, artists and speakers and traveled throughout the country supporting and taking part in Communist front meetings and in the program of the Party generally. They were alleged to be particularly active in the then paramount Communist Party objective, namely, defeat of the preparedness program.

Hemingway, according to a confidential source who furnished information on October 4, 1941, was one of the "heads" of the Committee for Medical Aid to the Soviet Union. This informant alleged that the above-mentioned committee was backed by the Communist Party.

(b1)

(C)

Dr. Alfred Kantorowicz listed Hemingway as a reference at the time he filled out his alien registration form. Kantorowicz is a German alien and has been reported to be one of the chief liaison men between the German Communists in Mexico and the German Communists in the United States. He was also allegedly the founder of the League of German Writers in Exile in Paris, France.

CONFIDENTIAL

OFFICE OF THE LEGAL ATTACHE

ALL INFORMATION CONTAINED
HEREIN IS UNCLASSIFIED
EXCEPT WHERE SHOWN
OTHERWISE

Classified by ~~39·1 CSK/04~~
Declassify on: OADR

CLASS. & EXT. BY ~~SA/1 DSK/9hw~~
REASON - FCIM 11. 12 4.2 (2)(3)
DATE OF REVIEW 10-26-89

EMBASSY OF THE
UNITED STATES OF AMERICA
HABANA, CUBA

June 26, 1943

Director,
Federal Bureau of Investigation,
Washington, D. C.

Re: ERNEST HEMINGWAY --
INTELLIGENCE ACTIVITIES IN CUBA

Dear Sir:

     As of interest to the Bureau, the following matters
affecting general intelligence activities are set forth.

1) Communist Attack on Ernest Hemingway

     SIS #360 has submitted a memorandum concerning the
attack in the Communist newspaper "Hoy" of April 25, 1943,
against Ernest Hemingway. The article is entitled, "The Last
Position of the Traitor Hemingway," and is written by Raul
Gonzalez Tunon.

     The article attacks Hemingway on several grounds.
First, it condemns him as being one of the "war tourists" who
went to Spain, not to seek the popular and eternal Spain, but
to seek curious, "effeminate", queer characters. Not finding
such characters in the Loyalist zone, they made friends with
the most "delirious" adventurers infiltrated in the CNT and
with the individualists of the Trotskyist group of the POUM.
On Hemingway's return to America, he published a book that was
"so miserable, so slanderous", that it met with excellent reception among the Fascists, the Trotskyists and the Munichists.
This was "For Whom the Bell Tolls." "The attacks on Andre
Marty...constitute a repetition of known slanders whose origin
must be sought in the propaganda office of Dr. Goebbels."

     Now, the article states Hemingway is a champion of the
race theory, in reverse. He advocates in the United States a
campaign for the sterilization of all Germans as a means of pre-
serving peace. That is, he wants to make this a racial war
against Germany. He shakes hands with Goebbels, who, trying to
prevent the disaster of the German people, says that "the skin
of every German is at stake in this war." This idea of Hemingway's
is a Trotskyist idea at the service of Nazism.

CONFIDENTIAL

Memorandum for Mr. Ladd
Page 9

CONFIDENTIAL

CONFIDENTIAL

(b1)

Hemingway has made this clear in regard to the film production
of his book "For Whom the Bell Tolls." He sold the movie rights to the
book more than two years ago; the picture was filmed and has gone through
several editing processes and according to Hemingway's latest information,
a final revision of the picture and reshooting of many scenes has resulted in the removal of all of what he considers the vital parts of the
story relating to the Spanish Civil War and reduced it to what he terms
a mere "Graustark romance." Hemingway has vigorously asserted that he
will soon go to Hollywood to find out who is responsible for this treatment of his book and when he finds out he will make an incident of it
which will cause the persons responsible to regret having ever inter-
fered with the story itself. Hemingway believes that influences which
he terms "Fascist" namely the Vatican and some elements in the United
States Department of State have been most influential in taking the teeth
out of his story.

Regarding Hemingway's position in Cuba, the Legal Attache
advises that his prestige and following are very great. He enjoys the
complete personal confidence of the American Ambassador and the Legal
Attache has witnessed conferences where the Ambassador observed Hemingway's
opinions as gospel and followed enthusiastically Hemingway's warning of
the probable seizure of Cuba by a force of 30,000 Germans transported
to the island in 1,000 submarines. A clique of celebrity-minded hero
worshippers surround Hemingway wherever he goes, numbering such persons
as Winston Guest, Lieutenant Tommy Shevlin (wealthy son of a famous Yale
football player), Mrs. Kathleen Vanderbilt Arostegui and several Embassy
officials. To them, Hemingway is a man of genius whose fame will be
remembered with Tolstoy.

CONFIDENTIAL

CONFIDENTIAL

FBI Secret Files

334

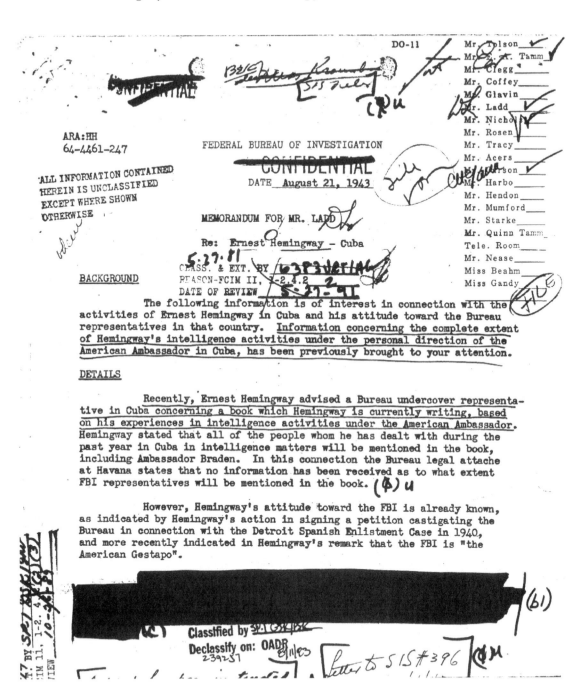

CONFIDENTIAL

CONFIDENTIAL

Mr. Ladd
Page 2

<u>ACTION</u>

No action is recommended in this matter at the present time, and the above information is being set out to supplement information previously called to your attention concerning Ernest Hemingway. (*) u

Respectfully,

C. H. Carson

We ought to try
& keep close to this
development.

CONFIDENTIAL

CONFIDENTIAL

CONFIDENTIAL

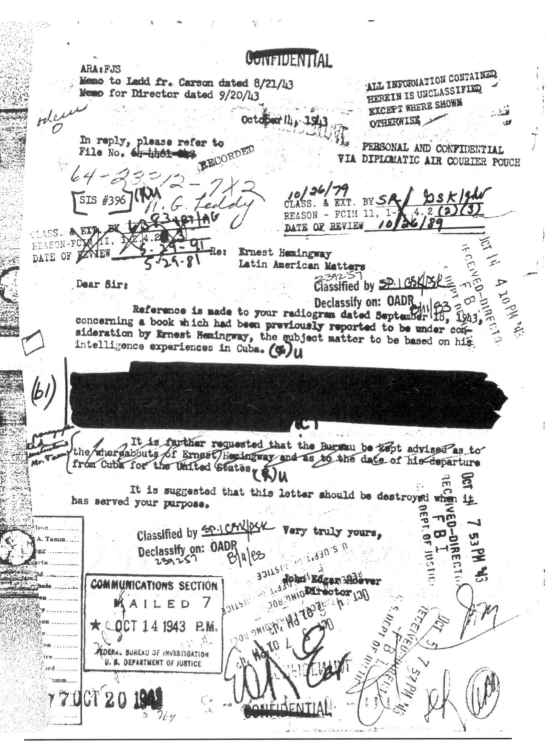

CONFIDENTIAL

ARA:FJS
Memo to Ladd fr. Carson dated 8/21/43
Memo for Director dated 9/20/43

ALL INFORMATION CONTAINED
HEREIN IS UNCLASSIFIED
EXCEPT WHERE SHOWN
OTHERWISE

October 14, 1943

In reply, please refer to
File No. 64-4461-843

PERSONAL AND CONFIDENTIAL
VIA DIPLOMATIC AIR COURIER POUCH

64-23312-7X2

[SIS #396]

10/26/79
CLASS. & EXT. BY SA /
REASON - FCIM 11, 1-4.2 (2)(3)
DATE OF REVIEW 10/26/89

CLASS. & EXT. BY
REASON-FCIM 11, 12.4.2
DATE OF REVIEW 5-29-81

Re: Ernest Hemingway
Latin American Matters

Classified by SP.1
Declassify on: OADR

Dear Sir:

Reference is made to your radiogram dated September 18, 1943, concerning a book which had been previously reported to be under consideration by Ernest Hemingway, the subject matter to be based on his intelligence experiences in Cuba. (S)U

(b1)

It is further requested that the Bureau be kept advised as to the whereabouts of Ernest Hemingway and as to the date of his departure from Cuba for the United States. (R)U

It is suggested that this letter should be destroyed when it has served your purpose.

Classified by SP.1
Declassify on: OADR

Very truly yours,

John Edgar Hoover
Director

COMMUNICATIONS SECTION
MAILED 7
★ OCT 14 1943 P.M.
FEDERAL BUREAU OF INVESTIGATION
U. S. DEPARTMENT OF JUSTICE

CONFIDENTIAL

FBI Secret Files

337

New York, 7, N. Y.

May 22, 1944

MR. HOOVER -

RE: ERNEST HEMINGWAY

Ernest is a great admirer of you
and the Bureau. In a conversation with an
Agent of this Office, he stated that he had
met several of the Bureau representatives
while in Havana, Cuba, and he thought that
they were of an unusually high type and,
further, that their work was most effective
there. He stated that he had been very
friendly with General Benitz, who was a
ranking political power in Cuba, and he
thought it was most amusing the General
should hold his present position inasmuch
as some years ago Benitz had acted in several
Hollywood pictures in which he played "Latin
lover" roles.

E. E. CONROY

ALL INFORMATION CONTAINED
HEREIN IS UNCLASSIFIED
DATE 10/26/79 BY SP-1 BSK/gbn

RECORDED
&
INDEXED

64-23312
F B I

32 JUN 7 1944

Hemingway Helped Spy, Saboteur Hunt

NEW YORK, Dec. 22 (P).—
Novelist Ernest Hemingway ran an underground "crime shop" in Cuba during World War II to help American agents track down saboteurs and spies aiding the enemy sink Allied shipping in the Caribbean Sea, it was disclosed today.

Spruille Braden, former Assistant Secretary of State, said that when he was Ambassador to Cuba in 1942, he arranged with Hemingway for the establishment of this counterspy apparatus.

The apparatus was headed, Braden said, by Gustavo Duran, an international mystery man and Hemingway's "inspiration" for the hero of "For Whom the Bell Tolls."

INDEXED-33

NOT RECORDED
133 JAN 7 1954

Times-Herald
Wash. Post
Wash. News
Wash. Star
N.Y. Herald Tribune
N.Y. Mirror

ALL INFORMATION CONTAINED
HEREIN IS UNCLASSIFIED
DATE 10/26/79 BY SP-1 BSK/9hn

Date:

5 8 JAN 12 1954

Hemingway's Suit

A lot of people in the writing game will understand why Ernest Hemingway has filed suit to prevent Esquire magazine from republishing some of his old stories about the Spanish Civil War. Back in those days, two decades ago, he was a strong supporter of the Loyalists against Generalissimo Franco, and the stories in question reflected his sentiment of that period. But now, even though he still adheres to that sentiment, he apparently wishes he had written them in a different way. Anyhow, he doesn't want to see them in print again in their original form, which makes him not unlike numerous lesser writers who are embarrassed when confronted with certain of their past works that look slightly unpolished or naive in retrospect.

Thus, speaking through his lawyer's brief, in a style not nearly so good as his own, Mr. Hemingway has had this to say: "It is respectfully submitted, and the court well knows, that the passage of time can affect the writings of authors either favorably or unfavorably. . . . Illustrative is the change in attitude of people to writings of men during the time Russia was our ally, to the present attitude of people to such men and their writings now that Russia is perhaps our greatest enemy." This is pretty turgid prose—prose which the Old Master obviously had nothing to do with, and which he has disavowed as a distortion of his own views—but it still makes its poignant point. Quite plainly, like many another literary fellow, Mr. Hemingway feels he has a right to revise some of his earlier pieces in a way designed to make sure that they will never return to haunt him.

However, even though Esquire has bowed to his suit, Mr. Hemingway must reconcile himself to the fact that it is not really possible for him, especially because of his stature, to stop the work of those who will keep on trying to compile and publish everything he has ever said or written. His position in that respect is well summed up in the following lines from an old American versifier:

"Careful with fire," is good advice we know;
"Careful with words," is ten times doubly so.
Thoughts unexpressed may sometimes fall back dead;
But God Himself can't kill them when they're said.

Tolson _____
Belmont _____
Mohr _____
Nease _____
Parsons _____
Rosen _____
Tamm _____
Trotter _____
W.C. Sullivan _____
Tele. Room _____
Holloman _____
Gandy _____

64-23313-A
NOT RECORDED
18 AUG 18 1958

Wash. Post and _____
    Times Herald
Wash. News _____
Wash. Star _A10_
N. Y. Herald _____
    Tribune
N. Y. Journal- _____
    American
N. Y. Mirror _____
N. Y. Daily News _____
N. Y. Times _____
Daily Worker _____
The Worker _____
New Leader _____

Date ___AUG 11 1958___

ALL INFORMATION CONTAINED HEREIN IS UNCLASSIFIED DATE 10/25/79 BY SP-1 BSK/gkh

52 AUG 19 1958

FD-36 (Rev. 12-13-56)

	Mr. Tolson
	Mr. Mohr
	Mr. Parsons
	Mr. Belmont
	Mr. Callahan
	Mr. DeLoach
	Mr. Malone
	Mr. McGuire
	Mr. Rosen
	Mr. Tamm
	Mr. Trotter
	Mr. W.C.Sullivan
	Tele. Room
	Mr. Ingram
	Miss Gandy

F B I

Date: **1/13/61**

Transmit the following in _____ **PLAIN**

(Type in plain text or code)

Via _____ **AIRTEL** _____

(Priority or Method of Mailing)

TO: DIRECTOR, FBI   PERSONAL ATTENTION

FROM: SAC, MINNEAPOLIS

RE: ERNEST HEMINGWAY
        INFORMATION CONCERNING

ERNEST HEMINGWAY, the author, has been a patient at Mayo
Clinic, Rochester, Minnesota, and is presently at St. Mary's
Hospital in that city. He has been at the Clinic for several
weeks, and is described as a problem. He is seriously ill,
both physically and mentally, and at one time the doctors
were considering giving him electro-shock therapy treatments.

████████████████████ Mayo Clinic, advised to
eliminate publicity and contacts by newsmen, the Clinic had
suggested that Mr. HEMINGWAY register under the alias GEORGE
SEVIER. ████████ stated that Mr. HEMINGWAY is now   (b7c)
worried about his registering under an assumed name, and is
concerned about an FBI investigation. █████████ stated that
inasmuch as this worry was interfering with the treatments
of Mr. HEMINGWAY, he desired authorization to tell HEMINGWAY
that the FBI was not concerned with his registering under
an assumed name ████████ was advised that there was no
objection.

3 - Bureau
1 - Minneapolis
WHW:RSK
(4)
cc - DeLoach

64-23312-18

ALL INFORMATION CONTAINED
HEREIN IS UNCLASSIFIED
DATE 10/29/79 BY SP-1 DSK/gん

11 JAN 24 1961

52 JAN 31 1961

Approved: _____ Sent _____ M _____ Per _____
        Special Agent in Charge

As Pegler Sees It:

He Was Never A Hemingway Fan

By WESTBROOK PEGLER

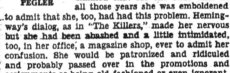

IT HAS BEEN my stubborn opinion that Ernest Hemingway was actually one of the worst writers in the English language during his time. It can be conceded that he invented a "style." But to me it was an ugly style, so barren of ordinary literary embellishment or amenity that it was confused and often incomprehensible.

He forswore the familiar "he said" and "he inquired." Things of that kind.

I freely volunteered to another professional writer, that early in Hemingway's fad I found myself thumbing back over half a dozen or more jerks of speech in quotation marks to determine which person was speaking at this moment.

To my comfort, my colleague exclaimed that for the first time in all those years she was emboldened to admit that she, too, had had this problem. Hemingway's dialog, as in "The Killers," made her nervous but she had been abashed and a little intimidated, too, in her office, a magazine shop, ever to admit her confusion. She would be patronized and ridiculed and probably passed over in the promotions and assignments as being old-fashioned or even ignorant.

I floundered in "The Sun Also Rises" and for years I had a reminder in the back of my intentions to try it again. This time, I would put forth a special effort to follow the meaning.

But eventually I said, "Oh, to Hell with Hemingway and his affectations."

I am a reasonably intelligent reader and if this great artist with his precious "style" could not exert himself to make his meaning clear to me, was I obliged to yield him precious hours out of my life and some precious measure of the measured vision of my eyes as homage to his reputation? Who created that reputation? Book reviewers and sellers.

After all, I had bought his book and had done him the courtesy of reading it. I did not owe him sacrifice to prove that I was equal to his tricky affectation.

He annoyed me also with profanity and vulgarity and when I pointed out that Ring Lardner had never told a dirty story and had shunned mucky stuff on paper, Hemingway's rejoinder did not dispose of Lardner. Hemingway answered that nevertheless people did speak as his characters spoke. True. But so did Lardner's and Lardner's ear for the language of ordinary Americans was as sensitive and true as Hemingway's. However, vulgarity in Hemingway was a minor fault.

PEGLER

64-23312

164-23312-A-
NOT RECORDED
176   JUL 19 1961

More than any other writer known in my time, Hemingway was the creature of a claque of sycophants, most of them book reviewers.

The eruption of shaving bubbles which engulfed us when he died was the gaseous emotional reaction of paltry people who thus acclaimed their own otherwise tentative or negative celebrity.

They stand for nothing. And nothing was the great standard which Hemingway had raised and fought for in his noncommittal uproars all those years.

Hemingway's obsession with pugilism as a personal activity was juvenile and brutal.

Professionals never strike a layman and Hemingway was equal to a fairly good professional heavyweight by Gene Tunney's serious opinion. Gene said Hemingway hit him as hard as any other man except Dempsey. Yet this man was a personal, physical bully and his adventures in and around battle, though exciting and dangerous, were only the routine experience of thousands of other men and kids all around him.

He was absolutely destitute of humor and his only affectionate souvenir to us is "Farewell to Arms."

Copyright, 1961, King Features Syndicate, Inc.

January 9, 1964

EX-105

REC-23 64 - 23312 - 19

(b7c)

Dear

    Thank you for your letter of January 6th, with enclosure. I can certainly understand Mary Hemingway's concern as well as your own. You may be certain this will be made a matter of official record.

    I will give Clyde your message and I know it will cheer him to learn you were thinking of him.

    In accordance with your request the envelope you sent is being returned.

    With every good wish,

        Sincerely,

        J. Edgar

MAILED 19
JAN 9 - 1964
COMM-FBI

Enclosure
1 - New York - Enclosures (2)
1 - Miami - Enclosures (2)
1 - Mr. Sullivan - Enclosures (2)

ALL INFORMATION CONTAINED
HEREIN IS UNCLASSIFIED
DATE 10/29/79 BY SP-1 DSK/ghw

(b7c) NOTE: is on the Special Correspondents' List.

JH:sis
(6)

Tolson
Belmont
Mohr
Casper
Callahan
Conrad
DeLoach
Evans
Gale
Rosen
Sullivan
Tavel
Trotter
Tele. Room
Holmes
Gandy

TELETYPE UNIT

0-19 (Rev. 1-30-74)

U.S. FIRM TO FILM SPECIAL IN CUBA

Castro Asks to Appear in TV Study of Hemingway

Bob Banner Associates, a television production company in Beverly Hills, Calif., has received permission from the Cuban Government to film portions of a television special about Ernest Hemingway, in Cuba.

The United States does not maintain diplomatic relations with Cuba, and the move by the Communist Government is regarded as highly unusual by broadcasting industry observers.

The Nobel Prize-winning novelist, who died in 1961, wrote about Cuba and lived there for many years. The special, "The House of Hemingway" will be filmed in part at the author's Cuban home and at some of his favorite island haunts.

Bob Banner Associates received permission to film in the Communist country after a personal telephone conversation between Dick Foster, producer of the show, and Premier Fidel Castro of Cuba, and a two-week visit by Mr. Foster to Cuba.

"It was really very simple," Mr. Foster said. "I placed a long distance call to Castro and, after a brief explanation to one or two aides," the producer found himself speaking to Mr. Castro.

Bob Banner, executive producer of the show, noted that "Hemingway is held in great regard by the Cubans" and that Premier Castro had "personally expressed a desire to make an appearance in the special."

Telegram Arrives

The show has not yet been sold to any television network, Mr. Foster said, because he was waiting until he received official confirmation. The confirmation arrived last Friday in the form of a telegram from the Cuban Government.

The 90-minute broadcast is being called an "entertainment documentary" and will include segments devoted to ivities that Hemingway in rd.

Mr. Foster would like to begin filming in early October in Ketchum, Idaho — another of the places where Hemingway lived— and then spend the last two weeks of the month in Cuba.

The telecast should be completed by Jan. 1, 1975, and be televised in the fall of 1975, Mr. Foster indicated.

He described the Hemingway home and library as being in excellent condition. "The home is spotless and all the memorabilia are displayed just the way they were left," he said.

In 1961, Mary Hemingway, the author's wife, gave the home to the people of Cuba. She is serving as a consultant to the television project.

The production company is speaking with such screen personalities as Ingrid Bergman, Marlene Dietrich and Gregory to appear in the special.

Center to St———

ALL INFORMATION CONTAINED
CLASSIFIED
D...10/29/79 SP-1905K/96w

64-23312-A-
NOT RECORDED
27. SEP 12 1974

File

105-340280

XEROX

A 1940 picture of Hemingway and Marlene Dietrich, the blond venus of Hollywood.

(John F. Kennedy Library)

James Baldwin (left) and Dempsey J. Travis, the author.

Chapter XVI

James Baldwin: The 5.7ft.Genius Is lOft. Tall Among Literary Giants

James Arthur Baldwin was born out of wedlock to Emma Berdis Jones on August 2, 1924 in the charity ward of the Harlem Hospital in New York City. Baldwin was sixteen years old when he accidentally discovered through eavesdropping that Reverend David Baldwin was not his biological father. The discovery caused him to lament over his illegitimate status for a long period of time. As a matter of fact he did not go public with his shame until 1961 at age 34 when he wrote a non-fiction book entitled: Nobody Knows My Name: More Notes of A Native Son.

The literary talents of James A. Baldwin began to surface at the third grade level at P. S. 24 in Harlem. The principal of the school was Gertrude Ayer the first Black to hold such a position in the New York public school system. She liked little Jimmy and took a very special interest in this gifted child. Whereas his stepfather told him he was dumb and the ugliest child he had ever seen. The old man cruelly nicknamed the boy Frog Eyes. When he was promoted from P. S. 24 to Frederick Douglass Junior High School his literary talents flowered through his contributions to the school newspaper, and with his short stories, editorials, and art works for the <u>Douglass Pilot</u> the school magazine.

At age 14 he was one of a very few Black boys selected to attend the very prestigious DeWitt Clinton High School in the Bronx where he excelled in class performance without the benefit of receiving high grades. Grading down Blacks in places where they are not expected by racist teachers was and still is a fact of life in America. The author recalls getting As on every test throughout the semester in an Advanced Harmony course but received a B+for the final grade. When the teacher was queried for an explanation she replied: "Your A's were all weak".

In the Clintonian, the DeWitt Clinton High School June 1942 senior yearbook, James Baldwin prophesied that he would be a novelist- playwright. His early training as a junior preacher in his stepfather's Fireside Pentecostal Assembly Church prepared him to be a riveting extemporaneous speaker. He said in the author's presence in the early 1980's in response to a question about his speaking ability during the Q & A period following his lecture at the Chicago Cultural Center. He said: *"I can't read a speech. It's kind of give and take. You have to sense the people you are talking to. You have to respond to whatever they hear in the fashion of a foot stomping gospel sermon on Sunday morning"*.

The author also had the opportunity to watch a telecast debate at Oxford University between James Baldwin and William Buckley in the late 1970s. Baldwin distinguished himself with his ability to address the subject of racism in America without rankle. His oratorical skills matched his writing ability when he expounded on the problems of American race relations from a psychological, colorless perspective.

James Arthur Baldwin died of stomach cancer at age 63 at his home in St. Paul de Vence in Southern France on Tuesday, December 1, 1987.

To the contrary, little Jimmy was brought home and laid to rest in Harlem, a venue that was central to much of his work. Three of his most important essays were created during the height of the civil rights struggles of the 1950s and 60s - Notes of A Native Son (1961) and The Fire Next Time (1963).

The following words were spoken about Baldwin after his transition:

Ralph Ellison said, "*America has lost one of its most gifted writers... And one of the most important essayists, black or white.*" Henry Louis Gates, a professor at Cornell University said, "*Mr. Baldwin's death was a great loss not only for black people, but to the country as a whole, for which he served as a conscience.*"

Poet and playwright Amiri Baraka commented: "*This man traveled the world like its history and its biographer. He reported, criticized, made beautiful, analyzed, cajoled, lyricized, attacked, sang, made us think, made us better, made us consciously human... He made us feel... that we could defend ourselves or define ourselves, that we were in the world not merely as animate slaves, but as terrifyingly sensitive measurers of what is good or evil, beautiful or ugly. This is the power of his spirits this is the bond which created our love for him.*" Juan Williams of the Washington Post wrote: "*The success of Baldwin's effort as a witness is evidenced time and again by people, black and white, gay and straight, famous and anonymous whose humanity he unveiled in his writings. America and the literary world are far richer for his witness. The proof of a shared humanity across the divides of race, class and more is the testament that the preacher's son, James Arthur Baldwin, has left us.*"

Selected writings

Fiction

Go Tell It on the Mountain. New York: Knopf, 1953.

Giovanni's Room. New York: Dial, 1956.

Another Country. New York: Dial, 1962.

Going to Meet the Man. New York: Dial, 1965.

If Beale Street Could Talk. New York: Dial, 1974.

Just Above My Head. New York: Dial, 1979.

Nonfiction

Autobiographical Notes. New York: Knopf, 1953.

Notes of a Native Son. Boston: Beacon Press, 1955.

Nobody Knows My Name: More Notes of a Native Son. New York: Dial, 1961.

The Fire Next Time. New York: Dial, 1963.

No Name in the Street. New York: Dial, 1972.

The Devil Finds Work. New York: Dial, 1976.

The Evidence of Things Not Seen. New York: Holt, Rhinehart, 1985.

The Price of the Ticket: Collected Nonfiction 1948-1985. New York: St. Martins, 1985.

A Dialogue. By James Baldwin and Nikki Giovanni. Philadelphia: Lippincott, 1973.

Little Man, Little Man: A Story of Childhood. By James Baldwin and Yoran Cazac. London: Joseph, 1976 / New York: Dial, 1976.

One Day When I Was Lost: A Scenario Based on "The Autobiography of Malcolm X. " London: Joseph, 1972.

A Rap on Face. By Margaret Mead and James Baldwin. Philadelphia: Lippincott, 1971.

Tell Me How Long the Train's Been Gone. New York: Dial, 1968.

Plays

The Amen Corner (first produced in Washington, D. C. at Howard University, 1955; produced on Broadway at Ethel Barrymore Theatre, April 15, 1965). New York: Dial, 1968.

Blues for Mister Charlie (first produced on Broadway at ANTA Theatre, April 23, 1964). New York: Dial, 1964.

Other

Contributor of book reviews and essays to numerous periodicals, including Harper's Nation, Esquire, Playboy, Partisan Review, Mademoiselle and New Yorker.

Sources

Books

The Black American Writer, Volume 2: Poetry and Drama, edited by C. W. E. Bigsby, Everett/Edwards, 1969.

Concise Dictionary of American Literary Biography: The New Consciousness 1941-1968, Gale, 1987.

Critical Essays on James Baldwin, edited by Fred Standley and Nancy Standley, G. K. Hall, 1981.

Dictionary of Literary Biography Gale, Volume 2: American Novelists Since World War II, 1978, Volume 8: Twentieth-Century American Dramatists, 1981, Volume 33: Afro-American Fiction Writers after 1955, 1984.

The Fifties: Fiction, Poetry, Drama, edited by Warren French,

Everett/Edwards, 1970.

James Baldwin: A Collection of Critical Essays, edited by Kenneth Kinnamon. Englewood Cliffs, NJ. : Prentice-Hall, 1974.

Pratt Louis Hill, James Baldwin. Boston: Twayne, 1978. Sylvander, Carolyn Wedin, James Baldwin, Frederick Ungar, 1980.

Bloom, Harold, ed. James Baldwin. New York: Chelsea House, 1986.

Campbell, James. Talking at the Gates: A Life of James Baldwin. New York: Viking, 1991.

Harris, Trudier. Black Women in the Fiction of James Baldwin. Knoxville, Tennessee, University of Tennessee Press, 1985.

Jennings, La Vinia Delois. Sexual Violence in the Works of Richard Wright, James Baldwin and Toni Morrison. University of North Carolina: Chapel Hill, 1989.

Leeming, David. James Baldwin. A Biography. New York: Knopf, 1994.

Macebuh, Stanley. James Baldwin: A Critical Study. New York: Third Press / Joseph Okpaku, 1973.

Moore, Gerian Steven. Modes of Black Discourse in the Narrative and Structure of James Baldwin's Fiction. University of Michigan, 1989.

O'Daniel, Therman B. James Baldwin: A Critical Evaluation. Washington, D.C. : Howard University Press, 1977.

Porter, Horace A. Stealing the Fire. The Art and Protest of James Baldwin. Connecticut: Wesleyan University Press, 1989.

Schnapp, Patricia Lorine. The Liberation Theology of James Baldwin. Bowling Green State University, 1987.

Standley, Fred L. and Louis H. Pratt ed. Conversation with James Baldwin. Mississippi, Jackson: University of Mississippi, 1989.

Troupe, Quincy, ed. James Baldwin: The Legacy. New York: Simon & Schuster, 1989.

Weatherby, William J. James Baldwin: Artist on Fire. New York: Donald I. Fine, 1989.

Weatherby, William J. Squaring Off: Mailer vs. Baldwin. New York: Mason/Charter, 1977.

Periodicals

New York Times, May 3, 1964; April 16, 1965; May 31, 1968; February 2, 1969; May 21, 1971; May 17, 1974; June 4, 1976; September 4, 1977; September 21, 1979; September 23, 1979; November 11, 1983; January 10, 1985; January 14, 1985; December 2, 1987; December 9, 1987.

Tri-Quarterly, Winter, 1965.

Washington Post, December 2, 1987; December 9, 1987.

Bieganowski, Ronald. "James Baldwin's Vision of Otherness in 'Sonny's Blues' and 'Giovanni's Room.' CLA Journal, 32, (September 1988), p. 69-80.

Clark, Michael. "Sonny's Blues: Childhood, Light and Art." CLA Journal, 29, (December 1985), p. 197-205.

Collier, Eugenia. "Thematic Patterns in Baldwin's Essays." Black World, 21, (June 1972), p. 28-34.

Courage, Richard A. "James Baldwin's 'Go Tell It On The Mountain': Voices of a People." CLA Journal, 32, (June 1989), p. 410-425.

Dance, Daryl O. "You Can't Go Home Again: James Baldwin and the South." CLA Journal, 18, (September 1974), p. 81-90.

DeGout, Yasmin Y. "Dividing the Mind: Contradictory Portraits of Homoerotic Love in 'Giovanni's Room'." African American Review, 26, (Fall 1992), p. 425-435.

Fuller, Hoyt W. "James Baldwin and the Black-Jewish Conflict." Black World, 20, (September 1971), p. 83.

Goldman, Suzy B. 'James Baldwin's 'Sonny's Blues': A Message in Music." Negro American Literature Forum, 8, (Fall 1974), p. 231-233.

Gross, Barry. "The Uninhabitable Darkness of Baldwin's 'Another Country': Image and Theme. " Negro American Literature Forum, 6, (Winter 1972) , p. 113-121.

Hughes, James M. "Black City Lights. Baldwin's City of the Just. " Journal of Black Studies, 18, (December 1987) , p. 230-241.

Lynch, Michael F. "Beyond Guilt and Innocence: Redemptive Suffering and Love in Baldwin's 'Another Country'. " Obsidian II: Black Literature in Review, 7, (Spring-Summer 1992) , p. 1-18.

Mosher, Marlene. "James Baldwin's Blues. " CLA Journal, 26, (September 1982) , p. 112-124.

Reilly, John M. "James Baldwin Making Literature Black. " Afro-American in New York Life and History, 11, (July 1987) , p. 53-61.

Warren, Nagueyalt. "The Substance of Things Hoped For: Faith in 'Go Tell It On The Mountain' and 'Just Above My Head'. " Obsidian II: Black Literature Review, 7, (Spring-Summer 1992) , p. 19-32.

Federal Bureau of Investigation

Freedom of Information/Privacy Acts Section

Subject: <u>James Baldwin</u>

PLEASE DO NOT REMOVE
THIS SLIP FROM EXHIBIT
NY 100-146553

ALL INFORMATION CONTAINED
HEREIN IS UNCLASSIFIED
DATE 5-22-89 BY

AN URGENT MESSAGE FROM:

Dear Friend:

As you are reading this letter, the young men and women shown above are in Mississippi performing an act of faith and courage that is so extraordinary that I find myself struggling for words to describe my feelings toward them.

They are some of the more than 1000 volunteers who have come from all over our country to spend this summer in the most terror-stricken area of the south -- Mississippi where 900,000 Negroes live in feudal conditions unimaginable to the outsider.

The gravest of dangers await these courageous workers. Some details of what they face are given in the enclosed article reprinted from Newsweek. The first of the summer volunteers have already been arrested; project offices have been attacked and even bombed. God knows what may happen between now, as I write this letter, and when you receive it.

All of us are waiting anxiously and still praying for the safety of the three young people who have disappeared.

And yet, they are coming; teachers, nurses, technicians, college students, legal advisors -- both Negro and white.

They are coming: on a unique mission, an unofficial peace corps for the south, bringing their skills and courage to communities which have been almost completely shut off from the American mainland.

(over please)

FBI Secret Files

These courageous young people will staff a wide range of programs whose goal is nothing less than to help bring the Mississippi Negro into the 20th century. Their undertakings will include: 1) the establishment of Freedom Schools teaching everything from the techniques of non-vidlent protest to technical skills and remedial reading; 2) expanded voter registration drives; 3) supporting Negro candidates for public office; 4) the creation of community centers across the state.

The director of the Mississippi Summer Project is Robert Moses, a leader of the Student Nonviolent Coordinating Committee. SNCC will be the driving force in carrying out the entire project. Bob Moses is a brilliant, 29-year old Negro who was educated at Hamilton and Harvard, then gave up an excellent teaching appointment to work in the civil rights movement.

Not many of us can leave jobs and families to spend a whole summer in Mississippi. But all of us can help see to it that these courageous young people have enough food to eat - sorely needed books and teaching materials - medicines for illness and injury- legal aid to keep them (or get them) out of jail.

These young people belong to us -- they are our sons and daughters. But just being proud of them won't help. Mayor Thompson of Jackson Miss., says "They won't have a chance." I ask you to help give them a chance by sending a generous contribution for the Mississippi Summer Project and to send it NOW. Please send as much as you can -- every dollar you can spare will be put to direct and immediate use.

Sincerely yours,

James Baldwin

James Baldwin

P.S. Time is so short - the need so immediate!
Please send your contribution now to me at
SNCC - 100 Fifth Ave., New York 11, N. Y.
Make all checks payable to SNCC.

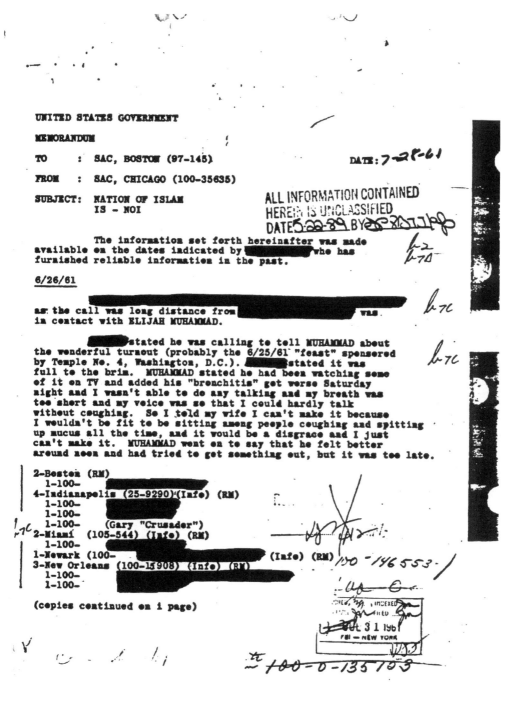

UNITED STATES GOVERNMENT

MEMORANDUM

TO : SAC, BOSTON (97-145)   DATE: 7-28-61

FROM : SAC, CHICAGO (100-35635)

SUBJECT: NATION OF ISLAM
IS - NOI

ALL INFORMATION CONTAINED
HEREIN IS UNCLASSIFIED
DATE 5-22-89 BY

The information set forth hereinafter was made
available on the dates indicated by ▮▮▮▮▮▮▮ who has
furnished reliable information in the past.

6/26/61

as the call was long distance from ▮▮▮▮▮▮▮ was.
in contact with ELIJAH MUHAMMAD.

▮▮▮▮▮ stated he was calling to tell MUHAMMAD about
the wonderful turnout (probably the 6/25/61 "feast" sponsored
by Temple No. 4, Washington, D.C.). ▮▮▮▮▮ stated it was
full to the brim. MUHAMMAD stated he had been watching some
of it on TV and added his "bronchitis" get worse Saturday
night and I wasn't able to do any talking and my breath was
too short and my voice was so that I could hardly talk
without coughing. So I told my wife I can't make it because
I wouldn't be fit to be sitting among people coughing and spitting
up mucus all the time, and it would be a disgrace and I just
can't make it. MUHAMMAD went on to say that he felt better
around noon and had tried to get something out, but it was too late.

2-Boston (RM)
  1-100-
4-Indianapolis (25-9290) (Info) (RM)
  1-100-
  1-100-
  1-100-   (Gary "Crusader")
2-Miami (105-544) (Info) (RM)
  1-100-
1-Newark (100-   (Info) (RM)
3-New Orleans (100-15908) (Info) (RM)
  1-100-
  1-100-

(copies continued on 1 page)

100-146553-1

100-0-135733

CG 100-35635

▉▉▉▉ told MUHAMMAD he would like to come out and
see MUHAMMAD next week. MUHAMMAD told ▉▉▉▉ he should call
towards the end of this week to see if he would still be here
as he had been thinking of going to Arizona until he gets
rid of the bronchitis. MUHAMMAD stated that medicine just
gave him temporary relief and added that he needs a long rest.
MUHAMMAD went on to thank ▉▉▉▉ and all the followers who
were in Washington yesterday and who carried out such an
orderly and wonderful mass meeting. MUHAMMAD added he was
proud of his followers. MUHAMMAD also wanted to make known
to ▉▉▉▉ his regrets that the officer here did not escort him
to the airport the last time he was here, adding it was
stupid of the officials and MUHAMMAD would not let it happen
again. MUHAMMAD stated he had bawed them out for this neglect,
adding they should have escorted him to the airport to show
their thanks for the good work he did here for a whole week
in his efforts to convert the "dead."

6/26/61

A Brother Minister, believed to be MALCOLM X
LITTLE, Minister of Temple No. 7, New York City, was in
contact with ▉▉▉▉▉▉ (believed to be ▉▉▉▉▉▉▉
and the Holy Apostle. MUHAMMAD thanked MALCOLM and the
other believers and followers for all the noble work they
did there (probably Washington, D.C.) after adding it was
wonderful. MUHAMMAD stated that "the whole world should
bear witness; there is no God but Allah and that MUHAMMAD
is his servant; that progress is being made in the wilderness;
that his name is being known in the wilderness where the dragon
of the evil world lives..." MUHAMMAD stated he would have put
aside a million dollars in cold cash if he could have been
there, but he wasn't able and Allah knows best. MUHAMMAD
stated he took worse on Saturday night and it would have been
impossible for him to get up on Sunday to make a speech.

MUHAMMAD then spoke about Brother BALDWIN, adding
he had heard him speak this morning and stated that he was
wonderful. MALCOLM stated he was just talking with Brother
BALDWIN. MUHAMMAD told MALCOLM to give him his best love and
he thought he was wonderful; that MALCOLM should tell him
if he had known his telephone number he would have called him
as soon as he was through looking at him. MALCOLM gave
MUHAMMAD telephone number WA 9-5921 for Mr. JAMES BALDWIN in
New York City. MALCOLM stated BALDWIN was very influential
among the intellectuals there.

- 2 -

CG 100-35635

pictures to ELIJAH. MUHAMMAD stated this would be very good, but he did not think they would start so soon.

No. ████████ mentioned "they" (believed to refer to Temple ████████ are going to move in 30 days. MUHAMMAD stated he knew and he was sure they would not have trouble finding another place.

████████ hoped that MUHAMMAD would be down there in August. MUHAMMAD stated he would be there if it was the will of Allah.

MUHAMMAD stated that ████████ had invited him to come there in September and he plans to do so if possible. ████████ stated that he ████████ usually fills up ████████ and is the most heard man on that side in that area, (possibly refers to Washington, D. C.).

7/14/61

brother at ████████ ████████ was in contact with a ████████ and asked for ████████ stated that sisters ████████ (indexed as ████████ are there with beige robes. ████████ told ████████ to send them home adding that they should have white ones.

7/15/61

████████ NOI) was in contact with Mr. BALDWIN (JAMES BALDWIN of New York City) and stated ELIJAH MUHAMMAD would like to have him for dinner on 7/16/61 at 4847 South Woodlawn. ████████ asked BALDWIN if he was appearing on TV tonight. BALDWIN stated he was at midnight. (JAMES BALDWIN, the author of "Nobody Knows My Name" appeared on IRV KUPCINET's "At Random" TV show at midnight 7/16/61).

- 4 -

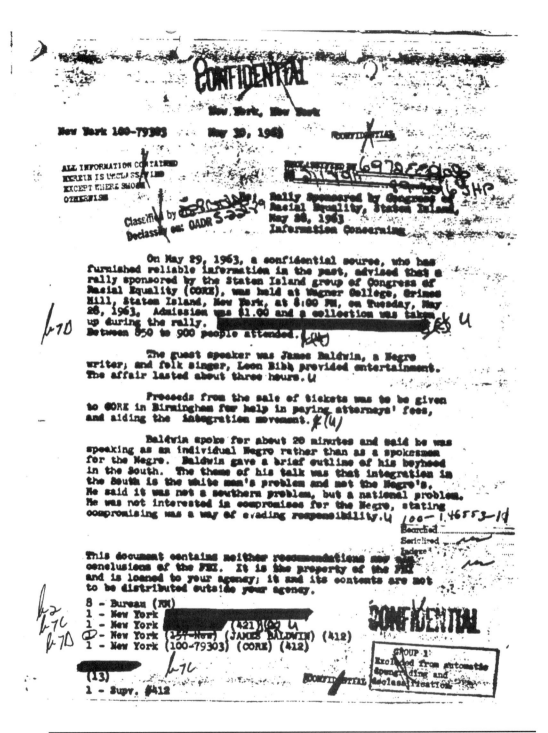

CONFIDENTIAL

New York, New York

New York 100-79303   May 29, 1963

CONFIDENTIAL

ALL INFORMATION CONTAINED
HEREIN IS UNCLASSIFIED
EXCEPT WHERE SHOWN
OTHERWISE

Classified by
Declassify on: OADR

Rally Sponsored by Congress of
Racial Equality, Staten Island,
May 28, 1963
Information Concerning

On May 29, 1963, a confidential source, who has
furnished reliable information in the past, advised that a
rally sponsored by the Staten Island group of Congress of
Racial Equality (CORE), was held at Wagner College, Grimes
Hill, Staten Island, New York, at 8:00 PM, on Tuesday, May
28, 1963. Admission was $1.00 and a collection was taken
up during the rally.
Between 850 to 900 people attended.

The guest speaker was James Baldwin, a Negro
writer, and folk singer, Leon Bibb provided entertainment.
The affair lasted about three hours.

Proceeds from the sale of tickets was to be given
to CORE in Birmingham for help in paying attorneys' fees,
and aiding the integration movement.

Baldwin spoke for about 20 minutes and said he was
speaking as an individual Negro rather than as a spokesman
for the Negro. Baldwin gave a brief outline of his boyhood
in the South. The theme of his talk was that integration in
the South is the white man's problem and not the Negro's.
He said it was not a southern problem, but a national problem.
He was not interested in compromises for the Negro, stating
compromising was a way of evading responsibility.

This document contains neither recommendations nor
conclusions of the FBI. It is the property of the FBI
and is loaned to your agency; it and its contents are not
to be distributed outside your agency.

8 - Bureau (RM)
1 - New York
1 - New York   (421)
1 - New York (157-New) (JAMES BALDWIN) (412)
1 - New York (100-79303) (CORE) (412)

(13)

1 - Supv. #412

CONFIDENTIAL

GROUP 1
Excluded from automatic
downgrading and
declassification

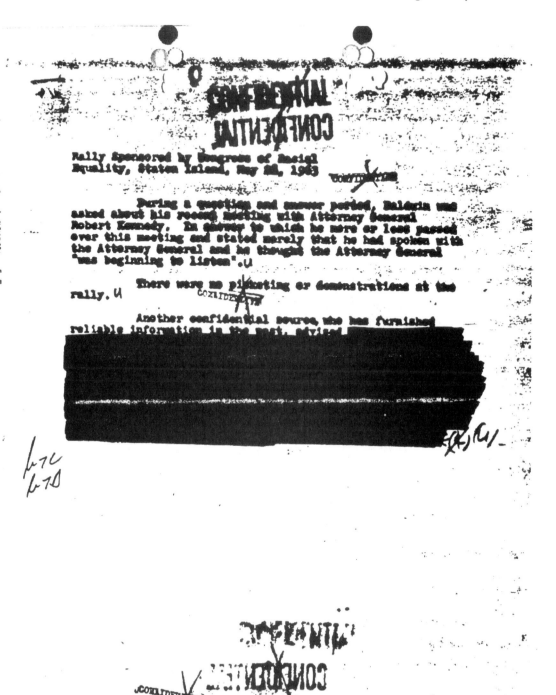

CONFIDENTIAL

Rally Sponsored by Congress of Racial
Equality, Staten Island, May 28, 1963   CONFIDENTIAL

During a question and answer period, Baldwin was
asked about his recent meeting with Attorney General
Robert Kennedy. In answer to which he more or less passed
over this meeting and stated merely that he had spoken with
the Attorney General and he thought the Attorney General
"was beginning to listen".

There were no picketing or demonstrations at the
rally.

Another confidential source who has furnished
reliable information in the past, advised

CONFIDENTIAL

(Mount Clipping in Space Below)

Baldwin's Message: 'Don't Hate Anyone'

Negro Author Returns to His Old School for Alumni Award

World-famous author James Baldwin made a sentimental journey yesterday back to the days 25 years ago when he was just an undersized adolescent who had a way with words.

He came home to JHS 139 in the heart of Harlem to receive a plaque as the school's alumnus of the Year. Baldwin was visibly moved at seeing many of his old teachers again after a quarter of a century away from the school.

Many expected Baldwin to deliver a fiery speech on Negro rights, as he has often done elsewhere. Instead, he offered fatherly advise to the youngsters sitting in the school auditorium.

Speaking of the present crisis in the Negro's struggle for equal rights, he said: "Remember when things get tough and ugly not to confuse power with morality. There is no moral value to either a black skin or a white skin. If someone wants you to

substitute your real past for an invented one, don't listen to them. It is important for you to be proud that your ancestors stood on the auction block. From the block to full equality is a journey no other people have ever taken.

"When you have a child, raise him not to hate anybody. What one seeks is not revenge. Revenge doesn't work. I know, I've tasted it."

The teachers and the youngsters gave the novelist and essayist a thunderous ovation. Baldwin was introduced by Lionel McMurren, once a classmate of Baldwin's at JHS 139, now on the faculty there.

(Indicate page, name of newspaper, city and state.)

26 N.Y. WORLD TELEGRAM AND THE SUN

Date: 6/21/63
Edition: METRO
Author:
Editor: RICHARD D. PETERS
Title: RACIAL SITUATIONS

Character:
or
Classification: 3U 100-386!00
Submitting Office: NYD

100-146553-14

SEARCHED_____INDEXED_____
SERIALIZED_____FILED_____
JUN 21 1963
FBI — NEW YORK

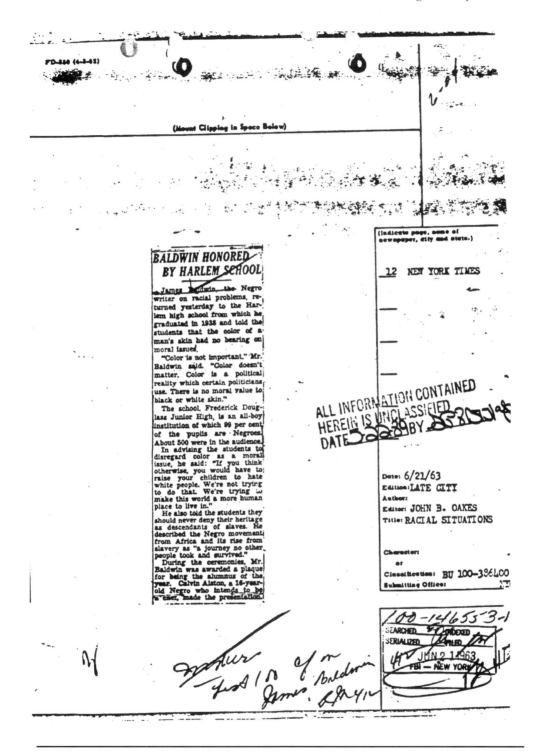

FD-350 (4-3-62)

(Mount Clipping in Space Below)

BALDWIN HONORED BY HARLEM SCHOOL

James Baldwin, the Negro writer on racial problems, returned yesterday to the Harlem high school from which he graduated in 1938 and told the students that the color of a man's skin had no bearing on moral issues.

"Color is not important." Mr. Baldwin said. "Color doesn't matter. Color is a political reality which certain politicians use. There is no moral value to black or white skin."

The school, Frederick Douglass Junior High, is an all-boy institution of which 99 per cent of the pupils are Negroes. About 500 were in the audience.

In advising the students to disregard color as a moral issue, he said: "If you think otherwise, you would have to raise your children to hate white people. We're not trying to do that. We're trying to make this world a more human place to live in."

He also told the students they should never deny their heritage as descendants of slaves. He described the Negro movement from Africa and its rise from slavery as "a journey no other people took and survived."

During the ceremonies, Mr. Baldwin was awarded a plaque for being the alumnus of the year. Calvin Alston, a 16-year-old Negro who intends to be a teacher, made the presentation.

(Indicate page, name of newspaper, city and state.)

12   NEW YORK TIMES

ALL INFORMATION CONTAINED
HEREIN IS UNCLASSIFIED
DATE _____ BY _____

Date: 6/21/63
Edition: LATE CITY
Author:
Editor: JOHN B. OAKES
Title: RACIAL SITUATIONS

Character:
or
Classification: BU 100-396400
Submitting Office:

100-146553-1
SEARCHED _____ INDEXED _____
SERIALIZED _____ FILED _____

JUN 2 1963
FBI — NEW YORK

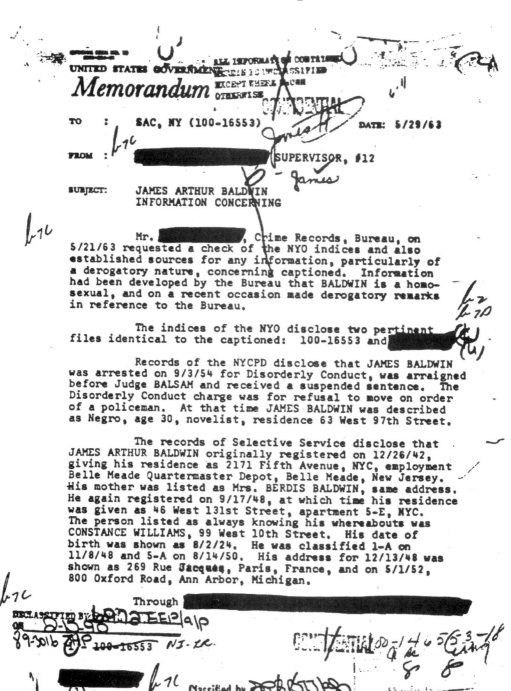

UNITED STATES GOVERNMENT

Memorandum

TO : SAC, NY (100-16553)   DATE: 5/29/63

FROM : ~~_____~~   SUPERVISOR, #12

SUBJECT: JAMES ARTHUR BALDWIN
INFORMATION CONCERNING

Mr. ~~_____~~, Crime Records, Bureau, on
5/21/63 requested a check of the NYO indices and also
established sources for any information, particularly of
a derogatory nature, concerning captioned. Information
had been developed by the Bureau that BALDWIN is a homosexual, and on a recent occasion made derogatory remarks
in reference to the Bureau.

The indices of the NYO disclose two pertinent
files identical to the captioned: 100-16553 and ~~_____~~

Records of the NYCPD disclose that JAMES BALDWIN
was arrested on 9/3/54 for Disorderly Conduct, was arraigned
before Judge BALSAM and received a suspended sentence. The
Disorderly Conduct charge was for refusal to move on order
of a policeman. At that time JAMES BALDWIN was described
as Negro, age 30, novelist, residence 63 West 97th Street.

The records of Selective Service disclose that
JAMES ARTHUR BALDWIN originally registered on 12/26/42,
giving his residence as 2171 Fifth Avenue, NYC, employment
Belle Meade Quartermaster Depot, Belle Meade, New Jersey.
His mother was listed as Mrs. BERDIS BALDWIN, same address.
He again registered on 9/17/48, at which time his residence
was given as 46 West 131st Street, apartment 5-E, NYC.
The person listed as always knowing his whereabouts was
CONSTANCE WILLIAMS, 99 West 10th Street. His date of
birth was shown as 8/2/24. He was classified 1-A on
11/8/48 and 5-A on 8/14/50. His address for 12/13/48 was
shown as 269 Rue Jacques, Paris, France, and on 5/1/52,
800 Oxford Road, Ann Arbor, Michigan.

Through

Classified by
Declassify on:

PUBLISHERS FIGHT BALDWIN BOOK BAN

3 Take Legal Action Against New Orleans Move

By HENRY RAYMONT

Three publishers here have retained attorneys to defend James Baldwin's novel, "Another Country," against a threatened ban in New Orleans on the ground of obscenity.

Criminal charges against shops selling the novel have been threatened by Edward Pinner, New Orleans assistant city attorney, who has called it "the most filthy and pornographic book I have ever read."

Richard Baron, head of The Dial Press, publisher of the hard-cover edition of the novel, said yesterday he had retained Horace Manges, attorney for the American Book Publishers Council, to head the legal battle. The novel, widely praised by critics, is about unfulfilled and rebellious artists in New York, and dwells on the fate of Negro intellectuals in America.

The Dell Publishing Company which put out the paperback edition, and Doubleday & Co. have hired Richard Galen and James F. Dwyer to work on the case.

Mr. Manges said he expected to hear next week if Mr. Pinner would press charges against Frank P. Rossitter, manager of the Doubleday Bookshop in New Orleans, and George E. Deville, assistant manager.

The two were arrested June 18 for having sold the book after the City Attorney's office had demanded its withdrawal. They were held an hour and released on parole.

The arrest has been criticized by other New Orleans authorities and newspapers and broadcasting stations there.

District Attorney James Garrison of New Orleans has said he does not believe the Doubleday employes committed an offense.

"I think there is no place in this city for censorship," he has said. "True, some persons may consider the book obscene. However, others may not and it should be left to the individual to decide."

If the criminal charges against the two are dropped, Mr. Manges said, he will seek a declaratory judgment by the New Orleans court to clear the book.

He said that the publishers and New Orleans bookstores had temporarily agreed to halt sales of the book until a court ruling had been obtained.

Mr. Baron said he had received reports of pressure on New Orleans bookstores and public libraries by the Citizens Council, a white-supremacist organization, to have them withdraw the novel.

Such pressure began, he said, shortly after Mr. Baldwin addressed a meeting of the Congress of Racial Equality at Tulane University in New Orleans.

It was the first time that an obscenity charge had been brought against the work of the 40-year-old writer, Mr. Baron asserted.

The charges against the Doubleday employes, filed with the New Orleans Municipal Court, are based on a city ordinance forbidding the sale of obscene literature.

BALDWIN SPEAKS AT PARIS CHURCH

Author Seeks Support for Civil Rights in U. S.

By PETER GROSE
Special to The New York Times

PARIS Aug. 18. — James Baldwin opened a civil rights appeal in The American Church in Paris today to show the solidarity of Americans living abroad with the March on Washington Movement.

The negro writer spoke to an overflow congregation in the interdenominational Protestant church immediately after the worship service.

He called for signatures on a petition to be handed to the American Embassy Wednesday after a silent march from The American Church on the Left Bank.

With this gesture, Mr. Baldwin gave Paris residents an opportunity to associate themselves with the March on Washington Aug. 28. More than 100 signatures were obtained immediately after the meeting.

"We cannot physically participate in this march." the petition said, "but we, like the rest of the world, have been tremendously stirred by so disciplined

Mottke Weissman

STARTS RIGHTS DRIVE: James Baldwin, who called on Americans in Paris to support Aug. 28 march on Washington with petitions.

an exhibition of dignity and courage and persistence.

"It is not easy to be an American abroad, nor is it easy to make coherent to those who are not Americans the nature and meaning of our struggle."

Among the early signatories were Anthony Quinn, the actor, now making a movie in Paris, and Hazel Scott, pianist.

"Segregation is not now, nor has it ever been, a regional matter." Mr. Baldwin told the church assemblage. "We in particular have an interest in turning America into the free country it has always claimed to be."

Mr. Baldwin, who has lived in Paris on and off for over 10 years, returned recently from the United States. He is now at work on a play.

The Paris campaign came into existence after an informal meeting last night at a nightclub run by Art Simmons, a jazz pianist.

"Those of us living here felt somewhat alienated from the struggle now going on in America, yet we wanted to show our sympathy and solidarity," said William Marshall, an actor from New York who, with Mr. Baldwin, called the meeting.

The Rev. Martin Van Buren Sargent, pastor of The American Church, sent his wife to meet Mr. Marshall and Mr. Baldwin and to offer the church's meeting room to open the campaign.

Arrangements were made so quickly that most of the regular congregation knew nothing of Mr. Baldwin's presence until Dr. Sargent announced the campaign at the morning service.

Word of Mr. Baldwin's scheduled appearance spread through the American community last night and many people not members of the church attended this morning.

About 200 families are enrolled in the church, but in the August vacation period most of the congregation are tourists.

James Baldwin Brings His Paris Petition

James Baldwin, the militant Negro author and part-time expatriate, came home yesterday in time to join Wednesday's civil rights march in Washington.

He arrived at Idlewild Airport last night with a petition urging the passage of civil rights legislation signed by 450 Americans in Paris. He said he planned to take the scroll to the Capitol to present it to "a high government official.

A reporter told him that Malcolm X and his Black Muslims had pulled out of the march, charging that it was government organized.

"That's not true," Mr. Baldwin said, "I'm very sorry to hear that he is leaving it for that reason."

Elaborating on the significance of the march, Mr. Baldwin said, "Ultimately, it will force the Republic to meet the challenge they should have met 100 years ago at the time of the Emancipation Proclamation."

Mr. Baldwin, who has lived most of the last nine years in Paris, said he plans to live in the U.S. for the "foreseeable future." His immediate plans include the direction of his own play, "blues for Mr. Charlie."

He expected to leave by plane for Washington at 4 p.m. today.

CLIPPING FROM THE

NY _____ Herald Tribune

EDITION _____ City

DATE _____ AUG 27 1963

PAGE _____ 2

FORWARDED BY NY DIVISION _____

NOT FORWARDED BY NY DIVISION _____ X

ALL INFORMATION CONTAINED
HERE IS UNCLASSIFIED
DATE 5/20/81

100-146553-29

UNITED STATES DEPARTMENT OF JUSTICE

FEDERAL BUREAU OF INVESTIGATION

New York, New York
September 24, 1963

In Reply, Please Refer to
File No.

New York 100-146553

SECRET

Re: James Baldwin
      Racial Matters; −
      Security Matter - C

On September 19, 1963, a confidential source who
has furnished reliable information in the past, advised that
on that date ████████████████████████████████
and James Baldwin (Negro author) held a discussion regarding
Baldwin's appearance on the USIA television program in
Washington on August 28, 1963. ████████████████████

████████████████ transcript and noted that Baldwin's remarks
regarding the Federal Bureau of Investigation (FBI) and Mr. Hoover
were not contained therein and ██████████████ assumed that
these remarks had been edited out. Baldwin stated that he
had witnesses to the statements that he had made on this
program. In recalling his statement regarding the FBI,
Baldwin stated that the substance of his remarks on this
program were "part of the problem in the civil rights
movement is J. Edgar Hoover" ████████████████
██████████ stated
that any legitimate critical opinion of the FBI is apparently
"off limits or taboo".

SECRET
Group 1
Excluded from automatic
downgrading and
declassification

100-146553-34

This document contains neither recommendations nor conclusions
of the FBI. It is the property of the FBI and is loaned to
your agency; it and its contents are not to be distributed
outside your agency.

<u>James Baldwin</u>

     Additionally, Baldwin ███████████ discussed Baldwin's public statement of September 18, 1963, issued at a press conference in New York City. According to the "New York Herald Tribune", September 19, 1963, Baldwin is quoted as bitterly criticizing the Kennedy Administration and the FBI for their "lack of action" following the Birmingham bombing, September 15, 1963. The "New York Times" of September 19, 1963, additionally quotes Baldwin as saying "I blame J. Edgar Hoover in part for events in Alabama. Negroes have no cause to have faith in the FBI". This source also stated that ██

████████████ advised Baldwin that Baldwin's press statements were a most significant contribution.

     Baldwin stated that he felt that Kennedy should go to Alabama and ████████████████████████████ added that Baldwin's press statement had been a very valuable contribution and that it reflected that general consensus of opinion of the majority of Negroes in Birmingham. Baldwin agreed that the feeling existed not only in Birmingham but elsewhere. Baldwin then spoke of something his sister had said to his mother, "Negroes are thinking seriously of assassinating Martin Luther King".

     In a further discussion of the Birmingham bombing ███ questioned the "efficacy of the FBI in cases like this". ███ stated that there had been 45 to 50 bombings since 1947 and not one had been solved. He further stated that "there has been a total absence of FBI infiltrating racist organizations".

- 2 -

NY 100-146553

THAT ANY LEGITIMATE CRITICAL OPINION OF THE FBI IS APPARENTLY "OFF LIMITS OR TABOO".

ADDITIONALLY, BALDWIN ████████ DISCUSSED BALDWIN'S PUBLIC STATEMENT OF NINE EIGHTEEN SIXTY THREE, ISSUED AT A PRESS CONFERENCE IN NEW YORK CITY. ACCORDING TO THE "NEW YORK HERALD TRIBUNE" NINE NINETEEN SIXTY THREE, BALDWIN IS QUOTED AS BITTERLY CRITICIZING THE KENNEDY ADMINISTRATION AND THE FBI FOR THEIR "LACK OF ACTION" FOLLOWING THE BIRMINGHAM BOMBING NINE FIFTEEN SIXTY THREE. THE "NEW YORK TIMES" OF NINE NINETEEN SIXTY THREE, ADDITIONALLY QUOTES BALDWIN AS SAYING "I BLAME J. EDGAR HOOVER IN PART FOR EVENTS IN ALABAMA. NEGROES HAVE NO CAUSE TO HAVE FAITH IN THE FBI". THIS SOURCE ALSO STATED THAT

- 2 -

SAC, NEW YORK (100-73250)   9/26/63

SA ████████████ b-7C

████████████
SM-C   b-7C ALL INFORMATION CONTAINED
                             HEREIN IS UNCLASSIFIED
                             DATE 5/23/08 BY ████████ b-2
                                                        b-7D

Identity of Source:
                                              ████████████
                                              (Conceal & paraphrase)

Reliability: Has furnished reliable
                                              information in the past.

Location: 100-73250-1A

On 9/20/63, source indicated that ████████████ was in
contact with JOHN KILLENS (ph). ████████████████████████████
██

KILLENS (ph) will again be in contact with ████████

Source advised on 9/20/63, that ████████ was in contact
with ████████████████ criticised KING (MARTIN LUTHER KING)
for allowing himself to be outmaneuvered by KENNEDY. ████████ indicated
that JOHN KILLENS (ph) and JAMES BALDWIN are going to blast KING today because of KING's actions in D.C.

On 9/20/63, source indicated that ████████████ was in
contact with JOHN KILLEN. They were critical of the results of the
meeting of the Civil Rights Leaders and the President. KILLEN felt
the man (President) hadn't done a thing and had been let off the
hook. ████████ though that ████████████ JAMES BALDWIN,
and KILLEN should meet prior to the meeting at 5:00 and plan strategy
on a statement to be released. The meeting was to take place at
3:30 pm in Room 440, Hotel Astor.

1 - NY 100-136585 (MARTIN LUTHER KING)
1 - NY 100-146553 (JAMES BALDWIN)
1 - NY 100-102397 (JOHN KILLENS)
1 - NY 100-73250

████████ b-7C

100-146553-39

SECRET

UNITED STATES DEPARTMENT OF JUSTICE

FEDERAL BUREAU OF INVESTIGATION

In Reply, Please Refer to
File No.

New York, New York
October 7, 1963

Communist Party, United States
of America (CPUSA)
Negro Question
Communist Influence in Racial Matters
Internal Security - C

On October 6, 1963, a confidential source, who has
furnished reliable information in the past, furnished
information which indicated that on that date, ████████
████████ expressed concern over James Baldwin (Negro author)
travelling to Birmingham, Alabama. ████████████
████████████ contact local airports to get time and flight
of Baldwin's plane to Birmingham. ████████████████
████████████████ to have him meet Baldwin, scheduled
to arrive at 7:25 p.m. the same date aboard United Airlines
flight from Newark, New Jersey.

████████████████████ was advised that
Baldwin arrived in Birmingham, but was not met by ████████
and is staying at the Gaston Hotel at Birmingham.

████████████████ advised that Baldwin had made
a telephone call to the Attorney General. Whether Baldwin
actually talked to the Attorney General, or the reason
for this contact is unknown by the source at this time.

SECRET
Group I

Excluded from automatic
downgrading and
declassification

100-146553-41

This document contains neither recommendations nor conclusions
of the Federal Bureau of Investigation (FBI). It is the
property of the FBI and is loaned to your agency; it and
its contents are not to be distributed outside your
agency.

9/24/63

On Sunday afternoon, 9/22/63, there was a demonstration at Foley Square, NYC, in protest against the recent bombing at a church in Birmingham, Ala. Members of the CP who were observed at this demonstration were ███

speeches which were made by NORMAN THOMAS, head of the Socialist Party and JAMES FARMER, head of CORE, and JAMES BALDWIN, the writer.

SECRET

UNITED STATES DEPARTMENT OF JUSTICE

FEDERAL BUREAU OF INVESTIGATION
New York, New York
October 10, 1963

In Reply, Please Refer to
File No. NY 100-151548

Communist Party, United States of
America (CPUSA)
Negro Question
Communist Influence in Racial Matters
Internal Security - C

On October 10, 1963, a confidential source, who
has furnished reliable information in the past, furnished
information which indicated that on that date, ██████████
██ had
been critical of Jimmy Baldwin's activities, and he mentioned
that Jimmy's sexual propensities are known. ██████████
██
██
██ Jim
Baldwin is a Negro author.

A second confidential source, who has furnished
reliable information in the past, advised on ██████████
██████████████ he identified a photograph of ██████████

SECRET
Group 1
Excluded from automatic
downgrading and
declassification

100 - 146553-50

This document contains neither recommendations nor conclusions
of the FBI. It is the property of the FBI and is loaned to
your agency; it and its contents are not to be distributed
outside your agency.

(Mount Clipping in Space Below)

JAMES BALDWIN

A New York Post Portrait—By FERN MARJA ECKMAN

(Indicate page, name of newspaper, city and state.)

21   NEW YORK POST

ARTICLE II

NOT FAR FROM the East River, in a second-floor apartment on East 3d St. where James Baldwin has been the intermittent guest in recent months of a German-born patent attorney, the Venetian blinds are drawn to bar the glare of the sun—and perhaps to simulate twilight, a time of the day the 39-year-old writer finds congenial.

The living room has the casual disarray of masculine housekeeping. One pair of shoes stands pigeon-toed on the gray-blue rug; another pair is lined up beside a bookcase stocked with French, German and English titles. A shirt and a tie are draped around the back of a chair. Empty cups and glasses dot the table tops.

It is early afternoon but Baldwin is still asleep. His secretary and closest friend, Lucien Happersberger, 31, a Swiss painter who commutes between his wife and two sons in Lausanne and Baldwin in New York or Paris, explains that the author went to bed at 7 a.m.

A reading of his just completed play, "Blues for Mr. Charlie," had occupied him until that hour. ("I always wanted to be an actor," he admits.) However, it is not unusual for Baldwin to retire just as the rest of New York is preparing to rise. He complains gloomily that his "night habits" are aggravated by the city of his birth.

A copy of the new manuscript lies open on the couch and on the cocktail table, next to an overladen ash tray, is a list of the characters dashed off in Baldwin's handwriting. "Me" is printed next to two of the roles and "David"—Baldwin's youngest brother, who is trying out for a part in the Actors Studio Theater production—next to three more.

Marie-France, a pert, young Frenchwoman married to the first-floor tenant, a ruffled apron inadequately covering her slacks and blouse, drifts about flicking a dust cloth at the furniture and chattering animatedly m Happersberger in French between his sessions at the telephone.

Date: 1/14/64
Edition: LATE CITY
Author: FERN MARJA ECKMAN
Editor: DOROTHY SCHIFF
Title: JAMES BALDWIN

Character: MISC INFO CON
or
Classification:
Submitting Office: NYO

Straightening a pile of magazines, Marie-France was absorbed in a pictorial weekly and sits down to thumb through it. She glances up with mild interest when the bedroom door opens and Baldwin emerges, cradling a coffee cup in his left hand, at precisely 12:45 p.m.

"Good morning," he says pleasantly. He smiles and moves across the room with big, easy, loose-hipped strides. He is wearing a white sweatshirt with three red stripes daubed on the back ("a joke—it means I'm a member of the U. S. Olympic Drinking Team"), black chinos and simple, expensive-looking sandals he bought in Puerto Rico last summer.

★　　★　　★

A HALF HOUR LATER, STILL NURSING HIS coffee, he gives his attention at last—only 70 minutes behind schedule—to the reporter. This amounts to punctuality for Baldwin. Flamboyantly disorganized, he can be relied upon to be hours late for appointments or not to show up at all, a habit that keeps his business associates on edge with anxiety.

As the day progresses, Baldwin swings through his regular daily cycle of liquid nourishment, sipping first coffee (his breakfast), then beer (from the can) and, finally Scotch augmented by a spoonful of water. It is growing dark before he starts to toy with eggs and toast.

"Jimmy," publicity woman Andrea Smargon remarked the other day, "is not an armored person." Baldwin pays unconscious tribute to the accuracy of the observation by ranging over a score of subjects, exposing each of them to the lightning play of his candor, wit, anger and eloquence.

He discusses love and hate ("equally terrifying"), marriage ("you know, I've been nearly married—three times"), Gide ("too defensive") and, with a burst of laughter that creases his thin cheeks into multiple folds, his own gullibility ("I don't care what the story is—any story, y'know, no matter what you're saying, it just fascinates me and, while I'm listening to you, I'll believe it").

Propping up his knees, he loops his arms around his jack-knifed legs and stares hard at the visitor. "I intend to become a *great novelist*," he says gravely. Baldwin is given to periodic reiteration of this ambition. Each time he sounds as though he were intoning a vow, possibly in defiance of critical insistence that he is primarily an essayist.

The reporter mentions that two of Baldwin's three novels, "Giovanni's Room" and the recent "Another Country," revolve around homosexuality, a circumstance that almost prevented the publication of the former. Baldwin corrects this: homosexuality, he points out, is also "implicit" in the boy's situation in "Go Tell It on the Mountain," his first book.

Unhesitatingly he then proceeds to explain the motivation for the recurrent theme in his fiction:

"There are two reasons for it, I think," he says. "Which are the same reason. The most brutal aspect of it, which is why people make such a fuss about the homosexuality in my novels—the real reason behind the fuss is that, no matter what they—I mean white people—say, I was once a Negro adolescent in this country.

"And, for example, when I hit the Village, one of the reasons why my years there were so terrifying was not only because of white *women*—but also because of white *men*. Who looked just like ———." He names a prominent national figure symbolic of conservatism, respectability and bumbling idealism.

"And I was a kid," Baldwin says furiously. "I didn't know any of the things I've since had to find out. People got mad at 'Another Country.' And the reason they got mad is because it's *true*. And it's much worse than that.

"It would not *ever* happen that way in any other country of the world—except, possibly, Germany. And in this country, what we call homosexuality is a grotesque kind of—of *waxworks*. You know? Which is the other side of what we call *heterosexuality* here."

His eyes blaze with contempt. "*Nobody* makes any connections—men or women, or men and men, nobody!" he says. "Parents and children—*nobody* makes any connections! So, naturally, you get, you know—you get this truncated, galvanized activity which *thinks* of itself as *sex*.

"It's not sex at all. It's pure desperation. It's clinical. Do y'know? It comes out of the effort to tell one's self a lie about what human life is like. It comes out of the attempt to cling to definitions which cannot contain anybody's life.

"American homosexuality is a waste primarily because, if people were not so frightened of it—if it wouldn't, you know—it really would cease in effect, as it exists in this country now, to exist. The only people who talk about homosexuality, you know, the way—in this terrible way—are Americans. And Englishmen and Germans. The Anglo-Saxons. The Puritans.

★　　★　　★

"IN ITALY, YOU KNOW, MEN KISS EACH OTHER and boys go to bed with each other. And no one is marked for life. No one imagines that—and they grow up, you know, and they have children and raise them. And no one ends up going to a psychiatrist or turning into a junkie because he's afraid of being touched.

"You know that's the root of the whole—of the American thing. It's not a fear of—it's not a fear of men going to bed with men. It's a fear of anybody touching anybody. That's what it comes to. And that's what's so horrible about it.

"If you're a Negro, you're in the center of that peculiar affliction—because anybody can touch you—when the sun goes down. You know, you're the target for everybody's fantasies.

"If you're a Negro, female whore, he comes to you and asks you to do for him what he wouldn't ask his wife to do—nor any other white woman. But you're a black woman." Hate, deadly, undisguised, seethes in his voice. "So you can do it—because you know how to do dirty things.

"And, if you're a black boy, you wouldn't believe the holocaust that opens over your head—with all these despicable—males—looking for somebody to act out their fantasies on. And it happens in this case—if you are 16 years old—to be you!"

The final word explodes, leaving Baldwin panting. The visitor, overwhelmed, gropes for an appropriate comment, fails, interjects weakly, "But, in Italy, they——"

"They understand," says Baldwin, cutting in, "that people were born to touch each other."

★　　★　　★

THE DOOR OPENS AND HIS BROTHER GEORGE, 35, a shy, handsome man, next to the author in age, enters. He stands there, holding on to the door-knob, in some way immobilized by the high-voltage arc of emotion still crackling through the room.

Then Baldwin nods at the newcomer. The tension snaps. "Hi," says George Baldwin gladly. As though released from a spell, he shuts the door behind him and walks in.

Jimmy Baldwin takes a deep breath. He reaches for a cigaret. The lighter flares, illuminating his slender, elegant hands. Then he pivots a little, picks up a turquoise pillow and thumps it—once, twice—against his sandaled foot.

——

Continued Tomorrow.

(Mount Clipping in Space Below)

JAMES BALDWIN

A New York Post Portrait—By FERN MARJA ECKMAN

ARTICLE V

IT WAS IN Europe that James Baldwin became an American.

In the U. S., he had felt himself an alien—and an enemy alien, at that. But, divided from the land of his birth by an ocean, liberated from the collective anonymity that transforms the Negroes of this country into invisible men, Baldwin reconciled himself to his identity.

The process was gradual. Breaking out of the ghetto, he was still its victim. He suffered from what he once described as the "profound, almost ineradicable self-hatred" with which this nation endows its black citizens. Perhaps it was inevitable that he should initially seek to forget his color: it was, after all, inextricably bound up in his mind and in his blood with the bitter humiliation he had endured at home.

During the eight years he lived abroad, Baldwin infrequently associated with Negroes. Then as now, his intimates, few in number, were usually white.

"When Jimmy was in his 20s in Paris," explains a Baldwin admirer, lowering his voice several decibels, "he thought seriously of never being a Negro again—certainly never a Negro in America."

Reality did not, of course, conform with this fantasy. Even life in sanctuary—and that is what France represented to him—was not devoid of dilemma. Confronted with Europe's abundant testimony to Western culture, Baldwin, searching in vain for a reflection of himself or his African heritage, despairingly concluded he was an interloper.

"What was the most difficult," he wrote later after merciless self-examination, "was the fact that I was forced to admit something I had always hidden from myself, which the American Negro has had to hide from himself as the price of his public progress; that I hated and feared white people. This did not mean that I loved black people; on the contrary, I despised them, possibly because they failed to produce Rembrandt. In effect, I hated and feared the world."

It is Baldwin's thesis that he has since purged himself of this hate and this fear. But the fury smoldering in his prose and flaring up in his speeches invites a measure of skepticism. Even while counseling peace, Baldwin communicates violence.

In any event, in Paris and, later, in the tiny Swiss village of Loche-les-Bains, James Baldwin came to recognize—and possibly even accept—both his nationality and his race.

(Indicate page, name of newspaper, city and state.)

39   NEW YORK POST

Date: 1/17/64
Edition: LATE CITY
Author: FERN M. ECKMAN
Editor: DOROTHY SCHIFF
Title: JAMES BALDWIN

Character: MISC. INFO. CO
or
Classification:
Submitting Office: NYO

100-146553-93

SEARCHED

FBI — NEW YORK

"SOMETHING *STRUCK* ME IN PARIS," THE 39-year-old author confessed the other day. "I didn't realize what a *puritan* I was until I found myself dealing with people, you know, whose morality was entirely different from my father's. Which was the morality I carried *around* with me, really. It was—it was really kind of *humiliating* to discover it.

"And I watched myself, you know. Just like any other little American, I was doing my best to avoid all the things which I thought of—that I'd been *brought up to believe* were amoral. But I couldn't—I couldn't, on the other hand, avoid realizing—because I was dealing with the streets of Paris, and with Arabs and Africans and French whores and pimps and *street boys*, you know—that there was something very beautiful, no matter how *horrible*.

"Y'know, I saw some — I saw some *tremendous things*. And some of those people were—very *nice* to me and, in a way, I owe them my *life*. D'you know? These were people, you know, that everyone else *despises* and *spits* on.

"And it was—it *humbled* me, in a way. It did something—very strange for me. It opened me *up*—to *whole areas* of life. Which—I would never have—*dared* to deal with in America. D'you know?"

WHAT PARIS OPENED UP TO HIM AND WHAT he dared to deal with is the material he ultimately worked into his three published novels:

"Go Tell It on the Mountain" (begun when he was 21 and completed a decade—or was it a lifetime?—later), "Giovanni's Room" (whose homosexual theme made timid New York publishers to shy off after issuing paternalistic warnings to Baldwin that they were rejecting the book for his own good, really, since publica-

tion would surely "wreck" his career) and the recent "Another Country" (a bestseller, acclaimed and damned in almost equal proportions).

Baldwin writes as he lives: hard. His labor-pains are always intense and prolonged. He tries to ease them by taking refuge, sometimes seriatim, in Istanbul, Corsica, Puerto Rico, Southern France, Switzerland, Fire Island, perhaps a friend's home in Connecticut or Westchester.

Yet, no matter how fast and how far he travels, he never escapes the pangs of creation.

There are always, as he confided not long ago in a letter, "the unforeseeable and demoralizing snags" that occur "when the writer, in working, disturbs one of his sleeping lions, the rage of which he's by no means prepared to face; or, to put it more simply, when the truth concerning one of his characters—or all of them—becomes crucially and unflatteringly involved with the truth about himself . . ."

THE PARIS IN WHICH HE MADE HIS DISCOM-forting discoveries was hardly the tourists' Paris.

Nor was it the artistic bohemia in which his gifted compatriots clustered. Plagued by hunger as well as sleeping lions, Baldwin shunned the company of his peers, convinced he would be patronized by colleagues possessed of influence, affluence or both.

In that hazardous period, he built solid relationships with James Jones, William Styron, Philip Roth ("I adore them") and, on a charged, on-again-off-again basis that is at once closer and more threatening, Norman Mailer. But the incestuous atmosphere of literary parties made Baldwin uneasy. And still does.

At 25, chronically skidding on the edge of starvation, he frequented a Left Bank bar where he could scrounge sandwiches and beer. There he met one day a lean, quiet, dimpled youth with a Charles Boyer voice and a talent for painting, Lucien Happersberger, 17, who had just run away from his home in Lausanne.

The two formed an alliance ("partly because, I suppose, I had the habits of an older brother, really") that continues to this day. Happersberger, whose 11-year-old son is Baldwin's godchild, currently serves as the writer's secretary, buffer and companion. "That's my best friend," says Baldwin, smiling at him affectionately.

Distance has lent the usual nostalgic enchantment to their early adventures, but at the time they were reminiscent of Gorki rather than Saroyan. Baldwin remembers a rainy Thursday in Paris when he and Happersberger hadn't eaten for a couple of days.

"We lived in this terrible place on Rue Jacob, way up on the top floor," Baldwin recalls, grinning. "Lucien and I went downstairs because we thought we could eat around the corner at this woman's restaurant. On credit. And it was *closed*." He begins to laugh. "And we had no cigarets. And no money. *Noth*-ing! And it really was *like* that."

"What did you do?" the reporter inquires.

The room resounds with Baldwin's laughter. "Why, we went back upstairs. It was *raining*." He rocks back and forth, helplessly, joyously, his huge eyes squeezed shut, laughing so hard that a tear courses down his cheek.

★ ★ ★

WHILE BALDWIN WAS GROWING THINNER AND shabbier on the streets of Paris—yes, and sometimes in its gutters—and learning to acknowledge his puritanical instincts and relishing his freedom and struggling with his autobiographical novel and selling an occasional essay, an editor back in New York buttonholed a psychologist-author

"Kenneth," Elliot E. Cohen of Commentary magazine said to Dr. Kenneth B. Clark, "there is a young man in Paris by the name of Jim Baldwin. If we can keep him alive, he will emerge as one of the greatest writers America has produced."

"What's his name again?" Clark asked.

"James Baldwin," Cohen said. "Don't forget it."

★ ★ ★

IN 1952, FOUR YEARS AFTER HE HAD EXILED himself from his native land, Baldwin decided to visit the U. S. He was intent upon pushing the sale of "Go Tell It on the Mountain," but he had another—an unspoken, interior—motive. He wanted to test the interaction between his country and himself.

The young writer had just enough money to pay his hotel bill or his ship fare. Bailed out of Paris by Marlon Brando ("he's a beautiful cat"), Baldwin arrived home stone-broke. His youngest brother, David, welcomed him at the pier with a $10 loan. Armed with borrowed cash and a borrowed suit, Baldwin prowled around New York.

"It was a nightmare," he says, whispering each word. "I'd been away just long enough—to have lost all my old habits, all my old friends, all my old con-

With Shelley Winters at a literary symposium.

nections, you know. So I came back into a kind of *limbo.*"

Knopf bought his book and Baldwin fled back to Paris. But the city of light had somehow dimmed in his absence. Paris had been his haven, his prop. Suddenly Baldwin required neither. He retired to a chalet belonging to Happersberger's family. There, in the Swiss Alps, he licked his wounds and brooded.

Baldwin had spent two weeks at the chalet the summer before but, to these villagers who had never seen another black man, he remained an exotic rarity. They fingered his hair; they touched his cheek to determine whether the color rubbed off; they roused in him "the rage of the disesteemed"—and a new maturity. In Loche-les-Bains, Jimmy Baldwin finally came of age.

"No road whatever will lead Americans back to the simplicity of this European village where white men still have the luxury of looking on me as a stranger," he wrote in a brilliantly perceptive essay that defined the nature of America's conflict and his own. "I am not, really, a stranger any longer for any American alive. One of the things that distinguishes Americans from other people is that no other people has ever been so deeply involved in the lives of black men, or vice versa."

Once James Baldwin had written those lines, the days of his expatriation had to be numbered.

IN THE WEEKEND EDITION: James Baldwin in America.

(Mount Clipping in Space Below)

~AMES BALDWIN

A New York Post Portrait—By FERN MARJA ECKMAN

(Indicate page, name of
newspaper, city and state.)

MAG 4   NEW YORK POST

Date: 1/19/64
Edition: WEEKEND
Author: FERN MARJA ECKMAN
Editor: DOROTHY SCHIFF
Title: JAMES BALDWIN

Character: MISC INFO CON
or
Classification:
Submitting Office: NYO

ARTICLE VI

ON ONE OF THOSE dismal, wet days when all Paris is submerged in gray and the entire population appears to be in mourning, James Baldwin trudged into the American Express office, praying he would find there a check from New York that represented salvation.

For economy's sake, the young author was then living in the village of Gallardon, near Chartres, pooling his skimpy resources with a Frenchman who painted, a Norwegian girl who sculptured and a German-African woman who wanted to write. On this occasion, it was Baldwin's turn to try his luck at reviving the communal exchequer. He had set out by bus, but a strike had obliged him to proceed on foot from the gates of Paris.

His mission proved a grotesque failure. No money awaited him. But 10 spanking-fresh copies of his first published work, "Go Tell It on the Mountain," did. Magnificently burdened with these testimonials to his success, Baldwin sloshed through the streets in rain-logged sandals to a bar in St. Germain des Pres.

Stacking his books on a table, he sat down behind the impressive array, dripping water into miniature puddles, cadging beer and waiting hopefully all day—alas, in vain—for some generous soul who would at least lend him enough money to get back to the country. "I was," Baldwin said recently, "absolutely broke and starving."

Ten years later, in the summer of 1963, now a literary figure of distinction with an income that justified his sporadic taste for caviar and champagne, Baldwin was driving up Park Av. with his publisher, Richard Baron of Dial Press, and his agent, Robert P. Mills.

Baron stopped for a red light. A blond girl in the next car, catching sight of Baldwin, held up a copy of "Another Country," then just off the press, and called out in a thick-as-honey Southern accent, "My daddy says the language is terrible but I think the book is great!" It was a memorable encounter and Baldwin loved every fleeting second of it.

Between those two incidents, Jimmy Baldwin's life had undergone a sea of change. In 1957, propelled homeward by a realization that "whatever's happening in your country is happening to you" and a mounting aversion for the woe-unto-the-U. S. lamentations of Paris' American contingent, Baldwin had returned "for good" to the land of his birth after more than eight years abroad.

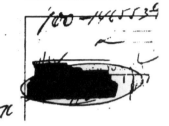

"I wasn't in the *least* prepared to come back *here*," Baldwin observed the other day. "But, on the other hand, I I was out of kilter in Paris too, because I couldn't get along with the bulk of the American colony—especially the American-*Negro* colony who, so far as I could see, spent most of their time, you know, sitting in bars and cafes, talking about how awful *America* was. And I didn't cross the *ocean* to do *that*, you know.

"And I wasn't prepared either to be used by the *French*—or any other European—as a stick to beat the U.S. over the *head* with. For, after all, it was *my* country. And France was really no *better*—you know, *my* country is. And for the French to complain, to want to be indignant about the way America's treated Negroes — seemed to me absolutely, you know, *hypocritical*—since I knew the way they treated their own black people."

★   ★   ★

LIKE A DEEP-SEA DIVER TRYING TO PREVENT the bends, Baldwin cautiously edged himself back into the U. S., spending nine sample months here in 1954.

Even so, the transition was jolting. It was hard for him to adjust to a system he was "determined not to adjust to." For a couple of months, he languished in a hotel room, moping, drinking too much, wondering what to do next.

"The thing to do, y'know, if you're really terribly occupied with—with *yourself*," he explained not long ago, "the thing to do is to, at any price whatever, get in touch with something which is *more* than you. Throw yourself into a situation where you won't have no I weep. So I went South. Because I was *afraid* to go South."

Baldwin was—and still is—"scared to death" in the Deep South. His terror springs from his unfamiliarity with the intricate code of behavior indulged in by both races there, a "weird kind of etiquette" that cannot be acquired "surface-wise."

Deliberately exposing himself to Southern segregation patterns, Baldwin crossed the Mason-Dixon line for the first time on an assignment from Look

magazine. The experience was painful but unexpectedly "beautiful." He found himself exhilarated and stirred by the day-to-day heroism of Negro civil rights crusaders.

"I suppose the depth of my involvement began then," he reflected. "Because I—was forced to *understand*—that people *talked* to me as though I were a messenger. To get—to get the message *out*."

On that initial journey, so long dreaded, so long fantasied, the forerunner of scores of others, each equally terrifying, Baldwin decided that the artist's role is to bear witness to what life is and what life does: "To speak for people who cannot speak—you are simply a kind of conduit."

The bitter grace of his first collection of essays,

Baldwin and Charlton Heston arrive for last August's
Washington March.

"Notes of a Native Son," had been triumphantly received. But Baldwin could still, with a fair degree of accuracy, entitle his second volume, "Nobody Knows My Name." It was this book, with its wrenching report on the Southern condition, that riveted the attention of students in the South.

"This was the point," Baldwin said, "where I meant something in their lives. And they began to *depend* on me more. And—it turned out that money could be raised on my name, y'know. And they needed money to pay all those terrible court costs. To get people out of jail, you know. And so I began donating my time to do that."

★   ★   ★

HE BEGAN THEN AND HE HAS YET TO STOP. At any hour of any day, Jimmy Baldwin can be deflected from the central and avowed purpose of his life with by an urgent request for his presence at integration rallies, emergency meetings—even protest marches, although he detests the military ceremony that attends such demonstrations.

At the legend of 1962, The New Yorker published the essay that forms the major portion of "The Fire Next Time." Almost overnight, Baldwin's cherished privacy was invaded by the brouhaha of public acclaim, his professional timetable, chronically disorganized, collapsed.

The opening of his new play, "Blues for Mr. Charlie," dedicated to the memory of his friend, Medgar Evers, the Mississippi field secretary for the N.A.A.C.P. who was murdered last June) has been indefinitely postponed, at least in part because Baldwin repeatedly delayed completion of the script to fulfill civil rights engagements.

Baldwin, who believes his own death at the hands of white supremacists is far from unlikely, was overwhelmed by Evers' ambush slaying. But neither that event, nor the tragic assassination of President Kennedy, ever for a moment shook his conviction that the force and dimension of the desegregation struggle must be inexorably expanded.

So total is Baldwin's commitment that his family (with the notable exception of his youngest brother, David, "my ally") and several of his associates periodically remind the essayist, novelist and playwright that his most effective battlepost is the typewriter, not the platform.

These confrontations are wearing for Baldwin, whose devotion to his mother and his eight brothers and sisters—emotional and financial—is unstinting.

"I've had this argument with them many, many times," Baldwin said recently. "And they're perfectly right so far as it *goes*. What they *overlook* is that it was exactly *because* I kept writing that all this happened.

"David and I had a tremendous fight with my sister Gloria, in a taxi, when she was saying what my *mother* said, you know: 'I don't want Jimmy in politics.' And David said, you know, 'Then you don't want Jimmy in the *world*.'"

In Baldwin's view, he is participating in a global "convulsion of nature" rather than a national movement. "I think of it as a *revolution*," he said, the tinkle of ice in his glass stilled for the moment.

"And I don't see any way of—of escaping your role, if you *have* one, in a revolution, y'know. It's up to you somehow to figure out how to do two things at once. It's—just—kind of difficult."

On a personal level, he is willing to settle for a compromise arrangement. He plans to buy a three-story house in New York (in which his mother will occupy one floor, his secretary—with his wife and two sons—the second, himself the third) and an apartment in Paris (anticipated cost: $25,000).

Then, continuing his transatlantic commuting, he could work six or seven months in France and spend the rest of the year here, "being a public figure."

Meanwhile, as "a holding operation," Baldwin moved just a few days ago from a friend's house on East Third Street to a spacious, seven-room, four-telephone establishment in a still-fashionable ("for the next five minutes") building on West End Avenue.

Renting suitable quarters was frustrating, even for such a celebrity as Baldwin. Vacancies were mysteriously filled as soon as landlords discovered the applicant was a Negro. On one occasion, Baldwin's Swiss secretary, Lucien Happersberger, was blandly

AND SO, LITERARY LION THOUGH HE IS, DIS-crimination still stalks Baldwin. But he requires no such stimulus to fire his rage. Jimmy Baldwin is a small man containing a monumental anger. Some-times he unleashes it at the well-intentioned as well as at the sinners.

Last October, when he was the Board of Educa-tion's guest speaker at PS 180, in Harlem, a white teacher, shy and earnest, made the mistake of in-quiring, "How would you define the role of the white liberal?"

Baldwin stared at him. In the modern idiom, and certainly in Baldwin's, "liberal" is a term of oppro-brium. "I don't really want to be abusive," the author finally remarked icily. "But what I really want to say is there is *no* role for the white liberal. He is really one of our *afflictions*."

From the predominantly Negro audience, there was a groundswell of laughter and applause. The teacher who had put the question slumped in his seat, crimson with embarrassment. Baldwin went in for the kill:

"The role of the white liberal in my fight is the role of the missionaries, of 'I'm trying to help you, you poor black thing, you.' The thing is—*we're* not in trouble. *You* are.

"I'd like to suggest that white people turn this around and ask what *white* people can do to help *themselves*. No white liberal knows what Ray Charles is singing about. So how can you help *me?* Work with yourself!"

This hostility, intricately interwoven through the labyrinthine Baldwin personality, reveals itself from time to time, inflaming some of his listeners, alienating others. But what Baldwin occasionally preaches is flatly contradicted by what he practices. Outside his family circle, he has only four real intimates; three of them are white. Carried away by rhetoric, he is apt to convey a distorted message.

Still, just the other day, expounding his theory that a worldwide race war is "more than probable" in our time, Baldwin, in Cassandra mood, dourly pre-dicted:

"People will have to make alliances on that basis, y'know. And someone like *me*, someone like *Lucien*"—Happersberger, just entering the room, looked startled—"will *perish*. In the *middle*. Because," said James Baldwin, the words surging up on a tide of passion, "I *can't* make my alignments on the basis of *color*."

Last of Six Articles.

Chapter XVII

Charlie Chaplin: The 20th Century's Funniest White Man

Following are things we ought to know about the movie star Charles Spencer Chaplin Jr. , the world's funniest white man. Firstly, what part of planet earth did he originate, and secondly what satellite launched him?

Chaplin Jr. , was born in Kennington, a suburb of London, England, April 16, 1889. His parents were Charles Spencer Chaplin and Hannah Harley Hodges Chaplin. He was educated in public schools in London and its provinces.

Chaplin's father and mother were vaudevillians. His mother's stage name was Lilly Harley. Her second marriage was to a Jewish bookmaker named Sydney Hawkes. Sydney Hawkes Jr. , Charlie's half-brother, was born of that union and assumed the Chaplin name. Hannah divorced Hawkes, and then formed an alliance with Wheeler Dryden (there is no record of their having married). In the absence of a stationary guardian, Charlie and Sidney were sent to live in the Lambeth Workhouse and a multiple of orphanages and poorhouses for two years. Young

Charlie had been identified with the theater since he was seven years of age in that he had been employed in vaudeville and the legitimate theater houses. His initial appearance on stage was as Billy, with William Gilette in a play entitled, <u>Sherlock Holmes</u>. His father died in England in 1902 when Charlie was only thirteen years of age and his mother died in August, 1928 in a Glendale, California sanitarium. She had been declared insane at the time.

Before Charlie reached the age of twenty-one, he was a vaudeville headliner in Great Britain and the United States. He entered the motion picture business in the United States in September 1910 at the age of 21 by invitation of Sennett Production and Associates. Under Chaplin's initial movie studio contract he was paid $150 a week.

On January 12, 1915, Chaplin was signed away from the Sennett Studios for a salary of $1,000 a week by the Essanay Company. In 1916 he was given a contract for $670,000 by the Mutual Film Company and was free to act and also produce his own moving pictures.

In December 1916, Chaplin refused to renegotiate a new contract with the Mutual Film Company and launched his own studio. He had found a financial angel who provided him with $1,000,000 for the production of eight pictures a year.

When he first arrived in Los Angeles he lived at the Stowell Hotel which was just one and a half steps above a flophouse. Julian Eltinge, a famous female impersonator of the stage, and for whom a New York theater was subsequently named encouraged Chaplin to move into the Los Angeles Athletic Club and it was there that he met Torachi Kono a Japanese American. The chemistry between the two men was positive enough for Chaplin to employ Kono on the spot as his secretary, chauffeur and handyman.

In 1918 Chaplin constructed his own studios in Hollywood and was the only member of United Artists Distributing Corporation who was also an independent producer.

Moving pictures in the early years were silent with printed dialogue at the bottom of the screen. There was always a piano player in the theater pit watching the movie and dialogue and playing mood music to fit the story line. Chaplin's personal magnetism and acting ability was displayed through his shuffling walk, the twirling of his trusted walking cane, a nervous smile, and very formal English mannerisms. His stage uniform was that of a "street tramp" in an old beat up derby hat, baggy pants, oversized floppy shoes, and an undersized coat jacket.

Chaplin's eyes and facial expressions projected a thousand different mental images in that he could make you laugh your head off in one minute and then make you cry in the next. He was indeed a genius of comedy, the only other comic in his class in the second decade of the twentieth century was Bert Williams, the first Black man to star in the Ziegfield Follies on Broadway. W. C. Fields, was a contemporary of both Chaplin and Williams, as a matter of fact, Fields worked in the Follies with Williams for four years. One day Fields who was a big time comedian in his own right said to Williams, "You are the funniest man I ever saw and the saddest man I ever knew. " Although Williams was the star of the Follies he replied, "I am just relegated, I don't belong. " Negroes were not accepted in the Actors Equity Association until several decades later. Jim Crow customs would not permit a Black man to bow in the front line along with the white members of the cast during the finale.

Up until 1925 it was mandatory that Blacks had to blacken their faces with greasepaint when they appeared before a white audience. They were not permitted to address a white audience directly. They would either talk out loud to themselves as if reciting poetry or to a Black second banana. On the other hand, if Black musicians were accompaning a white star like Sophie Tucker they could not be seen by the audience in that they had to play behind a screen. The establishment thought that if white and Black entertainers were seen together on the stage it would imply a notion of racial equality.

The first time this writer saw Charlie Chaplin was in 1925 in one of his earliest feature films entitled <u>The Kid</u> (1921). In that movie he introduced Jackie Coogan who became a leading child movie star during the roaring twenties. From 1925 forward I became a Charlie Chaplin and cowboy Tom Mix, the addict like millions of Americans old and young, Black and white in that I pleaded with my parents, Louis and Mittie Travis to take me to see every picture those actors appeared in at the States Theater, our neighborhood movie house which was located on the South Side of Chicago at 3507 South State Street. State Street was nicknamed the

Black Broadway of America by the brothers and sisters because of its reputation for highlighting such celebrities as Louis Armstrong, Butterbeans and Susie, Ethel Waters, Garbage, Bessie Smith, King Oliver, Jelly Roll Morton, Scott Joplin, Bert Williams, Fats Waller and Jack Johnson, the first Black heavyweight champion of the world and hundreds of others. Johnson owned the Café de Champion which was located several feet west of State Street at 31st Street. In 1912 his club became the first integrated (Black and Tan) nightclub in America.

In 1910 Shelton Brooks the famous ragtime piano player and composer was the house pianist at the Pekin Theater which was located at 2700 South State Street. It was on that venue that he composed Some of These Days (1910) which was popularized by Sophie Tucker when she introduced it at the White City Amusement Park located at 63rd and South Park in Chicago, she also adopted the song as her lifetime theme song. Brooks also wrote "The Dark Town Strutters Ball" while working on State Street in 1917 during World War I. The song's lyrics described State Street and the social activities of people of color on Saturday night.

Following my first opportunity of seeing Chaplin in The Kid, I subsequently saw him in a series of other movies including The Gold Rush (1925), The Circus (1928), City Lights (1931), Modern Times (1936) and The Great Dictator (1940).

Chaplin's activities during World War I appeared to have been confined to touring the United States with Mary Pickford, America's #1 sweetheart of the screen and her popular movie star husband Douglas Fairbanks in the summer of 1917. The actors paid their own expenses and were speaking on the behalf of the Liberty Loan War Bond drive.

On Chaplin's return from the war bond tour he met the woman who became his first wife, Mildred Harris. She was at that time sixteen years of age and he was 29. She was a guest in the home of Mary and Owen Moore, who at the time owned a house at Del Rey Beach, California. Charlie had never, in the deeper sense of the word, been in love with anyone except Hetty Kelly his British girlfriend who died before he could return to England and ask for her hand. Chaplin was infatuated with Mildred Harris but not in love. When he became tired of Mildred's lovemaking he did not jettison her, he simply moved her out of his home and purchased his wife and her mother a house of their own. That act freed him to hang out with a string of assorted young girls. After divorcing Mildred in 1924 he married Lita Grey who was also sixteen at the time. They had two sons, Charles Spencer Chaplin Jr. and Sidney Arthur Chaplin II. The couple was divorced in 1927. Chaplin's third wife was not a child but the mature and beautiful Paulette Goddard who was a budding movie star from whom he got a divorce in 1941. Sandwiched between his marriages, was a celebrated paternity suit which he lost because the DNA testing method had not been discovered as a mean of showing positive proof of parentage.

Early in 1942 during World War II following his divorce from Goddard he was placed on the FBI watch list of left wing individuals that were suspected of not being supportive of the United States war efforts against Germany, Italy and Japan.

During World War II Chaplin had a string of affairs with lonely American women. The first one to come to my attention was Edna Purviance, who came to Hollywood from Reno, Nevada. She was his first leading lady. Kono, his Japanese chauffeur picked her up every morning in route to the movie studio. They were a twosome in that she was seen with Chaplin at all of the great parties in Tinseltown. Between Edna and Oona, Charlie Chaplin's sexually active list of women became longer than a Hollywood call directory until he met Oona O'Neill the eighteen year old, daughter of the award winning playwright Eugene O'Neill who was opposed to her marrying the 54 year old Chaplin, and thus he disinherited his daughter. Chaplin was only one year younger than his future father- in- law.

O'Neill's works included <u>Morning Becomes Electra</u> (1931) and <u>Long Days Journey Into Night</u> (produced in 1956). He also won the 1936 Nobel Prize for Literature. In spite of O'Neill's objections Oona married Chaplin in 1943 and bore him eight children. Oona and seven of their eight children were at his bedside when he died on December 25, 1977. The final scene took place in a villa on his 37 acre estate overlooking Lake Geneva in Corsier- sur Vevey, Switzerland.

Federal Bureau of Investigation

Freedom of Information/Privacy Acts Section

Subject: <u>Charlie Chaplin</u>

Attention Mr. Hoo{ :-2-   L.A.File 180/1003

REPORT MADE AT:	DATE WHEN MADE:	PERIOD FOR WHICH MADE:	REPORT MADE BY:	
Los Angeles	Aug.15/1922	Aug.14,1922	A. A. HOPKINS:	

TITLE AND CHARACTER OF CASE:

CHARLIE CHAPLIN, et al.   Los Angeles, Cal.   COMMUNIST ACTIVITIES

FACTS DEVELOPED:

At Los Angeles, California:-

A reliable confidential info—   —in contact with the moving picture industry and also with the "Parlor Bolsheviki" groups of Los Angeles, Hollywood and Pasadena, reports that during the visit of WILLIAM Z. FOSTER to Los Angeles, a reception was given in his honor by CHARLIE CHAPLIN (the moving picture star) which reception was attended by many of the "Parlor Bolsheviki", and a large number of the radicals connected with the moving picture industry, as, for instance, WILLIAM DE MILLE, and ROB WAGNER.

CHAPLIN stated to FOSTER that neither himself nor the stars associated with him have any use for WILL HAYS. "We are against any kind of censorship, and particularly against Presbyterian censorship", he said laughingly, and showed his guests a pennant with the words: "Welcome WILL HAYS", which he had fastened over the door of the men's toilet in his studio.

At this reception, the great importance of moving pictures with their educational and propagandist appeal for the cause of the labor movement and the revolution was discussed, and several instances cited where radical ideas have been or are going to be embodied into moving pictures as well as legitimate plays.

MRS. KATE CRANE GARTZ, who was present at this recep-

REFERENCE:	COPIES OF THIS REPORT FURNISHED TO:
	Wash.-3; S.F.-1; Seattle-1; New York-2; File-1;

7—1169

A. A. Hopkins :   8/15/1922;   Page 2.

Re:- CHARLIE CHAPLIN: (Cont.)

tion, told that a Scenario writer by the name of HOCHSTETTER (or
some such name), had come to her and asked for a rather large sum
of money in return for which he could put some radical Communist
propaganda into scenarios in a manner that would do the greatest
possible good to the cause.

MRS. CLEWE, who for some time has been prominently identified with the TEACHERS COUNCIL movement, recently approached several of the wealthy radicals in this vicinity and asked them to support the MISSION PICTURES CORPORATION, a recently formed concern,
whose first picture was "SCIENCE OR GOD". This outfit intends to
produce a Socialist propaganda film called "ROBINSON CRUSOE, A SOCIAL
PIONEER ".

BRUCE ROGERS, notorious Communist agitator, recently sold
a scenario to LASKY. It is said that some one in Alaska turned
the manuscript over to him to sell it, but that ROGERS sold it
for his own account and pocketed the money. Since then he has quit
the FEDERATED PRESS.

As an instance of radical propaganda finding its way into
the stage, the radicals point to "THE FOOL", which recently ran at
the Majestic Theatre in Los Angeles, with RICHARD BENNETT, in the
role of a minister who takes it onto himself to settle a strike,
makes the Company accept the strikers' terms (which results in a loss
of millions of dollars to the concern) and does all kinds of other
impossible things in defiance of the existing social system, in an

A. A. Hopkins: Aug, 15,1922;   Page 8.

Re:- CHARLIE CHAPLIN (Cont.)

attempt to bring about the millenium, this FOOL being said to have
traits of Jesus as well as Postoevsky's Idiot, since HAUPTMANN's
DIE WEBER, the well known drama depicting the revolt of the striking
weavers in Silesia, no stronger labor propaganda is said to have
been produced for the stage.

One of the most effective scenes in the "FOOL" is the one
showing a Polish labor agitator in a fiery soap box speech against
the ten-hour day, and for better working conditions and higher
wages. The play was such a decided success here that BENNETT declared he was sorry he could not run it another couple of weeks. It
was being tried out here in Los Angeles previous to its being shown
in New York this coming season.

PLOTKIN, an organizer for the GARMENT WORKERS UNION
from the East, was recently sent to Los Angeles by the COMMUNISTS
to agitate among the Railroad strikers. Recently he went to CHARLIE
CHAPLIN with letters from MRS. KATE CRANE GARTZ, and MR.
BERCOVICI, to collect money for the Railroad strikers.

Copies of this report are sent to Washington and New York
with the request that this office be furnished with any information
available relative to PLOTKIN.

CONTINUED.

APPROVED
Leon Bone
SPECIAL AGENT IN CHARGE
LOS ANGELES, CAL.

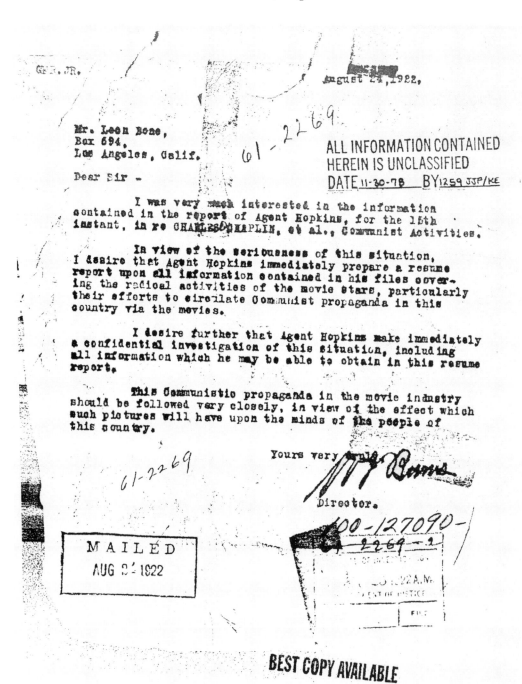

GFR. JR.

August 24, 1922.

Mr. Leon Bone,
Box 694,
Los Angeles, Calif.

61-2269

ALL INFORMATION CONTAINED
HEREIN IS UNCLASSIFIED
DATE 11-30-78 BY 1259 JJP/KE

Dear Sir -

I was very much interested in the information contained in the report of Agent Hopkins, for the 15th instant, in re CHARLES CHAPLIN, et al., Communist Activities.

In view of the seriousness of this situation, I desire that Agent Hopkins immediately prepare a resume report upon all information contained in his files covering the radical activities of the movie stars, particularly their efforts to circulate Communist propaganda in this country via the movies.

I desire further that Agent Hopkins make immediately a confidential investigation of this situation, including all information which he may be able to obtain in this resume report.

This Communistic propaganda in the movie industry should be followed very closely, in view of the effect which such pictures will have upon the minds of the people of this country.

Yours very truly,

Burns

Director.

61-2269

100-127090-
2269-2

MAILED
AUG 24 1922

BEST COPY AVAILABLE

WM. J. BURNS.
DIRECTOR.

GFR. JR.

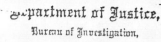

Department of Justice,

Bureau of Investigation,

Washington, D. C.

August 28, 1922.

MEMORANDUM FOR MR. HOOVER:

      I desire to call your attention to the attached extremely interesting report of Agent Hopkins, at Los Angeles, Cal., for the 15th instant, in re - CHARLIE CHAPLIN, et al., Communist Activities.

      This report would indicate that numerous movie stars are taking more than an active part in the Red movement in this country. Evidently they are endeavoring to organize a program for placing Communist propaganda before the public via the movies.

      In view of the seriousness of this situation, I directed a communication to the Los Angeles office on the 24th instant, requesting a detailed report covering all information which they have secured in the past on this subject, and all information which they may be able to obtain at the present time, as I am sure the Director will desire to submit the same to Mr. Will Hays.

      From the contents of Mr. Hopkins' report, it would appear that numerous stars have very little respect for Mr. Hays in his capacity as Director of the movie industry.

Respectfully,

Instructions fr   ial Agent Charles J.   e No. A-19(-)

REPORT MADE AT:	MADE:	PERIOD FOR WHICH MADE:	BY:
New York City	22	9/8/22	Joseph G. Tucker.

TITLE AND CHARACTER OF CASE:

IN RE: CHARLES CHAPLIN, ET AL., LOS ANGELES, CAL. - COMMUNIST ACTIVITIES.

Read by (1-2269

FACTS DEVELOPED: AT NEW YORK:

SEP 1 1922

Based upon report of Agent Hopkins of the J.Burns eles office,
dated August 15, 1922, in which mention is made of one Plotkin, said to
be an organizer for the Garment Workers' Union and to have been sent
Los Angeles by the Communist Party to agitate among the railroad strikers, and in which the request is made that such information as may be
available regarding this man be forwarded to that office, I today consult-
ed local files which show the following: GENERAL INTELLIGENCE

Plotkin in October, 1921, was active in the interests of the
Workers' League which preceded the present Workers' Party of America, and
was one of the speakers in behalf of the various candidates of the Workers' League and ran for office that year. At a disarmament meeting held
at the New Star Casino in New York on November 13, 1921, under the auspices of the Communist Party of America, Plotkin was one of the speakers
and pointed out to those present the need for a workers' republic to replace the present form of government. In November of that year he was
shown to have been an organizer for the Amalgamated Knit Goods Workers'
Union and a member of the Workers' League which operated under the Com-

100-127090-X3

DO NOT WRITE IN THESE SPACES

munist Party, Plotkin being one of the
delegates from the Amalgamated Knit
Goods Workers' Union to the Workers'
League. On November 6, 1921, Plotkin

FILE NO. 61-2-2269-2 RECORDED

BUREAU OF INVESTIGATION

DEPARTMENT OF JUSTICE

SEP 15 1922

ROUTED TO:

REFERENCE:	COPIES OF THIS REPORT FURNISHED TO:
	Washington (3) Los Angeles (2) New York (1)

JGT:EC

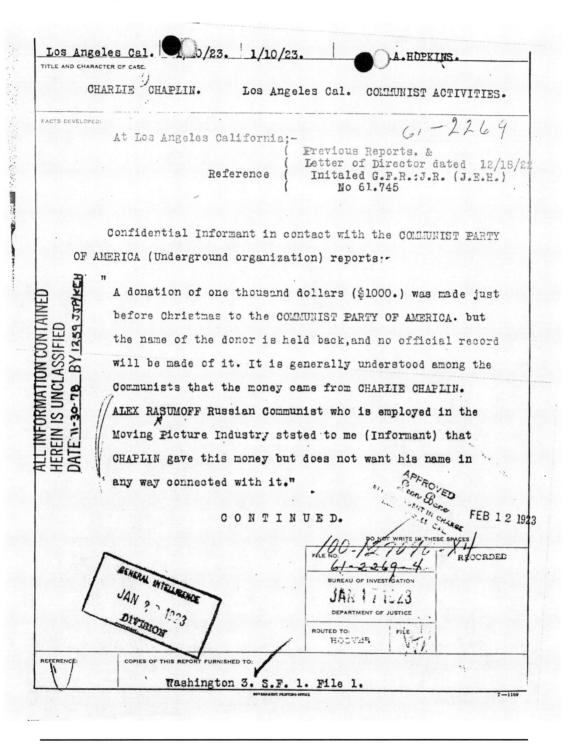

Los Angeles Cal. █0/23. 1/10/23. A. HOPKINS.

TITLE AND CHARACTER OF CASE:

CHARLIE CHAPLIN. Los Angeles Cal. COMMUNIST ACTIVITIES.

FACTS DEVELOPED:

At Los Angeles California:-

Reference (
    Previous Reports, &
    Letter of Director dated 12/18/22
    Initaled G.F.R.:J.R. (J.E.H.)
    No 61.745

61-2269

Confidential Informant in contact with the COMMUNIST PARTY

OF AMERICA (Underground organization) reports:-

"A donation of one thousand dollars ($1000.) was made just

before Christmas to the COMMUNIST PARTY OF AMERICA. but

the name of the donor is held back, and no official record

will be made of it. It is generally understood among the

Communists that the money came from CHARLIE CHAPLIN.

ALEX RASUMOFF Russian Communist who is employed in the

Moving Picture Industry ststed to me (Informant) that

CHAPLIN gave this money but does not want his name in

any way connected with it."

CONTINUED.

APPROVED

FEB 12 1923

ALL INFORMATION CONTAINED
HEREIN IS UNCLASSIFIED
DATE 11-30-78 BY 1259 JPT/KEN

FILE NO. 100-_____ RECORDED

61-2269-4

BUREAU OF INVESTIGATION

JAN 17 1923

DEPARTMENT OF JUSTICE

ROUTED TO: HOOVER   FILE

GENERAL INTELLIGENCE
JAN 2 ? 1923
DIVISION

REFERENCE:

COPIES OF THIS REPORT FURNISHED TO:

Washington 3. S.F. 1. File 1.

7—1169

Pravda, Jan. 12, 1923

THEATRE and MUSIC

CHARLIE CHAPLIN

by NICHOLAI LEBEDEV

We need laughter. During our minutes of rest and recreation along with lectures and sport we have the right to some time for laughter. Healthy, elementary muscular laughter.

So far we only laugh "seriously," "concretely," "crocodile" fashion. We are forced to laugh satirically and on command as testimony to the Worker and Peasant Inspection and G.P.U....

This was the reason for the great enthusiasm shown by the Sverdlovites and youth when the two mirthful children's pictures with Charlie Chaplin were shown in the moving theatre house at the Sverdlovsk University.

"Charlie Chaplin in the Theatre" and "Charlie Chaplin at Work" are the first two Chaplin films which have leaked through to us since the time of the war. The films are old in technic as well as time of filming. However, they are better than anything that has been sent to us by the Bourgeoisie West from among its millions of yards of movie films.

Without doubt Charlie Chaplin is the greatest of all movie actors. In performing the most difficult and most risky role - the creator of laughter - he happily avoids the shortcomings of the ordinary movie comedian actor. Charlie Chaplin does not have the banal insipidness of Max Linder. He lacks the degenerate idiotism of Toktalin (Durashkin), Prince and others. He does not have the

---

"dirt" and adultary found in French farce. He avoids the heavy
German humor. He does not have the greasy self-satisfaction of
the Russian comedian. Charlie Chaplin has learned the secret of
construction - serious physiognomy absurd body and accurate,
mathematical movie-trick. That is the artless machine of his
connoisseurship. And with its aid he creates masterpieces besides
which the Meierholdvsk "Rogonosets" and Forreger's experiments are
feeble epigonism.

What does Chaplin make one laugh at? At anything which
rates laughter. At trivialities and commonalities, deformity and
physical awkwardness and stupidity. In his comedies Chaplin surrounds
himself with human masks, grotesque figures, and he himself, perplexed
and awkward, rambles among them, makes unexpected paradoxical gestures
and ....: floods the faces of millions with uncontrollable laughter.

I do not know whether the Western bourgeoisie will consider
Chaplin one of their own when the Mayor of London meets him at the R. R.
station. But I do know that the American and European proletariat
loves and esteems "their Charlie" more than a hundred Chaliapins put
together. His films for all of their "party-lessness" can and must
be considered ours.

Charlie Chaplin is an old member of the Socialist Party of
America. According to the latest information (instruction) he has
joined the American Communists...

When we build a "laugh factory" (naturally this will be a
"movie factory") the Presidium of the Commissars of the International
will have to consider the request made by the group of Communist

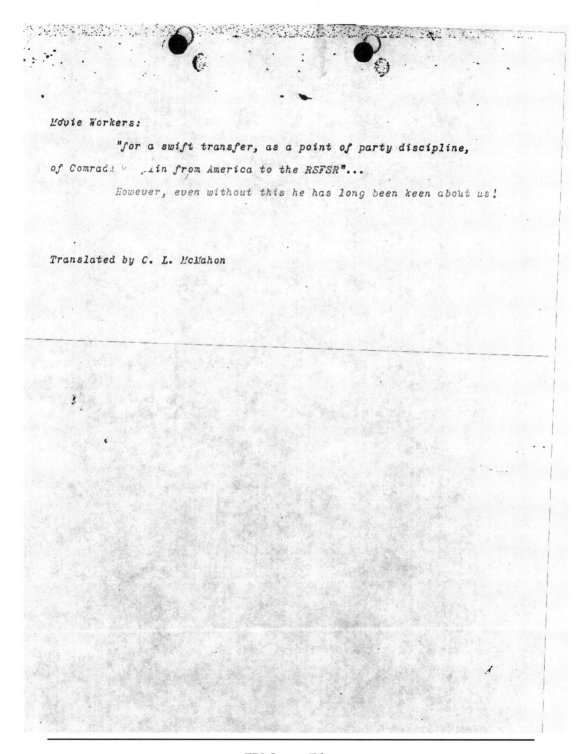

Movie Workers:

"for a swift transfer, as a point of party discipline,
of Comrade ⸻ ⸻in from America to the RSFSR"...

However, even without this he has long been keen about us!

Translated by C. L. McMahon

- 2 -

munists and fellow travellers (ANNA GOLDSBOROUGH, FRANK of the
Journal-American; TOM O'CONNOR and McMANUS of PM; ROSE RUBIN; etc.)
who were there in their capacity as sympathizers and not as working
press and inasmuch as I was supposed to be as enrapt as they were
in listening to CHAPLIN, I could not take many notes,--and certainly
not during his pro-Communist statements. However, I tried to
memorize them. In addition to the pro-Communist statements quoted
in the attached Times clipping, CHAPLIN stated: " We are fighting this
war to preserve art and culture. In Hollywood that will be a difficult
task. The moment we try to inject life into the movie art we have
trouble with the Hays office,- the moment you try to tell the people
the truth about life we run up against censorship......."

" We must be more tolerant of the Russian system. Let's stop
all this nonsense and evasion and call it what it is: the Communist
system. And that Communist system is a very convenient ally. They
have been very convenient for us up to now. They did the real fighting
for us. Why should anyone object to the Communist system? Two weeks
ago the head of the American Legion objected to HARRY BRIDGES speaking
at Harvard because he said that BRIDGES was a Communist. Apparently
this American Legion Commander still does not know that the Communists are our allies. Well, perhaps pretty soon this Commander will
be fighting side by side with the great Red Army,--and won't his face
be red then!- I am getting fed up with hearing people say: But the
Russians are not fighting for us,- they are fighting for themselves.

- 3 -

Well,- what nation is'nt? There is nothing wrong with that."

CHAPLIN then advocated a " united front" of "tolerance and
understanding for Russia and the Communist system from Thomas
Lamont of "Wall Street to Harry Bridges of the C.I.O."

Then came the passages quoted in the TIMES where CHAPLIN
said that it was high time to abandon political and economic
prejudices against our best ally the Soviet Union " since our
ally " (not allies, as stated in the Times!) " does not object
to our own ideals and form of government."

(I am quite sure that CHAPLIN used the singular and not the
plural. This plural was later cooked up by the Russian War Relief
publicity people under the direction of ANNA GOLDSBOROUGH (wife of
MILTON KAUFMAN) a Communist, formerly with TIME and now with RUSSIAN
WAR RELIEF and one of their publicity girls named MEHLER. Miss GOLDS-
BOROUGH with whom I spent two hours after the meeting together with
the above named group of newspaper people stated that the R.W.R.
crowd had been sitting on pins and needles lest CHAPLIN said anything
dangerous: he had been temperamental and refused to write an advance
in the transcripts for the papers
" and there were too many people present to do too much editing/in
case CHAPLIN made a bad break.")

CHAPLIN said:"The Communists like their system and communism
is what the Russians are fighting for and from the way they are fighting for it they must like it pretty well! "

Here again the Times story condenses because before CHAPLIN

- 5 -

salute to the " beloved Soviet Union."

Miss GOLDSBOROUGH told me later in the evening that RUSSIAN WAR RELIEF was at present pulling strings in Washington to have CHAPLIN go on a tour of Russia and she claimed that " our friends in t__ _tate _epartment will fix it that he gets the same cooperation that Willkie got.-"

She also told me that she is in charge of that part of press relations of R.W.R. which deals with the liaison with their 147 professional, fraternal, language, etc. sub-committees and the close to 400 community chests in various parts in the U.S which include R.W.R. in their budgets.- I also learned from her that she and two other people are doing a lot of ghost-writing for prominent people and even professional writers who write these days on Russia in magazines and newspapers. Miss GOLDSBOROUGH admitted specifically that many of these pieces have nothing to do with RUSSIAN WAR RELIEF and do not even mention it. She told me that any time I could sell a piece on Russia to a magazine she would see to it that the piece was written for me in her office and the only condition was that I make a substantial contribution to RUSSIAN WAR RELIEF from the fee which I got from the magazine.

b7D

EHW:PMC   December 23, 1942

ALL INFORMATION CONTAINED
HEREIN IS UNCLASSIFIED
DATE 11-30-78 BY 1259 JJP/KEH   MR. LADD

RE: CHARLES SPENCER CHAPLIN;
INTERNAL SECURITY - C.

On December 3, 1942, Charles Chaplin, the movie actor, addressed a dinner under the auspices of Russian War Relief, Incorporated, at the Hotel Pennsylvania in New York City. Confidential Informant ███████ covered this dinner and reported on Chaplin's speech in which Chaplin defended Communism and eulogized Russia.

During the dinner, Confidential Informant ███████ had occasion to talk with one Anna Goldsborough, who is described by the informant as a Communist. She is said to be in charge of press relations of Russian War Relief, Inc., dealing with the liaison of their professional, fraternal language, etc., sub-committees and the various community chests throughout the country.

During Miss Goldsborough's conversation with the informant, she advised that Russian War Relief, Inc., was presently "pulling strings in Washington to have Chaplin go on a tour of Russia." She is further said to have stated that "our friends in the State Department will fix it that he gets the same cooperation that Willkie got."

In view of the previous reported collaboration on the part of Chaplin with various front organizations, it is thought that the Bureau should know the background of any contemplated trip of Chaplin to Russia. In this connection, reference is made to the statement of Miss Goldsborough concerning the "friends" in the State Department who would arrange matters that Chaplin would get the same cooperation that Willkie got. It is suggested that you may wish to have the Liaison Section ascertain the circumstances surrounding any trip that Chaplin may make to Russia, as well as ascertain who is handling the matter in the State Department. This may in turn throw some light on the Party's entree into the State Department as well as make available to the Bureau the contemplated moves of Chaplin.

Mr. Tolson
Mr. E. A. Tamm
Mr. Clegg
Mr. Glavin
Mr. Ladd
Mr. Nichols
Mr. Rosen
Mr. Tracy
Mr. Carson
Mr. Coffey
Mr. Hendon
Mr. Kramer
Mr. McGuire
Mr. Harbo
Mr. Quinn Tamm
Mr. Nease   394
Miss Gandy

53 MAR 1 1943

Respectfully
&
INDEXED
N43
F. L. Welch

100 - 127090-1

FEDERAL BUREAU OF INVESTIGATION
JAN 12 1943
U. S. DEPARTMENT OF JUSTICE

Federal Bureau of Investigation
United States Department of Justice
Los Angeles, California
January 5, 1943

ALL INFORMATION CONTAINED
HEREIN IS UNCLASSIFIED
DATE 12-1-78 BY 1259 JJT/KEH

Director, FBI

RE; CHARLES CHAPLIN
Information Concerning

Dear Sir:

b7D In a recent conversation with [redacted] special service contact of this office, I inquired of him concerning the general reaction in the motion picture industry to the recent attacks against CHARLES CHAPLIN by WESTBROOK PEGLER.

b7D Subsequently, [redacted] advised me that ~~the re-~~ action was an unexpected one in view of the fact that CHAPLIN is not at all popular in the general motion picture colony, as he is regarded as stingy and unfriendly; however, in view of PEGLER'S attack against the actor's artistic ability, the tendency is for the motion picture people to defend him.

b7D [redacted] stated that regardless of PEGLER'S opinion, CHAPLIN very definitely is an artist and has been recognized as such all over the world, and undoubtedly because of their own artistic interests and for the protection of their own industry, they rallied somewhat to CHAPLIN'S defense against these recent attacks.

I thought you would be interested in knowing of this observation.

Very truly yours,

RBH:AB

R. B. HOOD
Special Agent in Charge

DEFERRED RECORDING

COPIES DESTROYED 1/14 59

RECORDED
INDEXED 100-127090

FOR VICTORY BUY UNITED STATES SAVINGS BONDS AND STAMPS

FEB 10 1943

JAN 11 1943

EX-46

COPY IN FILE

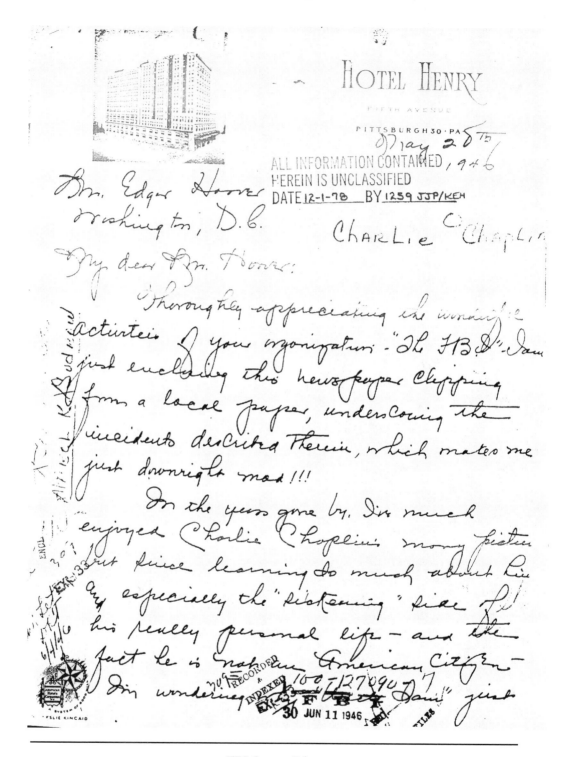

HOTEL HENRY

FIFTH AVENUE

PITTSBURGH 30 · PA

May 28th, 1946

ALL INFORMATION CONTAINED
HEREIN IS UNCLASSIFIED
DATE 12-1-78 BY 1259 JJP/KEH

Mr. Edgar Hoover
Washington, D.C.

Charlie Chaplin

My dear Mr. Hoover:

Thoroughly appreciating the wonderful activities of your organization - "The FBI" - I am just enclosing this newspaper clipping from a local paper, underscoring the incidents described therein, which makes me just downright mad !!!

In the years gone by, I've much enjoyed Charlie Chaplin's many pictures but since learning so much about him and especially the "sickening" side of his really personal life - and the fact he is not an American Citizen - I'm wondering

RECORDED
INDEXED 100-127090
EX F B
30 JUN 11 1946

LESLIE KINCAID

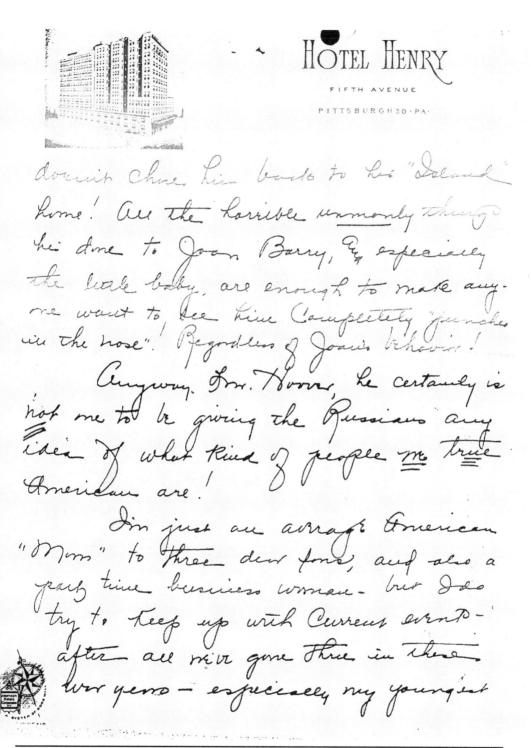

HOTEL HENRY

FIFTH AVENUE

PITTSBURGH 30 · PA ·

doesn't chase him back to his "Island"
home! All the horrible unmanly things
he's done to Joan Barry, & especially
the little baby, are enough to make anyone want to see him completely "punched
in the nose"! Regardless of Joan's behavior!

Anyway, Mr. Hoover, he certainly is
not one to be giving the Russians any
idea of what kind of people we true
American are!

I'm just an average American
"Mom" to three dear ones, and also a
part time business woman - but I do
try to keep up with current events -
after all we've gone thru in these
war years - especially my youngest

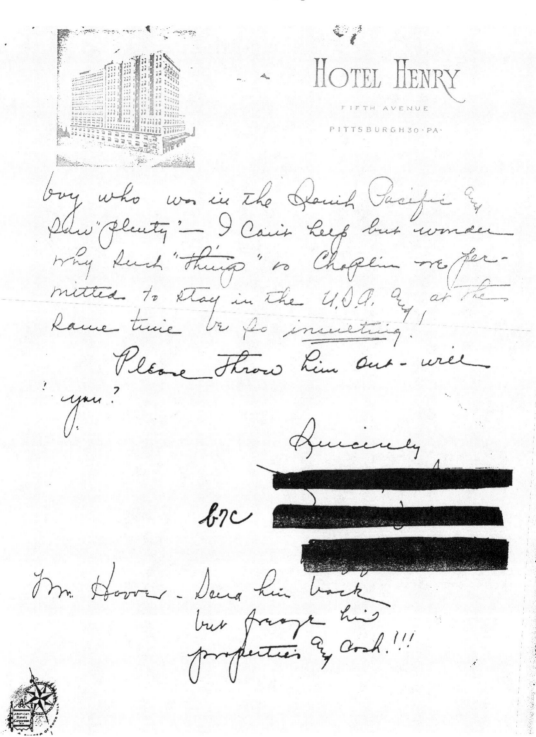

HOTEL HENRY

FIFTH AVENUE

PITTSBURGH 30 · PA·

boy who was in the South Pacific &
saw "plenty" — I can't help but wonder
why such "things" as Chaplin are permitted to stay in the U.S.A. & at the
same time be so insulting!

Please throw him out — will
you?

Sincerely

b7c

Mr. Hoover — Send him back
but freeze his
properties & cash.!!!

Reds Fete Hollywood Movie Stars

Special to the Sun-Telegraph

LONG BEACH, Cal., May 28.—Tingling with champagne a select group of Hollywood film luminaries applauded a Russian movie, "The Bear," about a water-drinking revolutionary at a weekend revel aboard a Soviet ship in Long Beach harbor.

The a — d the champagne— from 7 p. m. Sunday until 4 a. m. yesterday.

Prominently present was Charlie Chaplin, English film actor, who proposed toasts in Russian and referred to uniformed U. S. customs men as "the American Gestapo."

Others ... the party included Chaplin's young wife, formerly Oona O'Neill, daughter of Playwright Eugene O'Neill; Lewis Milestone, Russian-born director, and Mrs. Milestone; Actor John field and his wife, Mrs. Po field.

The champagne banquet— sumptuous in the Russian manner—was arranged by Alexander P. Grachev, representative of the Soviet Purchasing Commission in the United States.

It was held in a luxurious salon, which is a remarkable feature of the otherwise ordinary Russian tanker, SS Batumi, moored at Pier 49, Long Beach Harbor, and Vladimir Petroff, ship's captain, played host.

"The Bear" turned out to be a full-length talking feature about the struggles of the Russian people against the Czarists, whose decadence was demonstrated by their predilection for champagne parties. Its climax is a scene during the revolution in which the hero smashes hundreds of bottles of champagne.

Grachev told his guests that the champagne smashing is "a great dramatic effect" for Russian audiences, "very moral and uplifting" and putting the Soviet government in the light of favoring drinks of the common man.

"Nazdo Rovie!" (to your health) exclaimed Chaplin, hoisting a brimming goblet of champagne in one of the endless round of toasts.

The banquet table was arrayed with creamy borsch, blini, red and black caviar, huge smoked turkeys, hams and salmon from Russia and many other delicacies, including Russian canned crabmeat which Grachev said will shortly appear on the American market.

It comes from canneries recently taken from the Japs, he explained.

Bicycle Hits Boy, 5, Leg Seriously Hurt

Andrew Nyman, 5, of 27 Beech Dr., Bellevue, is in St. John's Hospital with a possible leg fracture suffered when he was run down by a bicycle last night on Davis Ave., North Side, police said. The rider was Buddy Welsh, police said.

Why wasn't Charlie Chaplin sent back

See Coal Pea

Chaplin at Red Ship Reve
Slurs U. S. Customs Mer

Calls Agents 'Gestapo'

Special to the N. Y. Journal-American.

LONG BEACH, Cal., May 28.—Tingling with champagne, a select group of Hollywood film luminaries, applauded a Russian movie about a water-drinking revolutionary at a weekend revel aboard a Soviet ship in Long Beach harbor.

The applause—and the champagne—continued from 7 p. m. Sunday until 4 a. m. Monday.

Prominently present was Charlie Chaplin, English film actor, who proposed toasts in Russian and referred to uniformed U. S. Customs men as "the American Gestapo."

Others in the party included Chaplin's young wife, formerly Oona O'Neill, daughter of playwright Eugene O'Neill; Lewis Milestone, Russian-born director, and Mrs. Milestone; actor John Garfield and his wife, Mrs. Roberta Garfield.

The champagne banquet sumptuous in the Russian manner—was arranged by Alexander Machev, representative of the Purchasing Commission in United States and of Amtorg, trading corporation, to present a special showing of a Russian film, titled "The Bear,"

was held in a luxurious salon, which is a remarkable feature of the otherwise ordinary Russian tanker, SS Batumi, moored at pier 49, Long Beach Harbor, and Dimar Petroff, ship's captain, acted host.

"The Bear" turned out to be a full-length talking feature about the struggles of the Russian

uestone, Russian-born director,
d Mrs. Milestone; actor John
rfield and his wife, Mrs. R?
ta Garfield.

'he champagne b a n q u e t
iptuous in the Russian man-
—was arranged by Alexander
is achev, representative of the
e Purchasing Commission in
nited States and of Amtorg,
trading corporation, to pre-
a special showing of a Rus-
film, titled "The Bear,"

was held in a luxurious salon,
h is a remarkable feature of
otherwise ordinary Russian
ker, SS Batumi, moored at
t 49, Long Beach Harbor, and
dmar Petroff, ship's captain,
yed host.

"The Bear" turned out to be a
l-length talking feature about
ne struggles of the Russian
people against the Czarists, whose
decadence was demonstrated by
their predilection for champagne
parties. Its climax is a scene
during the revolution in which
the hero smashes hundreds of
bottles of champagne.

Grachev told his guests that the
champagne-smashing is "a great
dramatic effect" for Russian audiences, "very moral and uplifting" and putting the Soviet Government in the light of favoring
drinks of the common man.

"Nazdc rovie!" (to your health)
exclaimed Chaplin, hoisting a
brimming goblet of champagne in
one of the endless round of toasts.

Brandy and vodka flowed freely
as the "decadent" sparkling wine,
but guests observed that the vodka
was labeled "made in Philadelphia."

The banquet table was arrayed
with thick borscht, blini, red and
black caviar, huge smoked turkeys,
hams and salmon from Russia,
and many other delicacies, including Russian canned crabmeat,
which Grachev said will shortly
appear on the American market.

It comes from canneries recently
taken from the Japanese, he explained.

Chaplin's "Gestapo" remark
came as he was leaving, when he
saw news cameramen waiting near
uniformed customs men headed
by N. E. Engeman, sergeant of the
law-enforcement section, Bureau
of Customs, U. S. Treasury Department.

"Oh, I see we are under the
power of the American Gestapo," said the actor.

Sgt. Engeman said his men were
present as a matter of course to
ake sure that no dutiable ar-
es, gifts or purchases were
ht ashore except under
circumstances.

AND ONE SAW RED! . . . scene wasn't supposed to be in script weekend champagne revel that Charl Chaplin and John Garfield, the mov actors, attended aboard a Soviet ship Long Beach, Calif., harbor. They we ught by camera in comradely pose a ey came off the ship. But the U. S Customs officer, at the left, didn't appe to relish their joy, for Chaplin had referred to Customs men as "the Americ Gestapo." *International News Ph*

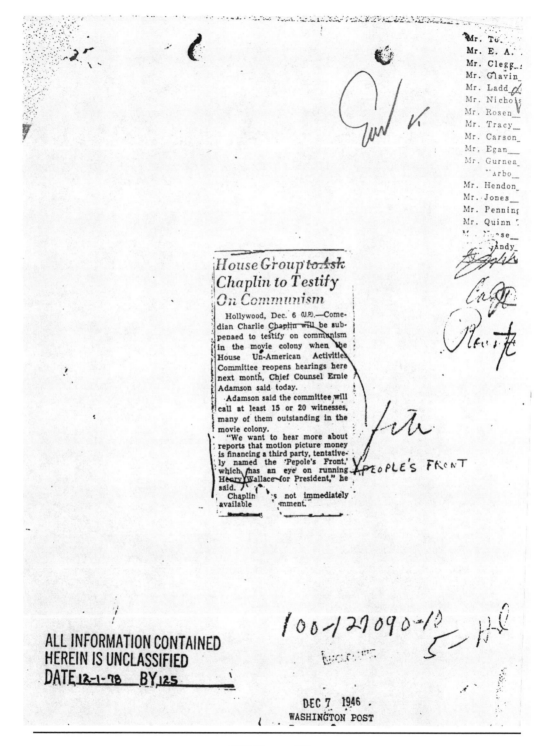

Mr. To.
Mr. E. A.
Mr. Clegg
Mr. Glavin
Mr. Ladd
Mr. Nichols
Mr. Rosen
Mr. Tracy
Mr. Carson
Mr. Egan
Mr. Gurnea
ʺarbo
Mr. Hendon
Mr. Jones
Mr. Penning
Mr. Quinn
M. ʺ ʺse
ʺndy

House Group to Ask Chaplin to Testify On Communism

Hollywood, Dec. 6 (U.P.).—Comedian Charlie Chaplin will be subpenaed to testify on communism in the movie colony when the House Un-American Activities Committee reopens hearings here next month, Chief Counsel Ernie Adamson said today.

Adamson said the committee will call at least 15 or 20 witnesses, many of them outstanding in the movie colony.

"We want to hear more about reports that motion picture money is financing a third party, tentatively named the 'Pepole's Front,' which has an eye on running Henry Wallace for President," he said.

Chaplin is not immediately available mment.

PEOPLE'S FRONT

100-127090-1?
5

ALL INFORMATION CONTAINED
HEREIN IS UNCLASSIFIED
DATE 12-1-78 BY 125

DEC 7 1946
WASHINGTON POST

'Eisler's Brother Is My Friend,' Chaplin Says

Charlie Chaplin, with all the suave aplomb of his new screen identity, the satanic "Monsieur Verdoux," yesterday nonchalantly told more than 100 reporters and photographers at a press conference that he is a friend of Hans Eisler, the Hollywood composer and brother of Communist Gerhart Eisler.

"I am a friend of Hans Eisler and I'm proud of it," said the white-haired comedian warmly. "I don't know his brother, but Hans Eisler is a fine artist, a great musician and a sympathetic friend."

Hans Eisler, a top-bracket composer in the movie colony, has for years been regarded as a Communist sympathizer and will be questioned when a House subcommittee on un-American activities opens its inquiry into Communist influence in Hollywood next month.

Previously, Chaplin denied emphatically that he is a Commuist, but said he might be called a Communist "sympathizer" for his "grateful memory" of what Soviet Russia did during the war.

The famed comedian, whose screen characterizations of a wistful tramp rocketed him to the capitalist class, added sardonically:

"If you step off the curb with your left foot you're branded as a leftist these days. I have no political views. I'm a movie comedian, not a politician."

The dapper little man declared he is against all dictatorships. Asked if this included Joe Stalin, he answered: "That depends on what you mean by dictatorship."

He has never been interested in becoming an American citizen, he said, because "I have never been a nationalist. You might call me a citizen of the world."

'CITIZEN OF THE WORLD'

Charlie Chaplin meets the press at the Hotel Gotham.
(International Photo)

Charlie Chaplin in regard to Hans Eisler

100-127090

ENCLOSURE

CLIPPING FROM THE

N.Y. Mirror

DATED APR 15 1947

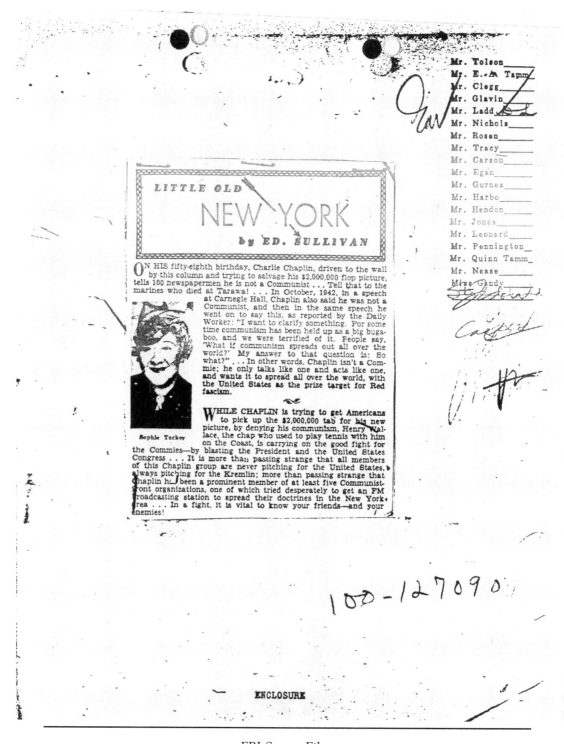

LITTLE OLD NEW YORK
by ED. SULLIVAN

ON HIS fifty-eighth birthday, Charlie Chaplin, driven to the wall by this column and trying to salvage his $2,000,000 flop picture, tells 100 newspapermen he is not a Communist ... Tell that to the marines who died at Tarawa! ... In October, 1942, in a speech at Carnegie Hall, Chaplin also said he was not a Communist, and then in the same speech he went on to say this, as reported by the Daily Worker: "I want to clarify something. For some time communism has been held up as a big bugaboo, and we were terrified of it. People say, 'What if communism spreads out all over the world?' My answer to that question is: So what?" ... In other words, Chaplin isn't a Commie; he only talks like one and acts like one, and wants it to spread all over the world, with the United States as the prize target for Red fascism.

Sophie Tucker

WHILE CHAPLIN is trying to get Americans to pick up the $2,000,000 tab for his new picture, by denying his communism, Henry Wallace, the chap who used to play tennis with him on the Coast, is carrying on the good fight for the Commies—by blasting the President and the United States Congress ... It is more than passing strange that all members of this Chaplin group are never pitching for the United States, always pitching for the Kremlin; more than passing strange that Chaplin has been a prominent member of at least five Communist-front organizations, one of which tried desperately to get an FM broadcasting station to spread their doctrines in the New York area ... In a fight, it is vital to know your friends—and your enemies!

100-127090

ENCLOSURE

b7D Former Confidential Informant ⬛⬛⬛⬛⬛⬛ in a report dated January 15, 1941, advised that in a number of the reviews made of Chaplin's picture, "The Great Dictator", it was pointed out that his closing speech was nothing more than subtle Communist propaganda. (61-7566-2197, pg.2) (U)

b7C The Army furnished a copy of a report dated June 19, 1942, reflecting the results of an investigation conducted by them into the activities of Private ⬛⬛⬛⬛⬛⬛⬛ In this report it is pointed out that ⬛⬛⬛ said on one occasion, "Sure, I'm a registered Communist. So is Harry Bridges. You take that guy Charlie Chaplin. He is a real guy. He is a member of the Party. Only a couple of weeks ago he gave a speech at a Communist meeting in San Francisco." (100-137829-3192) (U)

b7C ⬛⬛⬛⬛⬛⬛ address unknown, advised on August 6, 1942, that never in the history of the Communist Party have the hidden intellectual membership "thrown all caution to the wind and come out in the open for the very things that the Party is demanding." He then followed this report with a list of Communist members who were in this group of intellectuals and included the name of Charlie Chaplin in it. (100-3-45) (U)

b7D Confidential Informant ⬛⬛⬛ advised that on October 13, 1942, a meeting of the Fairfield Branch of the Communist Party was held at 1630 Bank Street, Baltimore, Maryland. It was announced at this meeting that the week of October 24, 1942, would be Stalingrad Week to honor the defenders of Stalingrad, Russia. The announcement indicated that it would be climaxed by a mass rally at the Fifth Regiment Armory, and Chaplin was to be the principal speaker.

(100-3-59-67, pg 43) (U)

CONFIDENTIAL

- 2 -

BEST COPY AVAILABLE

WHITE SLAVE TRAFFIC VIOLATION AND CIVIL RIGHTS AND DOMESTIC VIOLENCE VIOLATIONS BY CHAPLIN

100-7107C-11, PG 17 (U)

You will recall that the Bureau conducted an extensive investigation concerning Chaplin's activities with one Joan Berry in 1943 and 1944. During the course of this investigation it was learned that Chaplin authorized his studio to obtain railroad tickets for the transportation of Joan Berry and her mother to New York, leaving Los Angeles, California, on October 2, 1942, via the Santa Fe Railway. He left for New York himself on October 12, 1942. Chaplin took Berry to dinner in New York several tires following his appearance in New York on October 16, 1942, at the Artists Front to Win the War Rally. Thereafter, Berry returned to the Waldorf Astoria apartment of Chaplin, where the alleged immoral acts took place. The following day Chaplin gave Berry $300 to return to Los Angeles, California. She left for Los Angeles on October 28, 1942. Between the time she returned to Los Angeles and January, 1943, she had numerous trysts with Chaplin. On February 10, 1944, the Federal Grand Jury in Los Angeles returned a true bill of indictment against Chaplin, charging him with violation of the Mann Act in two counts. The first count charged him with transporting Berry to New York, and the second count charged him with transporting her from New York to Los Angeles. He was tried in Los Angeles, the trial commencing on March 21, 1944, and ending April 4, 1944, at which time he was acquitted.   31-68496-172, pg 1, 2
Ser 238 (U)

On February 10, 1944, a Federal Grand Jury at Los Angeles returned three indictments against Chaplin charging him and others with violations of Title 18, Sections 51, 52, and 58, United States Code, for conspiring to violate the civil

- 22 -   CONFIDENTIAL

CONFIDENTIAL

liberties of Joan Berry. The indictments were based on the activities of the subjects subsequent to the arrest of Berry on January 1, 1943, by the Beverly Hills Police Department through the person of Claude R. Marple. Thereafter, Robert Arden, admittedly acting for Chaplin, appeared before Captain W. W. White of the Beverly Hills Police Department with the request that Judge Charles J. Griffen send Berry out of California. On January 2, 1943, Berry was sentenced to 90 days by Griffen. The sentence was suspended on the condition that she leave Beverly Hills and pay her hotel bills. Judge Griffen had been advised by Arden that Chaplin would pay the bills and her transportation to New York. Thereafter, on January 5, 1943, Captain White escorted Berry to the train. Berry returned to California in April, 1943, and visited Chaplin's home on May 7, 1943, allegedly to advise him that she was pregnant by him. At that time one of the subjects, namely, Tim Durant, close friend of Chaplin, called the Beverly Hills Police Department and had her rearrested. The following day Judge Griffen sentenced Berry to thirty days in jail. On May 11, 1943, Durant, working in the interests of Chaplin, had Minna Wallis obtain the services of Judge Cecil D. Holland and was instrumental in getting Berry out of jail with the original idea of putting her in a sanitarium and thereafter sending her out of the state.
(31-68496-256, pg. 12) (U)

On May 15, 1944, Federal Judge J. F. T. O'Connor dismissed the charges against Chaplin when he was advised by United States Attorney Charles Carr that Carr had received written instructions from the Department of Justice to dismiss these charges. (31-68496-258) (U)

The records of the Identification Division do not contain any information concerning arrests of Chaplin other than for the charges set forth.
(31-68496-258, pg 2) (U)

On June 3, 1943, a suit was filed in the State Court in Los Angeles by Gertrude E. Berry, mother of Joan Berry, on behalf of Joan Berry's unborn child, seeking to obtain money from Chaplin for the support of this child. The child was born on December 23, 1943. (31-68476-9, pg. 21, 40) (U)

Investigation revealed that Chaplin was probably instrumental in procuring at least two abortions for Berry as a result of his associations with her. (31-68496-21) (U)

The Washington Post for August 4, 1945, said that the Los Angeles Court had declared that Chaplin was the father of the Berry child.
(31-68496-A) (U)

The Washington News, Washington, D. C., on April 9, 1945, said that Chaplin had been ordered to pay $75 a week for the support of the Berry child and $5,000 attorney fees. (31-68496-A) (U)

Mike Gold in his column, "Change the World", in "The Daily Worker" of January 19, 1945, said that the paternity suit against Chaplin by Joan Berry was a part of a campaign of character assassination started by the Hearst, McCormick, and Fascist Press of America when Chaplin produced "The Great Dictator", which lampooned Hitler and Mussolini.
(100-114353-17) (U)

- 23 -   CONFIDENTIAL

Pravda, Jan. 12, 1923

THEATRE and MUSIC

CHARLIE CHAPLIN

by NICHOLAI LEBEDEV

We need laughter. During our minutes of rest and recreation along with lectures and sport we have the right to some time for laughter. Healthy, elementary muscular laughter.

So far we only laugh "seriously," "concretely," "crocodile" fashion. We are forced to laugh satirically and on command as testimony to the Worker and Peasant Inspection and G.P.U....

This was the reason for the great enthusiasm shown by the Sverdlovites and youth when the two mirthful children's pictures with Charlie Chaplin were shown in the moving theatre house at the Sverdlovsk University.

"Charlie Chaplin in the Theatre" and "Charlie Chaplin at Work" are the first two Chaplin films which have leaked through to us since the time of the war. The films are old in technic as well as time of filming. However, they are better than anything that has been sent to us by the Bourgeoisie West from among its millions of yards of movie films.

Without doubt Charlie Chaplin is the greatest of all movie actors. In performing the most difficult and most risky role - the creator of laughter - he happily avoids the shortcomings of the ordinary movie comedian actor. Charlie Chaplin does not have the banal insipidness of Max Linder. He lacks the degenerate idiotism of Toktalin (Durashkin), Prince and others. He does not have the "dirt" and adultary found in French farce. He avoids the heavy German humor. He does not have the greasy self-satisfaction of the Russian comedian. Charlie Chaplin has learned the secret of construction - serious physiognomy absurd body and accurate, mathematical movie-trick. That is the artless machine of his connoisseurship. And with its aid he creates masterpieces besides which the Meierholdvsk "Rogonosets" and Forreger's experiments are feeble epigonism.

What does Chaplin make one laugh at? At anything which rates laughter. At trivialities and commonalities, deformity and physical awkwardness and stupidity. In his comedies Chaplin surrounds himself with human masks, grotesque figures, and he himself, perplexed and awkward, rambles among them, makes unexpected paradoxical gestures and ....: floods the faces of millions with uncontrollable laughter.

I do not know whether the Western bourgeoisie will consider Chaplin one of their own when the Mayor of London meets him at the R. R. station. But I do know that the American and European proletariat loves and esteems "their Charlie" more than a hundred Chaliapins put together. His films for all of their "party-lessness" can and must be considered ours.

Charlie Chaplin is an old member of the Socialist Party of America. According to the latest information (instruction) he has joined the American Communists...

When we build a "laugh factory" (naturally this will be a "movie factory") the Presidium of the Commissars of the International will have to consider the request made by the group of Communist

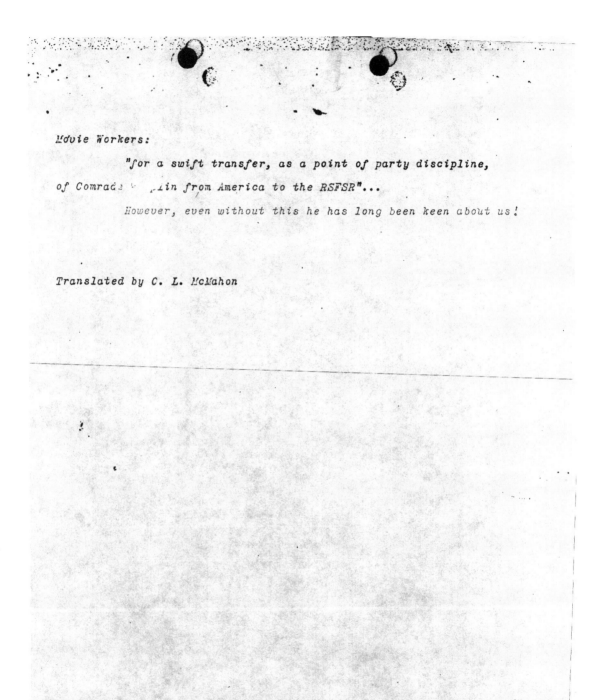

Movie Workers:

"for a swift transfer, as a point of party discipline,
of Comrade ⎯⎯⎯ ⎯in from America to the RSFSR"...

However, even without this he has long been keen about us!

Translated by C. L. McMahon

Chapter I

Books

Blackstock, Nelson. Cointelpro. New York: Pathfinder, 1988.

Dempsey, James X. and David Cole. Terrorism and The Constitution. Sacrificing Civil Liberties In The Name of National Security. Los Angeles, California: First Amendment Foundation, 1999.

Donner, Frank. The Age of Surveillance. New York: Putnam, 1979.

Donoyan, Jonathan. Conflict and Crisis. New York: Norton, 1977.

Goodwin, Doris Kearns. No Ordinary Time. New York: Simon & Schuster, 1994.

Lash, Joseph. Eleanor and Franklin. New York: Norton, 1971.

Lash, Joseph P. Eleanor: The Years Alone. New York: W.W. Morton & Company Inc.,1972.

O'Reilly, Kenneth. Racial Matters. New York: Macmillan Free Press, 1989.

Parmet, Herbert S. The Democrats: The Years After FDR. New York: Macmillan Publishing Co. Inc., 1976.

Summers, Anthony. Official And Confidential Life: The Secret Life of J. Edgar Hoover. NewYork: G.P. Putnam's Son, 1993.

Theoharis, Athan. Spying On Americans. Philadelphia: Temple, 1978.

Travis, Dempsey J. An Autobiography of Black Politics. Chicago, Illinois: Urban Research Press, Inc., 1987.

Travis, Dempsey J. The Duke Ellington Primer. Chicago, Illinois: Urban Research Press, Inc., 1996.

Travis, Dempsey J. They Heard A Thousand Thunders. Chicago, Illinois: Urban Research Press, Inc., 1999.

Memoirs by Harry S. Truman. Volume One: Year of Decisions. Garden City, N.Y.: Doubleday & Company, Inc., 1955.

Truman, Margaret. Harry S. Truman. New York: William Morrow & Company, Inc., 1973.

Newspapers

Author Claims Army Spied on Mrs. Roosevelt. Chicago Tribune, March 11, 1982.

Movie Director Recalls Blacklist in Guilty by Suspicion. Chicago Sun Times, February 24, 1991.

Nixon Tapes Trash Women, Minorities. Chicago Sun Times, December 27, 1998.

Federal Judge Clips Police Drive to Expand Spy Powers. Chicago Defender, October 4, 1999.

FBI File on Columnist Murray Kempton Is Released. New York Times, February 2, 2000.

Federal Documents

40,000 pages of FBI Files released under the Freedom of Information Act.

Municipal Documents

100 pages of the Chicago Police Red Squad Spy Files released under the Freedom of Information Act.

Chapter II

FBI Documents

40 preprocessed pages on Louis Armstrong released under the (Freedom of Information Act.) pursuant to Title 5, United States Code 552 and/or Section 552 a (Privacy Act).

Books

Allen,Walter C. The Music of Fletcher Henderson And His Musicians. Highland Park, New Jersey: W.C. Allen Publisher, 1974.

Anderson, Jervis. This Was Harlem. New York: Farrar Straus Group, 1981.

Armstrong, Louis. The Life and Times of Louis "Satchmo" Armstrong. New Jersey: Prentice Hall, 1954.

Balliett, Whitney. Night Creature. New York: Oxford University Press, 1981.

Bigard, Barney. With Louis and The Duke. New York: Oxford University Press., 1980.

Bogle, Donald. Toms, Coons, Mulattoes, Mamie, and Bucks. New York: Viking Press, 1973.

Claude Baker, Jean. Josephine: The Hungry Heart. New York: Random House, 1993.

Crow, Bill. Jazz Anecdotes. New York: Oxford University Press, 1990.

Dance, Stanley. The World of Earl Hines. New York: Charles Scribner's Sons, 1977.

Driggs, Frank & Harriet Lewine. Black Beauty, White Heat: A Pictorial History of Classic Jazz. New York: William Morrow, 1982.

Duberman, Martin Baums. Paul Robeson. New York: Alfred A. Knopf, 1988.

Editor Kernfield, Barry. The Blackwell Guide To Recorded Jazz. Boston, Mass: Cambridge Press, 1991.

Editors of Time-Life Books. This Fabulous Century, Volume II. New York: Time-Life Books, 1969.

Editors of Time-Life Books. This Fabulous Century, Volume III. New York: Time-Life Books, 1969.

Editors of Time-Life Books. This Fabulous Century, Volume IV. New York: Time-Life Books, 1969.

Ewen, David. American Popular Songs. New York: Random House, 1966.

Feather, Leonard. From Satchmo To Miles. New York: Stein & Day Publishers, 1989.

Gillespie, Dizzy. To Be or Not To Bop. New York: Doubleday & Company, 1979.

Gourse, Leslie. Louis' Children: America's Jazz Singer. New York: William Morrow & Company Inc., 1984.

Griffith, Richard. The Movies. New York: Simon & Schuster, 1957.

Hadlock, Richard. Jazz Masters of The Twenties. New York: The Macmillan Company, 1965.

Hammond, John. John Hammond On Record. New York: Summit Books, 1977.

Haskins, Jim. The Cotton Club. New York: Random House, 1977.

Hennessey, Thomas. The Black Chicago Establishment. Chicago, IL.: University of Chicago Press, 1969.

James, Burnett. Essays On Jazz. New York: De Capo Press, 1990.

Johnson, James Weldon. Black Manhattan. New York: Arno Press, 1968.

Jones, Max & John Chilton. Louis: The Armstrong Story 1900-1971. Boston-Toronto: Little, Brown and Company, 1971.

Kenny, William Howland. Chicago Jazz. New York: Oxford Press, 1993.

Lewis, David Leavering. When Harlem Was In Vogue. New York: Alfred A. Knopf, 1981.

Lowe, David. Lost Chicago. Boston: Houghton Mifflin Company, 1975.

Lyttelton, Humphrey. The Best Of Jazz II. New York; Taplinger Publishing, 1981.

Ostransky, Leroy. Oustanding Jazz. New Jersey: Prentice Hall, 1977.

Panassie, Hugues. The Real Jazz. New York: Smith & Durrell Inc., 1942.

Rose, Al. I Remember Jazz. Baton Rouge: Louisiana State University Press, 1987.

Schuller, Gunther. The Swing Era. New York: Oxford University Press, 1989.

Stearns, Marshall & Jean. Jazz Dance. New York: Schirmer Books, 1968.

Stewart, Rex. Jazz Masters of the Thirties. New York: Da Capo Paperback, 1972.

Tanerhaus, Sam. Louis Armstrong. New York: Chelsea House Publisher, 1989.

Taylor, Frank C. Alberta Hunter. New York: McGraw-Hill Book Company, 1987.

Terkel, Studs. Giants of Jazz. New York: Thomas Y. Crowell Company, 1957.

Tracy, Steven C. Langston Hughes And The Blues. Chicago: University of Illinois Press, 1988.

Travis, Dempsey J. An Autobiography of Black Jazz. Chicago, Illinois: Urban Research Press, 1983.

Travis, Dempsey J. Racism: American Style A Corporate Gift. Chicago, Illinois: Urban Research Press, 1991.

Travis, Dempsey J. The Louis Armstrong Odyssey. Chicago, Illinois: Urban Research Press, Inc. 1997.

Travis, Dempsey J. The Duke Ellington Primer. Chicago, Illinois: Urban Research Press, 1996.

Waters, Enoch P. American Diary. Chicago, Illinois: Path Press Inc., 1987.

Chapter III

FBI Documents

400 preprocessed pages on Josephine Baker released under the (Freedom of Information Act) pursuant to Title 5, United States Code 552 and/or section 552 a (Privacy Act).

Books

Baker, Jean-Claude and Chris Chase. Josephine: The Hungry Heart. Random House, New York, 1993.

Bricktop with James Haskins. Brick Top. New York: Macmillan Publishing Company, 1983.

Duber, Martin Bauml. Paul Robeson. New York: Alfred A. Knopf, 1989.

Ellington, Duke. Music Is My Mistress. New York: Da Capo Press, 1973.

Fitzgerald, Scott F. The Great Gatsby. New York: Charles Scribner's Sons, 1925.

Hancy, Lynn. Naked at The Feast: A Biography of Josephine Baker. New York: Dodd, Mead, 1981.

Rose, Phyllis. Jazz Cleopatra: Josephine Baker in Her Time. New York: Vintage Books, 1989.

Stearns, Marshall and Jean. Jazz Dance. New York: Schirmer Books, 1964.

Travis, Dempsey J. An Autobiography Of Black Jazz. Chicago: Urban Research Press, 1983.

Travis, Dempsey J. The Louis Armstrong Odyssey: From Jane Alley to America's Jazz Ambassador. Chicago: Urban Research Press, 1997.

Taylor, Frank C. and Gerald Cook. Alberta: A Celebration In Blues. New York: McGraw-Hill Book Company, 1987.

Newspapers

An Anniversary for Josephine Baker. The New York Times, October 2, 1989.

An American From Paris. The New York Times, January 30, 1994.

Taking Paris By Storm, With Bananas Flying. The New York Times, February 2, 1994.

Bouncing on Josephine's Musical Beds. Chicago Sun Times, Book Review. February 13, 1994.

The Magic and Myths of Josephine Baker. The New York Times, Book Review. February 20, 1994.

Chapter IV

FBI Documents

720 preprocessed pages on Leonard Bernstein under the (Freedom of Information Act). Pursuant to Title 5, United States Code 552 and/or 552 a (Privacy Act).

Books

Ames, Evelyn (Perkins). A Wind From the West; Bernstein and the New York Philharmonic Abroad [by] Evelyn Ames. Boston: Houghton Mifflin Co., 1970.

Bernstein, Leonard. Young People's Concerts, For Reading and Listening. New York: Simon and Schuster, 1962.

Bernstein, Leonard. The Infinite Variety of Music. New York: Simon and Schuster, 1966.

Bernstein, Leonard. The Joy of Music. London: Weidenfeld & Nicolson, 1968. Ewen, David. Leonard Bernstein, A Biography For Young People.

Bernstein, Leonard. Findings. London: Macdonald, 1982.

Briggs, John. Leonard Bernstein; The Man, His Work, and His World. Cleveland: World Pub. Co., 1961.

Burton, Humphrey. Leonard Bernstein. London: Faber and Faber, 1994.

Chapin, Schuyler. Leonard Bernstein: Notes From a Friend. New York: Walker, 1992.

Cone, Molly. Leonard Bernstein. New York: Crowell, 1970.

Ewen, David. Leonard Bernstein, A Biography For Young People. Philadelphia: Chilton Co., Book Division, 1960.

Freedland, Michael. Leonard Bernstein. London: Harrap, 1987.

Gradenwitz, Peter. Leonard Bernstein the Infinite Variety of a Musician. Leamington: Spa Berg, 1987.

Gruen, John. The Private World of Leonard Bernstein. New York: Viking Press, 1968.

Peyser, Joan. Leonard Bernstein. London: Bantam, 1987.

Reidy, John P. Leonard Bernstein. Chicago: Children's Press, 1967.

Robinson, Paul. The Art of the Conductor. London:Macdonald, 1982.

Secrest, Meryle. Leonard Bernstein: A Life. London: Bloomsbury, 1995.

Venezia, Mike. Leonard Bernstein / written and illustrated by Mike Venezia. New York; London: Children's Press, 1997.

Chapter V

FBI Documents

208 preprocessed pages on Adam Clayton Powell under the (Freedom of Information Act) pursuant to Title 5, United States Code 552 and/or Section 552 a (Privacy Act).

Books

Baker, Jean-Claude and Chris Chase. Josephine: The Hungry Heart. New York: Random House, Inc., 1993.

Bardolph, Richard. The Negro Vanguard. New York: Rhinehart and Company, Inc., 1959.

Berman, William C. The Politics of Civil Rights In The Truman Administration. Columbus, Ohio: Ohio State University Press, 1970.

Duberman, Martin Baum. Paul Robeson. New York: Alfred A. Knopf, 1988.

Garrow, David. Bearing The Cross. New York: William Morrow and Company, Inc., 1986.

Haygood, Wil. The King of The Cats: The Life and Times of Adam Clayton Powell Jr. New York: Houghton Mifflin, 1993.

Myrdal, Gunnar. An American Dilemma. New York: Harper & Bros., New York, 1944.

Powell, Adam Clayton. Adam Clayton Powell: The Political Biography of An American Dilemma. New York, Athenem: 1991.

Powell Jr., Adam Clayton. Adam by Adam, The Autobiography of Adam Clayton Powell Jr. New York: The Dial Press, 1971.

Powell Jr., Adam Clayton. Keep The Faith, Baby! New York: Trident Press, 1967.

Rampersad, Arnold. The Life of Langston Hughes Volume II: 1941-1967 I Dream A World. New York: Oxford University Press, 1988.

Travis, Dempsey J. Autobiography of Black Politics. Chicago: Urban Research Press, 1987.

Travis, Dempsey J. The Duke Ellington Primer. Chicago: Urban Research Press, 1996.

Waters, Enoc P. American Diary: A Personal History of The Black Press. Chicago: Path Press, 1987.

Chapter VI

FBI Documents

10 preprocessed pages on Tennessee Williams under the (Freedom of Information Act). Pursuant to Title 5, United States Code 552 and/or 552 a (Privacy Act).

Books

Asibong, Emmanuel B. Tennessee Williams: The Tragic Tension. Devon: Stockwell, 1978.

Boxill, Rodger. Tennesse Williams. New York: St.Martin's, 1987.

Gunn, Drewey Wayne. Tennessee Williams: A Bibliography. Metuchen, N.J.: Scarecrow, 1980.

Horst, Franz. American Playwrights Drama. New York: Hill, 1965.

Leverich, Lyle. Tom: The Unknown Tennessee Williams. New York: Crown Publishers, 1995.

McCann, John. S. The Critical Reputation of Tennessee Williams: A Reference Guide. Boston: Hall, 1983.

Miller, Jordan Y., ed. Twentieth Century Interpretations of A Streetcar Name Desire: A Collection of Critical Essays. Englewood Cliffs: Prentice-Hall, 1971.

Rader, Doston. Tennessee, Cry of the Heart. Garden City, N.Y.: Doubleday, 1985.

Reed, Rex. People Are Crazy Here. New York: Delacorte, 1974.

Saddik, Annette J. Politics of Reputation: The Critical Reception of Tennessee Williams' Later Plays. New York: Fairleigh Dickinson University.

Smith, Bruce. Costly Performances: Tennessee Williams: The Last Stage. New York: Paragon House, 1990.

Spoto, McDonald. The Kindness of Strangers: The Life of Tennessee Williams. New York: Little Brown, 1985.

Spoto, Donald. The Kindness of Strangers: The Life of Tennessee Williams. New York: Ballentine, 1986.

Chapter VII

FBI Documents

235 preprocessed pages on Richard Wright under the (Freedom of Information Act). Pursuant to Title 5, United States Code 552 and/or 552 a (Privacy Act).

Books

Abcarian, Richard. Richard Wright's Native Son: A Critical Handbook. Belmont,

California: Wadsworth, 1970.

Adams, Timothy Dow. Telling Lies in Modern American Autobiography. Chapel Hill, N. C.: University of North Carolina Press, 1990.

Bone, Robert A. Richard Wright. Minneapolis: University of Minnesota Press, 1969.

Ciner, Elizabeth J. "Richard Wright's Struggles with Fathers." In Richard Wright: Myths and Realities, edited by C. James Trotman. New York: Garland, 1988.

Davis, Allison. Leadership, Love and Aggression. New York: Harcourt Brace Jovanovich, Publishers, 1983.

Ellison, Ralph. "The World and the Jug". Shadow and Act. New York: Random House, 1964.

Fabre, Michel. The Unfinished Quest of Richard Wright. Translated by Isabel Arzun. New York: William Morrow, 1973.

Gates, Jr. Henry Louis Edited, and K.A. Appiah Richard Wright: Critical Perspectives Past and Present. New York: Amistad Press, Inc., 1993.

Green, Gerald. "Black to Bigger". In Proletarian Writers of the Thirties, edited by David Madden. Carbondale, Ill.: Southern Illinois University Press, 1968.

Howe, Irving. "Black Boys and Native Sons". A World More Attractive. New York: Horizon, 1963.

Hughes, Carl M. The Negro Novelist. New York: Citadel Press, 1953.

Kinnamon, Keneth. The Emergence of Richard Wright: A Study in Literature and Society. Urbana, Ill.: University of Illinois Press, 1972.

Richard Wright and Maya Angelou. "In Belief vs. Theory in Black American Literary Criticism, edited by Joe Weixlmann and Chester J. Fontenot. Greenwood, Fla.: Penkevill, 1986.

Littlejohn, David. Black on White: A Critical Survey on Writing by American Negroes. New York: Viking Press, 1969.

Mootry, Maria K. "Bitches, Whores and Woman Haters: Archetypes and Typologies in the Art of Richard Wright". In Richard Wright: A Collection of Critical Essays, edited by Richard Macksey and Frank Moorer. Englewood Cliffs, N.J.: Prentice Hall, 1984.

Redding, Saunders. "The Alien Land of Richard Wright". In Soon One Morning, edited by Herbert Hill. New York: Alfred A. Knopf, 1965.

Stepto, Robert B. "I Thought I Knew These People: Richard Wright and the Afro-American Literary Tradition". In Chant of Saints, edited by Michael S. Harper and Robert B. Stepto. Urbana, Ill.: University of Illinois Press, 1979.

Walker, Margaret. Richard Wright, Demonic Genius: A Portrait of the Man, a Critical Look at His Work. New York: Warner / Amistad Books, 1988.

Williams, John A. The Most Native of Sons. Garden City, N.J.: Doubleday, 1970.

Wright, Richard. Native Son. New York: Harper & Brothers Publisher, 1940.

Wright, Richard. Black Boy: A Record of Childhood and Youth. New York & London: Harper & Brothers Publishers, 1937.

Chapter VIII

FBI Documents

475 preprocessed pages on Walt Disney under the (Freedom of Information Act). Pursuant to Title 5, United States Code 552 and/or 552 a (Privacy Act).

Books

Canemaker, John. Treasurers of Disney Art, ed. New York: W. Rawls, 1982.

Finch, Christopher. The Art of Walt Disney. Los Angeles: Disney, 1973.

Greene, Katherine and Richard. The Man Behind the Magic: The Story of Walt Disney. New York: Viking Press, 1991.

Schroeder, Russell Editor. Walt Disney: His Life In Pictures. New York: Disney Press, 1960.

Letters

A letter dated July 16, 1936 to Walt Disney from J. Edgar Hoover indicating he would be pleased to be of service to him throughout his lifetime.

A congratulatory missive dated November 9, 1956 from FBI Director J. Edgar Hoover to Walt Disney.

A letter dated November 26, 1956 from Walt Disney to Hoover thanking him for his complimentary letter of November 9th.

A FBI teletype encoded message dated December 15, 1966 suggesting a letter of sympathy be sent to the widow, Lillian. Disney had died earlier that day from complication of cancer of the lungs.

A telegram extending his heart felt sympathy dated December 15, 1966 was sent to Mrs. Walt Disney from John Edgar Hoover.

Note: Mr. Disney was on Hoover's special correspondents' list of persons he addressed by their first name. His name was deleted upon the notification of his death.

Newspapers & Magazines

New York Times. "What's In A Naming?" May 8, 1993.

National Enquirer. "Disney: Hollywood's Unstable Genius Was A Hard-Drinking, Drug-Using Weirdo. May 1993.

Chicago Tribune. "Walt Disney, Grace Kelly, J. Edgar Hoover- No One's Safe From A Sleazy Life After Death." July 13, 1993.

Chapter IX

FBI Documents

38 preprocessed pages on Nat King Cole and Dorothy Dandrige under the (Freedom of Information Act). Pursuant to Title 5, United States Code 552 and/or 552 a (Privacy Act).

Books

Epstein, Daniel Mark. Nat King Cole. New York: Farrar, Straus and Girou, 1999.

Gourse, Leslie. Unforgettable: The Life and Mystique of Nat King Cole. New York: St. Martin Press, 1991.

Haskin, James, with Kathleen Benson. Nat King Cole. New York: Stein and Day, 1984.

Teubig, Klaus. Straighten Up And Fly Right: A Chronology And Discography of Nat King Cole. Westport, CT.: Greenwood Press, 1994.

Travis, Dempsey. An Autobiography of Black Jazz. Chicago: Urban Research Press, 1983.

Interviews

Kenneth Blewett, April 7, 1982.
Eddie Plique, September 13, 1982.
Henry Fort, February, 1983.
Marty Faye, February, 1983.
Baldwin Tavares, June, 1983.
Nancy Wilson, June, 1983.
Billy Eckstine, July, 1983.

Notes:

Memorandum from Gene Howard's King Cole Trio Bio File 102347 and the author's personal diary.

Chapter X

FBI Documents

415 preprocessed pages on Adlai E. Stevenson under the (Freedom of Information Act). Pursuant to Title 5, United States Code 552 and/or 552 a (Privacy Act).

Books

Baker, Jean H. The Stevensons. New York, London: W.W. Norton and Company, 1996.

Fitzgerald, Kathleen Whalen. Brass: Jane Byrne and The Pursuit of Power. Chicago, Illinois: Contemporary Books, Inc., 1981.

Fremon, David K. Chicago Political Ward by Ward. Bloomington, Indiana: Indiana University Press, 1988.

Granger, Bill and Lori. Fighting Jane Bryne. New York: The Dial Press, 1980.

O'Connor, Len. Clout: Mayor Daley and His City. Chicago, Illinois: Contemporary Books, Inc., 1975.

Phillips, Cabell. The Truman Presidency: The History of A Triumphant Succession. New York: The Macmillan Company, 1966.

Rakove, Milton L. We Don't Want Nobody Nobody Sent. London: Indiana University Press. Bloomington and London, 1979.

Royko, Mike. Boss: Richard J. Daley of Chicago. New York: E.P. Dutton & Co. Inc., 1971.

Newspapers

From FBI Files: Hoover's Grudge Match With Stevenson. Chicago Tribune, May 30,

1999.
Blazing A Trail For The New Frontier. Chicago Sun Times, January 4, 2000.
Adlai Made An Impression. Chicago Sun Times, January 30, 2000.
An Appreciation of Adlai- Democrat, Statesman, Visionary. Chicago Tribune, February 6, 2000.

Chapter XI

FBI Documents

52 preprocessed pages on Duke Ellington under the (Freedom of Information Act). Pursuant to Title 5, United States Code 552 and/or 552 a (Privacy Act).

Books

Anderson, Jervis. This Was Harlem. New York: Farrar Straus Elroux, 1982.
Bigard, Barney. With Louis and the Duke: The Autobiography of a Jazz Clarinetist, ed. Barry Martyn. New York: Oxford University Press; London: Macmillan, 1985.
Calloway, Cab and Bryant Rollins. Of Minnie the Moocher and Me. New York: Thos Y. Crowell Co, 1976.
Chilton, John. Who's Who of Jazz. New York: Time-Life Records Spec. Ed., 1978.
Collier, James Lincoln. Duke Ellington. New York: Oxford University Press, 1987.
Cripps, Thomas. Slow Fade to Black. New York: Oxford University Press, 1977.
Dance, Stanley. The World of Duke Ellington. New York: Charles Scribner's Sons, 1970; London: Macmillan, 1971.
Dance, Stanley. The World of Earl Hines. New York: Charles Scribner's Sons, 1977.
Driggs, Frank & Harris Lewine. Black Beauty, White Heat: A Pictorial History of Classical Jazz. New York: Wm. Morrow, 1982.
Dubin, Arthur D. Some Classic Trains. Milwaukee: A Kalmback Publication, 1964.
Ellington, Duke. Music Is My Mistress. New York: Doubleday & Company, Inc., 1973.
Ellington, Mercer & Stanley Dance. Duke Ellington In Person: An Intimate Memoir. New York: Da Capo Press, 1978.
Feather, Leonard. The Encyclopedia of Jazz. New York: Da Capo Press, 1960.
Floyd, Jr., Samuel A. The Power of Black Music. New York: Oxford University Press, 1995.
Gabbard, Krim (editor). Representing Jazz. Duke University Press, 1995.
George, Don. Sweet Man: The Real Duke Ellington. New York: G.P. Putnam's Sons, 1981.
Gleason, Ralph J. Celebrating the Duke, an Atlantic Monthly Press Book. Boston, Toronto: Little Brown and Company, Boston, Toronto 1975.
Hajdu, David. Lush Life. New York; Farrar Straus Giroux, 1996.
Hare, Maud Cuney. Negro Musicians and Their Music. New York: Da Capo Press, 1974.
Hasse, John Edward. Beyond Category. New York: Simon & Schuster, 1993.
Hinton, Milton & David G. Berhger. Bass Line. Philadelphia: Temple University Press, 1988.
Jewell, Eric. Duke: A Portrait of Duke Elllington. New York: W.W. Norton, 1977.
Jones, LeRoi. Blues People. New York: Wm. Morrow, 1963.
Nicholson, Stuart. Reminiscing In Tempo: A Portrait of Duke Ellington. Boston: Northern University Press, 1999.
Ruff, Willie. A Call To Assembly. New York: Penquin Books, 1991.
Shapiro, Nat & Nat Hentoff. The Music Makers. New York; Da Capo Press, 1957.
Stewart, Rex. Boy Meets Horn. Ed. Claire P. Gordon. Ann Arbor: University of Michigan Press, 1991.
Stewart, Rex. Jazz Masters of the 30's. New York: Da Capo Press, Inc., 1972.
Travis, Dempsey J. An Autobiography of Black Chicago. Chicago: Urban Research Press, Inc., 1981.
Travis, Dempsey J. An Autobiography of Black Jazz. Chicago: Urban Research Press, 1983.
Travis, Dempsey J. The Duke Ellington Primer. Chicago: Urban Research Press, 1996.
Tucker, Mark (editor). The Duke Ellington Reader. New York: Oxford University Press, 1993.

Chapter XII

FBI Documents

355 preprocessed pages on John Lennon released under the (Freedom of Information Act.) pursuant to Title 5, United States Code 552 and/or Section 552 a (Privacy Act).

Books

Abrams, M.H. gen ed. The Norton Anthology of English Literature. New York: W.W.Norton & Company, Inc. 1968.
Brown, Peter and Stephen Gaines. The Love You Make: An Insider's Story of The Beatles. New York: New American Library Penguin Books, 1983.
Bugliosi, Vincent and Curt Gentry. Helter Skelter. New York: Bantam Books, 1975.
Campbell, John and Henry Mordon Robinson. A Skeleton Key To 'Finnegan's Wake'. New York: Harcourt Brace & Company, 1944.
Carroll, Lewis. The Complete Works of Lewis Carroll. New York: The Modern Library by Random House Inc, 1916.
Cirlot J.E. Dictionary of Symbols. - trans. by Jack Sage. New York: Philosophical Library, 1971.
Coleman, Ray. Lennon. New York: McGraw-Hill, 1985.
Dowlding, William. Beatle Songs. New York: Fireside by Simon & Schuster, 1983.
Fawcett, Anthony. John Lennon: One Day At A Time. New York: Grove Press, 1976.
Fulpens, H.V. The Beatles: An Illustrated Diary. New York: Perigree Books, 1982.
Gaines, Steven. Heroes and Villains: The True Story of the Beach Boys. New American Library, 1986.
Gaskell, G.A. Dictionary of All Scriptures and Myths. New York: Avenel Books, Julian Press, 1981.
Goldman, Albert. The Lives of John Lennon. New York: William Morrow & Company Inc., 1988.
Harrison, George with Derek Taylor. I Me Mine. New York: Simon & Schuster, 1980.
Hockinson, Michael J. The Ultimate Beatles Quiz Book. New York: St. Martin's Press, 1992.
Jobes, Gertrude. Dictionary of Mythology, Folklore, and Symbols. Part One. New York: The Scarecrow Press, Inc., 1962.
Joyce, James. Finnegan's Wake. New York: Viking Press, 1939.
Lewisohn, Mark. The Beatles: Recording Sessions. New York: Harmony Books, 1988.
McCabe, Peter and Robert D. Schonfeld. Apple to the Core. New York: Pocket Books, 1972.
McCartney, Michael. The Macs: Mike McCartney's Family Album. New York: Delilah Books, 1972.
Marsh, David and Kevin Stein. The Book Of Rock Lists. New York: Dell Rolling Stone Press, 1981.
Norman, Philip. Shout! The Beatles in Their Generation. New York: Warner Books, 1982.
O'Grady, Terence J. The Beatles, A Musical Evolution. Boston, Mass: Twayne Publishers, 1983.
Patterson, R. Gary. The Great Beatle Death Clues. London England: Robson Books Ltd. 1996.
Pawlowski, Gareth L. How They Became The Beatles; A Definitive History of the Early Years. New York: E.P. Dutton, 1989.
Poundstone, William. Big Secrets. New York: Quill, 1983.
Riley, Tim. Tell Me Why: A Beatles Commentary. New York: Alfred A. Knopt, 1988.
Salewicz, Tim. McCartney. New York: St. Martin's Press, 1986.
Schaffner, Nicholas. The Beatles Forever. New York: McGraw-Hill, 1978.
Schultheiss, Tom. A Day In The Life: The Beatles Day By Day. Michigan: Pierian Press, 1980.
Sheff, David. The Playboy Interviews With John Lennon & Yoko Ono. New York: Berkley Books, 1981.
Shotton, Pete with Nicholas Shaffner. The Beatles, Lennon, And Me. New York: Stein And Day, 1984.
Stannard, Neville. The Long and Winding Road. A History of the Beatles on Record. New York: Avon Books, 1984.
Suczek, Barbara. 1972. The Curious Case of the Death of Paul McCartney. Urban Life and Culture. Vol. 1. Sage Publications, 1972.
Taylor, Derek. It Was Twenty Years Ago Today. New York: Fireside, 1987.

Chapter XIII

FBI Documents

22 preprocessed pages on Billie Holiday under the (Freedom of Information Act) pursuant to Title 5, United States Code 552 and/or Section 552 a (Privacy Act).

Bibliography

Books

Albertson, Chris. Bessie. New York: Stein and Day, 1972.

Blesh, Rudi. Eight Lives in Jazz: Combo, U.S.A. New York: Hayden Book Company, Inc., 1972.

Bogle, Donald. Toms, Coons, Mulattoes, Mammies & Bucks: An Interpretive History of Blacks in American Films. New York: Bantam Books, Inc., 1974.

Chilton, John. Billie's Blues: The Story of Billie Holiday, 1933-1959. New York: Stein and Day, 1975.

Chilton, John. Billie's Blues, The Billie Holiday Story. 1933-1959. New York: DaCapo Press, 1975.

Collier, James Lincoln. The Great Jazz Artists. New York: Four Winds Press, 1977.

DeVeaux, Alexis. Don't Explain. New York: Harper & Row Publishers, 1980.

Drimmer, Melvin. Black History: A Reappraisal. New York: Doubleday, 1969.

Duffy, William. Lady Sings The Blues, Billie Holiday. Garden City, New York: Doubleday & Company, 1956.

Feather, Leonard. From Satchmo to Miles. New York: Stein and Day, 1974.

Feather, Leonard. The New Edition of the Encyclopedia of Jazz. New York: Bonanza Books, 1960.

Gleason, Ralph J. Celebrating The Duke & Louis, Bessie, Billie, Bird, Carmen, Miles, Dizzy, & Other Heroes. New York: Dell Publishing Company, Inc., 1976.

Grant, Joanne, ed. Black Protest: History, Documents, and Analyses from 1619 to Present. New York: Fawcett World Library, 1975.

Hammond, John. John Hammond on Record. New York: Summit Books, 1977.

Harris, Middleton A., Morris Levitt, Furman, and Ernest Smith. The Black Book. New York: Random House, 1973.

Hentoff, Nat. The Jazz Life. New York: Dial Press, 1961.

Holiday, Billie, with William Dufty. Lady Sings the Blues. New York: Doubleday, 1956.

Hughes, Langston and Milton Meltzer. Black Magic: A Pictorial History of the Negro in American Entertainment. Englewood, New Jersey: Prentice-Hall, Inc., 1967.

Jones, Hettie. Big Star Fallin' Mama: Five Women In Black Music. New York: Viking Press, 1974.

Jones, LeRoi (Amiri Baraka). Black Music. New York: William Morrow and Company, 1967.

Jones, LeRoi (Amiri Baraka). Blues People: Negro Music in White America. New York: William Morrow and Company, 1963.

Moore, Carman. Somebody's Angel Child: The Story of Bessie Smith. New York: Dell Publishing Company, Inc., 1975.

Schiffman, Jack. Uptown: The Story of Harlem's Apollo Theatre. New York: Cowles Book Company, Inc., 1971.

Schoener, Allon. Harlem on My Mind. New York: Random House, 1969.

Travis, Dempsey J. Autobiography of Black Jazz. Chicago, Illinois: Urban Research Press, 1983.

Travis, Dempsey J. The Louis Armstrong Odyssey. Chicago, Illinois: Urban Research Press, 1997.

Magazine

Strange Fruit. Vanity Fair, September 1998.

Chapter XIV

FBI Documents

556 preprocessed pages on Lorraine Hansberry released under the (Freedom Of Information Act) pursuant to Title 5, United States Code 552 and/or section 552 a (Privacy Act).

Books

Abramson, Doris E., Negro Playwrights in the American Theatre; 1925-1959, New York: Columbia University Press, 1969.

Carter. Steven R., Hansberry's Drama: Commitment Amid Complexity. Urbana: University of Illinois Press, 1991.

Cheney, Anne, Lorraine Hansberry. New York: Twayne, 1984.

Davis, Arthur P., From the Dark Tower: Afro-American Writers, 1900-1960. Washington: Howard University, 1960.

Periodicals

Black American Literature Forum, Spring 1983, pp. 8-13.

Commentary, June 1959, pp. 527-30.

Freedomways (special issue), 19:4, 1979.

New Yorker, May 9, 1959.

New York Times, January 13, 1965; October 5, 1983, p.C24.

New York Times Review of Books, March 31, 1991, p. 25.

Theatre Journal, December 1986.

Time, January 22, 1965.

Village Voice, August 12, 1959.

Washington Post, November 7, 1986.

Chapter XV

FBI Documents

254 preprocessed pages on Ernest Hemingway released under the (Freedom of Information Act) pursuant to Title 5, United States Code 552 and/or section 552 a (Privacy Act).

Books

Baker, Carlos. Ernest Hemingway: Critiques of Four Major Novels. New York: Scribner's, 1962.

Baker, Carlos. Ernest Hemingway: A Life Story. New York: Scribner's, 1969.

Baker, Carlos. Hemingway, The Writer As Artist. Princeton, New Jersey: Princeton University Press, 1972.

Baker Carlos, ed. Ernest Hemingway: Selected Letters. New York: Granda, 1981.

Benson, Jackson J. Hemingway: The Writer's Art of Self - Defense. Minneapolis; The University of Minnesota Press, 1969.

Brenner, Gerry. Concealments in Hemingway's Works. Columbus: Ohio State University Press, 1983.

Bruccoli, Matthew J. Scott and Ernest: The Authority of Failure and the Authority of Success. New York: Random House, 1978.

Buckley, Peter. Ernest. New York: Dial Press, 1978.

Burgess, Anthony. Ernest Hemingway and His World. New York: Scribner's, 1978.

Cowley, Malcolm, ed. Hemingway. New York: The Viking Press, 1944.

Donaldson, Scott. By Force of Will: The Life and Art of Ernest Hemingway. New York: Viking, 1977.

Falco, Joseph M. The Hero in Hemingway's Short Stories. Pittsburgh: University of Pittsburgh Press, 1968.

Fenton, Charles Andrews. The Apprenticeship of Ernest Hemingway: The Early Years. New York: Farrar, Straus and Young, 1954.

Flora, Joseph M. Hemingway's Nick Adams. Baton Rouge: Louisiana State University Press, 1982.

Gajdusek, Robert E., ed. Hemingway's Paris. New York: Scribner's, 1978.

Gellens, Jay. Twentieth Century Interpretations of "A Farewell to Arms". Englewood Cliffs, N.J.: Prentice-Hall, 1970.

Gurko, Leo. Ernest Hemingway and The Pursuit of Heroism. New York: Crowell, 1968.

Hemingway, Ernest. Men Without Women. New York: Scribner's, 1927.

Hemingway, Ernest. Death in the Afternoon. New York: Scribner's, 1932.

Hemingway, Ernest. Green Halls of Africa. New York: Scribner's, 1935.

Hemingway, Ernest. To Have and Have Not. New York: Scribner's, 1937.

Hemingway, Ernest. The Fifth Column, and the First Forty-nine Stories. New York: Scribner's, 1938.

Hemingway, Ernest. For Whom the Bell Tolls. New York: Scribner's, 1940.

Hemingway, Ernest. Across the River and Into the Trees. New York: Scribner's, 1950.

Hemingway, Ernest. The Old Man and the Sea. New York: Scribner's, 1952.

Hemingway, Ernest. The Sun Also Rises. New York: Scribner's, 1954.

Hemingway, Ernest. A Farewell to Arms. New York: Scribner's, 1957.

Hemingway, Ernest. In Our Time. New York: Scribner's, 1958.

Hemingway, Ernest. A Moveable Feast. New York: Scribner's, 1964.

Hemingway, Ernest. The Snows of Kilmanjaro, and Other Stories, New York: Scribner's, 1970.

Hemingway, Ernest. Islands in the Stream. New York: Scribner's, 1970.

Hemingway, Ernest. The Nick Adams Stories. New York: Scribner's, 1972.

Hemingway, Ernest. Winner Take Nothing. New York: Scribner's, 1983.

Hemingway, Gregory. Papa: A Personal Memoir. Boston: Houghton Mifflin, 1976.

Hemingway, Lencester. My Brother Ernest Hemingway. Cleveland: World Publishing, 1962.

Chapter XVI

FBI Documents

1,221 preprocessed pages on James Baldwin released under the (Freedom of Information Act) pursuant to Title 5, United States Code 552 and/or section 552 a (Privacy Act).

The following is a selected bibliography on James Baldwin from the holdings of the Vivian G. Harsh Collection of Afro-American History and Literature, Woodson Regional Library, Chicago Public Library, 9525 South Halsted Street.

Books

Amen Corner. A Play. New York: Dial, 1968.

Another Country. New York: Dial, 1962.

Blues for Mister Charlie. A Play. New York: Dial, 1964.

The Devil Finds Work. New York: Dial, 1976.

A Dialogue. By James Baldwin and Nikki Giovanni. Philadelphia: Lippincott, 1973.

The Evidence of Things Not Seen. New York: Holt, Rinehart, 1985.

The Fire Next Time. New York: Dial, 1963.

Giovanni's Room. New York: Dial, 1956.

Go Tell It On the Mountain. New York: Knopf, 1953.

Going To Meet the Man. New York: Dial, 1965.

If Beale Street Could Talk. London: Joseph, 1974/ New York: Dial, 1974.

Just Above My Head. New York: Dial, 1979.

Little Man, Little Man: A Story of Childhood. By James Baldwin and Yoran Cazac. London: Joseph, 1976 / New York: Dial, 1976.

No Name in the Street. New York: Dial, 1972.

Nobody Knows My Name. New York: Dial, 1961.

Notes of a Native Son. Boston: Beacon, 1955.

One Day When I Was Lost: A Scenario Based on "The Autobiography of Malcolm X". London: Joseph, 1972.

The Price of the Ticket: Collection Nonfiction, 1948-1985. New York: St. Martin's, 1985.

A Rap on Face. By Margaret Mead and James Baldwin. Philadelphia: Lippincott, 1971.

Tell Me How Long the Train's Been Gone. New York: Dial, 1968.

Chapter XVII

FBI Documents

1,985 preprocessed pages on Charlie Chaplin released under the (Freedom of Information Act) pursuant to Title 5, United States Code 552 and/or section 552 a (Privacy Act).

Books

Bessy, Maurice, and Florey, Robert. Monsieur Chaplin, ou le rire dans la nuit, Jacques Damase, Paris, 1952.

Bessy, Maurice, and Livio, Robin. Charles Chaplin, Denoel, Paris, 1972.

Bowman, William Dodgson. Charlie Chaplin. His Life and Art, Routledge, London, 1931. Reprint: New York: Haskell, 1974.

Brown, Albert T. The Charlie Chaplin Fun Book, 1915.

Brownlow, Kevin. The Parade's Gone By. New York: Alfred A. Knopf, 1968/ London: Secker & Warburg 1968.

Chaplin, Charles. A Comedian Sees the World. New York: Crowell, 1933.

Chaplin, Charles. My Autobiography. London: The Bodley Head, 1964/ New York: Simon & Schuster, 1964/ Harmondsworth: Penguin Books, 1966/ New York: Fireside Books, 1978. Translations in Arabic, Armenian, Bulgarian, Chinese, Czech, Danish, Dutch, Finnish, French, Georgian, German (publication in Austria. West Germany and East Germany). Greek, Hungarian, Icelandic, Italian, Japanese, Latvian, Norwegian, Polish, Portuguese, Rumanian, Russian, Serbo-Croat, Spanish, Swedish.

Chaplin, Charles. My Early Years. London: The Bodley Head, 1979. The first eleven chapters of My Autobiography.

Chaplin, Charles. My Life in Pictures. Introduction by Francis Wyndham. London: The Bodley Head, 1974/ New York: Grosset & Dunlap, 1976.

Chaplin, Charles. My Trip Abroad, New York: Harper & Brothers, 1922. Translations in Bulgarian, Chinese, Czech, French, German, Polish, Portuguese, Russian, Spanish, Swedish, Yiddish.

Chaplin, Charles. My Wonderful Visit. London: Hurst & Blackett, 1922. English edition of My Trip Abroad.

Chaplin, Charles, Jr. (with N. and M. Rau) My Father Charlie Chaplin. New York: Random House, 1960/ London: Longmans, 1960.

Chaplin, Michael. I Couldn't Smoke the Grass on My Father's Lawn. London: Leslie Frewin, 1966/ New York: G.P. Putnam's Sons, 1966.

The Charlie Chaplin Book. New York: Street & Smith, 1915.

The Charlie Chaplin Book. New York: Sabriel Sons & Co., 1916.

Codd, Elsie. 'Charlie Chaplin's Methods' in Cinema: Practical Course in Cinema Acting in Ten Complete Lessons, Volume II, Lesson 2. London: Standard Art Book Company, 1920.

Cooke, Alistair. 'Charles Chaplin' in Six Men. New York: Alfred A. Knopf, 1977/ London: The Bodley Head, 1978/ New York: Berkley Publishing Corporation, 1978/ Harmondsworth: Penguin Books, 1978.

Cotes, Peter and Niklaus, Thelma. The Little Fellow. The Life and Work of Charles Spencer Chaplin. Foreword by W. Somerset Maugham. London: Paul Elek, 1951/ New York: Philosophical Library Inc., 1951. Reprint: New York: Citadel Press, 1965.

Dell, Draycott M. The Charlie Chaplin Scream Book. London: Fleetway, 1915.

Delluc, Louis. Charlot, Maurice de Brunoff, Paris, 1921. English translation by Hamish Miles: Charlie Chaplin, John Lane/ London: The Bodley Head, 1922.

Florey, Robert. Charlie Chaplin. Ses debuts, ses films, ses aventures. Preface by Lucien Wahl. Collection 'Les Grands Artistes de l'Ecran'. Paris: Jean-Pascal, 1927.

Fowler, Gene. Father Goose. The Story of Mack Sennett. New York: Covici Friede, 1934.

Gallagher, J.P. Fred Karno, Master of Mirth and Tears. London: Robert Hale, 1971.

Gifford, Denis. The Movie Makers. London: Macmillan, 1974/ New York: Doubleday, 1974.

Gold, Michael. Charlie Chaplin's Parade. New York: Harcourt, Brace & Co., 1930.

Haining, The Legend of Charlie Chaplin. London: W.H. Allen, 1983. Anthology of writings by or about Chaplin.

Hembus, Joe. Charlie Chaplin und seine Filme. Eine Dokumentation. Munich: Wilhelm Heyne, 1972/ 1973.

Hoyt, Edwin P. Sir Charlie. London: Robert Hale, 1977.

Huff, Theodore. Charlie Chaplin. New York: Henry Schuman, 1951/ London: Cassell, 1952. Reprints: New York: Pyramid Books, 1964/ New York: Arno Press, 1972.

Jacobs, David. Chaplin, The Movies and Charlie. New York: Harper & Row, 1975.

Jacobs, Lewis. The Rise of the American Film. New York: Harcourt, Brace & Co., 1939.

Kerr, Walter. The Silent Clowns. New York: Alfred A. Knopf, 1975.

Lahue, Kalton C. World of Laughter. Oklahoma, Norman, 1966.

Lahue, Kalton C. Kops and Custards. Oklahoma, Norman, 1967.

Leprohon, Pierre. Charlot, ou la Naissance d'un Mythe. Paris: Editions Corymbe, 1935.

Index

Index

Other Books by Dempsey J. Travis

Don't Stop Me Now

An Autobiography of Black Chicago

An Autobiography of Black Jazz

An Autobiography of Black Politics

Real Estate Is The Gold In Your Future

"Harold" The Peoples' Mayor

Racism: American Style, A Corporate Gift

I Refuse To Learn To Fail

View From The Back Of The Bus During WWII

The Duke Ellington Primer

Louis Armstrong Odyssey

Racism: Round 'n' Round It Goes

They Heard A Thousand Thunders

The Life And Times Of Redd Foxx

Victory Monument: The Beacon Of Chicago's Bronzeville

URBAN RESEARCH PRESS, INC.

WWW.URBANRESEARCHPRESS.COM

ISBN 0-941484-31-9